A Young Doctor's Manual

A Young Doctor's Manual

Dr. R.P. Gupta

Ocean Paperbacks

A Division of Ocean Books Pvt. Ltd.

ISO 9001:2008 Publishers

Published by
Ocean Paperbacks
A Division of Ocean Books Pvt. Ltd.
4/19 Asaf Ali Road,
New Delhi-110 002 (INDIA)
e-mail: info@oceanbooks.in

ISBN 978-81-8430-283-7
A Young Doctor's Manual
by Dr. R.P. Gupta

Edition
First, 2014

Price
Rs. 400.00 (Rs. Four Hundred only)

Printed at
Bhanu Printers, Delhi

Dedicated to
My Teachers, My Parents,
My Family Members
and To All My Colleagues

PREFACE

The purpose of writing this book to put my experience of fifty years and practical tips, to pen down for benefits of young fresh graduates of medicine and surgery. Every young doctor should read this book which will help him for safe sojourn during internship and house job. It is no replacement for a textbook of surgery but it has practical tips which will help in difficult circumstances to help the patient.

Now a days, so many candidates go to Russia or China for medical education. When they return to India, they don't have much practical knowledge and this book will help them a lot in taking care of their patients. I hope it will fulfill the gap in practical knowledge and benefit all young doctors.

It will help the novice to step into the shoes that he is expected to wear to become a successful and above all a good doctor, sympathetic towards all—his patients and their relatives and with his colleagues and other members of his profession. Moreover, he will gain knowledge from an experienced surgeon which will help him handle any situation with ease and fulfill his professional goal.

This book is intended for everyday use by senior students, young doctors in hospital, and by lone practitioners working in underdeveloped countries and in rural areas. In a rapidly changing and even more complex subject such as surgery, at times it is difficult for a young doctor to retain a clear view of some of the guiding principles of good medical practice. Common sense must be exercised in the application of recent advances. Compassion must be shown to all patients and to their worried relatives. If costs are to be contained. Awareness of the escalating expenses of modern surgical care is essential. Doctors must take a conscious effort to keep down the cost of the drugs which they use. Investigations that are not strictly necessary should be avoided.

My sincere thanks to Mr. Tilak Raj Nanda, Mr. Bishan Singh Kiroula and many other colleagues who guided and helped me in safe sojourn in my early period of surgical training.

—Dr. R.P. Gupta

CONTENTS

DUTIES OF A YOUNG DOCTOR

Smoking

Smoking is dangerous to health, and doctors should set an example to the public by not smoking. A house-surgeon should never smoke in front of patients, or in parts of the hospital where he may be seen by members of the public. Cigarettes should not be sold in hospital, and **any patient who is going to have a general anaesthetic should be encouraged to stop smoking completely.** A major operation provides a good opportunity to give up the damaging habit permanently.

Time Keeping

Patients in an acute surgical ward need to have a doctor readily available at all times. One of the first tasks of a new house-surgeon is to check up in detail on the suggested duty or off-duty rota in his hospital. He has to make certain that there is continuous medical cover for his patients, 24 hours per day, 7 days a week. Consultation with other junior colleagues usually enables a safe and satisfactory rota to be worked out. Senior medical and nursing staff should be informed about the proposed rota.

When on duty, the doctor should endeavour to be punctual. This usually means being in the ward 30 minutes before the consultant is expected, so that the latest state of the patients may be ascertained. **Reliability and punctuality** are major factors in a young doctor's chances of promotion. If for any reason he has to absent himself from his usual place of work while on duty, the house-surgeon should tell the ward sister and hospital telephonist exactly where he can be quickly contacted in an emergency. All emergency admissions must be seen without delay.

Responsibility and Consultation

Assuming immediate responsibility for a ward full of sick patients for the first time is a daunting prospect. The consultant and other members of the team realize this, and will advise and support a new house-surgeon. After a few weeks, when he knows all the patients thoroughly and has become accustomed to the ward routine and hospital procedures, the house-surgeon becomes more confident and a valuable link-man in the team. If he is ever in doubt about a ward technique or how to proceed, the house-surgeon should ask a more senior doctor for advice and help—that is how an apprenticeship system works. The young doctor should know his own limitations, without at the same time allowing himself to become a nuisance to others. It is not always easy to strike the right balance.

The consultant in-charge will generally want to know at once of any unusual happening in his ward such as an accident, sudden death, unexpected complication, threatening relatives or anything that may lead to litigation later. Always inform the consultant of any late major changes in the plans made for the next day, for example cancellation of an operating list caused by illness, strikes or staff shortages.

Relations with Staff and Relatives

Relations with Family Doctors

The family doctor should always be treated courteously, and his telephone calls answered promptly. He is in a unique position to provide vital information about a patient that he may want to admit. Besides noting down the patient's history and personal particulars, ask his doctor about previous episodes, drugs given, family history and social circumstances. There can rarely be any justification in refusing a request for an admission made by an outside doctor. When there is no other general hospital in the district, then the patient *must* be admitted, and somehow a bed be found for him in the hospital.

It is good practice for the surgeon to send the family doctor a letter at the time of any operation. If the practitioner wants to visit his patient in hospital, he should be made welcome and given full information. When the patient goes home, the house-surgeon should give him a note to hand to his doctor briefly indicating: (1) the diagnosis, (2) treatment, (3) dosage of any drugs suggested, (4) arrangements for follow-up or after-care. **One of the more senior members of the team normally sends a detailed, typed letter as soon as possible after the patient's discharge.**

Relations with Nursing and Other Staff

Patients sometimes confide in nurses information which they have been afraid to tell the doctor. Nurses often gain considerable insight into home circumstances, and an experienced nurse may be almost as good as a medical social worker in sorting out the patient's domestic problems. The intelligent house-surgeon can learn a lot from the nursing staff. He should always be considerate and polite towards them. Try to avoid interviewing patients in bed at times when nurses are known to be serving meals, dispensing drugs or giving out bed-pans. Student nurses appreciate the doctor in the ward explaining a patient's symptoms and treatment to them when time permits.

A surgical ward which has a permanent physiotherapist and medical social worker attached to it is very fortunate. The house-surgeon is responsible for telling them about foreseeable problems and co-operating with them in the management of complications and other difficulties. They should be alerted at an early stage, and be kept informed of progress. Verbal communications are always better than written messages. It is profitable for the house-surgeon to build up a good personal relationship with other skilled technicians such as biochemists, radiographers and electrocardiographers—their services are frequently required in a surgical unit.

Relations with Relatives

It is not uncommon for relatives to be even more worried than the patient who is admitted to hospital. Consequently, they should be handled carefully and with sympathy. The doctor's first duty is always lies towards his patient. First find out exactly what is the degree of kinship between relative and patient. If the relationship is close and there is no reason to suspect that the relative may take any action that would be against the patient's best interests, then the relative should be given a short, simple account of the medical condition and prognosis. Stick to the truth and do not pretend to be a prophet. A close relative should be notified of any sudden deterioration in the condition of a patient, and of course of a patient's death.

Sometimes relatives become unreasonable and make a nuisance of themselves. That is the time to be firm and to enlist the support of a senior doctor. A tired patient may need to be protected from excessive visits by unthinking relatives.

Relations with the Police

While the first duty of a doctor is lies towards his patient, he also does have a civil responsibility to help the police when appropriate. Information should not be divulged to the police hastily; snap disclosures over the telephone should be avoided. Such information may be used in court proceedings. Ideally, witnessed consent should be obtained from an adult patient before medical information concerning him is given to the police. If the young doctor finds that there is a conflict between his obligations to preserve confidentiality on the one hand and to do his civil duty on the other, he should say nothing, but ask the police to contact the senior surgeon or hospital medical administrator next morning.

Note-Taking

Good patient records are essential for correct diagnosis and management, and for follow-up and research purposes at a later date. They form a useful index of the standard maintained in a surgical unit, and some institutions for higher surgical training take ward records into account when deciding whether or not a hospital post should be recognized for training purposes. **Good records are invaluable for the preparation of insurance reports and in any legal proceedings.**

Notes about patients should be written legibly at once and not left until later. Several systems are in use. All should include simple statements: (1) of what did the patient complain; (2) duration of complaint; (3) how it began, etc.

It is advisable to record specific dates and times. There may be several different symptoms to be dealt with in sequence. Ask the patient about any industrial injury or hazard for which he may be able to claim compensation. Has he had any adverse reactions to drugs in the past? A provisional diagnosis should be suggested after the first round of questions and investigations. At the end of a ward admission, the definitive diagnosis is written down, along with the arrangements for aftercare.

The problem-orientated medical record is frequently advocated, but has not been widely adopted. Each patient has in his case notes a master problem list—this is a simple column of defined problems (with dates) and firm diagnoses. Problems can be secondary to other problems and may be active or passive. Investigation and diagnosis are conducted in a dynamic and logical manner.

The Department of Radiodiagnosis

The house-surgeon is involved both in requesting radiological investigations and in the preparations of his patients for the same. He must also ensure that the results of the investigations are made known to the senior member of the surgical team as quickly as possible.

Request Form. When ordering an X-ray, the request form should (1) indicate the provisional diagnosis, (2) mention relevant clinical findings such as a palpable mass or jaundice, (3) give details of any operation on the relevant part, (4) show the dates of any previous radiological studies, (5) mention factors which may be of practical importance in carrying out the investigation, e.g. a stiff hip or gross obesity before, and (6) stating clearly which particular investigation is required, if need be after consultation with the radiologist.

Avoidance of Accidental Irradiation of an Early Pregnancy

Female patients of childbearing age should be asked about the possibility of early pregnancy. If there is any doubt, X-ray examination should be avoided (except in dire emergency) until pregnancy tests have been performed. Some hospitals confine irradiation of the lower abdomen in females to the 10 days following the first day of a menstrual period—The Ten Day Rule.

Types of Radiological Investigation

Radiology is a rapidly expanding speciality. New techniques are constantly being developed. The house-surgeon is not expected to know the details of performing all the types of investigation and therapy which can now be practised in a modern radiology department. He should, however, possess an understanding of the role of radiology in the study of patients under his care, and of the relative merits of and place for the different types of investigation and of interventional radiology.

1. Straight X-ray

A straight X-ray is useful for fractures, in chest diseases, the acute abdomen, with opaque foreign bodies, etc.

2. Contrast Studies

Contrast studies are useful for outlining hollow organs or channels with compounds containing opaque barium or iodine. In the alimentary tract, they may be complementary to endoscopic studies. In some systems such as the biliary tract contrast studies have been largely superseded by ultrasonic (or CT) scans.

3. Ultrasonic Scanning

This involves no irradiation and has now achieved a high degree of accuracy in detecting fetal abnormalities, cysts, abscesses, abdominal masses, biliary and pancreatic disease, congenital and valvular lesions of the heart, and in imaging major arteries.

4. Computerized Tomography (CT scan)

This is expensive, but valuable in intracranial lesions, mediastinal and abdominal masses (particularly in obese subjects), lymphomas and retroperitoneal tumours. CT scans should only be ordered after consultation with the radiologist.

5. Nuclear Magnetic Resonance (NMR)(MRI)

There is no radiation hazard. Helpful in detecting hepatic tumours and in central nervous system diseases. Tissue characterization may be possible.

6. Isotope Imaging

Isotope imaging depicts changes of a functional nature. Useful for demonstrating thyroid uptake, bone metastases, pulmonary emboli, myocardial ischaemia, intracardiac shunts and differential renal function and bone scanning.

Interventional Radiology

The radiologist can now undertake therapeutic procedures under direct visual control, e.g. aspirating renal cysts, embolizing bleeding vessels, dilating arterial stenoses (transluminal angioplasty), percutaneous biopsies of bones or tumours and removal of retained biliary calculi.

Digital Radiography

The development of television enhancement systems using digital electronics and improved electronic recording enables an image to be stored (e.g. on video disc) and be handled by a computer. These techniques may replace conventional X-ray films.

Requesting Another Opinion

When the surgeon wants advice from a colleague in another ward or department, first ascertain if that person is available. If the matter is urgent, a personal visit is made to the other doctor and the nature and urgency of the situation explained to him. This is more courteous than an impersonal letter sent through the hospital mail. When the matter is less urgent, a tactful, factual letter can be delivered by hand to the unit where advice is being sought. It is unwise to rely on important letters reaching the correct specialist by entrusting them to impersonal delivery services. A telephone call can supplement a written communication.

Prescribing Drugs

This is a task that has to be performed carefully and with attention to detail, particularly when dealing with controlled and other dangerous drugs. On the drug prescription card commence with: (1) the date, then insert (2) the pharmaceutical name of the drug, (3) the dose in metric units, (4) the route, (5) the times of administration, and finally, (6) sign the entry. Usually it is inadvisable to mark drugs to be given 'as required', but an experienced ward nursing sister can be given some discretion with regard to mild laxatives and domestic types of analgesics. When a drug is discontinued, the date should be written down and signed. It is bad medical practice to administer drugs longer than is necessary, and furthermore they are costly—the house-surgeon should frequently review the prescription card for each patient.

Any unusual reaction to a drug is noted on the prescription card and on the front of the patient's case notes.

Ward Rounds

The resident doctor should go round all the patients under his care first thing each morning, checking not only on temperatures and intravenous infusions, but also on such mundane matters as urine output and bowel function. He should note the number of empty beds, particularly if his ward is to receive emergency cases that day.

The time of the nursing staff is just as valuable as that of the doctors. Rounds should not normally be started when meals are about to be served. If the registrar and senior registrar are available, they should go to round with the house-surgeon, and not expect the senior nurse to accompany each of them on separate rounds. When the consultant goes to round, the house-surgeon should have all the case notes and latest results available for inspection and discussion.

Nowadays, many house-surgeons will be off duty in the evening, but their ill patients still need careful supervision. Before he leaves the ward, the house-surgeon must make a clear arrangement with another doctor in the surgical team, or with a colleague in an adjacent ward, to visit his ward in the late evening. It is important to tell the senior nurse whom to contact in case of difficulty, and leave a prominent note to this effect—nurses go off duty too!

Discharging a Patient

When possible, a patient should be told a few days before it is likely that he will be able to leave hospital. He can then tell his relatives and make arrangements. It is very expensive to keep a patient in a hospital bed. The house-surgeon should show intelligent anticipation in each case and try to ensure that every patient gets home to his family as soon as it is medically safe for him to do so. Before the patient leaves the ward, the doctor needs to check on the state of any incision and make sure that the patient is fit to make the journey. A patient should not be sent home to an empty house after an operation. If he has any doubts about the home circumstances, the house-surgeon is advised to contact the patient's family doctor by telephone.

Patient Taking His Own Discharge (Discharge at Request or LAMA)

A patient of sound mind has the right to decide what treatment he will accept and when he will leave hospital. If the doctor considers it medically unsafe for the patient to leave hospital, he should reason and explain to the patient in front of a witness. The consequences of his action having been explained, if the patient still insists on leaving, he should be asked to sign a form acknowledging that he is leaving contrary to medical advice. This form is duly witnessed. If the patient refuses to sign the form, then the doctor and witness sign it, noting down the patient's refusal to accept advice and to complete the form.

When the patient is considered to be of unsound mind, the duty psychiatrist should be called at once.

Operating Lists

Consent

Each patient having an operation has to sign a consent form after the nature of the operation has been explained to him—informed consent. The house-surgeon must give this explanation in simple terms. It is most important that the patient understands what is involved, particularly if a limb or breast is to be removed, an external intestinal stoma established, or the patient rendered sterile.

The patient has to agree that the operative and anaesthetic techniques can be varied as considered necessary, and no undertaking is given that the procedure will be performed by any particular doctor.

Marking

With bilateral structures, limbs, etc., the side to be operated on must be clearly marked beforehand with a felt pen. Remember that a swelling may seemingly vanish once the patient is under a general anaesthetic.

Timing

On taking up the appointment, the house-surgeon must find out from permanent members of the team approximately how long it takes the surgeon to perform different operations. Surgeons vary greatly. One may complete a straightforward gastric operation in 40 minutes, while another surgeon takes twice as long. The change-round time between cases for the anaesthetist involved also has to be taken into account. By adding these various times together, always try to ensure that the complete elective operating list can be safely completed within the allotted duration of the operating session. Theatre nurses, orderlies and anesthetists are entitled to their off-duty. Only for a genuine emergency should they be asked to stay on beyond the limit of their restored duty time.

Confidentiality

Always remember that information gained about a patient is confidential and should only be divulged readily to professional personnel directly concerned with the patient's management.

Be on guard when inquiries are made by employers, lawyers and insurance companies. Ask the patient if he wishes them to be told about his medical condition, and where appropriate get his written consent. If, in doubt, refer the request for information to the consultant in charge.

Protection Against Litigation

For their own protection, all doctors are strongly advised to belong to a medical protection society. This is often a condition of employment. Litigation is becoming more common. Keep your society informed of any change of address.

Death Certificates

When the cause of a patient's death is known, the necessary certificate should be issued to the distressed relatives as soon as possible. They should not be kept waiting—the house-surgeon should leave some less urgent task to complete the certificate.

The formalities for recording deaths with Central Government authorities vary in different parts of the world. The main purpose is to provide accurate information on the causes of deaths within the different countries. Health-care resources and research can then be directed towards tackling the principal killing disease. Every 10 years the World Health Organization revises its classification of the causes of death.

The certificate is in two parts: Part I lists the sequence of fatal events, while Part II records other conditions present which may have diminished the patient's chances of survival, but did not directly contribute to the patient's death.

The immediate cause of death is inserted on the first line of Part I, e.g. broncho-pneumonia, peritonitis or myocardial infarction. The second line shows the cause or reason for the first entry, e.g. hemicolectomy or perforation. A third entry may be made to complete the sequence, e.g. indicating that the reason for the hemicolectomy was carcinoma of sigmoid colon or that the perforation was of a chronic duodenal ulcer. For some patients, only the first line needs to be completed, for example, carcinoma of lung when the diagnosis had been confirmed earlier by biopsy, and the patient's lungs and liver were clearly full of metastases. When possible, information should be provided on the primary site of a tumour, whether the condition was acute or chronic, or in the case of an earlier accident, whether it occurred at home or on a public road.

Part II might include generalized diseases such as chronic bronchitis, diabetes and hypertension. The house-surgeon also records if an autopsy was performed, and whether or not he or another doctor saw the body. The Registrar of Deaths may later seek clarification or amplification.

In some cases of death from natural causes, it is not possible to complete the certificate in the detail outlined above. A patient may die from a widespread anaplastic neoplasm, the primary site being unknown. This is a natural death. It is only unnatural, unexplained or violent deaths that have to be reported to the police.

Death Certificate to be Give at Time off Death for Cremation

A confirmatory medical certificate which has to be completed by a doctor on duty. This has just to mention name of patient, age, sex, time and date. When patient died at the place (hospital name) and immediate cause of death.

When death is to be determined on the basis of brain death, the diagnosis should be arrived at by the following combination of doctors.

(a) A consultant who is in-charge of the case or, in his absence, his deputy, who should have been registered for five years or more and have had adequate previous experience in the care of such cases, and

(b) One other doctor, of comparable seniority.

Neither doctor should be a member of the transplant team and their findings, opinion and the time of death should be recorded in the case notes. The tests of brain death should be repeated at least once. Thereafter artificial ventilation and heart beat should be maintained until the removal of the organs is completed by the transplant surgeon; he also must have satisfied himself that the donor is dead.

Important Duties of a Duty Doctor and How to Carry Them Out

Discharging the Patient

For patient discharge, four steps are necessary:

1. **Follow-up** – Arrange follow-up instructions for all discharged patients. This can be as simple as telling the patient to call his or her own doctor if any problems occur. In general, anyone sent home with a potentially serious problem such as chest pain or abdominal pain, should be given very clear instructions regarding what specific problems need a doctor's attention, whom to see or call, and when to call. Whenever possible, contact the physician you want the patient to see in follow-up to ensure that these instructions can be carried out in a timely manner. **PEARL: You must provide an interpreter for non-English-speaking patients.** If no one is available (e.g. a friend, relative, or staff member), a long-distance telephone carrier is usually able to provide this service.
2. **Warning Signs** – Remember that your diagnosis may be wrong or the patient's condition may deteriorate. Therefore, give all patients a list of problems or warning signs that require immediate return to the hospital. For example, a patient with right lower quadrant pain, who seems well enough to go home but might conceivably have appendicitis, should be told: "If the pain becomes more severe or you develop repeated vomiting or fever, come back here immediately."
3. **Medication** – Specify what medication should be taken, and give specific instructions regarding how and when to take medications. **PEARL: Avoid the use of medical abbreviations. Don't write doses and timing of medications**

in medical "jargon." Avoid terms such as bid, tid, and q/h.

4. **Specific instructions** – Give specific instructions regarding allowable or desirable activities and diet, as well as use of special measures (e.g. ice pack, heating pads), as appropriate.

Signing Out

At the beginning and end of each shift, you will go through a ritual handing-off of responsibility for patients, known as "sign-out." When you are leaving, it's a good idea to prepare for this. Check all of your patients' charts to ensure that you've written your note, make all the telephone calls or consult calls you can (because you know the patient best), and make sure that the workup (e.g. labs, X-rays) is being carried out. Before signing out, walk by the rooms to check that you haven't forgotten a particular patient (yes, this happens!). At sign-out, make sure the on-coming person who will take over for your patient knows what has been done, what needs to be done, and what you think is going on with the patient. Conversely, when you are coming in, make sure that you get all this information, and ask for it if you don't get it. Smooth sign-outs are vital for proper patient care and flow! For giving one, you should go from bed to bed and give instruction. **Never give or takeover on a sheet of paper without going to the patient bed.**

What You Wear and Carry

While you are working, what you wear and carry can make a difference in your ability to do your job. Clothing should be neat, clean, and functional. Avoid necklaces, dangling earrings, scarves, and ties (in most places); patients or visitors with behavioral problems may grab these, seriously injuring you in the process. Also avoid wearing anything of great value such as an expensive watch or grandma's ring. They could easily be damaged or stolen in the hectic environment of the hospital duty. Always wear comfortable shoes—as an experiment, try wearing poorly fitting shoes for one shift and see how you feel!

Equipment you burden yourself with should serve a real purpose. In most cases, you won't need a tuning fork or ophthalmoscope; the first is seldom needed, and the second is usually mounted on the wall in each room. A good stethoscope is vital, and it is the only piece of equipment many carry. It can also double as a reflex hammer. A good penlight can be useful—even more so a working pen but a cheap one, because it may very well end up permanently "borrowed". A good pair of heavy duty shears is quite helpful ("paramedic shears") for cutting bandages, clothing, and so on. Using index cards to keep track of each patient will help you to keep your thoughts organized. Most important, bring your wits, enthusiasm, and energy—you will find them taxed but stimulated in the organized chaos of the hospital. □

THE DIFFICULT PATIENT

Pre-hospital Considerations

- Consider hypoglycemia and obtain a blood sugar with Gluco meter in all violent patients.
- Police assistance may be required for transport of violent patients.

The "difficult patient" arouses feelings of animosity and hostility in the health-care provider. Such patients include those who are verbally or physically abusive, intoxicated, suicidal, homeless, malodorous, and self-abusive. Often, the health-care provider has negative feelings either before he or she meets the patient, based on the nurse's report or the patient's chief complaint, or immediately upon entering the patient's room. These patients, however, need your attention most. **PEARL: Remember that the patient's abnormal behaviour may be the result of a serious underlying disease, even in psychiatric patients.** Also, because of their social isolation, these patients are at risk for developing many serious illnesses. Therefore, a thorough evaluation is always required. The somnolent alcoholic patient lying in your ED may simply be drunk, but also might be suffering from a subdural hematoma, hypoglycemia, or a brain abscess. **PEARL: Exclude hypoglycemia in all violent patients.**

The Violent Patient

It is always best to try to identify potentially violent patients before they actually become violent. **PEARL: Predictors of violence include male gender, drug or alcohol abuse, and history of violence.** The following are conditions in which violent behaviour should be anticipated:

- Alcohol or drug abuse
- Acute psychotic or manic disorder
- History of violent behaviour
- Antisocial personality
- Severe psychomotor agitation (e.g. pacing, yelling)
- Restraints already in place or patient brought in by police.

PEARL: Potentially violent patients require rapid attention, which often helps to diffuse their anger. All angry patients should be considered potentially violent. These patients should be isolated from other patients and visitors. Offering a comfortable chair or food may help. Never argue with a potentially violent patient. Also, never touch the unrestrained violent patient before obtaining permission, and always stand at least an arm's length away.

Physical Restraint

An actively violent patient must be restrained for his or her own protection from serious injury, as well as for the protection of the health-care providers. Carefully document in the patient's chart why the restraint was necessary. Restraining the patient also facilitates patient evaluation, which might otherwise be impossible. Never turn your back on or stay alone in a closed room with a potentially violent patient. Leave the door open, and do not stand in the way if the patient attempts to bolt out of the room. Also, always leave yourself an easy avenue of exit. Some patients, if placed in a quiet environment, can be "talked down." In other instances, a show of force is enough to subdue a potentially violent patient.

Enter the room with confidence, and explain to the patient in a strong, steady tone that you are there to help. If the patient refuses to stay calm, say you will need to use a restraint. Usually, at least five people are required to physically restrain a violent patient. Each member of the team should be assigned one limb, and all members should approach the patient simultaneously. The patient should then be put into a strong four-point restraint and a posey (a thick cloth device intended to restrain the trunk). Placing patients on their side helps to prevent aspiration, although the supine position with elevated head is more comfortable and facilitates the examination. Explain to the patient that you are using a restraint to avoid further injury to anyone. All violent and suicidal patients should be searched for weapons (which may be concealed in their undergarments).

Chemical Restraint

Physical restraints usually are sufficient, but often the violent patient requires a chemical restraint as well such as a major (neuroleptics) or minor (benzodiazepines) tranquilizer. This protects the patient from injuries (e.g. rhabdomyolysis) due to struggling against the restraint and can facilitate evaluation.

Neuroleptics are particularly effective, having relatively few side effects such as cardiorespiratory depression. Haloperidol 5 mg IV or IM every 10 to 20 minutes is used most commonly. Note that IV use of haloperidol is not yet approved by the FDA. Droperidol, which has a more rapid onset and fewer adverse reactions than haloperidol, also can be given in doses of 2.5 mg IV or IM every 10 minutes. All neuroleptics can cause an acute dystonic reaction, which should be managed with diphenhydramine 50 mg IV or benztropine 2 mg IV.

Benzodiazepines can cause respiratory depression, yet are safer to use when seizures are a possibility (e.g. in those with alcohol withdrawal, antidepressants, cocaine abuse). Lorazepam 1 mg IV or IM every 5 to 10 minutes or midazolam 0.5 to 1.0 mg IV can be given as needed. If you choose benzodiazepines, be prepared to intubate the patient if necessary. Use a cardiac monitor and pulse oximetry to monitor the patient. Frequent reassessment of the patient is required. **PEARL: Rapid chemical restraint may be obtained by combining a butyrophenone with a benzodiazepine.** A combination of lorazepam 2 mg and haloperidol 5 mg or droperidol 2.5 mg is more effective than either drug alone.

Differential Diagnosis

The differential diagnosis of violent behaviour can be remembered by the **mnemonic FIND ME**, as shown in Table 1.

Table 1. Differential Diagnosis of Violent Behaviour; FINDME

F	Functional disorders Schizophrenia Paranoia Mania Antisocial or borderline personality disorders Post-traumatic stress disorder
I	Infections Meningitis Encephalitis Sepsis
N	Neurologic disorders Head injuries Seizures (especially temporal lobe) Neoplasms Vasculitis
D	Dementia Drug-related disorders. **PEARL: Consider a drug reaction, especially in the elderly.** Alcohol intoxication or withdrawal PCP (phencyclidine) Cocaine Amphetamines LSD (lysergic acid diethylamide) Anticholinergics Opioid withdrawal Sedative hypnotic withdrawal γ-Hydroxybutyrate
M	Metabolic disorders Electrolyte abnormalities Acute renal or hepatic failure Hypothermia or hyperthermia Hypoxia Vitamin deficiencies Hypertensive encephalopathy
E	Endocrine disorders Hypoglycemia Thyroid storm Cushing's disease Workup

Workup

Extensive workup is indicated in the violent patient with a suspected organic cause. Table 2 presents several findings to help distinguish organic from functional causes of violence. **PEARL: Abnormal vital signs, disorientation, altered mental status, and lack of psychiatric history suggest an organic cause of violence.**

The following tests should be considered in the workup: CBC, electrolytes, renal function tests, liver function tests, osmolality, CT scan of the head, lumbar puncture (LP; especially if the patient has fever or signs of meningeal irritation), ethanol level, and urine toxicology screen or blood toxicology (or both).

After underlying medical conditions are ruled out, violent patients should be seen by a psychiatrist.

The Intoxicated Patient

An alcoholic patient presenting with an altered mental status may be suffering from any of the following conditions:

- Acute intoxication with ethanol or mixed substances such as methanol, ethylene glycol, and/or cocaine.
- Subdural hematoma or any other intracranial structural lesion.
- Hypoglycemia, ketoacidosis, or electrolyte imbalance.

Table 2. Comparison of Findings in Functional and Organic Disorders

	Functional	*Organic*
Age of onset	15-45 yr	Any age
Acuity	Days to weeks	Acute
Prior psychiatric history	Often present	Often absent
Vital signs	Usually normal	Often abnormal
Physical examination	Usually normal	Often abnormal
Level of alertness	Usually normal	May be abnormal
Orientation	Usually normal	Often abnormal
Speech	Normal or pressured	Often abnormal
Delusions	Often present	Absent
Hallucinations	Auditory	May be visual or tactile
Memory	Usually normal	Often abnormal short-term

- CNS infection.
- Thiamine deficiency with acute Wernicke's encephalopathy.
- Delirium tremens.
- Any other medical problem unrelated to intoxication.

All known alcoholic patients or patients with alcohol on their breath who present with an altered mental status should undergo a thorough physical examination to rule out any significant underlying diseases. Ascertain the following:

- Is there evidence of trauma?
- Is there nuchal rigidity?
- Is the patient febrile?
- Are there focal neurologic findings or signs of increased intracranial pressure?
- Were there any focal or new-onset seizures?

All intoxicated patients should have a rapid glucose determination by a glucometer. Consider obtaining a blood alcohol level. Most patients with an altered mental status should receive thiamine 100 mg IVP, $D_{50}W$ 50 mL IV (if glucose is low or unmeasurable), and naloxone 2 mg IV as indicated. Continue to reassess these patients every 15 to 30 minutes for signs of deterioration. If the patient's blood alcohol level is not high, immediately proceed with an extensive workup for an altered mental status including blood labs, head CT, toxicology screen, and possibly an LP.

Indications for an urgent head CT in alcohol-dependent patients include:

- Focal or new-onset seizures
- Evidence of head trauma
- Signs of increased intracranial pressure or focal neurologic findings on examination
- An unimproved or deteriorating level of consciousness.

If the initial alcohol level is high and the patient's level of consciousness improves, usually no further workup is necessary. As a rough estimate, non-alcohol-dependent patients metabolize alcohol at a rate of 15 to 20 mg/dL per hour. In alcohol-dependent patients, the metabolism is enhanced, and the clearance increases to 25 to 30 mg/dL per hour. **PEARL: Remember that alcohol-dependent patients may have very high blood alcohol levels while acting completely sober.**

The Homeless Patient

Because of poor nutrition and hygiene, inaccessible medical care, and lack of social supports, otherwise benign illnesses can develop a malignant course among the homeless. Also, these patients tend to present for treatment much later in the course of their disease and, therefore, often have a more serious illness. Soft tissue infections, pneumonia, and dehydration (which might otherwise be managed outside the hospital) can require inpatient care because of poor patient compliance and lack of stable medical follow-up.

Lack of adequate shelter exposes the homeless to the extreme elements and their associated conditions such as frostbite, trench foot, hypothermia, heat exhaustion, and heat stroke. Therefore, a rectal temperature should be measured, especially during the cold months. Other commonly encountered problems in the homeless include malnutrition, skin ulcers, lice, scabies, alcohol abuse, trauma, viral hepatitis, tuberculosis, and mental illnesses.

If the patient is being discharged, a follow-up should be arranged. We recommend using social services to help arrange for proper disposition. If no alternative care is possible, have the patient come back for a follow-up.

□

BURNS

Pre-hospital Considerations

- All patients require 100% O_2 via nonrebreather mask.
- Cool burns with cold water, then cover with a sterile or clean sheet.
- Avoid excessive cooling with ice, especially with burns over a large area.
- Do not cover burned skin with any creams or oinments.
- Chemical burns require copious irrigation.

Burns are the result of thermal injury and are caused by scalding fluids, steam, fire, electricity, or chemicals. In the past, fluid loss was a major cause of mortality; today, **inhalational injury** and **sepsis** are the major contributing factors. Therefore, in addition to aggressive fluid management, early recognition of inhalational injury and appropriate management are paramount. **Remember, too, that the patient may also have other significant injuries and should be managed as for any other multiply injured patient.**

The prognosis of burn victims depends on the patient's age, the extent of the burn [percentage of body surface area (% BSA)], the burn depth, the presence of associated inhalational injury, and the patient's past medical history. Therefore, every one of the latter factors must be assessed.

History

Include the following information in the patient's history.

- What caused the injury?
- What kind of material was combusted?
- Did the injury occur in a closed space?
- Is there any evidence of inhalation injury?

- Was the patient conscious at the scene?
- What treatment was already given at the scene and en-route (e.g. O_2, fluids)?
- Does the patient have any underlying medical illnesses or immunocompromised conditions?

Initial Assessment and Management of the Burn Victim

Airway

Immediately determine whether there are any signs of present or impending airway compromise. Facial edema, singed nasal vibrisae, perioral burns, and carbonaceous sputum should all increase your degree of suspicion of inhalational injury. Laryngeal edema can develop rapidly, making endotracheal intubation very difficult or impossible. **PEARL: Assume all patients with flame injuries in a closed space have an inhalation injury and may need immediate intubation.** Therefore, if there is any suggestion of airway compromise, intubate the patient with the largest endotracheal tube possible. If there is already significant laryngeal edema making intubation impossible, perform a cricothyroidotomy.

Breathing

Inhalational injury secondary to toxic fumes or steam as well as carbon monoxide or cyanide poisoning should always be suspected. All patients should receive 100% supplemental O_2 while ABGs and carboxyhemoglobin levels are being obtained. For a more detailed review of carbon monoxide and cyanide poisonings, patients who fail to maintain adequate oxygenation (PaO_2 60 mm Hg on 100% O_2) or ventilation ($PaCO_2$ > 50 mm Hg) require intubation and mechanical ventilation.

Circulation

Burns cause significant external fluid loss as well as large internal fluid shifts. Rapidly assess the patient's hemodynamic stability. **PEARL: Establish I.V. access with at least two large-bore I.V. catheters, preferably through intact skin (IVs can be placed through injured skin if no other sites are available).** Femoral lines or saphenous venous cut-downs present a high risk for infection or thrombosis and should be avoided. Monitor urine output closely using an indwelling urethral catheter.

Fluid Resuscitation

The patient's fluid requirements during the first 24 hours can be estimated with the Parkland formula.

2 to 4 mL/kg of lactated Ringer's lactate per % BSA (up to 50%) burned should be given during the first 24 hours (only second- and third-degree burns should be considered in calculating percentage of BSA). Half of the requirements are given within the first eight hours from the time of the injury (*not* from the time of presentation). Make adjustments based on clinical parameters such as vital signs, urine output, and central venous pressure.

Assessment of the Burn

Depth

Burns are classified according to depth:

- **First-degree burns** involve only the epidermis, causing erythema and pain.
- **Second-degree burns** involve the epidermis and part of the dermis, causing blistering and severe pain.
- **Third-degree burns** involve the epidermis and all elements of the dermis as well as subdermal tissues.

They are characterized by coagulation of blood vessels and white or brown, shiny, leathery skin. These burns do not blanch and usually are not painful because the nerves are destroyed.

Percentage of Body Surface Area

This can be estimated roughly by using the patient's palm, which equals 1% of the total BSA, as a reference. In adults, use the "rule of nines":

Head = 9%
Anterior trunk = 18%
Posterior trunk = 18%
Upper limb = 9%

Anterior lower limb = 9%
Posterior lower limb = 9%
Genitalia = 1%

In children, the head is larger and the lower limbs smaller in proportion to adults (Fig. 1).

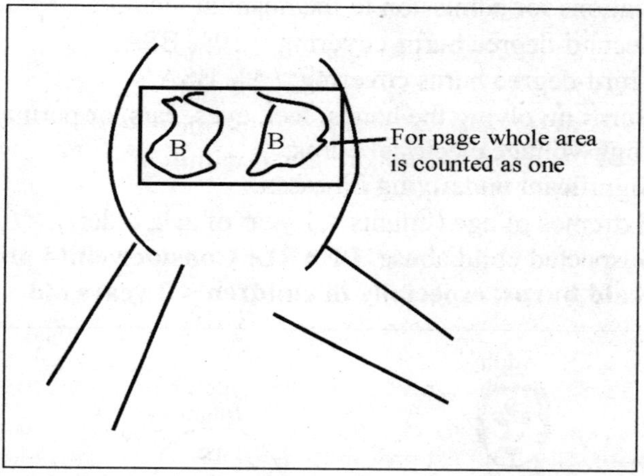

Fig. 1.

If burns are not in continued on abdomen chest extremeties, then measure with palm.

Palm is 1% of burn area. If second degree burns are there, the intervening areas is also conted as burned are as the blood supply is cut off from both sides.

Local Treatment of Burns

In third-degree burns, eschars (necrotic burned tissues) are stiff and, if circumferential, can compromise circulation (in the limbs) or breathing (in the trunk). **PEARL: If there is any evidence of vascular or respiratory compromise, perform an escharotomy.** Use a #10 scalpel along the sides of the arms, legs, digits, or chest as required (Fig. 2). Anesthesia is not necessary, and the incision should be deep enough to allow the scar to expand and the subcutaneous fat to bulge, thus improving circulation or ventilation.

Cleanse second-degree burns with a balanced crystalloid solution. Ruptured blisters should be gently debrided; however, unruptured blisters should be left intact. Then, cover the burns with a sterile dressing. If the patient is to be discharged, use an antimicrobial cream such as bacitracin or silver sulfadiazine.

Disposition

Indications for admission to the hospital include:

- Second-degree burns covering > 10% BSA.
- Third-degree burns covering > 5% BSA.
- Burns involving the hands, feet, eyes, ears, or perineum.
- High-voltage electrical burns.
- Significant underlying illnesses.
- Extremes of age (infants < 1 year of age, elderly > 65 years).
- Suspected child abuse. **PEARL: Consider child abuse with scald burns, especially in children < 3 years old.**

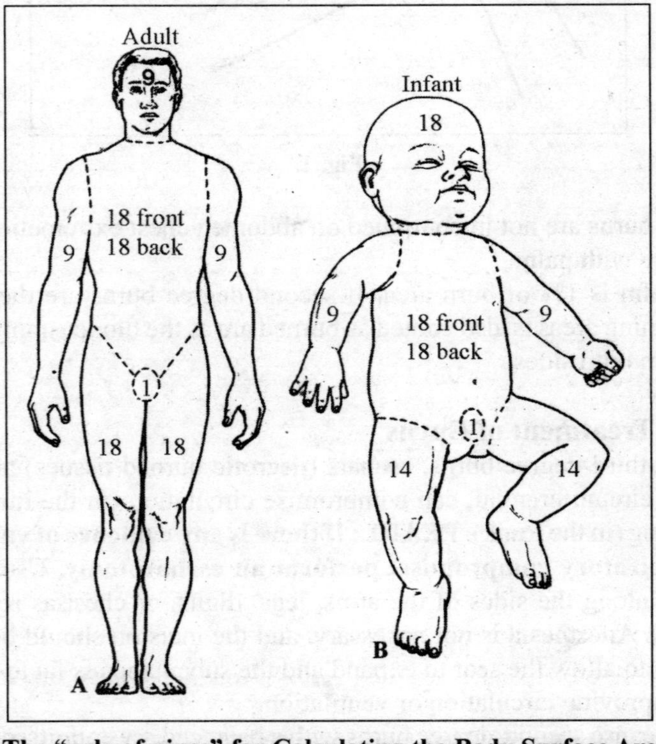

Fig. 2: The "rule of nines" for Calculating the Body Surface Area in an Adult (A) and a Child (B).

All wounds should be reevaluated within 48 hours. Systemic antibiotic prophylaxis is not indicated. Give tetanus prophylaxis in accordance with the guidelines presented.

Pearls for Management of Burn Patient

(1) Intravenous fluids: 2 cc/kg/% of burn in 1st 24 hrs

In 1st 8 hrs 1/2 colloid

(1/3rd Blood if Burn 1 > 30 %) + half crystalloids + remaining plama) Dextran or Plasmaran **(Take blood sample for cross matching before giving Dextran)**

In next 16 hrs — One half of total colloid and remaining half of total crystalloids

Next 24 hrs — Same as 1st 24 hrs

(2) For Deep Burns: Blood must be given

Rate of Drip

Amount of fluid in litres in 24 hrs × 12
= No. of drops/per minute

(3) If burns are more than 50%

Calculate fluid only for 50% of burns

Sign of Patient Recovery

(1) Patient is quiet.

(2) Thirst is relieved.

(3) Urine is 25-30 cc/hrs.

(4) Patient is warm.

(5) Peripheral circulation is good.

Maximum loss of fluids in 1st eight hrs it stops after 48 hrs after that resorption starts. In patient with 10-15% burn can give oral fluid only.

In patients with 15-30% of burns—Put it cannula for I.V. drip can skip blood transfusion?

If > 30% burns—Must give blood transfusion

(3) Sedation – Morphia 15 mg for an adult I.V.

(4) Tetanus toxoid

(5) High protein diet

(6) Antibiotics

(7) Local care of burns

(8) Oxygen therapy in extreme burns are if face or respiratory area is involved—3-5 litres/hr

(9) Chart temp., pulse and respiration and blood pressure.

□

TRAUMA

Pre-hospital Considerations

- Rapid transport of all trauma patients to the nearest trauma center is imperative.
- All multiple-trauma patients should be immobilized with a stiff collar and backboard and receive 100% oxygen with a non-rebreather mask.
- Large-bore I.V. access should be established en-route to the hospital, if possible, to minimize the amount of time spent at the scene.
- Rapid infusion of crystalloids should be considered in all hemodynamically unstable patients.

General Principles

In no other situation is it more important to perform a rapid and thorough assessment than in the multiply injured patient. **Your goal is to identify and initiate management for those salvageable injuries that can cause death (if unrecognized) during the first "golden hour."** Although the assessment and management of the multiply injured patient is presented here in a sequential manner in order of priority, in the clinical setting, multiple steps should be addressed simultaneously.

History

Trauma can be divided into two major types: *blunt* and *penetrating.* Blunt trauma is often multiple and occult, whereas penetrating trauma is more limited and readily apparent. Therefore, patients with blunt trauma have greater mortality and morbidity secondary to a delay in diagnosis.

Ascertaining the mechanism of initial trauma can help you to predict the types and severity of resulting injuries. Each type of trauma injury is associated with a distinct set of circumstances. Therefore, one must gather all of the following relevant information:

- **Motor vehicle accidents:** What was the direction of impact; appearance of vehicle (body, windshield, steering wheel, and column); use of restraining devices, seat belts, and/or air bags; and estimated speed at impact (remember energy equals mass times velocity squared)? Ejection of the patient from the vehicle or the death of another passenger significantly increases the likelihood that the patient has serious injuries. Also, try to estimate the degree of external blood loss at the scene.
- **Falls:** From what height and onto what type of surface did the patient fall?
- **Penetrating trauma:** Where was the patient injured? What weapon was used? What was the estimated distance of the patient from the weapon? What was the velocity and caliber of the bullet?

Other important information that should be considered in your evaluation includes damage to structures surrounding the trauma victim at the scene, extrication problems, injuries suffered by others in the same event, events preceding the injury, recent alcohol or drug use, and last oral intake of food or beverage. Also obtain a history of prior illnesses, surgeries, medications, immunizations, and allergies.

Patient management consists of a rapid primary evaluation, resuscitation of vital functions, a more detailed secondary evaluation, and finally, the initiation of definitive care.

The Primary Survey: Assessment of the ABCDEs

During the initial stage of patient evaluation and assessment (the primary survey), you must recognize life-threatening conditions and initiate management simultaneously. Once a problem is identified, it must be addressed before proceeding to the next stage. The mnemonic ABCDE will help you to remember the sequence of patient evaluation during the primary survey: A: airway; B: breathing; C: circulation; D: disability; and E: exposure.

Airway and Cervical Spine

Cervical spine (C-spine) injuries are present in approximately 1% to 2% of all blunt trauma patients and in 5% to 10% of patients with head trauma. **PEARL: It is safest always to assume a C-spine fracture is present.** Excessive motion of the unstable C-spine (both hyperextension and hyperflexion) can cause further neurologic damage.

Rapidly assess the upper airway for obstruction. Use the chin lift and/or jaw thrust to establish airway patency. Look in the mouth for foreign bodies, debris, and vomitus. If the airway is compromised, rapid-sequence induction (RSI) with in-line C-spine immobilization is the preferred method of airway control.

The following is a summary of RSI in the patient with trauma:

1. **Preoxygenate** with 100% O_2.
2. **Pretreat** with vecuronium (0.01 mg/kg IV), lidocaine (1.5 mg/kg IV), and fentanyl (3 to 5 µg/kg JV).
3. **Induce** with etomidate (0.3 mg/kg IV, with multiple injuries) or thiopental (3 to 5 mg/kg IV in isolated head injuries).
4. **Paralyze** with succinylcholine (1.5 mg/kg I.V.). Children under age 5 should be pretreated with atropine 0.01 mg/kg I.V.
5. **Perform orotracheal intubation** with C-spine immobilization.

If you are unable to intubate the patient because of obstructive lesions, you must perform needle or surgical cricothyroidotomy through the cricothyroid membrane. You can find this membrane by locating the suprasternal notch and advancing your finger cephalad in the midline. The first hard cartilaginous structure you encounter is the cricoid cartilage. The soft cricothyroid membrane is immediately above this and below the thyroid cartilage (the "Adam's apple," Fig. 1).

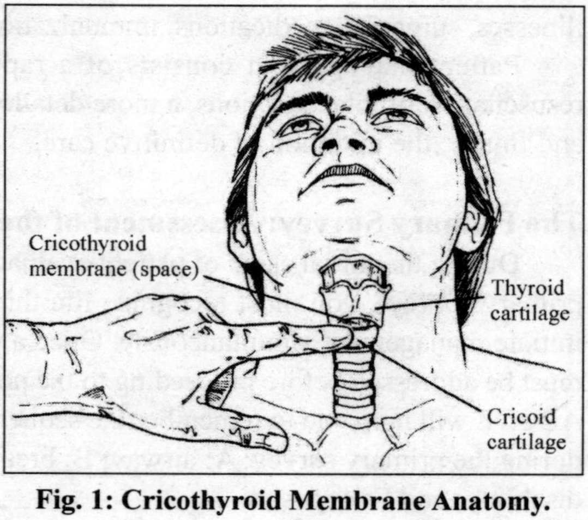

Fig. 1: Cricothyroid Membrane Anatomy.

Needle cricothyroidotomy is

performed by inserting a large-bore angiocatheter attached to a 10-mL syringe through this membrane at a 45° angle in the caudal direction. Aspirating for air while advancing can help prevent cannulation of the esophagus or the soft tissues. The hub of the angiocatheter should be connected to a 3-mm endotracheal tube adapter or to a 3-mL syringe and 7.5-mm adapter, which enables ventilation with a BVM (Fig. 2). Use of a jet insufflator at a pressure of 50 pounds per square inch (psi), however, is the most effective method to ensure adequate oxygenation and ventilation. Use this method only as a temporizing agent because it can result in hypercarbia after 30 minutes.

Surgical cricothyroidotomy is the definitive surgical airway. A midline superficial vertical incision is made between the suprasternal notch and the thyroid cartilage. After the cricothyroid membrane is identified, a horizontal incision is made through it by gently puncturing it with the tip of a # 11 blade. This opening then is enlarged with a surgical clamp, and a 6-mm endotracheal tube (or specialized tracheostomy tube) is inserted between the spread ends of the clamp (Fig. 3). Avoid surgical cricothyroidotomy in children younger than 8 years old because of their small airways.

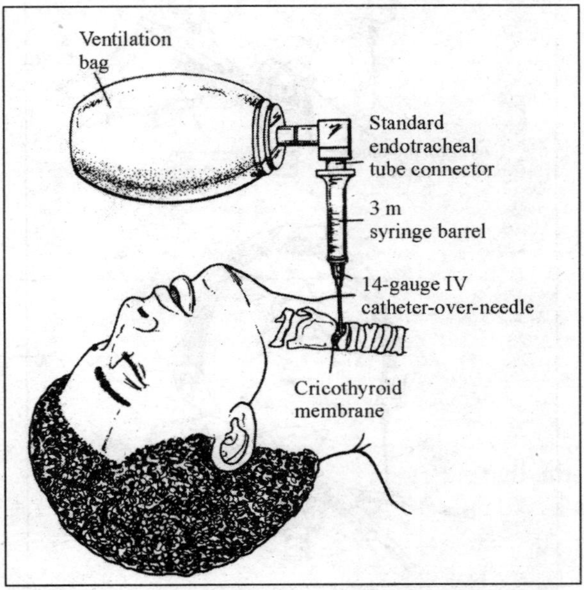

Fig. 2: Needle Cricothyroidotomy.

Breathing

During this stage, attempt to identify the three traumatic conditions that most often severely compromise ventilation: (1) tension pneumothorax, (2) open pneumothorax, and (3) large flail chests with an underlying pulmonary contusion. Examine the chest and assess for adequacy of air exchange:

- Is the chest wall moving?
- Is the movement symmetric?
- Are there any obvious injuries (e.g. open wounds, contusions, abrasions)?
- Auscultate below the armpits bilaterally for the presence of breath sounds.
- Is the trachea midline?

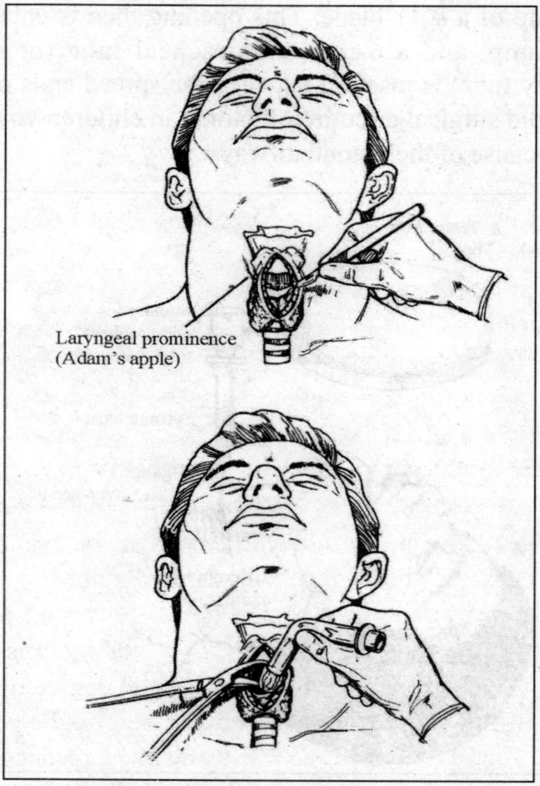

Fig. 3: Surgical Cricothyroidotomy.

- Is there jugular venous distention?
- Is there paradoxic motion of a flail segment of the chest?

If you suspect a tension pneumothorax (i.e. respiratory distress, absent breath sounds, deviated trachea and mediastinum, elevated central venous pressure, and poor peripheral perfusion), insert a #18- or #16-gauge angiocatheter attached to a fluid-filled syringe in the second intercostal space at the mid-clavicular line. The appearance of air bubbles in the fluid-filled syringe both confirms and decompresses a pneumothorax (remember that the patient will need a more definitive chest tube placed after you complete your primary survey). If you find an open-chest wound, an occlusive dressing should be placed immediately. If one is already in place or if on placing an occlusive dressing the patient's respiratory status suddenly deteriorates, remove the occlusive dressing and insert a chest tube before reapplying an occlusive dressing.

All trauma patients should receive supplemental 100% O_2 via a non-rebreather masks.

Circulation

Significant external bleeding should be identified and controlled during the primary survey by direct manual pressure on the wound. Do not blindly insert surgical clamps in wounds in an attempt to stop bleeding. Peripheral perfusion is assessed by examining the patient's level of consciousness, pulse, BP, skin, urine output, and ABGs (for a detailed discussion of assessing tissue perfusion).

Hemorrhagic shock secondary to acute blood loss is the most common cause of shock in trauma patients. Other causes of shock should always be considered, however, especially if the patient is not responding to treatment. *Cardiogenic shock* may be due to underlying cardiac disease or may be the result of a cardiac contusion or pericardial tamponade. *Neurogenic shock* should be considered in patients with relative bradycardia and warm skin. *Hypovolemic shock* is divided into four stages of increasing severity based on the degree of blood loss. Table 1 is a useful classification of shock based on the percentage of volume lost, the average blood loss, and the presence of clinical parameters.

Table 1: Classification of Stages of Hypovolemic Shock

Class	*Blood Loss*	*Physical Examination Findings*	*Therapy*
I	15% (750 mL)	Normal	Ringer's lactate, normal saline
II	15%-30% (750-1500 mL)	Normal BP, tachycardia, anxious	Ringer's lactate, normal saline
III	30%-40% (1500-2000 mL)	May be hypotensive, tachycardia, confused/combative, metabolic acidosis	Ringer's lactate, normal saline *plus* Packed red blood cells (PRBCs)
IV Profound shock	> 40% (> 2000 mL)	Obvious hypotension, tachycardia, coma	Ringer's lactate, normal saline *plus* PRBCs

Early recognition of the shock state, aggressive fluid management, and identification and correction of the underlying cause are the cornerstones of management. In many trauma patients, this means getting them to the operating room as soon as possible. **PEARL: Don't delay the transport of an unstable patient to the operating room to complete physical, radiologic, or lab assessment (all may be completed in the operating room).**

Intravenous Access

Intravenous access must be established as soon as possible with at least two large-bore peripheral IVs (#14- or #16-gauge angiocatheters). Central venous catheters are not part of the initial resuscitation unless no other access is available. They may play an important diagnostic and monitoring role later in the management, but they are rarely required during the primary survey.

The following are sites for IV access *in order of preference* (remember that this is not the time to save the "best" veins for last to demonstrate your skills as a phlebotomist):

1. **Antecubital veins,** which usually are easy to visualize or palpate.
2. **Other peripheral upper-extremity veins** in the forearm or hand. The cephalic vein, located over the lateral radial aspect of the wrist, is often a good choice.
3. **Saphenous venous cutdown.** Perform a 2-cm horizontal incision, 1 cm anterior and 1 cm proximal to the medial malleolus at the ankle. Isolate the greater saphenous vein by blunt dissection with a curved hemostat, and cannulate with a large-bore angiocatheter (Fig. 4).
4. **The femoral vein,** which is located medial to the femoral artery distal to the inguinal ligament. If no pulse is palpable, insert the needle distal to the inguinal ligament one finger breadth medial to the halfway point between the anterior superior iliac spine and the pubic tubercle (Fig. 5). An 8F catheter should be introduced into the vein over a guide wire. This may be faster and easier than a saphenous venous cutdown.
5. **Subclavian or internal jugular vein,** whichever you are more comfortable with. Use an 8F short catheter. Beside ultrasound,

using a 7.5 MHz transducer may help locate the veins in different situations.

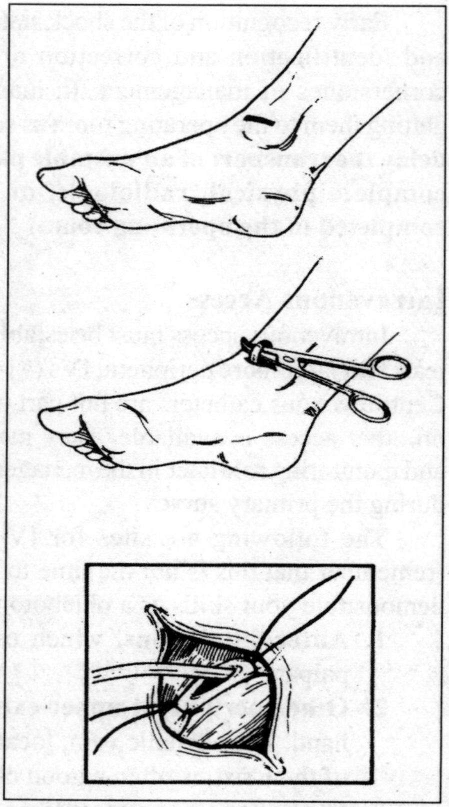

Fig. 4: Saphenous Venous Cutdown.

Fluids

Although the issue of crystalloids versus colloids is controversial, crystalloids should be the initial choice in shock. **PEARL: Don't be afraid to push fluids in patients with head or spinal cord injuries who are hemodynamically unstable.** Either normal saline (NS) or lactated Ringer's solution may be used. As a rule, three times as much crystalloids are required to replace the loss of a given amount of blood. Begin by giving a 2-liter fluid bolus as rapidly as possible (rapid infusion pumps are available in some emergency departments). Further fluid management is determined by the response to this initial fluid challenge. **PEARL: Give blood to hemodynamically unstable patients not responding to crystalloids.** If the patient remains hypotensive, give blood. Although type-specific blood is preferable (usually available within 10 minutes), type O-negative blood should be given if the patient is hemodynamically unstable.

Blood is most often given as packed red blood cells (PRBCs). Generally, give 2 U of fresh frozen plasma for every 6 U of PRBCs transfused. With very rapid infusion of blood, both platelets and calcium chloride may be required. *Note that blood products must be diluted with NS, not lactated Ringer's solution.* **PEARL: Avoid overly**

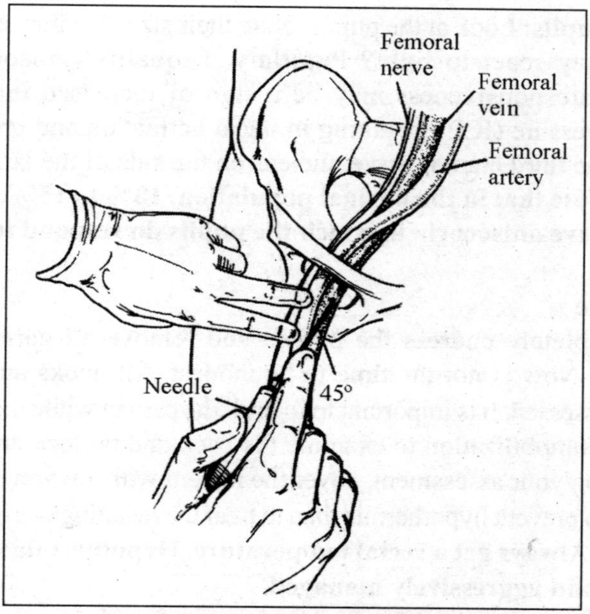

Fig. 5: Femoral Vein Cannulation

aggressive fluid resuscitation in the hemodynamically stable patient with head or spinal cord injuries.

Disability

During the primary survey, a brief neurologic evaluation, including level of consciousness and a pupil examination, should be performed:

1. The patient's level of consciousness can be described using the AVPU method:

   A alert

   V responds to *vocal* stimuli

   P responds to *painful* stimuli (pain should be applied above the clavicles such as supraorbital pressure)

   U unresponsive to all stimuli.

   The GCS is rarely necessary in the primary survey; it is used during the secondary survey. If the patient is to be intubated and paralyzed, however, rapid GCS assessment is essential for the neurosurgeon. Often it is enough to say, "Open your eyes," and note the response to noxious stimuli such as IV attempts.

2. **Pupils:** Look at the pupils. Note their size. Are they equal? Do they react to light? Pupillary inequality (anisocoria) or unresponsiveness may be a sign of increased intracranial pressure (ICP), resulting in uncal herniation and pressure on the third cranial nerve nucleus on the side of the larger pupil. **Note that in the normal population, 10% to 15% of people have anisocoria in which the pupils do respond to light.**

Exposure

Completely undress the patient and remove all garments and jewellery. Now is not the time to be modest. All nooks and corners must be assessed. It is important to log roll the patient while maintaining C-spine immobilization to examine the back and buttock areas. After completing your assessment, cover the patient with a warm blanket. It is easier to prevent hypothermia than to treat the resulting complications. **PEARL: Always get a rectal temperature. Hypothermia should be avoided and aggressively managed.**

Monitoring

All patients in shock should be connected to a cardiac monitor and pulse oximetry. Place an automated BP monitor or an arterial line. If the patient remains hypotensive, consider inserting a central venous pressure catheter to assess for elevated right-sided pressures that may be caused by pericardial tamponade or for very low pressures that require more aggressive fluid or blood resuscitation.

Resuscitation

Although presented separately, resuscitative efforts should be instituted while the primary and secondary surveys are being performed.

The following elements should be part of the resuscitation of all trauma patients:

- **O_2:** All patients should receive supplemental O_2 via a nonrebreather mask.
- **IV access:** All patients should have at least two peripheral large-bore IVs established, as described previously in this chapter under IV Access (i.e. in patients in hypovolemic shock). When

inserting an IV, blood should be drawn immediately for type and cross-match as well as for a baseline complete blood count (CBC), chemistry, and amylase. Seriously injured patients should have a hematocrit. If you insert an angiocatheter and have difficulty obtaining the required amount of blood, draw blood from the femoral artery to avoid wasting precious time.

- **Urinary output:** Output should be monitored after an indwelling urethral catheter is placed. Attempts should be made first to obtain a spontaneously voided urine because urethral catheterization can cause injury and some bleeding. **PEARL: Always examine the genitalia and perform a rectal examination before inserting a urethral catheter.** Contraindications to urinary catheterization include blood at the external meatus, perineal or scrotal hematoma, and a high-riding or non-palpable prostate. If a urinary catheter cannot be placed, the patient will need an emergent retrograde urethrogram.
- **Ryles tube:** Gastric catheters should be considered at this point. Aspiration of blood suggests gastrointestinal injury. Emptying the stomach also reduces the risk of aspiration and relieves pressure on the diaphragm that can limit adequate ventilation. In cases of significant nasal trauma or suspected skull fracture, an orogastric tube should be placed (because of the risk of a nasal approach leading to intracranial intubation). Early placement of a gastric catheter also enables administration of oral contrast when an abdominal computed tomographic (CT) scan is required.
- **Radiologic trauma screen:** A screen should be obtained, including a cross-table lateral view of the neck, a supine anteroposterior view of the chest, and a pelvic view. It is easiest to film all three areas in rapid succession before having the technician develop the films. All other X-rays should be performed after stabilization and performance of a more detailed secondary survey.
- Ultrasound of whole abdomen.
- CT scan of chest and whole abdomen.

The Secondary Survey

The secondary survey consists of a thorough head-to-toe evaluation of the patient including assessment of vital signs. **PEARL: Continually reassess the patient's vital signs, airway, and endotracheal tube placement.** This survey must not be performed before initial patient stabilization. A complete description of the secondary survey can be found in the ATLS manual. Several often-neglected areas are highlighted.

Head

- Paper clips bent in two can be used to create eyelid re-tractors when eye opening is difficult.
- Epistaxis (nosebleed) should be tamponaded with a nasal tampon.
- A nasal septal hematoma should be drained with a #18-gauge needle or a #11 blade.
- A hemotympanum is the most common clinical finding in basilar skull fractures.

Central Nervous System

The patient's level of consciousness, based on the GCS, should be assessed (Table 2). The neurologic status should be reassessed repeatedly (every 10 to 15 minutes) for signs of deterioration.

Increased ICP with herniation is suggested by the following signs and symptoms:

- GCS < 8
- Unequal pupils (anisocoria > 1 mm) in a patient with an altered mental status.
- Cushing's, triad (hypertension, bradycardia, and abnormal respirations).
- Deteriorating neurologic status.
- Significant edema or midline shift visualized on a head CT scan.
- Lateralizing neurologic signs.

The following measures will help decrease ICP:

1. Elevate the head of the bed to 30° if shock has been corrected.

Table 2: The Glasgow Coma Scale

1. Best Verbal Response	
None	1
Incomprehensible sound	2
Inappropriate words	3
Confused	4
Oriented	5
2. Eye Opening	
None	1
To pain	2
To command	3
Spontaneously	4
3. Best Motor Response	
None	1
Abnormal extension	2
Abnormal flexion	3
Withdrawal	4
Localizes	5
Obeys commands	6
Total Score	**3-15**

2. Intubate and hyperventilate the patient *down* to a $PaCO_2$ of approximately 30 mmHg by ventilating the patient 20 times per minute (once the $PaCO_2$ drops below 30 mmHg, significant cerebral vasoconstriction will occur and cause a decreased perfusion pressure that can cause more ischemic damage).
3. Give mannitol 1 g/kg IV rapidly (avoid in the hypotensive patient).
4. Sedate the patient; give morphine sulfate 0.1 mg/kg IV every hour.
5. Paralyze the patient; give vecuronium or pancuronium 0.1 mg/kg IV every hour.
6. Maintain normothermia. (If patient is febrile, give antipyretics.)

Indications for a head CT scan in the multiply injured patient include:

- Head injury with skull penetration.

- Any alteration in the level of consciousness.
- A clear history of substantial loss of consciousness with memory deficit.
- Focal neurologic findings or lateralization on examination
- Recurrent vomiting.
- Increasing headache.

Any patient with significant signs or symptoms suggesting intracranial injury should be admitted for observation and possibly a second head CT scan in 24 hours, even if the initial CT scan is negative.

Maxillofacial Trauma

Palpate for areas of tenderness and instability. Grasp the upper teeth and assess for mid-face instability. Have the patient open and close his or her mouth and assess for malocclusion.

Cervical Spine

Radiographic evaluation of the C-spine should include a cross-table lateral film, an anterior-posterior film, and an open mouth view (odontoid film). If despite normal plain films you still suspect injury, additional films or scans of the neck [e.g. oblique, flexion-extension, CT, or magnetic resonance imaging (MRI)] may be performed. All seven vertebrae, including the C7 to Tl alignment, must be visualized. To facilitate visualization of the lower vertebrae, pull down on the patient's arms while obtaining the cross-table lateral film. If either of the arms is injured, wrap a long sheet around the shoulder from front to back and apply traction in the direction of the feet. If you still cannot see all the cervical vertebrae, a "swimmer's" view is recommended.

No X-ray is indicated if all of the following criteria are fulfilled:

- The patient is alert.
- The patient is not intoxicated.
- There are no significant distracting injuries (i.e. an extremity fracture).
- There is no mid-line neck tenderness.
- The patient denies having any neck pain.

Remove the cervical collar and ask the patient to move his or her head. If the patient has severe pain or great difficulty, obtain films.

Chest

The presence of deformities, ecchymosis, subcutaneous emphysema, and unequal breath sounds can suggest significant thoracic pathology.

Distant heart sounds and distended neck veins can indicate cardiac tamponade (in the presence of hypovolemia, however, neck veins may not be distended). Indications for chest tube placement include:

- Penetrating trauma to the chest: Don't forget that high abdominal and flank injuries can also invade the pleural cavity.
- Hemothorax or pneumothorax.
- Subcutaneous emphysema and multiple rib fractures, especially if the patient is to be taken to the operating room and ventilated with positive pressure.

If a chest tube is indicated, insert a large chest tube (#34F) anterior to the mid-axillary line at the level of the fifth intercostal space (at the level of the nipple in men or at the level of the inframammary fold in women) (Fig. 6A).

Prep and drape the chest at the site of insertion and, if time allows, locally anesthetize the skin and rib periosteum with 1% lidocaine. Make a horizontal 2- to 3-cm incision over the rib below the predetermined space. Then bluntly dissect through the subcutaneous tissues over the top of the rib, and carefully puncture the parietal pleura with the tip of a large clamp. Insert your finger into the incision, and to avoid further injury, perform a 360° sweep, feeling for organs (lungs, heart, liver, spleen) and adhesions before inserting the chest tube.

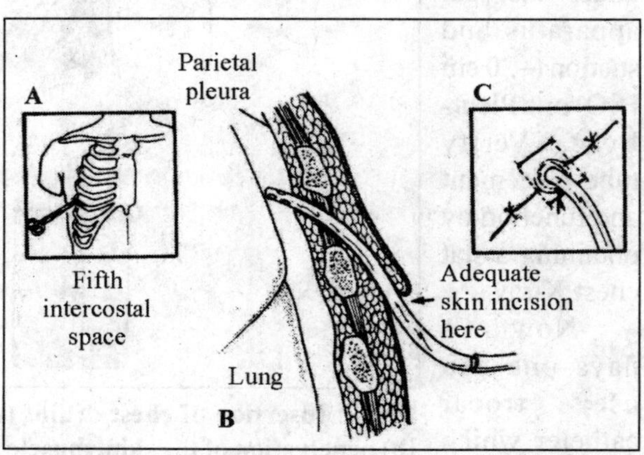

Fig. 6: Chest tube placement. (A) Location of chest tube insertion. (B) Tunnel the tube through the subcutaneous tissue and above the rib superior to the site of insertion. (C) Secure the tube with a pursestring suture.

Because most trauma

patients have a combined pneumothorax and hemothorax and are usually supine, direct your chest tube posteriorly, superiorly, and medially. Make sure all side holes are within the pleural cavity. Look for condensation in the chest tube. Do not let go of the tube until it is adequately secured with a #0 silk or mersilene suture and adhesive tape (Fig. 6C). The end of the chest tube should be attached to an underwater seal apparatus and suction (–20 cm H_2O) or a Pleur-Evac. Verify tube placement and function by obtaining a stat chest X-ray.

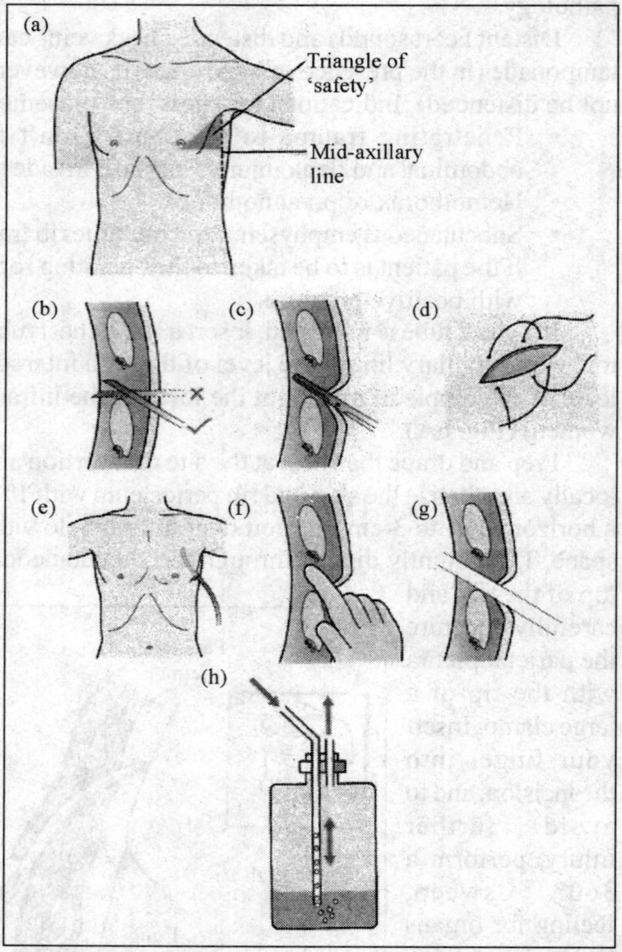

Fig. 7: Insertion of chest drain: (a) triangle of safety; (b) penetration of the skin, muscle and pleura; (c) blunt dissection of the parietal pleura; (d) suture placement; (e) gauging the distance of insertion; (f) digital examination along the tract into the pleural space; (g) withdrawal of central trochar and positioning of drain; (h) underwater seal chest drain bottle.

Now a days one can use trocar catheter which one easy and more simpler to put in.

Abdomen

Focus on determining whether an abdominal injury exists and surgical intervention is required. Frequent re-assessments help you to identify any change in the patient's condition. The abdominal examination involves the following:

- **Inspection:** Are there any obvious penetrating injuries or evisceration of intra-abdominal organs (which usually are absolute indications for operative intervention)? (Some institutions are selective in cases of stab wounds.) Are there any significant abrasions or contusions indicating injury? Is the abdomen distended?
- **Palpation for areas of tenderness, rigidity, or masses:** Always perform a rectal examination for evidence of obvious rectal tears, pelvic fractures, or blood. Note the rectal tone and the position of the prostate gland.

Diagnostic Aids

The choice of abdominal CT, bedside ultrasonography, or peritoneal lavage for the evaluation of abdominal trauma is controversial and often institution-dependent. CT (with and without oral and IV contrast) gives the most specific anatomic information and allows assessment of the retroperitoneal space as well. If the patient is too unstable to be transferred to the CT scanner, however, peritoneal lavage or bedside ultrasound should be chosen. Performance of a rapid bedside ultrasound that allows early detection of intra-abdominal blood has become more acceptable and readily available in many institutions.

Indications for abdominal imaging include:

- Equivocal abdominal findings (e.g. in the presence of fractured ribs or lumbar spine fracture).
- The presence of head injury, intoxication, or paraplegia, which make the abdominal examination unreliable.
- Necessity of other lengthy evaluations or surgery (which precludes frequent reassessment).
- Unexplained hypotension. **PEARL: Never presume that hypotension is caused by a head injury.**

If you choose to perform a peritoneal lavage, we suggest that you use a semiopen technique with an incision through the skin and

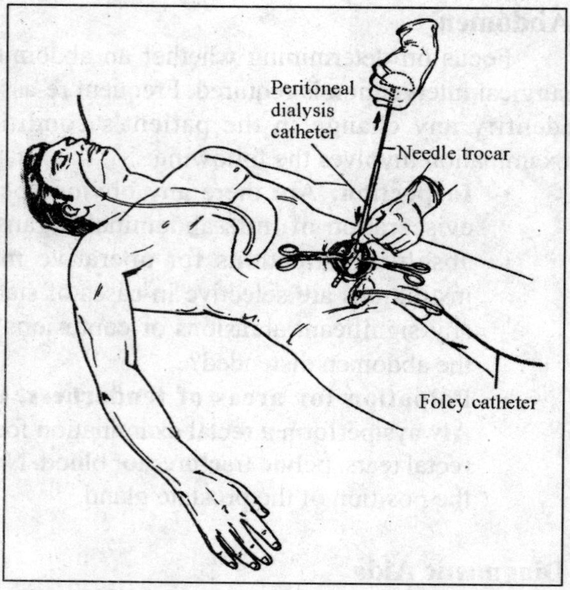

Fig. 8: Peritoneal lavage. An assistant should place traction on the transversalis fascia and peritoneum.

subcutaneous tissue before inserting a peritoneal dialysis catheter over a trocar. Have an assistant apply traction and elevate the abdominal wall with a pair of clamps. This will make using the peritoneal trocar easier and safer. Peritoneal lavage should be performed below the umbilicus in the midline (Fig. 8). Always decompress the stomach and bladder with a gastric tube and urinary catheter before performing lavage to avoid damage to these organs. Aspirate for blood or obvious enteric contents. If none is present, instill 1 liter of warm crystalloid (10 mL/kg in children) and then drain by gravity.

The following findings on peritoneal lavage often indicate the need for exploratory laparotomy:

- > 5 mL of gross blood on aspiration.
- Obvious enteric contents (food, feces).
- Appearance of peritoneal fluid in urinary catheter or chest tube.
- 100,000 RBCs/mL of peritoneal lavage fluid.
- 500 white blood cells (WBCs)/mL of peritoneal lavage fluid.
- Amylase > 175 U (controversial).

Surgery is also indicated in the unstable patient with evidence of intra-abdominal fluid on ultrasonography. Abdominal imaging should never be performed when early surgical intervention is clearly indicated, as in the hemodynamically unstable patient with evidence of abdominal trauma or in the patient with unequivocal peritoneal irritation.

Pelvis and Perineum

Urine should be obtained for a urine dipstick, which if negative, reliably rules out hematuria. Remember that a positive dipstick may also be caused by hemoglobinuria (usually pink) or myoglobinuria (usually cola colored). Therefore, if the dipstick is positive, send urine for microscopic analysis to confirm the presence of hematuria. Isolated microhematuria in the hemodynamically stable patient does not require further workup. **PEARL: Perform a digital vaginal examination in female patients, looking for blood and evidence of a pelvic fracture.** Priapism in men suggests spinal cord injury.

Extremities

Inspect all extremities for swelling, ecchymosis, or obvious deformities. **PEARL: Palpate and document all extremity pulses.** All peripheral pulses should be assessed. If pulses are not palpable, try using a portable Doppler. Emergency arteriography should be considered in the presence of an arterial bleeder, an expanding hematoma, or a penetrating trauma in proximity to a major blood vessel.

Log roll the patient as a unit while immobilizing the head and neck, and inspect and palpate the thoracic and lumbar spine for areas of swelling, deformity, or tenderness. Don't forget to look between the buttocks for evidence of injury.

□

CLOSED HEAD INJURY

A. The neurologic examination is a critical part of the primary survey recommended by the American College of Surgeons Advanced Trauma Life Support protocols. Maintenance of airway, breathing, and circulation are of utmost importance.

B. Brain injury is thought to occur in two phases. The first phase occurs at the time of impact and is irreversible. The second phase occurs from that moment on and is caused by effects ultimately related to poor cerebral perfusion or oxygenation of the penumbra. Injury occurring during the latter phase may be ameliorated by intervention.

C. Data suggest that maintaining a cerebral perfusion pressure (cerebral perfusion pressure equals mean arterial pressure minus intracranial pressure) greater than 70 mmHg, an intracranial pressure less than 20 mmHg, PCO_2 of 30 to 35 mmHg, and a pO_2 of greater than 60 mmHg may helplessen secondary brain injury.

D. Injury to the central nervous system is often assessed by the Glasgow Coma Scale (GCS). The GCS measures motor response, verbal response, and eye opening. Motor response is graded as follows: commands (6 points), localizes (5 points), withdraws to pain (4 points), decorticate or flexor posturing (3 points), decerebrate or extensor posturing (2 points), and no response (1 point). Verbal response is graded as follows: oriented (5 points), confused (4 points), inappropriate (3 points), incomprehensible sounds (2 points), no response (1 point). Eye opening is graded as follows: spontaneous (4 points), open to voice (3 points), open to pain (2 points), no response (1 point). The best score is 15 and the worst score is 3. Although this scale measures global function and consciousness, it is not sensitive to focal neurologic deficits or pupillary reactivity that may alter treatment. Repeat neurologic examinations are crucial to clinical decision making. Deteriorating findings on examinations may indicate the need for urgent neurosurgical intervention.

E. Confounding factors such as chemical paralysis or alcohol intoxication will often obscure a single neurologic assessment.

F. Decreased mental status or level of consciousness may indicate the need for intracranial pressure monitoring. If serial neurologic examinations are not possible (e.g. because of sedation), intracranial pressure should be monitored by a fiberoptic pressure transducer or ventriculostomy. A GCS score of 8 or less is an indication for intracranial pressure monitoring. Certainly, any patient with a significant head injury and the need for an operative procedure should be monitored for intracranial hypertension throughout that operation.

G. Patients who are fully alert and who have a normal examination may be observed. Patients who have had a seizure should be monitored closely. In the setting of intracranial hemorrhage, prevention of early post-traumatic seizures may be managed by phenytoin given for 1 week; however, this does not appear to alter the incidence of late onset (more than seven days) seizures.

H. Intubation and hyperventilation to a PCO_2 of 30 to 35 mmHg decreases intracranial pressure; however, a PCO_2 below this level is thought by some to be harmful because it might exacerbate cerebral ischemia. Osmotic diuretics such as mannitol also aid in decreasing intracranial pressure with intermittent doses. Glucocorticoids such as dexamethasone are not recommended in severe head injury. Elevation of the patient's head in reverse Trendelenburg is a simple maneuver to decrease intracranial pressure while maintaining spine precautions. Care should be taken to ensure that the cervical collar is not so overly snug that jugular venous outflow is impaired. Computed tomography (CT) is sensitive for most traumatic intracranial pathology. Repeat CT should be performed if there is obvious intracranial pathology on the initial scan or if the neurologic examination changes. **Scans performed within a few hours of injury may not accurately reflect intracranial pathology.** Diffuse axonal injury may not show any manifestations on CT scans.

I. If a focal neurologic deficit cannot be explained by CT, carotid injury should be suspected and radiographic evaluation (e.g. angiography, CT angiography, or magnetic resonance angiography) should be performed.

J. Patients with normal CT scans and normal neurologic examinations who are not under the influence of drugs or alcohol may be observed or sent home under the direct supervision of a responsible individual. A post-traumatic seizure warrants observation in the hospital. Concussion can be graded by several scales; these generally take into account confusion, loss of consciousness, amnesia, and duration of symptoms. Estimates of the duration of unconsciousness before arrival to the hospital are often unreliable; however, post-traumatic amnesia correlates with the severity of concussion and with prognosis. Patients with a loss of consciousness should undergo a CT scan. Postconcussive syndrome may ensue after trauma and may last days to months. Headache, nausea, dizziness, vertigo, short-term memory loss, difficulty with concentration, irritability, and fatigue are manifestations of this syndrome. These symptoms gradually resolve; however, if they are associated with focal neurologic deficits or if they persist, a repeat CT scan is indicated. In addition, severe headache during the days following trauma is another indication for a repeat CT scan. Return to sports after concussion should await complete resolution of any and all symptoms related to the injury. Resuming activity before resolution of symptoms may result in severe damage even if the second head injury is mild.

K. Intracranial hemorrhages are evacuated via craniotomy depending on the extent of the mass effect and the neurologic examination. Posterior fossa pathology often requires urgent neurosurgical intervention. Closed depressed skull fractures may be repaired electively depending on the cosmetic deficit.

Important Pearls in Management of Headinjuries

Management

(1) AIRWAY
(2) Bleeding
(3) Perforation of any viscera
(4) Bladder
(5) Nutrition
(6) Fluid and electrolyte balance
(7) External injury

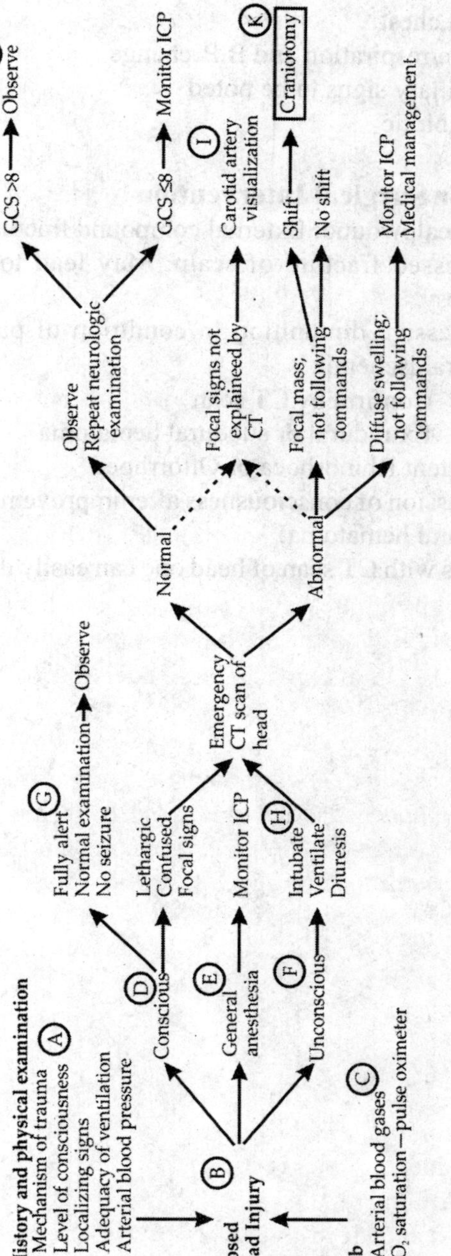
History and physical examination
Mechanism of trauma
Level of consciousness
Localizing signs
Adequacy of ventilation
Arterial blood pressure
A
Closed Head Injury
B
Lab
Arterial blood gases
O2 saturation—pulse oximeter
C
Conscious
D
General anesthesia
E
Unconscious
F
Fully alert
Normal examination → Observe
No seizure
G
Lethargic
Confused
Focal signs
Monitor ICP
Intubate
Ventilate
Diuresis
H
Emergency CT scan of head
Normal
Abnormal
Observe
Repeat neurologic examination
GCS >8 → Observe
J
GCS ≤8 → Monitor ICP
Focal signs not explained by CT
Carotid artery visualization
I
Focal mass; not following commands
Shift → Craniotomy
K
No shift
Diffuse swelling; not following commands
Monitor ICP
Medical management

(8) Flail chest
(9) Pulse/respiration and B.P. change
(10) Pupillary signs to be noted
(11) Antibiotic

Indication for Surgical Intervention

(1) Any scalpwound: External compound fracture of scalp bone.
(2) Depressed fracture of scalp: May lead to post traumatic epilepsy.
(3) Progressive dimunition in condition of patient indicating cerebral ischemia
Confirm by CT scan
Extradural or subdural hematoma
(4) Persistent Rhinorhoea or Ottorrhoea
(5) Regression of consciousness after improvement (posibility of subdural hematoma).

Nowadays with CT scan of head one can easily decide whether to operate of not.

□

CERVICAL SPINE FRACTURES

A. Recognition of a cervical fracture is of paramount importance. Neck or midscapular pain, muscle spasm, or neurologic deficit in the setting of trauma should raise suspicion for a cervical fracture. Change in level of consciousness or drug use can sometimes obscure these clues, but mechanism of injury should also alert the physician to the possibility. Motor vehicle accidents, falls, and diving accidents are common causes of cervical spine fractures. Gunshot wound victims do not usually sustain spine fractures unless the trajectory of the bullet nears the spine. Some studies have also found an association between head injury and cervical spine fractures, most commonly in the upper cervical spine.

B. Neurologic deficit will alter treatment options. Motor or sensory deficit, absence of rectal tone, loss of bulbocavernosus reflex, priaprism, paradoxical respirations (use of accessory muscles), or bradycardia and hypotension (neurogenic shock) are indicators of cervical spine injury. Monoplegia or a Homer's sign are more suggestive of a brachial plexus injury. Progressive neurologic deficit demands emergent imaging (e.g., X-ray, CT, or MRI) followed by intervention.

The role of methylprednisolone in spinal cord injury was studied in the NASCIS I, II, and III trials. Although still controversial, there is evidence to suggest that high-dose methylprednisolone sodium succinate given within eight hours of injury may facilitate neurologic improvement, more so in incomplete spinal injury. Benefit was seen after an intravenous loading dose of 30 mg/kg over 15 minutes followed by 5.4 mg/kg/hour infusion for 24 hours if given up to 3 hours after injury, or 48 hours if given from three to eight hours after injury. Decreased neurologic recovery was noted if methylprednisolone was administered more than eight hours after injury. Although some studies have shown a higher incidence of adverse events after use of high-dose methylprednisolone, a systematic review did not reveal any significant increase in complications; however, those patients receiving treatment for 48 hours may be at higher risk for pulmonary complications (reported in NASCIS III). There is also some evidence to suggest that maintenance of a mean arterial pressure greater than 85 mmHg for seven days postinjury may improve neurologic outcome.

C. The presence of neck or mid-scapular pain should prompt a thorough radiographic work-up. Plain films are often used first for screening. Abnormalities on plain film lead to more detailed investigation with thin-cut CT scans and reconstructions. Helical CT may be more efficacious and cost effective for screening in trauma patients. MRIs or angiograms are sometimes indicated to rule out ligamentous or vascular injury. If no fracture is elucidated but pain persists, patients should be maintained in a cervical collar until pain resolves and flexion/extension X-rays can be obtained. Care should be taken to ensure that all radiographs are of adequate quality and that all segments of the cervical spine including the cervicothoracic junction are well visualized.

D. Marked subluxation generally requires reduction. Most clinicians will proceed with CT evaluation of the fracture site first, but in the presence of a neurologic deficit, early reduction may be attempted. Traction is applied through a halo ring or Gardner-Wells tongs. After reduction is achieved, traction should be removed in order to prevent overdistraction or further neurologic injury. Generally, 5 to 19 pounds of weight per cervical level are utilized. Neurologic recovery has not been clearly proven to be related to early decompression or surgical intervention.

E. Patients who are cooperative and awake, and who are neurologically intact without pain, can usually be evaluated with plain films. Radiographic abnormalities in this scenario should be assessed for age of defect as well as for stability. Thin-cut CT scans with reconstructions and flexion/extension X-rays often assist with the diagnosis.

F. Patients with neurologic deficits but no bony abnormalities should be evaluated with MRI or CT myelogram. Acutely herniated disks, epidural hematomas, or spinal cord injury without radiographic (X-ray) abnormality (SCIWORA) may be diagnosed by these studies.

CT myelograms should be performed both above and below any complete block in order to fully assess any pathologic process.

G. The decision to treat a patient with external fixation or surgical fusion is generally based on the degrees of bony and ligamentous disruption.

H. If the fracture is markedly unstable or displaced, or there is extensive ligamentous injury, surgical fusion is usually necessary. Anterior or posterior approaches depend on the nature of the injury itself.

I. Compressive lesions generally require surgical intervention. Patients with canal compromise and no neurologic deficit or an incomplete neurologic injury may be considered for surgical treatment for decompression. Anterior decompressions usually take the form of diskectomy or vertebrec-tomy/corpectomy. Posterior decompressions are achieved by laminectomy. Decompressions may be followed by open reduction or fusion depending on the injury.

J. Surgical or open reduction is performed if alignment cannot be achieved by traction. Locked facets represent one type of injury often reduced in the operating room. Other injuries such as fracture dislocations may require multiple interventions (e.g. anterior decompression, anterior fusion, and posterior fusion). A full radiographic evaluation better defines fracture patterns that, in turn, dictate treatment options.

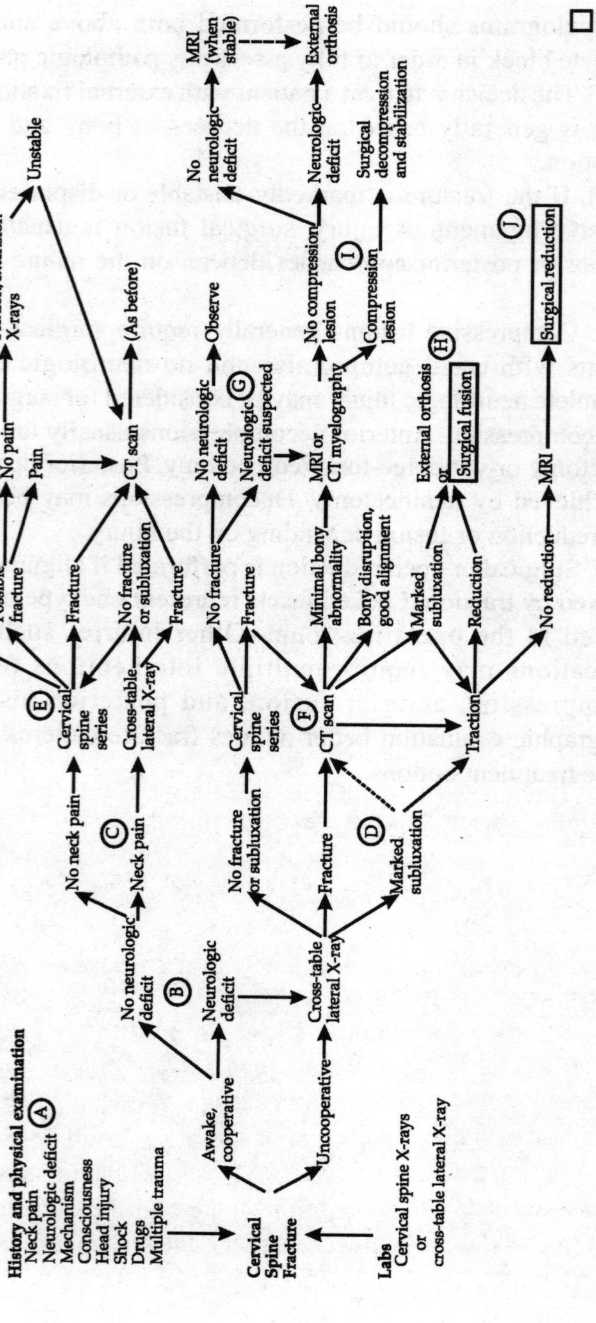
History and physical examination
Neck pain
Neurologic deficit
Mechanism
Consciousness
Head injury
Shock
Drugs
Multiple trauma
A
Cervical Spine Fracture
Labs
Cervical spine X-rays
or
cross-table lateral X-ray
Awake, cooperative
Uncooperative
No neurologic deficit
Neurologic deficit
B
Cross-table lateral X-ray
No neck pain
Neck pain
C
No fracture or subluxation
Fracture
Marked subluxation
D
Cervical spine series
E
Cross-table lateral X-ray
No fracture
Possible fracture
Fracture
No fracture or subluxation
Fracture
Observe
Observe
Repeat X-ray if pain returns or persists
No pain
Pain
Flexion/extension X-rays
Stable
Unstable
CT scan
(As before)
Cervical spine series
No fracture
Fracture
No neurologic deficit
Observe
Neurologic deficit suspected
G
F
CT scan
Minimal bony abnormality
Bony disruption, good alignment
Marked subluxation
MRI or CT myelography
H
No compression lesion
Compression lesion
I
No neurologic deficit
Neurologic deficit
MRI (when stable)
External orthosis
Surgical decompression and stabilization
Traction
Reduction
No reduction
External orthosis or
Surgical fusion
MRI
Surgical reduction
J

DROWNINGS

Pre-hospital Considerations

- Consider hypothermia in all drowning victims.
- Consider C-spine injuries in all drowning victims, and immobilize patients with stiff collar and backboard.
- Support ABCs with oxygen, and assist ventilation, if required.

Drowning is defined as death from suffocation after submersion in water, whereas *near drowning* refers to survival after submersion. *Delayed drowning* or *secondary drowning* occurs when a patient who was apparently doing well after surviving submersion suddenly deteriorates. There is a bimodal distribution of those at risk, patients under three years of age and teenagers. Alcohol and drug abuse plays a significant role in many drowning and near-drowning cases, especially among youths. In submersion accidents involving diving injuries, concomitant cervical spine injuries are common and must be excluded. **PEARL: Rule out spinal injuries in all victims of drowning.** Myocardial ischemia, seizures, and hypothermia may also be factors in submersion accidents and should always be considered. In approximately 15% of cases, laryngospasm causes death due to asphyxia, referred to as "dry drowning."

In the past, much emphasis was put on differentiating between freshwater and saltwater drowning. In most cases, however, the quantity of aspiration is not large enough to cause significant electrolyte shifts or hemolysis; *hypoxemia* is the major cause of morbidity and mortality. Hypoxemia can result from surfactant washout (leading to atelectasis), ventilation-perfusion mismatch, or damage to the alveolar capillary membrane. Non-cardiogenic pul-monary edema can result from direct pulmonary injury.

History

In obtaining the patient's history, ask the following questions.

- How long was the patient under water?
- What was the temperature of the water?
- Did the patient require resuscitation?
- Was there a diving/shallow water injury?
- How soon did resuscitation begin?
- Does the patient have any underlying diseases such as ischemic heart disease, seizures, or diabetes?
- Was there any evidence of drug or alcohol ingestion before the accident?

Management

Assessment of the patient's ABCs with C-spine precautions and immobilization should be performed as soon as the patient arrives at the hospital. **PEARL: Obtain pulse oximetry and a chest X-ray in all but asymptomatic patients.** Always look for associated injuries or underlying causes. **PEARL: All patients need supplemental O_2.** Patients who are obtunded or who remain hypoxic ($PO_2 < 60$) despite O_2 therapy must be intubated and mechanically ventilated. Patients often require positive end-expiratory pressure (PEEP) to achieve adequate oxygenation. Hypotensive patients should receive aggressive fluid resuscitation, but central venous pressure monitoring may be required to avoid overhydration and pulmonary edema. **Measure a rectal or esophageal temperature to rule out hypothermia,** which may be either the cause or the result of the near-drowning. The following investigations should be obtained: C-spine, CBC, KFT, LFT, PT, PTT, urinalysis, ECG, ABGs, and a chest X-ray. Note that the chest X-ray may or may not be helpful early on; often, radiologic findings lag behind changes in the ABGs. A nasogastric tube should be placed to empty the stomach and to avoid any further aspiration. Placement of a urethral catheter will help monitor urinary output. Repeated boluses of sodium bicarbonate (1 mEq/kg IV push) should be given, as required, for metabolic acidosis (pH < 7.10). Antibiotics and steroids are not indicated. Arrhythmias, which often result from hypoxia and acidosis, should be treated with appropriate antiarrhythmics.

Indications for Admission

All patients who are hypoxemic and require O_2 must be admitted to the hospital. Asymptomatic patient without evidence of significant submersion can be discharged. Asymptomatic patients who have had a significant submersion or mildly symptomatic patients should be observed in the emergency department for several hours and can be discharged if their chest X-ray and oxygenation level remain normal.

□

RYLES TUBE INSERTION

Indications

(1) For feeding purposes.

(2) To remove contents of the stomach in case of obtruction or poor gastric emptying.

Procedure

- Take a disposable ryles tube.
- Ask patient if he has any nasal problem like polyp or deviated septum.
- Put on sterile gloves.
- Spray 10% xylocaine in both nostrils and in posterior part of throat and pharynx.
- Keep a glass with sterile water in it.
- Now put xylocaine gel in both the nostrils and apply some gel on the tip of the ryles tube and for clear six inches on its distal end.
- Now gently push the tip of Ryles tube in one nostril and it should smoothly go in the pharynx. If it does not go, then try to push it in the another nostril and let it come in the pharynx.
- Ask the patient to open mouth and see the Ryle tube in the pharynx.
- Now give a sip of water and ask the patient to keep in the mouth.
- Try to push the Ryle tube gradually and ask the patient to swallow this sip of water which is in the mouth. If the tube does not go down try to repeat the procedure again as above and you will be able to place the Ryles tube in the stomach.

Confirmation of Tube in the Stomach

(1) Take about 20 ml of air in a syringe. Put chest piece of stethoscope on the stomach area and put the air through the Ryle tube. If you hear gurgling sound then tube is in the stomach.

(2) Suck the Ryles tube with a 20 ml syringe and if fluid comes out, then tube is in the stomach.

Fixing the Tube

Once confirmed that your tube is in right place then take a nasal fixator (pre-prepared), it is of Dyonoplast cut it the form of U shape. The broad piece goes on the nose on both ends, one after the other are wrapped around the Ryles tube close to the nostril.

Difficult Insertion

At time you will find that your repeated tries fail and the tube coils in the mouth only.

Take size 7 non-cuffed endotracheal tube and check that the Ryles tube goes through it smoothly.

Apply xylocaine gel on the distal half of endotracheal tube and put the ryles tube half way down the endotracheal tube.

Now gradually push the endotracheal tube in the throat and push it. It will go in the oesophagus and once you are in oesophagus and patient is not coughing then push the Ryles tube gradually in the stomach after lubricating it.

Now check the tube for proper placement and if confirmed that it is in the stomach, then pull the endotracheal tube from the nose and now fix the Ryles tube on the nose with tape as describe above.

How to Pullout a Ryles Tube

When asked to pull out a Ryles tube—

- Put on gloves.
- Remove the tape from the nostril.
- Take patient in the confidence and take a large towel and hold the tube near the nostril with one end of the towel and than gradually pull it out to that its ends are in the towel and no

contents fall on the patient or bed. It all remains in the towel only.

- Now clean the nostril of the patient with spirit or acetone so that the sticky material for the nostril is removed.

□

VENEPUNCTURE AND CENTRAL LINE AND OTHER MINOR PROCEDURES

Venepuncture

Skill at obtaining venous blood samples can only be learned by practice. The skill is important as the more traumatic the venepuncture, the less the confidence felt by the patient during future management.

Any suitable vein in the antecubital fossa or the dorsum of the hand may be selected—a Y-junction is usually best. A tourniquet is applied above the proposed site, but is left in place for as short a time as possible and is not used at all if serum calcium is to be estimated. The skin injection site is thoroughly cleaned with spirit. The vacuum in the disposable syringe is released and the needle is rapidly inserted through the skin some 3-4 mm distal to the entry site on the vein. The needle is then passed proximally into the vein, at which point there is a characteristic feeling of 'give,' and blood may be drawn back. The tourniquet is then released. Once the sample has been obtained, the needle is withdrawn and pressure applied for 2-3 min (Fig. 1).

In obese patients, a distended vein may have to be palpated by the experienced finger. Occasionally, a *femoral vein stab* (Fig. 2) is required, but leg veins should be avoided if possible both for venepuncture and for infusion purposes. To perform a stab, the femoral artery is palpated in the groin, the skin is cleaned and the needle is inserted just medial to the femoral pulse. If back pressure is applied as the syringe is depressed, both the feel and the obtaining of venous blood confirms entry into the vein.

Arterial Puncture

To obtain arterial blood for blood gas analysis, strict local asepsis is essential. The femoral artery is the site of choice. The pulse is felt by

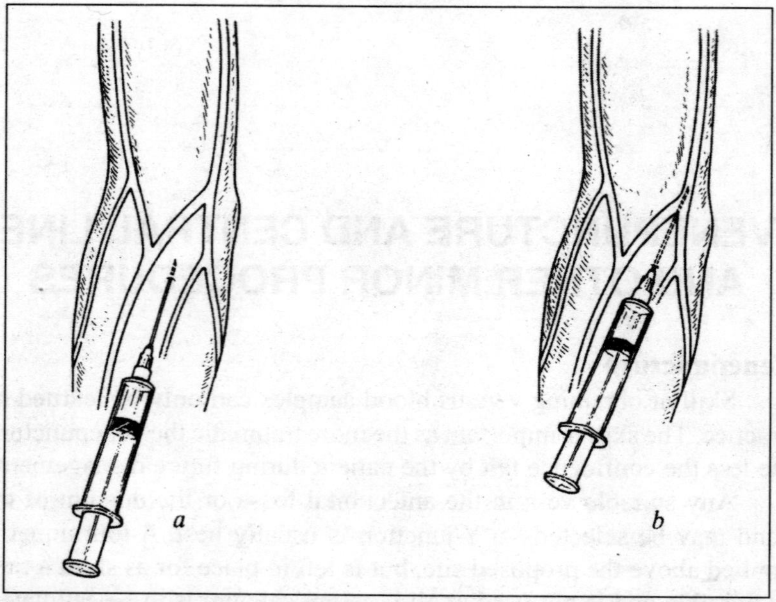

Fig. 1: Venepuncture, (a) Needle inserted 1 cm distal to Y-junction in antecubital fossa, (b) Needle enters vein at confluence.

two fingers of one hand lying longitudinally and the needle is then inserted between the fingers. One can feel the needle entering the artery and bright red arterial blood enters the syringe under arterial pressure. Once the needle is removed, the syringe must be sealed at once by bending the needle to 90° to prevent contamination with room air. Firm pressure is applied over the puncture site for 3 min.

Nowadays radial artery is also punctured with experienced anaesthetist to get arterial blood for blood gas analysis. The needle is bent immediately after withdrawing it.

Intravenous Infusion

The principles involved in venepuncture are also applied to setting up a fluid infusion except:

(a) It is kind to infiltrate some local anaesthetic at the skin puncture site and if the skin is at all tough to use a scalpel to nick the skin to facilitate entry of the cannula.

(b) If at all possible, a site away from the antecubital fossa is preferable as elbow flexion may displace the cannula.

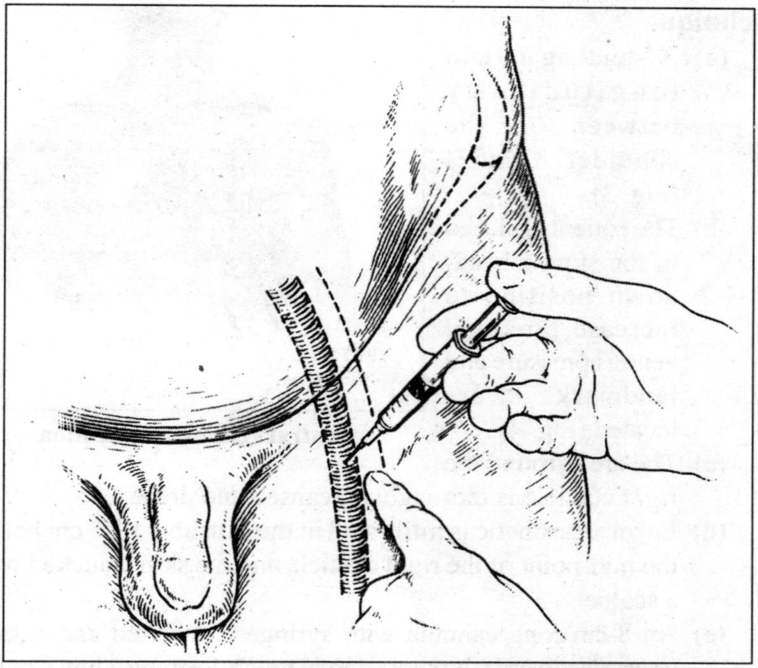

Fig. 2: Femoral triangle venepuncture. A watching finger palpates the artery lateral to the femoral vein 1 cm distal to the inguinal ligament.

(c) Firm fixation of the cannula and the IV set are essential to minimize night calls to attend to problems!

Various cannulae are available and only by trial will personal preference be determined. It is vital to check infusion sites for: (1) thrombophlebitis, (2) tissue collection of fluid and to change the site if either is found. Local symptomatic therapy may be required. Great care must be taken when changing infusion bottles to minimize the risk of bacterial contamination and to avoid air embolism.

Central Venous Cannulation

Whether for central venous pressure monitoring or for total parenteral nutrition, strict asepsis using full theatre sterile techniques is essential if a central vein is to be cannulated.

Of the three most popular—subclavian puncture; internal jugular puncture; antecubital fossa puncture and cannula passage proximally—the first is the easiest to master, with least morbidity.

Technique

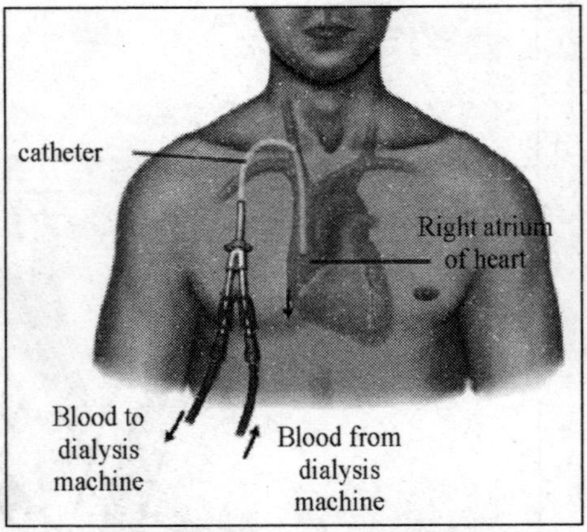

Central vein catheterization

(a) A sandbag is laid longitudinally between the shoulder blades (Fig. 3).

(b) The patient is placed in the supine head-down position to increase proximal venous pressure and landmarks are located (Fig. 4).

(c) The area around the *right* clavicle is thoroughly cleansed and draped.

(d) Local anaesthetic is infiltrated in the skin about 2.5 cm below the mid-point of the right clavicle and the skin is nicked with a scalpel.

(e) An 8-cm long cannula with syringe is inserted and passed upwards towards the suprasternal notch, keeping a line parallel to the medial one-third of clavicle (Fig. 5). If slight backward pressure on the syringe is maintained, the vein can be identified by the feel on entry plus the delivery of venous blood. A guide wire is directed through the cannula into the vein and a silicone catheter of 16-cm length is passed over the guide wire and

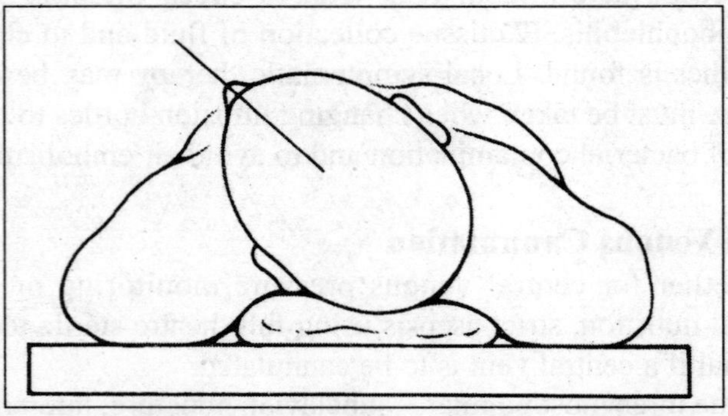

Fig. 3: Central venous cannulation. A sandbag is placed between the shoulders and the patient's chin is turned to the left.

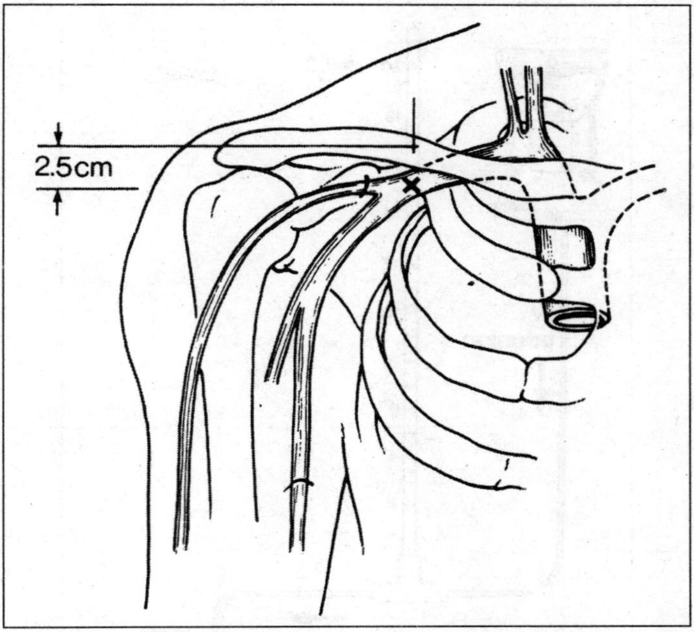

Fig. 4: Relationship of the right subclavian vein to the clavicle and the first rib.

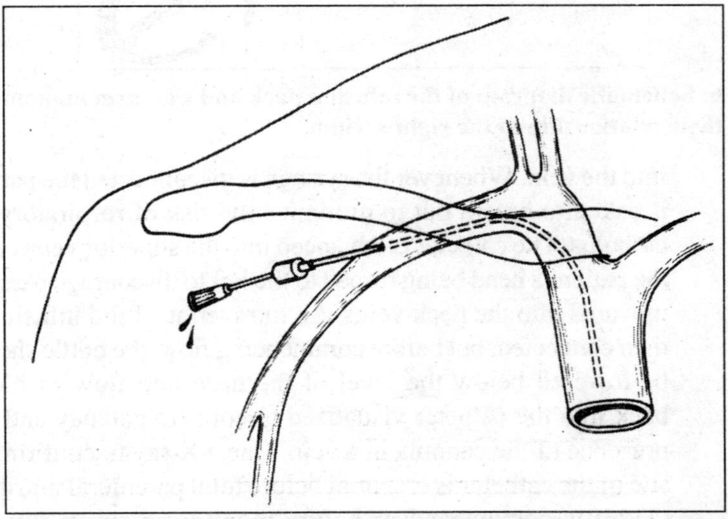

Fig. 5: Cannula inserted parallel to the medial one-third of the right clavicle.

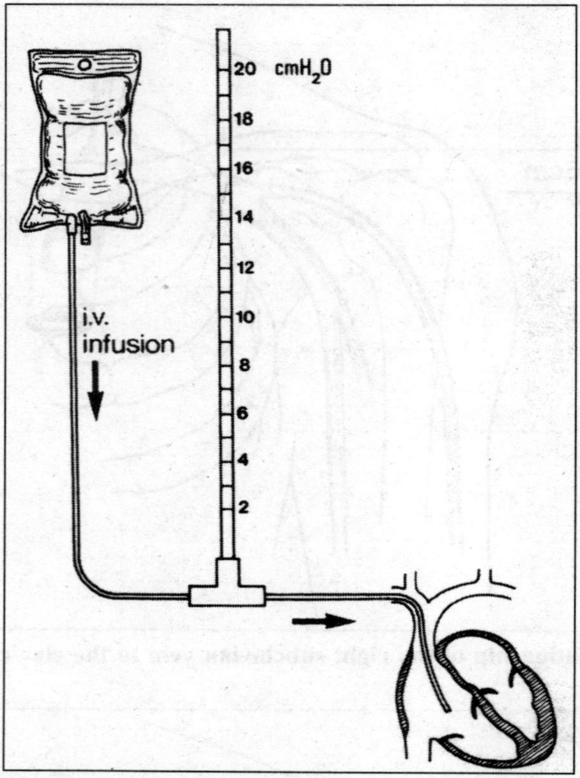

Fig. 6: Schematic diagram of the infusion pack and side-arm manometer and their relationship to the right atrium.

into the vein. Whenever the syringe is disconnected the patient is asked to breath out to minimize the risk of respiratory air embolus. The catheter is advanced into the superior vena cava, the patient's head being turned to the left to discourage passage upwards into the neck veins. An intravenous fluid infusion is then connected, but before commencing flow, the bottle should be lowered below the level of the head and flow of blood back into the catheter visualized to confirm patency and the presence of the cannula in a vein. Chest X-ray to confirm the site of the catheter is essential before total parenteral nutrition (TPN) is commenced or before monitoring starts. Fix the Catheter to skin close to site of insertion in skin.

Central Venous Pressure (CVP) Monitoring

Clear fluids only should be infused if CVP monitoring is required. A reference point marking the position of the right atrium is used to measure zero and CVP can be read from a simple side arm manometer in cm H_2O (Fig. 6). It is important:

(a) To alter reference point as the patient's position changes.
(b) To make allowance for the effect of assisted ventilation which tends to increase CVP.
(c) To remember that CVP is *not* an absolute measurement, but is only valuable as a method of assessing response to fluid infusion. **Whenever a central venous cannula is removed, the tip should be sent for bacteriological investigation culture and sensitivity.**

Venous Cutdown (Fig. 7)

Very occasionally in a shocked patient neither peripheral nor central venous cannulation is possible. If so, it is possible to identify a vein in a standard anatomical site by cutdown.

Under aseptic conditions, the area is cleaned and locally anaesthetized. A transverse incision is made in the skin and is deepened until a reasonably sized vein is identified. The vein is dissected free and two linen ties passed around it. The distal is firmly tied: only one throw is made in the proximal. The vein is opened using a fine scalpel or scissors and a venous cannula inserted carefully. The proximal thread is then tied firmly and a fluid infusion commenced. Standard skin closure is performed.

Blood Culture

Using strict aseptic conditions, a venepuncture specimen of 20 ml is obtained. Taking a fresh needle, an aliquot of blood is injected into culture medium bottles for aerobic and anaerobic culture and the bottles are placed in an incubator at 37°C (98.6°F).

Samples are obtained from each bottle for plating and for microscopy as appropriate. The sensitivity of any bacteria to antibiotics is determined.

The best time to obtain positive blood cultures is at the peak of a pyrexia, and cultures should be repeated with each subsequent spike.

Biochemical Testing of Blood

The only standard test essential in the house surgeon's expertise is the measurement of blood sugar using glucometer.

Other tests are done in the laboratory, but it must be ensured that the correct tube is used for the estimation required. The number of

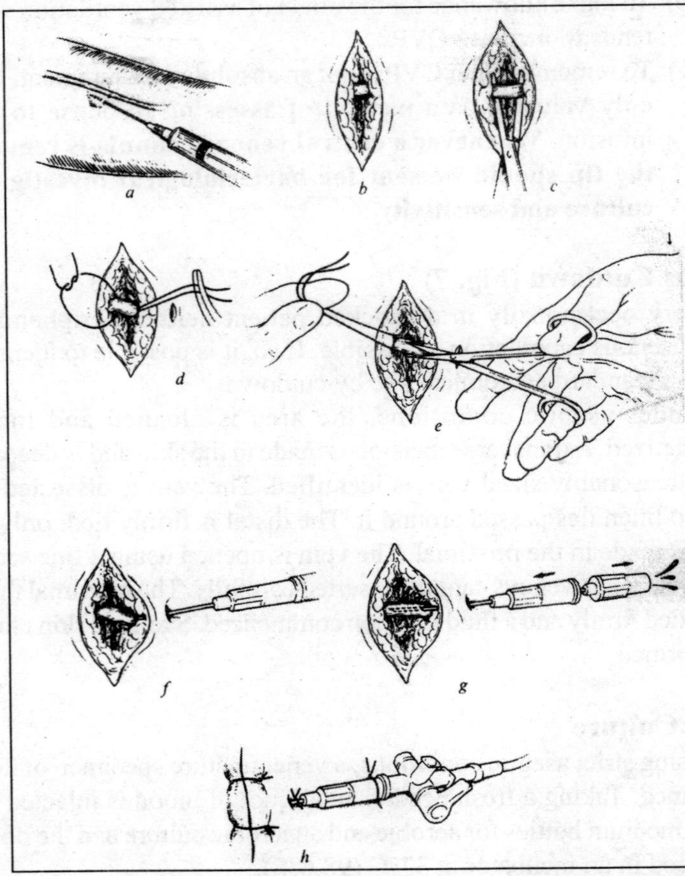

Fig. 7: Venous cutdown. (a) Infiltrating local anaesthetic in forearm. (b) Incision at right-angles to vein. (c) Clearing vein. (d) Sling stitches around vein. (e) Making nick in vein for large cannula. (f) Inserting cannula, (g) Removing stilette. (h) Three-way tap and infusion line attached to cannula. Main incision sutured, and two sutures securing cannula in position.

venepunctures should be kept to the minimum possible. The needle must be removed before blood is transferred from the syringe to the tube in order to minimize trauma to red cells.

Risks of Hepatitis

Where there is any possibility of viral hepatitis, it is essential that the doctor wears gloves and pays particular attention to the avoidance of spillage or contamination. All tubes must be identified and placed in a polythene bag. The laboratory forms should make the fact of possible viral hepatitis very clear.

Cyst Aspiration and Cytology (Breast)

The most common site for aspiration is the breast. The area is cleaned: the cyst focalized with the left fingers and a needle is inserted into the cyst cavity. The fluid is aspirated to dryness. If no fluid is obtained, it is worthwhile to continue aspiration as the needle is withdrawn as a specimen can be obtained for cytology. On removal, the syringe is detached from the needle; air is aspirated; needle and syringe are reconnected and any cells in the needle can be expelled onto a clean slide by emptying the syringe of air. The specimen is dried and sent to the cytology laboratory for staining and microscopy. If the cyst does not resolve on aspiration, if it recurs or if it contains blood, cytological examination by an expert is essential, followed by formal biopsy. If the breast cyst is emptied completely, the patient should nonetheless be checked clinically in four weeks.

Lumbar Puncture

Before embarking on lumbar puncture, it is essential to ensure that there are no clinical signs of raised intracranial pressure nor any fundal signs such as papilloedema. As in all procedures, the steps involved are explained carefully to the patient, who then lies on the left side with hips (Fig. 8) and neck flexed. An aseptic technique is essential. After carefully washing and gloving the hands, thoroughly clean the skin overlying the lumbar spine and towel the area. Identify the posterior superior iliac spine and palpate the space between two lumbar spines just distal to this level. Infiltrate about 2 ml of 1% plain lignocaine. The lumbar puncture needle and trocar (Fig. 9) are inserted and passed in the mid-line upwards and then straight to enter the spinal canal. The sensation of 'give' is characteristic both as ligamentum flavum and outer dura are penetrated. If leg pain is complained of, withdraw the needle a little and reinsert it more centrally. Fluid is obtained on removing the trocar. Cerebrospinal pressure can be measured using a simple manometer and fluid sent to the laboratory for biochemical (sugar and protein) and bacteriological investigation. The needle is removed: a firm dressing is applied and the patient is kept supine in bed for 24 hours.

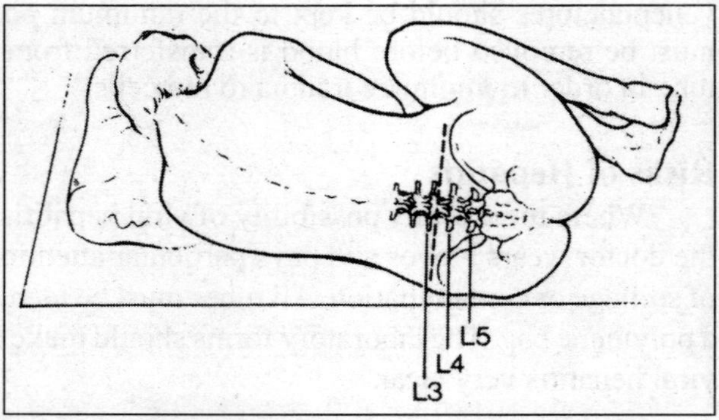

Fig. 8: Position for performing lumbar puncture.

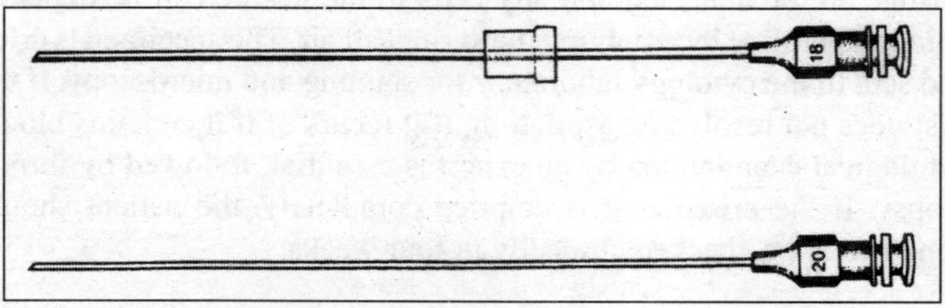

Fig. 9: Lumbar puncture needles; the larger with a marker.

Abdominal Paracentesis

The following technique is used:

1. To obtain a specimen of ascitic fluid for diagnostic purposes.
2. To allow drainage of such fluid causing symptoms.
3. To assist in the diagnosis of intra-abdominal trauma, or more recently, of acute pancreatitis.

The procedure is explained to the patient and the abdominal wall cleaned thoroughly with antiseptic solution. The entry site of choice is mid-way between anterior superior spine and umbilicus (Fig. 10) but particular care is required where there are scars from previous surgery. The site chosen is infiltrated with local anaesthetic down to peritoneum and a needle attached to a syringe or a special peritoneal dialysis catheter is inserted along the line used infiltrated with local analgesia to enter the peritoneal cavity.

Specimens of fluid are sent for biochemical, bacteriological and cytological examination.

Care must be taken not to remove too much fluid too quickly lest hypovolaemia results.

Where there is minimal fluid and either trauma or pancreatitis are suspected, lavage of the cavity is performed using a fixed volume of warmed normal saline and the effluent is examined for blood and/or amylase.

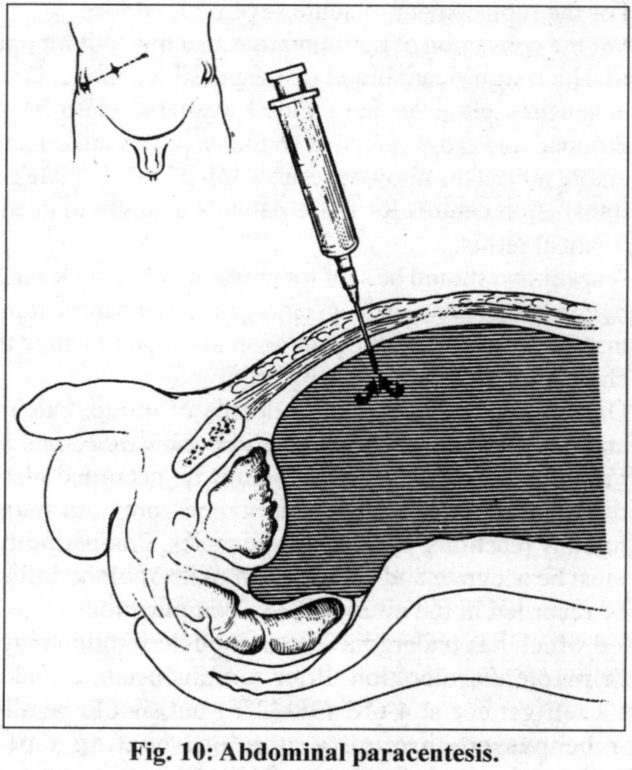

Fig. 10: Abdominal paracentesis.

□

BLOOD TRANSFUSION

Recent developments in the blood transfusion service have allowed separation of the individual components, e.g. platelets, fresh frozen plasma, antihaemophilic factor, and clearly these have specific indications. In general surgical practice, whole blood transfusion is indicated:

1. For the replacement of acute severe blood loss.
2. For the correction of perioperative anaemia, but for operations in which significant blood loss is possible, but not common, it is sensible either to have blood available or to have serum grouped and cross-matched so that supplies are on hand in an emergency. This allows preservation of an adequate supply in transfusion centres for those patients actually in need.

In practical terms:

1. A specimen should be sent for cross-matching at least 24 hours before surgery except in an emergency when more rapid cross-matching may allow the provision of blood in which there is a check of major compatibility only.
2. Once blood is available, the details of group, batch number and expiry date *must be carefully checked and compared with the patient's details.* These should be accorded also on the request form—name, age, unit number, previous transfusions had any reactions, previous pregnancies. Compatibility checks must be accurate and details of all units of blood infused must be recorded in the notes lest any complications arise.

Blood which has undergone excessive deterioration may show a pinkish or purple discoloration. Prior to transfusion, blood must be stored in a refrigerator at 4-6°C (38-42°F) but should be allowed to warm or be passed through a standard heating coil before administration. Massive infusion of cold blood may cause irreversible cardiac arrest.

Administration

Blood is given by the same technique as described previously, accurate fluid balance being ensured. Where large quantities are prescribed, a filter ought to be used to remove particles resulting from storage. The rate of infusion is indicated by:

1. The patient's requirements.
2. The patient's tolerance of the fluid load.

It is usual to infuse the first 100-200 ml more slowly to allow observation of major reactions. Where only correction of anaemia is required, rather than acute replacement, slower rates are preferable, or packed cells in which some plasma has been removed may be used as an alternative. Where rapid transfusion is required, a pneumatic pump may be used, but is potentially dangerous.

Risks of Transfusion

1. Fluid overload. This can be avoided by clinical monitoring the jugular venous pressure, oedema, or better by CVP measurements in at risk patients.
2. Pyrexial reactions. These are not uncommon and are usually mild. They may respond to simple injection of antihistamine, but if not, or if severe, the transfusion should be stopped and the blood returned to the laboratory with full details of the reaction.
3. Transmission of such diseases as viral hepatitis or syphilis were once well recognized. Careful monitoring has meant the virtual abolition of infected blood, but where suspected, replacement with crystalloid infusion, introduction of a broad-spectrum antibiotic and bacteriological analysis of the blood are all essential.

Incompatibility Reactions

Reactions are uncommon but are commoner, after multiple blood transfusions. Onset may be sudden with rigors, dyspnoea and backache. The volume of blood required to produce a reaction is very variable. Later problems are jaundice and renal dysfunction.

If such a reaction is suspected, the transfusion must be stopped immediately and the bag of blood returned to the laboratory with full details, and further cross checks are requested.

In treatment, clear fluids should be infused and urine output maintained by diuretic or by the infusion of 500 ml of 10% mannitol.

Problems of Storage

1. Storage reduces red cell concentration of 2,3-diphosphoglycerate, with increased affinity of the haemoglobin molecule for oxygen, i.e. oxygen delivery is reduced.
2. Red blood cell haemolysis results in hyperkalaemia and in jaundice.
3. The citrate used in storage may result in consumption of calcium and so produce hypocalcaemia. Therefore, 10 ml calcium gluconate should be injected intravenously after every five units of whole blood.
4. Stored red cells are less deformable and this may impede capillary flow. In severe shock, this must be borne in mind.

Collection of Blood

The transfusion service can provide a taking set and either a plastic pack or a sterile bottle containing anticoagulant, e.g. disodium citrate 2-5 g and dextrose 3 g in 120 ml of pyrogen-free water.

A swab soaked in 0.05% chlorhexidine in 70% alcohol should be placed on the top of the rubber closure and left for two min. The needle of the air outlet should be inserted through one of the quadrants marked into the appropriate port on the bag. The bottle needle of the taking set should be pushed fully through the other quadrant marked. If the needle of the air outlet is blocked, e.g. by a plug of rubber, a potentially dangerous situation exists. Blood will flow into the bottle until the pressure of air in the bottle equals the pressure of blood in the vein. If the pressure in the sphygmomanometer is now released, air will pass from the bottle into the vein. A fatal air embolism can result. The tubing should always be clamped before the pressure in the sphygmomanometer is released.

The donor lies with arm abducted. The venous return is occluded with a sphygmomanometer cuff inflated to 40-60 mmHg on the upper arm. The skin over a suitable antecubital vein is cleaned with 0.5% chlorhexidine in 70% alcohol. An injection of local anaesthetic (1-2 ml of 1% lignocaine) is made and the needle is inserted into the vein.

When 420 ml of blood have been collected the tubing is clamped, the sphygmomanometer cuff is removed, a sterile swab placed over the skin puncture point and the needle removed. The donor should keep his arm straight, and exert pressure on the swab with the thumb of his other hand for three min.

Blood may also be collected in a plastic bag, the spring balance showing when 300-400 g have been collected.

□

ENEMA

To give enema is an art. One has to learn it properly. Enema can be of following types:

1. Plain-water enema
2. Soap-water enema
3. Proctoclysis enema
4. Olive-oil enema

Plain-water Enema: One litre water in taken in an enema can. Enema tube tip is lubricated with xylocaine jelly in the anal region and using a glove, insert the enema tube gently in the anal can for 2-3 inches. The patient has to be in left lateral position and the enema can is hanged on I.V. stand about six ft high from the bed and the fluid is slowly allowed to go in the rectum and colon. Once the can is empty, remove the tube from anus and let the patient lie flat on his/her back. The patient if mobile will go to the toilet in 5-10 minutes or make him sit on a commode near the bed.

Soap-water Enema: If you wish to give soap-water enema, then dissolve about 20 z of liquid soap in 1 litre of water in enema can and give it by the same process as described above.

Proctoclysis Enema: This is ready-made enema which comes in a polythene bag attached to a tubing. Now put on a glove and apply xylocaine jelly on the anus and lubricate the tip of the enema bag and gradually introduce the tip of the tube with glove in the anal canal. Now press the contents of the polythene bag containing enema in the rectum and anal canal till the content of the bag are completely emptied out. Remove the tube from the anal can and let him lie flat. Within 15-30 minutes patient should get the urge to pass motion and go to the toilet.

Olive-oil Enema: When patient has been hospitalized for long period and scybala are present in the large gut, then give olive oil enema. Mix two ounce olive oil in 1 litre of water enema can. Now put one glove and give the contents of the can as enema slowly over 10-15 minutes and let the patient lie flat.

Manual Evacuation of Rectum and Anal Canal

Put on gloves—double pair and then push 20 zs of glycerine in the anal canal. Then using the index finger of the right hand, try to bring out scybala for the anal canal gradually one by one. One has to be careful so anal canal muscles should not be injured.

□

URETHRAL CATHETERIZATION

The proper use of the urethral catheter is the most important single factor in the successful management of bladder and prostatic cases: Misuse can cause disaster.

In male, a brusque forcing of the catheter may bruise the urethra and cause copious bleeding, while cruder effort will tear a false passage and result in failure to enter the bladder. Both misdemeanours may lead to a stricture. This mechanical disaster is equalled only by the introduction of infection. The bladder is especially liable to infection if it has been distended for a long time. Imperfect aseptic technique is inexcusable.

Types of Catheter

The introduction of the plastic catheter has brought many advantages (Fig. 1). The old-fashioned red-rubber catheters were irritant to the urethra and strength was obtained at the expense of internal diameter.

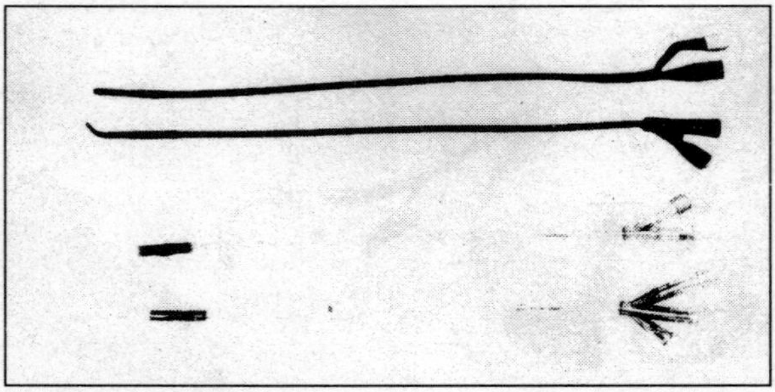

Fig. 1. Various types of urethral catheter. From above downwards; simple latex with Foley ballon. Tiemann with balloon.

Foley Catheter

The latex Foley catheter (Fig. 2) is of softer material and has an inflatable bulb near its end so that on distension (with water), the latter is held within the internal meatus. The bulb capacity varies from 5 to 30 ml and is clearly marked on each catheter. The disadvantages of the Foley catheter are that its lumen is relatively small and, despite the thickness of its wall (in which the inflation channel is fully incorporated), it remains only semi-rigid. It cannot therefore be used to overcome serious urethral obstruction. In such a case, it is better to use a Tiemann balloon catheter made of neoplex. Metal introducers should not be used in the conscious patient. By nature of its softness, the latex Foley catheter will collapse if firm suction is applied so its use is not recommended if much bleeding and clot obstruction are likely. Uneven distension of the balloon with consequent angulation of the tip may sometimes interfere with drainage, but nevertheless this type of catheter is extremely valuable, especially in female cases, and is widely used. A combination of Gibbon catheter and Foley balloon is available (Fig. 3).

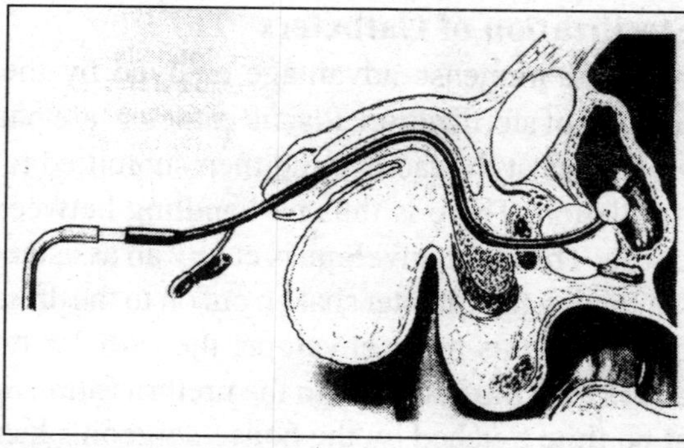

Fig. 2: Foley's balloon-ended self-retaining catheter in place.

Fig. 3. Gibbon catheter with Foley balloon.

Sizes of Catheters

Catheters and bougies are calibrated according to two main scales. The widely used French (or Charriere) scale is a direct indication of the external circumference in millimetres. For simple drainage in cases of adult urinary retention, an 18F catheter should be used. This permits free drainage of the urethral secretions but prevents meatal stenosis, and is comfortable for the patient.

Sterilization of Catheters

The immense advantage enjoyed by the modern catheter is its method of sterilization. Plastic catheters are packed in a series of sealed envelopes at the factory and then submitted to sterilization by gamma irradiation. There is thus no handling between manufacture and time of use. The outer envelope is cut by an assistant and the inner envelope containing the catheter shaken out on to the dressing trolley. After cutting or tearing this inner envelope, the catheter itself is made to protrude and is then introduced into the urethra from within the envelope, being at no time touched by the house-surgeon's hands.

Catheterization for Retention

In cases of acute (painful) retention of urine or where difficulty in catheterization is expected, there is every reason to relieve the patient's anxiety and discomfort by suitable sedation. If the patient is much distressed, give an injection of diazepam, 10 mg IV (dosage for men of average build). In male, the glans penis should be carefully cleansed, the foreskin being withdrawn and all smegma wiped away. Aqueous chlorhexidine (strength 1%) is preferred for this purpose. Holding the penis in the left hand, the anterior urethra is anaesthetized and lubricated by injecting a gel of 1% lignocaine and 0.25% chlorhexidine via the external meatus (Fig. 4).

After the lubricant has been injected, it should be massaged well down the urethra for a few moments before a penile clamp is applied. The latter should be left in place for two min to allow the anaesthetic to act and the house-surgeon should use the time to wash his hands again. In some units, the use of sterile disposable gloves has become routine and there is much to recommend this practice. The penis is then wrapped in a sterile swab and held in the left hand, while the tip of the catheter, lubricated and held vertically in the envelope in the right hand, is gently introduced down the urethra. As the bulb of the urethra is reached, the penis should be rotated down into the line of the patient's body and the catheter further introduced towards the bladder. This manoeuvre is only necessary with the more rigid catheters. If a stylet is present, it should now be removed and a sample of the urine collected in a sterile bottle for laboratory analysis.

In difficult cases, it is often helpful to place a sandbag under the patient's buttocks so that the curvature of the bulbous urethra is diminished. Once the catheter has been introduced into the bladder and a specimen of urine taken, it should immediately be connected to the drainage bag or bottle. In cases of acute retention due to prostatic hypertrophy or stricture and where there is no bleeding, the use of a uri-bag with the Gibbon-type catheter is advised. This has but one junction so that the risk of introducing infection is minimized. The bag is light, may be hooked on to the side of the bed and is easily handled by the nursing staff during bed making. Moreover, on account of its

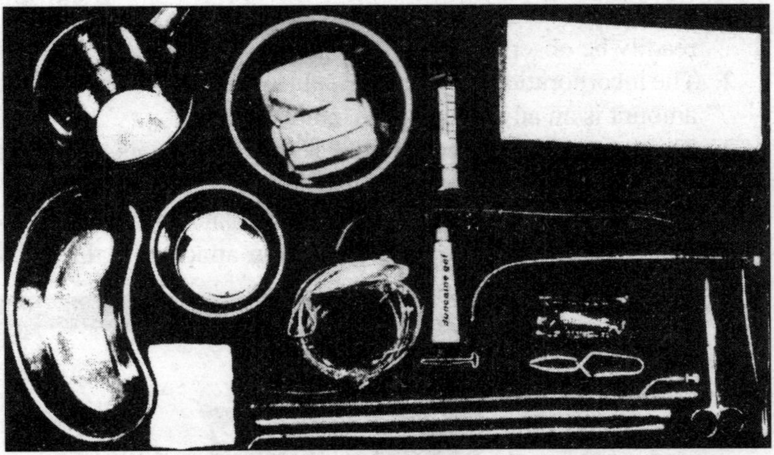

Fig. 4: Catheterization trolley. On the left are receptacles and galley pots containing swabs and chlorhexidine. A variety of catheters are at the bottom; above them is a tube of local anaesthetic, penile clip, spigot, metal urethral bougie and catheter introducer. On the right are sterile glove packet (top), scissors and forceps for no-touch technique.

lightness, the ambulant patient can carry the bag about with him so that his activity is in no way curtailed. It is important, however, that it should be carried well below the level of the bladder!

Securing the Catheter

If a small catheter of the Foley type has been used, the balloon should immediately be distended to the requisite volume, thus rendering it self-retaining. At this stage, it is imperative to replace the prepuce over the glans penis otherwise paraphimosis may develop. A small protective dressing of ribbon gauze or lint smeared with flavine emulsion is then applied to the external meatus.

Sterile disposable collecting bags for urine vary in their efficiency. and cost. The following features are important:

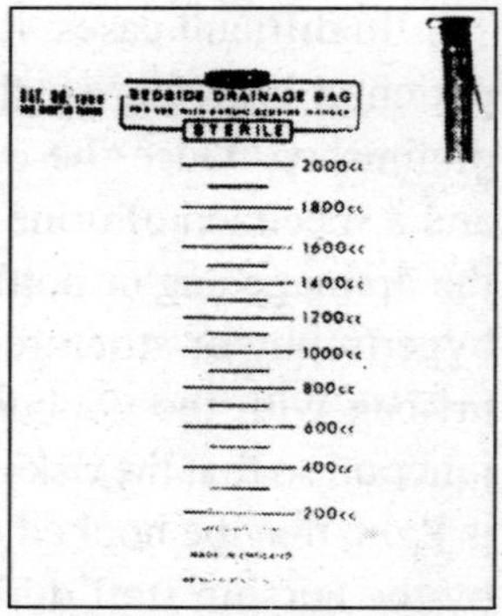

Fig. 5: Disposable drainage bag.

1. They should preferably be made of transparent material so that the quality and quantity of drainage can readily be observed.
2. The incorporation of a printed scale to register the approximate amount is an advantage.
3. They should be so constructed as to avoid seams which may leak when the bag becomes distended.
4. Provision should be made for a carrying handle which can either be used by the patient (if ambulant) or attached to the side of the bed.
5. The junction of the collecting tubing with the bag should be reinforced or capable of support in such a way as to avoid angulation with consequent obstruction of drainage.

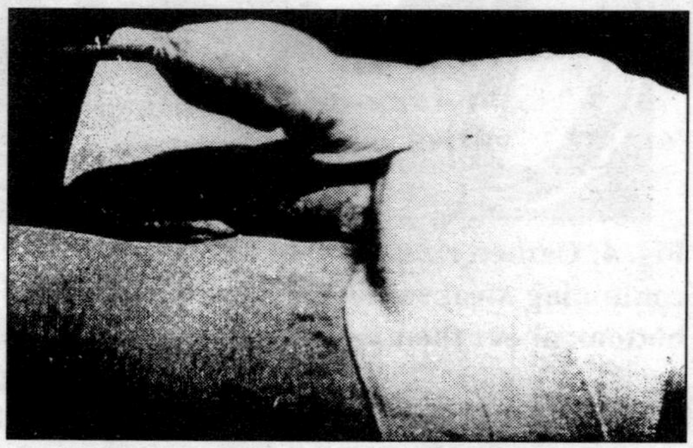

Fig. 6: Tubegauz penile dressing and catheter.

6. An adequate length of collecting tubing of sufficient calibre should be attached.

Failed Catheterization

When catheterization fails to relieve retention, the bladder must be drained suprapubically. As a temporary measure, suprapubic aspiration may be performed or a fine catheter introduced by the Supracath (Fig. 7).

Suprapubic Catheterization

1. Suprapubic Stab Cystotomy

If it is thought that temporary suprapubic drainage is required for only a few days, then suprapubic stab drainage should be carried out. An intradermal weal of 1% xylocaine is raised in the mid-line two fingerbreadths above the pubis. The intended track through the abdominal wall into the distended bladder is then infiltrated with the same anaesthetic agent and after making a small incision through the skin a 12F Argyle trocar-catheter is introduced firmly and steadily through the abdominal wall and into the bladder. The trocar is then withdrawn and the retaining balloon inflated. This is an extremely effective method of relieving painful retention of urine.

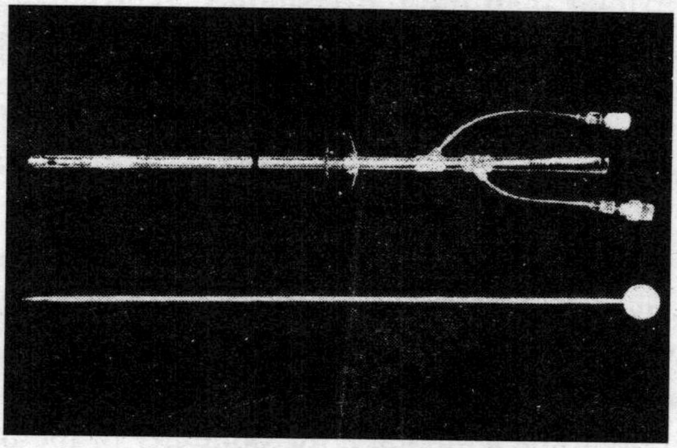

Fig. 7: Argyle suprapubic catheter.

2. Formal Suprapubic Cystostomy

Owing to improvement in the quality of urethral catheters, and to the better control of infection by chemotherapy, the need for permanent suprapubic cystostomy drainage has nowadays greatly diminished. In most cases, where corrective surgery is excluded by senility or intercurrent disease, continuous drainage with an indwelling urethral catheter of the latex Foley type is generally to be preferred. When, however, catheterization is impracticable for mechanical reasons, or fails to provide free drainage on account of debris or clot in the bladder, formal suprapubic drainage may be called for.

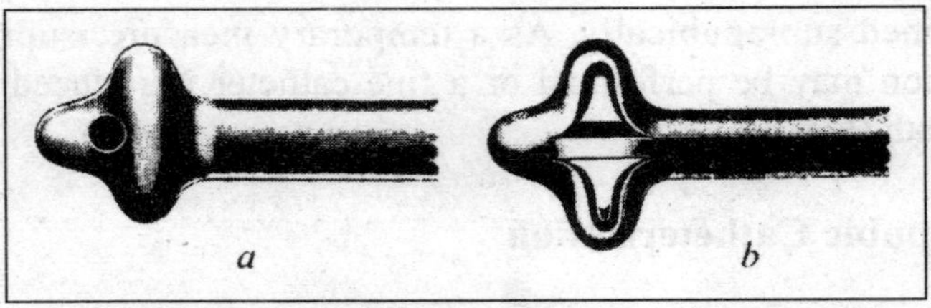

Fig. 8: (a) De Pezzer catheter; (b) Malecot catheter.

Technique

The procedure, which should be carried out in the operating theatre, consists of the introduction of a large self-retaining catheter, at least 32F of the De Pezzer or Malecot type (Fig. 8). These catheters are nowadays made of latex rubber which retains its resilience and is less irritant than the old-fashioned red-rubber variety. Encrustation is minimal and the risk of the material perishing and the expanded head breaking off in the bladder when the catheter is changed has all but been eliminated.

Percutaneous suprapubic cystostomy can be done nowaday with disposable sets.

Formal suprapubic cystostomy should always be carried out well away from the symphysis pubis and preferably at a point at least half-way between the latter and the umbilicus. If a retaining belt is going to be worn, it will 'sit' more comfortably at this level, while if drainage is only to be temporary, the obliquity of the track will encourage more rapid closure after the catheter is withdrawn.

The formal operation may be performed under either general or local anaesthesia, infiltrating 1% lignocaine subcutaneously and into the abdominal wall at the above-mentioned site. The bladder is distended. A 4-cm vertical incision is then made through the skin and between the rectus muscles. The peritoneum is swept cranially with a swab, the recti being gently retracted laterally. Two catgut stay stitches are inserted into the bladder wall and, using a scalpel, a small stab incision is made between them. Excess bladder fluid is sucked away and a 22 or 24 gauge Foley catheter introduced. If a Malecot or De Pezzer catheter is used, it should be introduced by placing the tip of a long haemostat into the lumen of the catheter via one of the drainage openings and pulling the catheter up tightly so as to reduce the calibre of the expanded end (Fig. 9).

Care should be taken to advance the catheter sufficiently within the cavity of the bladder to avoid extrusion as the latter contracts (Fig. 10). On the other hand, the expanded end should not be allowed to dangle like the clapper of a bell, as intermittent contact with the sensitive trigone may cause considerable discomfort.

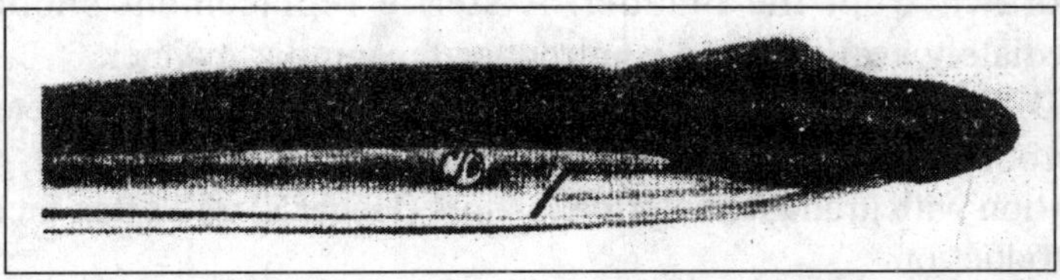

Fig. 9: Method of stretching a De Pezzer catheter with a haemostat.

The stay stitches may then be crossed and tied to ensure a snug fit for the emerging tube. A few interrupted stitches complete the closure of the small abdominal incision; a skin stitch may help secure the tube.

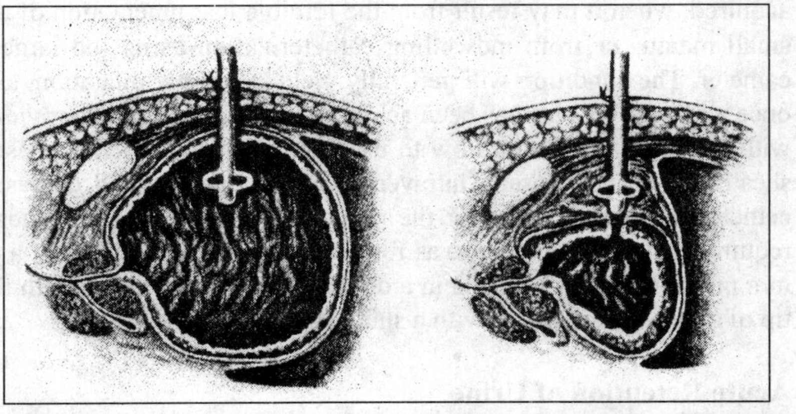

Fig. 10: Unless the expanded end of the catheter is pushed well into the bladder it will be dragged out as the bladder contracts, for the catheter is fixed to the skin by a stitch.

Changing the Tube

When permanent suprapubic drainage has been established, it becomes necessary to change the tube from time to time. If latex catheters are used, an interval of between three and four weeks is usually sufficient and a gentle wash-out with sterile saline (using a 50-ml disposable syringe) should be given through the new catheter to ensure that drainage is satisfactory.

To remove the tube, a blunt-ended introducer is inserted into the lumen and advanced as far as it will go. The catheter is pulled up tightly over the introducer so as to straighten out the expanded end and then withdrawn from the bladder. A sterile replacement should be immediately available and is introduced in similar manner.

Difficulty may sometimes occur when the previous catheter has fallen out and the fistulous track has contracted. In such an event, gentle dilatation with graduated uterine dilators (Hegar's) will often facilitate reintroduction.

It must be emphasized that nowadays permanent suprapubic cystostomy is seldom justified.

Meatal Stenosis

Narrowing of the external meatus may be either congenital or acquired, when it may result from the forcible instrumentation of the small meatus or from indwelling catheterization using too large a catheter. The condition will generally yield to regular dilatation, and once a reasonable size has been achieved, the patient can be provided with a dilator and taught how to use it himself: the tapering plastic sheaths in which disposable intravenous needles are supplied, or plastic catheter spigots are ideal for the purpose. Should a meatal stenosis require immediate treatment, as for the relief of acute retention, a 6-mm incision should be made in a downward direction either with the tip of a pair of scissors or with a small scalpel.

Acute Retention of Urine

Paramount among the commoner urological emergencies requiring immediate attention is acute urinary retention. The combination of a painfully distended bladder with inability to void distinguishes the condition from:

1. Chronic retention in which the distension, though often greater, is painless and associated with ineffectual frequency or overflow incontinence.
2. Oliguria or anuria when little or no urine is passed but the bladder remains empty.

Except in unconscious patients or in traumatic cases with severe shock, acute retention is unlikely to be overlooked. Even in such circumstances, routine clinical examination immediately reveal the distended viscus. Uncertainty may yet occasionally arise on account of obesity, abdominal distension from other causes or where the bladder has become displaced, as following previous surgical excision of the rectum. In a majority of cases, however, the condition is self-evident and some idea of the more usual causes (excluding postoperative retention) may be gleaned from Table 2.

Table 2: Analysis of 300 Consecutive Cases of Acute Retention in a General Hospital

	No. of cases
Benign prostatic hyperplasia	193
Malignant disease of the prostate	39
Urethral stricture	23
Phimosis	14
Vesical tumour (clot retention)	9
Inflammation (cyst-prostatitis)	4
Impacted urethral calculus	3
Rupture of urethra	2
Papilloma of urethra	1
Spinal injury	4
Neurological disease	4
Miscellaneous (drugs, constipation, etc.)	4

Careful attention to the history, antecedent urinary symptoms or disease and recent use of drugs, e.g. alcohol, antispasmodics or sympathomimetics, as well as to the age of the patient and the circumstances in which retention has occurred, will often suggest the cause. Further evidence must be sought by clinical methods, always including rectal examination. The information thus gained will in most cases reveal the diagnosis and indicate the appropriate means of relief.

As will be seen from Table 2, a majority of cases stem from some form of prostatic obstruction which, even where drugs or neurological disorders are implicated, often coexists as an essential component. Stricture has nowadays become less common because of the better treatment of urethral inflammation and trauma. Among the elderly uncircumcised, however, inflammatory phimosis (particularly in diabetics) remains a not unusual cause of obstruction.

Management of Acute Retention

Irrespective of the cause, the presence of a painfully distended bladder calls for early relief. Except in obvious cases of hysteria and occasionally others where no obstructive cause is immediately apparent, attempts to induce voluntary voiding are generally a waste of time. Traditional remedies such as sedation or sitting in a hot bath are rarely effective and even if successful seldom bring more than temporary relief. Similar objections apply to the use of parasympatheticomimetic drugs such as carbachol which, in addition to carrying certain risks, may only increase discomfort.

It should be clearly recognized that with few exceptions the onset of retention reflects the presence of an underlying obstructive lesion for which admission to hospital and further investigations will be required. The practice of relieving the condition by catheterization in the casualty department and then discharging the patient to await events is only mentioned to be condemned.

1. Outside Hospital

Nowadays, except in isolated areas, transfer to hospital is generally practicable within a few hours and it is unlikely that the patient will come to any harm during this period if adequately sedated. Such a course is strongly to be recommended as avoiding the risk of infection, etc. contingent on an immediate attempt to decompress the bladder in unfavourable surroundings. In adverse circumstances, however, the latter may have to be considered, the choice lying between catheterization and suprapubic aspiration. Briefly, the factors influencing a decision will be (1) the presumed nature of the obstruction, (2) the availability of suitable equipment (catheters, aspirating needles, etc.), and (3) the period likely to elapse before hospitalization can be effected. Generally speaking, catheterization is to be preferred and is more readily accepted by the patient as a logical method of relief. The risk of infection can be reduced by appropriate chemotherapy and when, as for example at sea, some delay can be foreseen before further assistance is obtainable, the catheter should be left indwelling.

Continued or repeated suprapubic aspiration, on the other hand, is fraught with the hazard of extravasation and can only be condoned as a short-term expedient or as a forced alternative where attempts at urethral instrumentation have failed. In the latter case, it circumstances permit, the deliberate performance of open cystostomy drainage may well prove preferable.

2. Inside Hospital

On arrival at hospital, management becomes more clearly defined. All cases with acute retention should be admitted forthwith and any thought of relieving the condition in the casualty department must be rigorously excluded. Once in bed and following suitable sedation, the conditions are favourable for an attempt at catheterization. Strict attention to asepsis is obligatory. Unless there is good reason to believe that the cause is purely temporary (e.g. drugs, alcoholic excess), the catheter should be left indwelling while further investigations are being undertaken.

If catheterization fails, preparation should be made for a further attempt under general anaesthesia. Suprapubic aspiration as an alternative has little or no place in hospital practice save when an anaesthetic is precluded or in occasional cases of acute urethral inflammation.

Subsequent Investigation

Once the distended bladder has been relieved, the emergency is over. Continued catheter drainage affords an opportunity for further study and the planning of definitive treatment. Three factors affect the latter:

1. The nature of the obstruction.
2. The condition of the remainder of the urinary tract (including renal function).
3. The overall clinical status of the patient.

The pattern of investigation should thus be arranged accordingly. The essential urological investigations include:

1. Laboratory analysis of the urine, including bacteriology and sensitivities.
2. Haemoglobin estimation, blood grouping and saving of the serum for cross-matching.

3. Estimation of blood urea, creatinine, serum acid and alkaline phosphatase (bearing in mind that raised values of acid phosphatase may follow recent palpation of the prostate or urethral instrumentation).

With regard to other systems, simultaneous investigation and restorative therapy should be carried out as indicated. It is unnecessary to carry out intravenous urography in every case of acute urinary retention. If there is a clear-cut history of increasing prostatism and physical examination and blood values are normal, the expense of this examination may be saved. In such a case, the chances of intravenous urography revealing any serious pathology are so remote as to make the examination unjustified.

Chronic Retention of Urine

As the name implies, this condition carries little of the urgency associated with the acute variety. Nevertheless, the effect of longstanding incomplete obstruction is to produce more severe damage to the upper urinary tract. Impaired renal function and an added susceptibility to infection render it vital that such cases should be investigated and treated with extra caution. Although, as in the acute variety, benign prostatic enlargement remains the commonest cause, the relative frequency both of urethral stricture and prostatic cancer is somewhat increased. The possibility of neurogenic dysfunction should also be considered.

Investigation

Time given to preliminary investigation is generally well spent and any attempt to relieve the distended bladder is better postponed until the diagnosis is reasonably assured. In addition to full clinical examination, laboratory studies should be carried out as outlined above, but, in addition, excretion urography is needed. This, however, should not be done until the level of nitrogen retention is known, so that an appropriate dose of contrast may be given. A degree of anaemia is common in chronic urinary retention with renal failure and this will need correction before surgery is undertaken.

Treatment

1. Benign Prostatic Enlargement

As well as treatment of any aetiological factor (drugs, diabetes, etc.) free catheter drainage should be instituted under full aseptic precautions. The need for slow decompression has been overstressed. The potential hazards of haemorrhage and suppression following the rapid release of longstanding tension are generally more than counterbalanced by the benefits of unobstructed drainage and early mobility. Nevertheless, some caution is merited in cases with severe uraemia. Close attention should be paid to the fluid balance and electrolyte requirements: sometimes a marked sodium diuresis follows the relief of longstanding obstruction. This must be watched for by daily measurement of blood and urine electrolytes and urine volume.

In Adults

The indications here are recurrent balanitis (sometimes associated with diabetes mellitus), phimosis and following the relief of paraphimosis by dorsal slit (Fig. 11). The technique is similar to that outlined above but it is wiser to keep the patient in hospital for four or five days.

It is helpful to prescribe stilboestrol 5 mg b.d. over the operative period to prevent painful erections.

Paraphimosis

Usually, this condition is already far advanced when the patient is first seen and efforts to reduce the constricting band by the injection of hyaluronidase or the application of a 1-1000 adrenaline compress are doomed to failure.

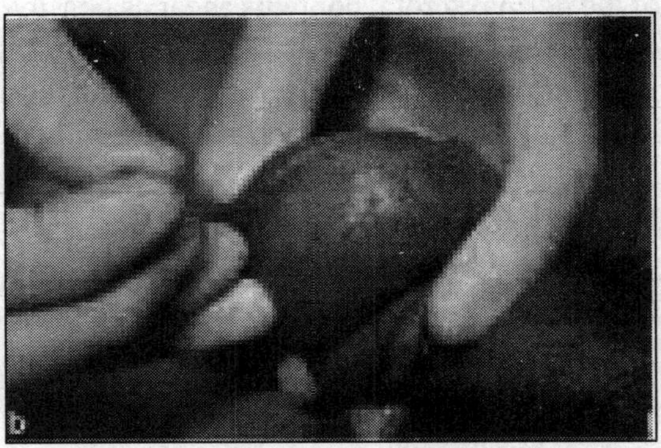

Fig. 11:A method of forcible reduction of a paraphimosis.

Reduction

A short-acting anaesthetic should be given and a gentle but firm attempt made to reduce the paraphimosis (Fig. 11).

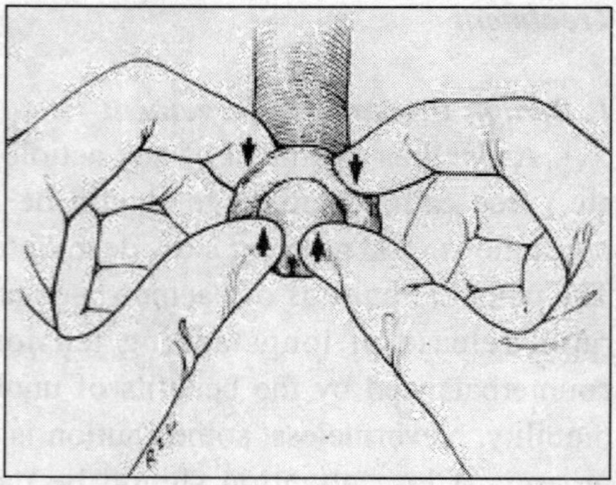

Fig. 12: Alternative method of forcible re-duction of a paraphimosis.

The tyre-like swelling of foreskin is firmly compressed for 2-3 min. Firm, even pressure all round is needed. Then, with the index and middle fingers of each hand behind the swelling and the thumbs giving counterpressure on the tip of the glans, an attempt is made slowly and steadily to draw the foreskin forward (Fig. 12).

If this fails and the local condition is not too unfavourable, an immediate circumcision may be performed. Alternatively, and in all longstanding cases, it is better merely to perform a dorsal slit and carry out an elective circumcision at a later date when all oedema and inflammation have subsided.

Aspiration of Hydrocele

A prerequisite to successful treatment is to establish the position of the normal scrotal contents as far as possible and to define the extent of the hydrocele.

Put on a pair of sterile gloves. Clean the skin with Betadine. Now in the fluctuation area, insert a needle and gradual aspirate the fluid.

Urinary Catheterization

Indications

1. To empty the bladder in case of urinary retention.
2. In patients who are operated under general, spinal or epidural anesthesia.
3. To measure urinary output in a seriously ill patient, or patients who can't pass urine on their own.

Procedure

Collect the following:

1. One pair of sterile gloves of your size.
2. Sterile Foley's catheter of size 16 or 18.
3. Xylocaine jelly tube.
4. Catheterisation tray containing one red rubber sterile catheter and two bowls.
5. One 10 ml and other 20 ml sterile syringe.
6. Normal saline about 50 ml.

Procedure

— Open the glans in males and clean the meatus with Betadine solution.

— Now put on your gloves and put a draw sheet on the patient with a central hole through which external genitalia can be brought out.

— Now insinuate the xylocaine jelly in the meatus after lubricating the lip of meatus with the jelly.

— About 10 ml of jelly should be put in one bowl.

— Once the whole jelly tube has been inserted, pinch the penis so that the jelly flows in urethra for 4-5 minutes.

— Now open the sterile Foleys catheter on the sterile sheet and lubricate the tip and distal shaft with xylocaine jelly.

— Insert the tip of the catheter in the urethra and smoothly push it in the urethra. Gradually, it will go in the bladder. If you fail to put it in urethra completely, then at the point of obstruction, rotate it and put in again and see if you can push it in. At times in stricture the opening is not central but on one side and by rotating the tip you might succeed pushing it in.

— Once the catheter is in then put 5 ml of saline with a syringe in to balloon and pull the catheter to the internal meatus and see in the other bowl if the urine come out or not.

— If urine comes out, then connect the catheter outlet to the urine bag.

— If no urine comes out, then with 20 ml syringe, suck the jelly out of catheter and urine will start coming out immediately.

— The jelly, being thick, blocks the catheter at time it need to be sucked or pushed in the bladder.

Foleys Catheterization

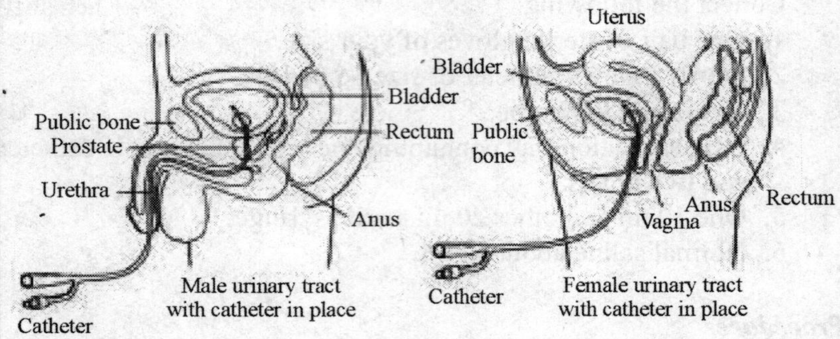

— You may take 20 ml of saline in other syringe and push it in bladder. You will find that urine comes out and now connect the catheter to the bag.

— Now clean the glans and the penis of any jelly with agauge piece.

— Pull back the skin of the glans.

— Put notes in the file of the urine catheterization and check how much urine came out after catheterization.

Difficulties in Removing a Foley's Catheter

— You will come across condition at time when you want to remove a Foley catheter and the water does not come out from the balloon even after using a syringe for suction.

How to Tackle this Problem

1. Take about 0.5 ml ether in a syringe and push it to the balloon. Once this goes inside the bulb, the balloon ruptures. You can pull the catheter out now. Don't push more than 0.5 ml of ether.
2. If this process does not workout, then take a rigid thin wire which come with small size catheter and unbent that now push it gradually in to the balloon of catheter once the balloon is punctured then the catheter can be pulled out.
3. If still difficult, when the above and techniques don't work, then take the patient to X-Ray Deptt. Under ultrasound guided

push a needle in the balloon from suprapubic region and suck the contents of balloon and the pull the catheter out. One can also put the needle and syringe through the anal canal and rectum and puncture the balloon from there.

□

PULMONARY EMBOLISM

The pain of a pulmonary embolism (PE) is usually pleuritic but can be dull, mimicking a myocardial infarction (MI). These patients often complain of associated dyspnea. They may have hemoptysis. A history of immobility (e.g. a long plane flight), CHF, any underlying malignancy, or the use of cigarettes or birth control pills may be suggestive of PE. A personal or family history of deep venous thrombosis or a PE should raise your index of suspicion.

Physical examination may reveal tachypnea or tenderness and swelling in the legs. Less than half of patients with a PE are tachycardic, and their heart rates should not be used as a basis for diagnosis of PE. The ECG most commonly shows non-specific ST-T changes or an $S_1Q_3T_3$ pattern. The chest X-ray may be normal, or it may show the classic "Hampton's hump" of pulmonary infarction (a wedge-shaped, pleural-based density) or Westermark's sign (increased central vascular markings with peripheral oligemia). An elevated hemidiaphragm may be seen. Blood gases usually show an increased A-a gradient and desaturation; however, 10% to 15% of patients may have totally normal blood gas values. **PEARL: Blood gas values never substitute for a V/Q scan or a CT angiogram.**

The treatment for PE is I.V. heparinization, which should be started immediately if the diagnosis is strongly suspected, even before further diagnostic testing. An I.V. bolus of 80 U/kg followed by a continuous infusion of 18 U/kg per hour should be given and adjusted to achieve a partial thromboplastin time (PTT) 1.5 to 2 times the normal. Low-molecular-weight heparin (enoxaparin 1 mg/kg every 12 hours), given subcutaneously, is now also being used.

The diagnosis of PE can immediately be established in patients with a deep vein thrombosis by an abnormal lung V/Q scan, an abnormal CT angiogram, or pulmonary angiography. The diagnosis of a PE is excluded in the patient who has a low clinical suspicion and a normal V/Q scan. If the scan is abnormal in any way (i.e. with low or intermediate probability), the patient will need further tests to exclude a PE. Only the patient with high clinical suspicion and a high-probability scan should be treated for PE with-out further studies. Recently, there has been a trend toward use of Helical angiography. This modality identifies most PE as well as other diagnoses; however, it is less sensitive for peripheral PE.

Non-invasive studies of the legs looking for deep venous thrombosis also can be useful. In most cases, we start with lung scanning, followed by leg studies if the scan is non-diagnostic. If the leg studies are negative but we still strongly suspect PE, we then get a pulmonary angiogram. A proposed diagnostic approach to PE is presented.

Pneumothorax

Patients with pneumothorax can complain of sharp and pleuritic chest pain, often with associated dyspnea. Often, they are young, thin men. The lung examination may not show any abnormality, but the chest X-ray is usually diagnostic. It is sometimes helpful to get an end-expiratory film, which accentuates the abnormality. **PEARL: In children or uncooperative patients, a lateral decubitus film with the affected side up may also accentuate a pneumothorax.** Treatment usually involves placing a chest tube or a smaller "pigtail" catheter into the pleural space. **PEARL: If the pneumothorax is under tension, the patient is likely to be in serious trouble.**

□

APPLICATION OF BANDAGES

A bandage is defined as a piece of material used to cover, support, immobilize, or exert pressure to a part of the body. Good and effective bandaging can be learned only by frequent practice. It is worth mastering, for a well-applied bandage is greatly appreciated by the patient.

Bandages are used for many purposes: as a first-aid measure in the treatment of the injured, particularly to control bleeding; to immobilize a part or restrict its movement; to afford support; to hold splints securely; and to prevent or reduce swelling. They are also used to protect a surgical wound against infection, to hold surgical dressings or other local applications in place, and to assist in the correction of a deformity.

Before applying a bandage, the following considerations must be kept in mind:

1. The type and purpose of the bandage.
2. The comfort of the patient.
3. The most natural position of the part to be bandaged.
4. The neatness and the economy of the bandage.

Roller Bandages

There are many new proprietary bandages available which are proving effective and easy to apply. However, some roller bandages still have a place in hospital and general medical practice, and for this reason are included in this chapter. A roller bandage is defined as a length of material wound into a compact firm roll.

Size

Various lengths and widths are used according to the part to which the bandage is to be applied (Table 1).

Material

A roller bandage may be improvised from any material but those available commercially utilize a variety of materials, natural and synthetic. Special bandages will be described later in the chapter.

Table 1: Guide to Approximate Dimensions of Bandages used for Various Parts of the Body

	Length		*Width*	
Part of body	*Yards*	*Centimetres (approx.)*	*Inches*	*Centimetres (approx.)*
Toe or finger	1-3	90-270	0.75-1	1.8-2.5
Head	6	540	2-4	5-10
Arm	6	540	2-2.5	5-6.25
Leg	6-9	540-810	2.5-3	6.25-7.5
Trunk	6-9	540-810	4-6	10-15

Although the open-weave cotton bandage, is still available, it has largely been superseded by an open mesh conforming bandage, frequently incorporating materials such as nylon, polyester and viscose Equally, the cotton crepe bandage, light and woven in such a way as to allow considerable elasticity, tends to be replaced by the crepe knit bandage made of 60% nylon and 40% viscose. Both can be applied easily so that uniform pressure is maintained over the area covered.

Application

Before starting to apply a roller bandage the patient should be placed in a comfortable position and the part to be bandaged should be in the natural position if permitted. The person applying the bandage, should stand in front of the patient and the part to be bandaged. A tightly rolled bandage should be used and only a short length, not more than 5-7.5 cm (2-3 in), unrolled at a time so that full control of the bandage is maintained.

Starting just below the part to be covered, the outer surface of the bandage is placed next to the skin, and two turns initially will firmly anchor the bandage. The bandage should be applied in an upward direction whenever possible and from within outwards for a limb. Absorbent material ought to be placed between two skin surfaces to absorb perspiration and to avoid friction. All prominences should be well padded. Particular care should be taken that the bandage is applied with even tension over the whole area. It should be borne in mind that the degree of pressure required will vary according to the purpose for which the bandage is used. One-third of each turn of the bandage should be left uncovered.

The bandage should be finished with a complete turn and fixed securely with a strip of inexpensive adhesive strapping or sellotape; with the end of the bandage, which is split and tied; with a safety-pin, taking care that it will not cause harm; or by sewing the end with needle and cotton.

Mistakes

When applying a bandage, every effort should be made to avoid the following:

1. A wet bandage, as it will shrink when dry.
2. Uneven tension of the bandage as it is being applied—a very tight bandage will interfere with the circulation of blood and cause death of tissue—a loose bandage will become displaced.
3. Reverse turns over a prominence or wound as they will not 'give' at all and can cause the patient discomfort and pain.
4. Use of too much bandage which will cause discomfort and is expensive.
5. Incorrect securing of the end of the bandage, which may do harm.

Basic Turns

There are five turns commonly used in roller bandaging:

1. *Circular.* When the bandage is carried horizontally around the part. It is used mainly for securing a bandage at the beginning and end. It should not be used around a limb as it could interfere with the circulation of blood.
2. *Spiral.* When the bandage is carried spirally up the limb. It is applied over parts that are of uniform thickness as for the finger and the upper arm.

3. *Reverse spiral.* When a spiral bandage has a reverse turn. It is used for parts of varying dimensions, e.g. the forearm (Fig. 1).
4. *Figure-of-eight.* When each complete turn of the bandage forms a figure-of-eight. It consists of overlapping turns, each of which crosses at a mid-point and ascends or descends alternately. It is used over joints and as an alternative to the reverse spiral. A spica is a modification of the figure-of-eight turn when one loop is much larger than the other.

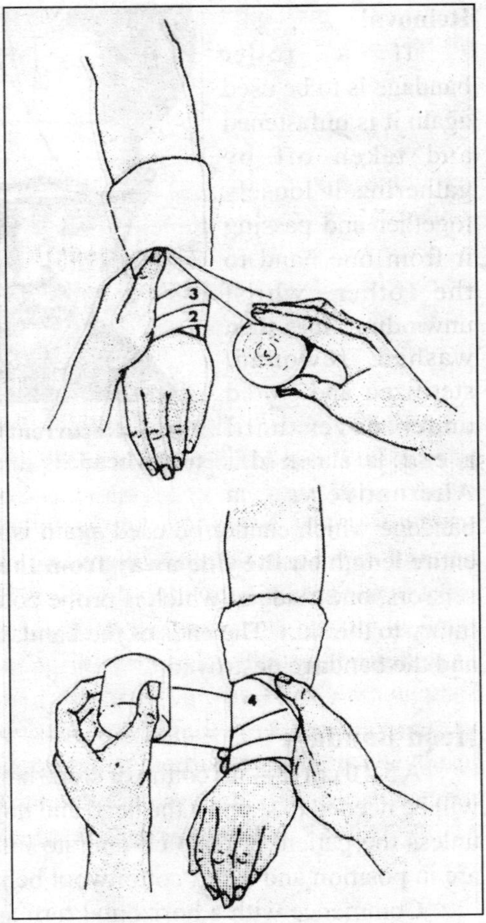

Fig. 1: A reverse spiral turn.

5. *Recurrent.* When a series of alternating turns are made. After one or two spiral turns the initial turn is made across the middle of the area to be covered and the succeeding turns pass to and fro over the end on first one side, then the other, of the initial turn until the entire area is covered. Finally, the bandage is completed with one or two spiral turns. This pattern is useful when applying a bandage to the stump of an amputated limb, or to the head (Fig. 2).

Removal

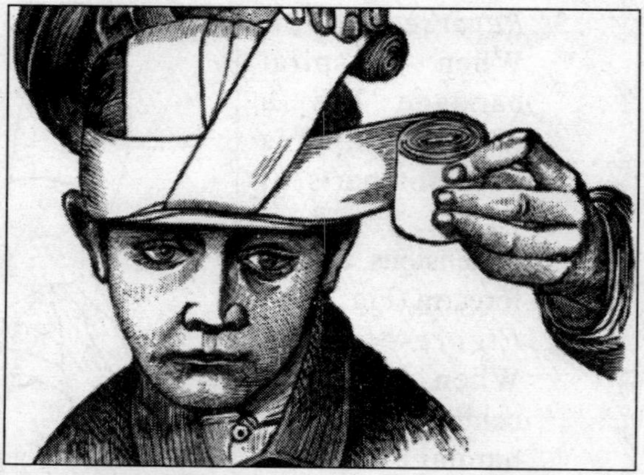

Fig. 2: Recurrent turns when applying bandage to the head.

If a roller bandage is to be used again it is unfastened and taken off by gathering it loosely together and passing it from one hand to the other whilst unwinding. It is then washed, rewound, sterilized and stored under cover until required. Alternatively, a bandage which cannot be used again is removed by cutting along its entire length **on the side away from the injury or wound.** A special scissors, one blade of which is probe pointed, should be used to avoid injury to the skin. The ends of the bandage are then carefully gathered and the bandage destroyed.

Head Bandage

A 5-10 cm (2-4 in) cotton or crepe bandage is required. An assistant will be needed to support the head and hold in place the recurrent turns unless the patient is fit to co-operate fully. Ensure that the dressings are in position and insert cottonwool behind the ears.

Commence with a horizontal turn around the head, beginning at the right ear, carry it backwards low on the occiput and forward over the left ear, across the forehead to the starting point. Repeat. Over the starting point make a reverse turn and guide the bandage over the centre of the head to the left ear. (Sometimes the central bandage is continued down the left side of the head under the chin and up the right side of the head over the right ear, up over the head to one side of the first turn to the left ear and then continued as already described.) Here reverse the bandage again and guide it back over the head to one side of the central bandage to the right ear. Pass the succeeding turns to and fro over the head on first one side, then the other of the central bandage until the head is covered. Finish with two horizontal turns round the head and fix in front with a safety-pin or adhesive strapping (Fig. 2).

This bandage is frequently used in neurosurgical units, but in some instances it has been superseded by the appropriate application of either cotton/rayon or elastic net tubular bandage.

Eye Bandage

A 5 cm (2 in) woven edged bandage is used. Place the bandage against the forehead above the affected eye, pass it horizontally around the head towards the sound eye and above the ears, bringing it low on the occiput and forward to the starting point. Here, take it over the back of the head under the ear on the affected side and up over the inner edge of the dressing to the centre of the forehead. Care is needed to keep the edge of the bandage clear of the sound eye. Take the bandage obliquely across the side and down the back of the head and again up over the eye. Finally, after two or three such turns make one horizontal turn around the head and secure the end of the bandage on the forehead. Crepe bandages are used when pressure is needed (Fig. 3).

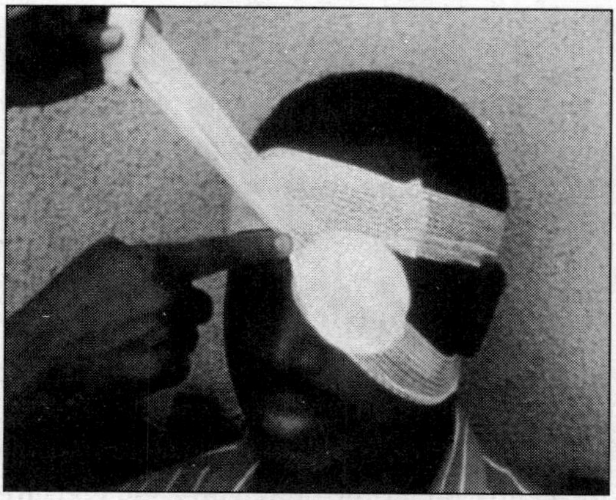

Fig. 3: Bandage to left eye.

Ear Bandage

Take a 5 cm (2 in) bandage; cut off a length of approximately 22.5 cm (9 in) and lay it vertically across the patient's forehead. Fix by placing the free end of the bandage over the dressing and taking one and a half turns around the head; then carry the bandage from a point above the ear on the sound side obliquely downwards low on the occiput and forwards to cover the lower edge of the dressing on the affected side. Continue to carry the bandage forwards and upwards across the horizontal turn and over the front and side of the head. Repeat the complete turn, bringing the first part a little higher each time over the dressing, and the second part a little nearer the forehead over the head. Finish with a complete horizontal turn around the head. The strip is then tied tightly to fix the end of the bandage and to prevent any slipping (Fig. 4).

Fig. 4: Bandage to left ear.

The application of the single ear bandage to each side in turn is most practical when both ears require dressings.

If used for a mastoidectomy, a crepe bandage may be applied for the first 24 hours when it can be replaced by an open-weave cotton bandage for a few days.

Barrel Bandage for Fractured Jaw

A barrel bandage may be used for a fractured jaw. Take approximately 150 cm (60 in) of a 7.5 cm (3 in) bandage and place the centre under the chin, carry the ends to the top of the head and tie with the first loop of a reef knot; loosen and separate the loop bringing one-half over the forehead and the other low on the occiput. The ends are now taken to the top of the head and tied securely with a reef knot (Fig. 5).

Fig. 5: A barrel bandage.

Shoulder Bandages

There are two ways of applying a spica to the shoulder. If the dressing is low over the joint the ascending spica is used; conversely, if the dressing is high on the shoulder a descending spica should be used.

Ascending Spica

Insert a pad of absorbent cotton wool in each axilla. A 7.5 cm (3 in) bandage is used. Commence by taking a spiral turn around the upper part of the arm on the affected side, follow with two reverse spirals and carry the bandage across the back and under the opposite arm well below the axilla, across the front of the chest and over the shoulder. Then take the bandage under the arm from behind forwards, up over the shoulder, and across the back again. Repeat these turns until the dressing is covered and secure in front. If the dressing is not extensive the reverse spiral turns on the arm can be omitted (Fig. 6).

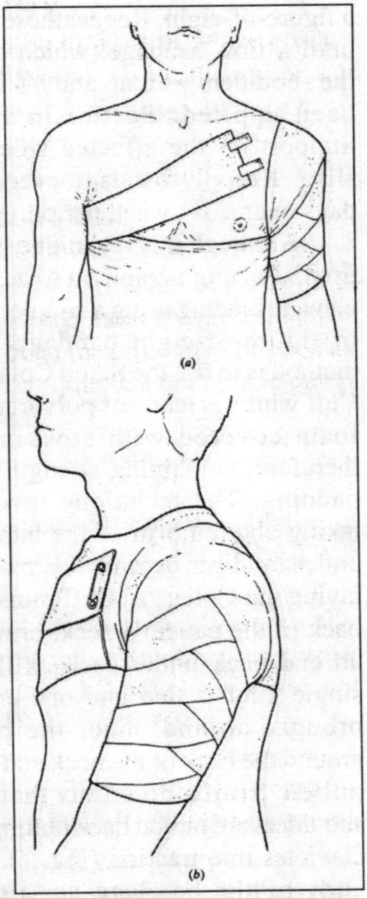

Fig. 6: Bandage of left shoulder—ascending spica.

Descending Spica

The bandage is similar to that already described for an ascending spica but the figure-of-eight turns work downwards to cover the entire dressing and it is secured on the arm.

Bandage for Fracture of the Clavicle

Use a 10 cm (4 in) (i.e. cotton and wool weft) bandage. The patient sits with shoulders braced back, arms flexed and hands resting on hips. The person who is applying the bandage stands behind the patient. Place large pads of wool over the shoulders and under the axillae. Start in front of the sound shoulder. Take the bandage across the back, under the axilla, and up in front of the affected shoulder. Continue across the back under the axilla and up in front of the sound shoulder to complete a figure-of-eight. Repeat these turns until a firm bandage, which draws the shoulders well up and back, has been applied. Secure in front. Support on the affected side in a sling. Reapply bandage every few days over a 3-4 week period.

Although this technique is still used, it is more common to achieve clavicle bracing using a simpler form of figure-of-eight bandage. One method is to use the Seton Collar 'n' Cuff which is made of polyurethane foam covered with stockinette, therefore, combining strength with padding. The technique involves taking about 1.5 m of the bandage and, standing behind the patient, laying the Collar 'n' Cuff round the back of the patient's neck, bringing an end back under each axilla. A single knot is tied and one end is brought up and under the piece around the back of the neck and then pulled firmly down so that the shoulders are pulled back putting the clavicles into traction (Fig. 7). The ends of the bandage are firmly secured using either the fasteners provided or by tying a knot, first removing the foam from the two tails. In this way a flatter more comfortable knot will be achieved.

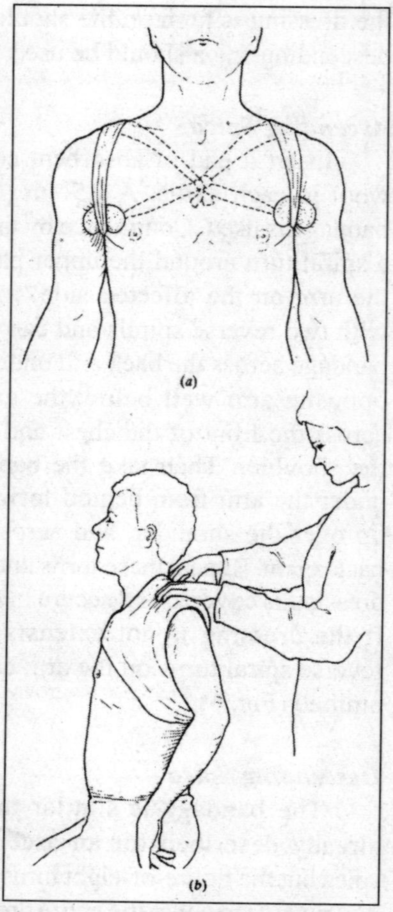

Fig. 7: (a) and (b) Bandage for fracture of the clavicle.

Bandages for the Upper Limb

Whole Arm

A 6.25 cm (2.5 in) bandage is used. Turn the hand palm downwards and bend the elbow. Start with a spiral turn around the wrist, from within outwards. Then fix the bandage by taking one turn around the hand followed by a figure-of-eight turn, one loop being around the knuckles and the other around the wrist. Now make one spiral turn around the wrist and begin to reverse. Continue up as far as the elbow, keeping the turns near the centre of the arm to avoid pressure on the bone (alternatively, figure-of-eight turns can be used). Change to figure-of-eight turns over the elbow. Either continue these turns to the top of the arm or reverse again after the elbow is passed. Finish with a spiral turn and secure.

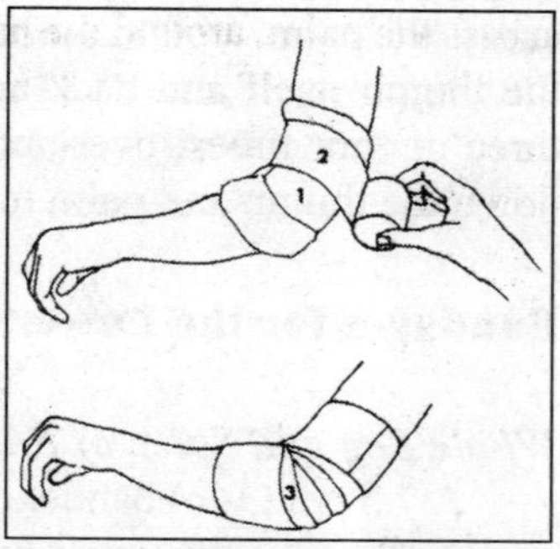

Fig. 8: Bandage to elbow - spica.

Spica of Elbow

Use a 6.25 cm (2.5 in) bandage. Start with two spiral turns around the elbow so that the point of the elbow rests in the middle of it. Continue the bandage with figure-of-eight turns, working above and below the point of the elbow until the dressing is covered. Finish above the elbow with a spiral turn and secure (Fig. 8).

Spica of Thumb

Where there has been a thumb or thenar muscle injury it is usual to use Elastoplast strapping 2.5 cm (1 in) in order to achieve support. Commencing below the distal interphalangeal joint, two turns around the thumb are applied in an anti-clockwise direction on the left thumb and clockwise on the right thumb. The strapping is carried straight

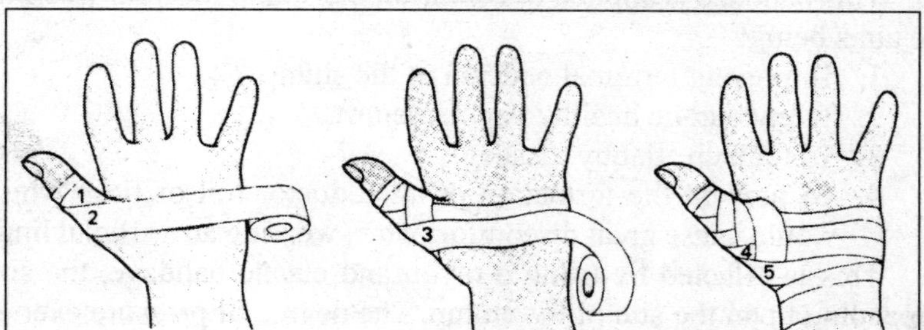

Fig. 9: Bandage to thumb of left hand—spica.

across the palm, around the hand and over the base of the thumb, around the thumb itself and back-across the palm. These turns are repeated three or four times, overlapping each other by at least half, working down the thumb and palm towards the wrist (Fig. 9).

Bandages for the Lower Limb

Whole Leg and Spica of Knee and Heel

A 7.5 cm (3 in) bandage is used. A similar technique is employed as described for the upper limb.

Knee Pressure Bandage

A 7.5 cm (3 in) crepe knit bandage is used. The patient lies in the dorsal recumbent position with knee extended and his heel resting on a wedge. Wrap a thick layer of wool around the knee. Apply two or three firm circular turns of the bandage around the knee, add another layer of wool, then two or three more firm circular turns of bandage. Repeat until a firm unyielding bandage has been applied. This bandage is used to control and reduce swelling, for immobilization of the knee following injury, and as a postoperative measure.

Sprained Ankle

As a temporary measure only, a crepe knit bandage may be applied, and the method of application is similar to that described for the more effective adhesive strapping bandage.

Bandaging an Amputation Stump

This bandage is applied to condition the stump for limb wearing, the aims being:

1. To prevent terminal oedema of the stump.
2. To encourage healthy venous return.
3. To tone up 'flabby' tissue.
4. To prevent the formation of an adductor roll of flesh which would cause great discomfort when wearing an artificial limb.

This is effected by using a rayon and elastic bandage, the size depending upon the site of the stump. The degree of pressure exerted by the bandage depends upon the patient's ability to tolerate the pressure but it must be applied from the time of amputation.

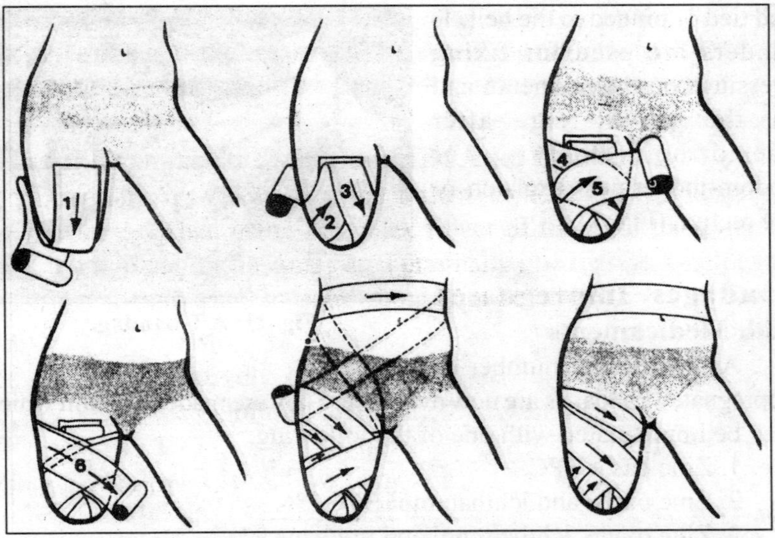

Fig. 10: Bandage to an above-knee stump of an amputated limb.

Below-knee Stump

Figure-of-eight turns are used commencing above the lateral tibial condyle, then bandaging diagonally across the front of the stump to the medial distal corner. The bandage is then taken firmly up along the posterior aspect of the stump, care being taken to place fixing turns around the limb only above the joint, leaving the patella exposed.

Above-knee or Through-knee Stump Bandaging

This may be carried out as shown in Fig. 10 and described by Seton Products Ltd., who recommend the use of the Elset 'S' bandage.

Incorrect stump bandaging is one of the major causes of delayed rehabilitation following amputations and it may be necessary to obtain the advice of the Limb Fitting Service on this matter.

Special Bandages

The T-bandage

This bandage may have one tail (single) or two tails (double) attached to a belt. The belt is passed around the waist and secured. The single or double tails are passed between the legs, which are extended, and tied or pinned to the belt. T-binders are used for fixing dressings on the perineum and in the groin, e.g. after haemorrhoidectomy or abdom-inoperineal excision of the rectum (Fig. 11).

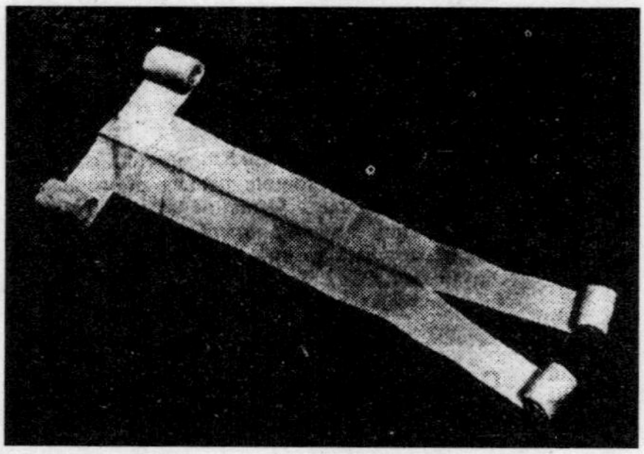

Fig. 11: A T-bandage.

Bandages Impregnated with Medicaments

An increasing number of impregnated bandages are now available. They are made of cotton which may be impregnated with one of the following:

1. Zinc paste BPC.
2. Zinc oxide and ichthammol BPC 2%.
3. Zinc oxide, ichthammol and urethane 2%.
4. Zinc oxide, calamine 5.75% and urethane 2%.

These bandages are used to protect and soothe the skin and to promote healing of wounds, in particular eczemas, dermatitis and gravitational ulcers. They also act as a buffer between a compression bandage (when used) and the skin and thus prevent skin damage. Detailed instructions are supplied with the bandages.

Cotton Crepe (Elastocrepe)

This is a smooth-surface cotton crepe bandage which provides greater compression and support than the ordinary crepe bandage. It stretches to nearly twice its length but regains its original length readily. This elasticity gives firm but controlled compression, and is particularly useful for this purpose when applied in conjunction with the impregnated bandages already described.

□

DIAGNOSIS AND MANAGEMENT OF CIRCULATORY ARREST

1. Sudden loss of consciousness, occasionally with convulsions.
2. Appearance—combination of pallor, cyanosis and skin blotching—the patient looks dead.
3. Absence of respiration—there may occasionally be irregular gasps.

   The diagnosis should be strongly suspected from the above factors in a *few seconds,* and should be confirmed in a further 10-15 sec by finding:
4. Absence of femoral pulses (usually more easily ascertained than absence of carotid pulses).
5. Dilatation of the pupils.

Note that sudden loss of consciousness occurs in fainting but there is *bradycardia* in such circumstances.

Treatment

1. Call for help, oxygen and resuscitation equipment (Fig. 1).
2. Make patient lie flat, e.g. removing any pillows from the bed.
3. Thump the precordium hard with the ulnar border of the clenched fist (this may act as a stimulus to restart an arrest in asystole).
4. *Immediately* proceed to carry out external cardiac compression, applied over the lower third of the sternum (Fig. 2).
5. If single-handed, interrupt cardiac compression after 10 sec to apply expressed air resuscitation by mouth-to-nose (easier than mouth-to-mouth) respiration or by the use of an artificial airway, e.g. Brock's airway.

6. Provided there are sufficient assistants, the patient is best placed on a firm surface—the floor makes endotracheal intubation and the setting up of I.V. infusion difficult, and a firm bed-board under the trunk is better.
7. Elevate the legs.
8. Pass an endotracheal tube (8 or 9 mm for an average adult) and inflate the cuff (Fig. 3). Administer oxygen by means of a reservoir bag and valve, or a self-inflating bag such as the Ambu. If intubation is not possible, apply a face mask with the head fully extended, and give oxygen by intermittent positive-pressure ventilation (this tends to be difficult for untrained personnel).

   One inflation of the lungs should be given for eight cardiac compressions. *Caution*: Make sure endotracheal intubation has been achieved, otherwise oxygenation will be inadequate and gastric rupture may occur.

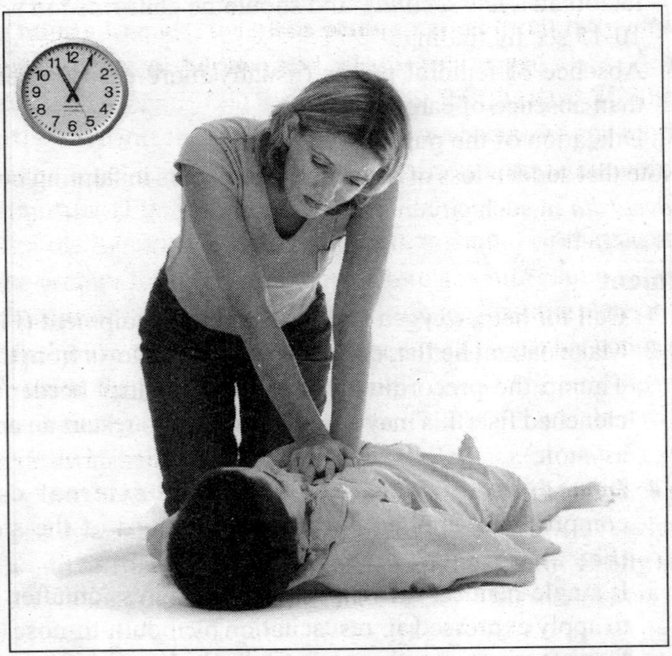

Fig. 1: (a) Lay patient flat on firm bed or floor; (b) Strike the precordium with the fist; (c) Call for assistance; (d) Note the time.

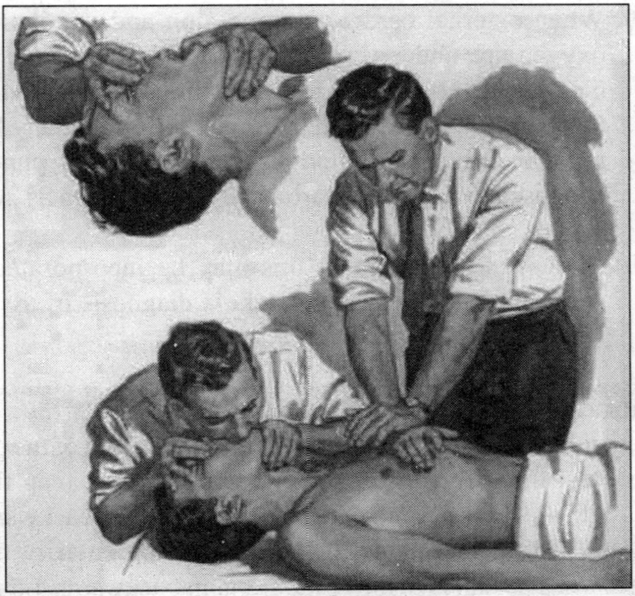

Fig. 2: (a) Elevate legs; (b) External cardiac massage—press lower sternum backwards 60 times/min; (c) Mouth-to-nose or mouth-to-mouth respiration—nostrils pinched.

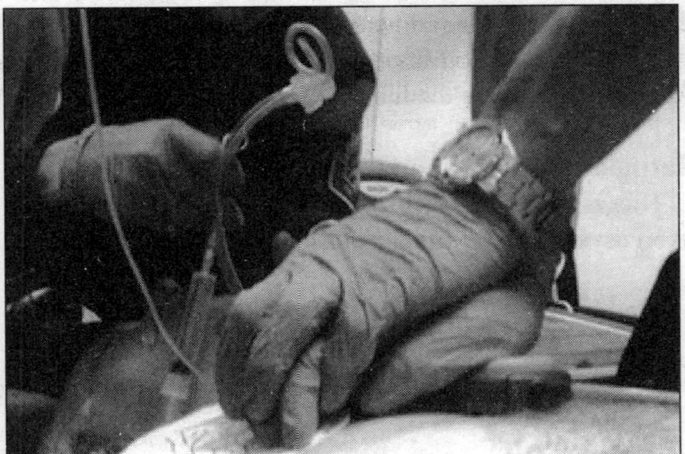

Fig. 3: (a) Intubate the patient and ventilate 8 times/min with oxygen; (b) Continue external massage; (c) Connect up cardioscope; (d) Set up I.V. infusion of sodium bicarbonate, 4.2% or 8.4%.

9. When external cardiac compression and ventilation with oxygen are under way, set up an I.V. infusion of sodium bicarbonate (100 mmol in 10 min initially). Immediate cut-down at the elbow without aseptic technique may be more rapid than repeated attempts at percutaneous puncture of collapsed veins. The bicarbonate may be given as 200 ml of a 4.2% solution.
10. Connect ECG monitor (this may be incorporated in the defibrillating equipment). Make a diagnosis of asystole or ventricular fibrillation.

Technique of External Cardiac Massage

Press with the heel of the hand over the lower third of the patient's sternum. Rest the other hand on top of the first and keep the arms straight. With a sharp jerky movement, press vertically backwards once per second, lifting the hands off the chest momentarily between compressions. The aim is to move the sternum backwards 4-5 cm with each compression. In an old person one or more ribs are frequently broken, but mechanical damage to the myocardium or liver must be avoided. Only one hand, and much less force is needed in a young child. Check whether the compressions produce a palpable carotid pulse.

If only one person is present, interrrupt cardiac massage every eight strokes to inflate the lungs.

Treatment of Arrhythmia

This is aimed at early defibrillation, with the possible need to convert asystole to ventricular fibrillation initially.

Ventricular Fibrillation

Apply external defibrillator (DC countershock-synchronized) starting at 200 joules (Wsec) in an adult, 50 joules in a younger child.

Precautions

1. Disconnect ECG machine from patient.
2. Continue external cardiac compression and ventilate until the defibrillator is completely prepared for use.

3. Apply electrode jelly to the external electrodes to prevent skin burning.
4. Apply the electrodes to the chest, so that the electrical discharge passes through the largest bulk of heart tissue, i.e. one electrode at the base of the heart (to right of upper sternum) and the other over the estimated area of the apex of the heart, usually the sternal angle.
5. Make certain that nobody is in direct or indirect electrical contact with the patient before activating defibrillator.
6. Resume cardiac compression and ventilation *immediately* while awaiting the reappearance of the ECG pattern.

If the first shock is unsuccessful in stopping fibrillation, increase the current to 300 joules and try again. Further attempts are made after infusing another 100 ml of 8.4% sodium bicarbonate solution; if this fails, lignocaine in a dose of 1-2 mg/kg body-weight may be given in resistant cases.

If fine fibrillation persists on the ECG, it may be made coarser by giving 2-5 ml of 1-10000 adrenaline hydrochloride intravenously, and then repeating the DC shocks or giving propranolol, 5 mg.

External cardiac massage and ventilation of the lungs are continued between the shocks.

Treatment of Asystole

Give an intracardiac injection of 3-5 ml of 1-10000 adrenaline hydrochloride into the left ventricle and continue external massage. The adrenaline may strengthen the myocardial contraction if and when it is re-established. Should spontaneous beating not recommence in 3-4 min, then give 10 ml of 10% calcium gluconate intravenously. If now the heartbeat starts, but the blood pressure remains low, inject 100 mg hydrocortisone intravenously or use pressor drugs, e.g. metaraminol 1-5 mg intravenously. After spontaneous heartbeat has been restored careful supervision is needed:

1. Monitor patient's ECG.
2. Record blood pressure and temperature every 15 min.
3. Count respiratory rate; check adequacy of respiration.
4. Check acid-base status several times and correct metabolic acidosis.

5. Watch urinary output. Insert urethral catheter.
6. Be prepared for further episodes of cardiac arrest.

When to Stop Unsuccessful Resuscitation

Patients have returned to a normal life after an hour of cardiac massage. Recovery is unlikely, however, if spontaneous beating of the heart has not recommenced within 30 min of the start of resuscitative efforts. Certainly, no junior doctor should cease his efforts in under 30 min. The decision to stop is best taken by the anaesthetist and senior clinician together. Frequent repetition of the steps outlined above for the treatment of ventricular fibrillation usually brings success. Asystole carries a worse prognosis. If after giving adrenaline, calcium and then hydrocortisone there is no sign of electrical activity on the ECG, the prognosis is gloomy.

Other Measures

Periods of anoxia cause cerebral oedema, which may interfere with the circulation to the brain and lead to permanent brain damage; they may also adversely affect renal function. To counteract these tendencies hypothermia and dehydration therapy may be used.

1. *Hypothermia.* The brain's oxygen requirements decrease sharply as the body temperature is lowered. If consciousness is not regained shortly after the heart is restarted, if there are other neurological changes or hyperpyrexia, then the patient should at once be cooled down 3-5°C to 32-35°C (89.6-95.0°F), by placing packs of broken ice around him at an early stage or if available by the use of a circulating blanket. Small doses of chlorpromazine (12.5 mg) I.V. may be used to help this process. Accurate monitoring of the core temperature is necessary and smaller doses of drugs are needed by the hypothermic patient.
2. *Dehydration Therapy.* Urinary output can be increased by giving 500 ml of 10% mannitol intravenously. This loss of fluid from the body may, as with dexamethasone, reduce the tendency to cerebral oedema. The latter must be used with caution because it may interfere with wound healing. If arrest has lasted more than 10 min give 50 ml of 50% dextrose intravenously.

3. *Plasma Expander.* If the cardiac arrest was precipitated by hypovolaemia, a plasma expander, e.g. 500 ml of 6% Macrodex, may be infused intravenously.

Table 1. Drugs and solutions that may be required in the treatment of cardiac arrest. They should all be present on the resuscitation trolley

Drugs
Adrenaline injection, BP, 1-10000, 1-ml ampoule × 5
Ampoules of sterile water, 10 ml × 10
Hydrocortisone, 100-mg vials × 2
Metaraminol, 1 mg/ml, 10-ml vial × 1
Noradrenaline injection, 2-ml ampoules × 4. Dilute to 1-10000
Procaine hydrochloride, 1% in 10-ml ampoules × 2
Lignocaine hydrochloride, 1% plain, 10-ml ampoules ×2
Procaine amide 100 mg/ml, 10-ml vial × 1
Calcium gluconate 10%, 10-ml ampoules × 5
Propranolol 5 mg, ampoules × 2
Digoxin 2 mg, ampoules × 2
For Anaesthesia
Thiopentone 0.5 g
D-Tubocurarine 15 mg, ampoules × 3
Atropine 0.6 mg, ampoules × 4
Neostigmine 0.5 mg, ampoules × 6
Intravenous Fluids
Normal saline
Dextrose 5%
Macrodex 6% in saline
Macrodex 6% in dextrose
Sodium bicarbonate 8.4% (or 42%) 250-ml bottles × 2
Mannitol 20%, 500-ml bottle
Glucose 50%, 50-ml ampoules × 4

Intracardiac Injections

With effective cardiac massage and an intravenous line established, it should usually be unnecessary to inject drugs into the heart, a manoeuvre which is difficult and potentially dangerous because:

1. The average disposable hypodermic needle is almost always too short.

2. A needle may cause a pneumothorax.
3. There may be puncture of an anterior descending branch of one of the coronary arteries.

Clinical Features

Activity of the accessory respiratory muscles and stridor are the two cardinal features of incomplete respiratory obstruction. The first merely signifies respiratory effort and is thus not specific, the latter is the consequence of air rushing through a greatly narrowed passage and is not only specific but is usually a harbinger of early doom unless something is done. In drawing of the intercostal, spaces may or may not be present. Incomplete respiratory obstruction does not necessarily imply respiratory insufficiency, although the one is likely to follow hard upon the other. There is not much difficulty in diagnosing complete obstruction—convulsive respiratory effort, cyanosis, unconsciousness, convulsions and circulatory arrest are the sequelae over a period of less than 2 min.

Recognition of Respiratory Insufficiency

The definition of respiratory insufficiency is biochemical and biophysical—an abnormal state of arterial blood gases. It follows that it has no clear-cut symptoms or physical signs—indeed it represents a final common state that results from a wide variety of causes. In surgical patients, the usual but not invariable situations are:

1. Inadequate mechanical ventilation from either poor or ineffective movement of the chest wall.
2. Blocked respiratory passage by retained sputum or aspirated vomit with subsequent distal absorptive collapse. To this may be added either the ineffective movement of pre-existing lung disease or the consequent effects of oedema in an infected lung in circumstances where massive inappropriate respiratory efforts are being made.

Given the common underlying causes, the surgeon's job is to recognize the presence of respiratory insufficiency in individual circumstances. When dyspnoea or cyanosis is present there is little difficulty, but before these have supervened respiratory insufficiency is usually well marked. Thus, PO_2 may fall from the normal 100 mmHg to 60 mmHg before saturation is significantly reduced (and cyanosis consequently apparent); a further small fall may precipitate severe desaturation (*see* Fig. 4 for details). This 'slippery slope' of the oxygen dissociation curve should be constantly in the mind's eye of all those dealing with respiratory insufficiency.

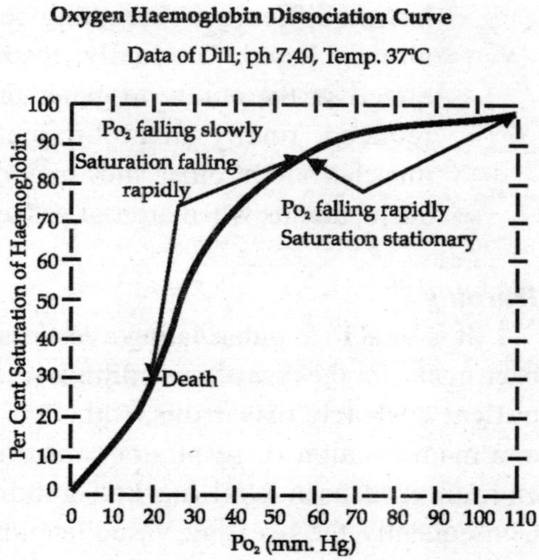

Fig. 4: The oxygen dissociation curve. Initially PO_2 falls rapidly without change in saturation but at a PO_2 of approximately 60 mmHg large changes in saturation take place for small changes in PO_2. This is the 'slippery slope'.

In the absence of gross signs, what other guides are present for the clinician? Restlessness and disorientation are two of the most valuable. Although both may have many causes, among the commonest in surgical wards is hypoxia. Sudden changes in mental states should at once raise the question: Is hypoxia present or has hypercarbia developed?

3. Increasingly, the so-called adult respiratory distress syndrome or 'post-traumatic pulmonary insufficiency'. This is a complex problem in which pulmonary capillary microaggregates and interstitial oedema combine to reduce compliance, interfere with gas exchange and raise pulmonary artery pressure. The usual cause is sepsis and trauma.
4. Respiratory insufficiency may also occur in the surgical patient as a consequence of fatigue. The sequence of events is seen in the malnourished patient with reduced energy stores who is

having difficulty in breathing because of some of the factors already listed. Gradually, respiratory effort becomes less effective; the ability to generate an explosive cough is also reduced; finally anaerobic metabolism of the respiratory muscles and at other sites may develop. There is a period in such patients when arterial gas tensions are normal.

Warning

It is vital to avoid sedating a restless patient until a diagnosis has been made, for the **incautious administration of sedatives to a hypoxic patient is clearly disastrous.** Although *hypercarbia* is mentioned as one manifestation of respiratory insufficiency, it is not commonly encountered as a well-marked syndrome in surgical patients. Consequently, the sweating, vasodilatation and drowsiness that go with a very high PCO_2 (80-90 mmHg) are rarely seen. The explanation is that the surgical patient is not often underventilating in the sense that he has an inadequate stimulus to his respiratory centre or an inadequate mechanical response. Usually, he is trying hard to breathe in the face of a situation which involves hypoxia and because of the free diffusibility of carbon dioxide, he may even produce respiratory alkalosis in association with a low PO_2 and clinical deterioration.

Aids to the Diagnosis of Respiratory Insufficiency

A chest X-ray is mandatory. It may show the basal collapse consolidation characteristic of the patient with postoperative sputum retention and raised diaphragm; a fluid collection; or the patchy consolidation increasing to 'total whiteout' of adult respiratory distress syndrome.

The final diagnosis rests on proving the definition—abnormality of blood gases—by direct measurement of PO_2 and PCO_2. Both these are now well within the capacity of most hospital biochemical organizations who will provide, in addition, information about hydrogen ion concentration. To produce such results, the laboratory must be provided with an iced, rapidly transported (less than 1 h old), anaerobically drawn arterial blood sample, although some techniques can make use of capillary blood.

Techniques of Arterial Puncture

Femoral, brachial or radial arteries may be used, but the last is to be preferred in that harm is not likely to follow. A short-bevelled 21 gauge needle is attached to a 10-ml syringe wetted with heparin 1000 u/ml so that the needle is filled with this solution. The skin is stretched with the thumb and forefinger of the free hand (Fig. 5), and the artery fixed so that its pulsation can be felt and if possible seen just proximal to the digit of the operator which is pressed against the skin. A quick skin puncture is made at a moderate angle. The needle is then advanced steadily and obliquely into the artery which offers firm resistance. Entry into the lumen of the vessel is signified by a rise of the plunger of the syringe which then fills under arterial pressure alone; failure to detect the added resistance of the arterial wall implies that the needle is lying either to one or other side of the vessel and a fresh puncture should be made. The needle is sharply withdrawn, the syringe capped to avoid aeration of the sample, and firm pressure applied to the puncture site for three minutes by the clock. The results should be available within five min.

In complicated circumstances for repeated sampling, a fine cannula should be threaded into the artery and filled with heparin solution 500 u/ml. Needle-cannulae combinations which have the needle outside the cannula should not be used for this purpose as the needle puncture is not always free from leakage. A cannula such as an Intramedicut is satisfactory, but indwelling cannulae should always be removed as soon as possible because thrombosis is a common complication.

Acidosis

Acidosis—a raised blood hydrogen ion concentration in respiratory insufficiency—is the consequence of:

1. Underventilation with a rise in PCO_2 which in turn displaces the equation
$$CO_2 + H_2O = H_2CO_3 = H^+ \text{ and } HCO_3^-$$
to the right, and
2. The metabolic hydrogen ion production which is the result of anaerobic metabolism in the hypoxic patient with the production of lactic acid.

Both are of particular importance in that they render the patient more susceptible to acute cardiovascular disturbance such as fibrillation, arrest and peripheral circulatory failure. The exact dissection of the relative contributions to acidosis of respiratory and metabolic components rests on the correct application of one of the acid-base nomograms commonly used in hospital practice. Because these vary according to the apparatus used (and also the taste of the resident expert) they will not be considered here. However, circumstances will help: underperfusion should suggest the presence of metabolic acidosis; hypoventilation should suggest respiratory acidosis.

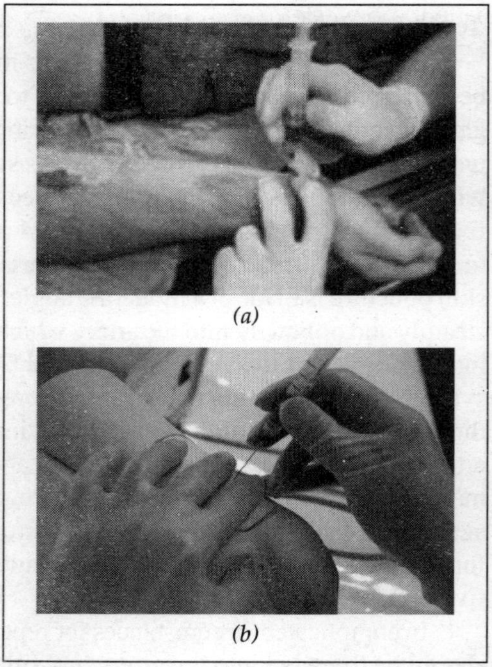

Fig. 5: Method of fixing (a) the femoral and (b) radial arteries for arterial puncture.

Oxygen Saturation Measurement

When facilities for full blood-gas analysis are not available, saturation measurements are of some use in determining oxygenation. It must be remembered, however, that as already stated, arterial desaturation is a situation of advanced respiratory failure and requires most urgent and effective management. Absence of desaturation must not lull anyone into a false sense of security.

Prevention and Treatment of Respiratory Obstruction

Predisposing factors should be avoided. The unconscious patient is usually at risk and must be nursed on his side or semiprone. Where this is impossible (e.g. when other injuries such as fractured femur coexist), prophylactic intubation or tracheostomy should be undertaken (*see below*).

When acute obstruction is diagnosed, an airway must be re-established forth with. Often this is simple—pulling forward the tongue digitally or with a towel clip (which pierces the tongue without damaging it) and then maintaining forward displacement of the jaw (Fig. 6). In the deeply unconscious patient, an airway may be inserted, but it is far better to insist that someone is delegated to maintain the jaw forward than to insert an airway casually and hope for the best.

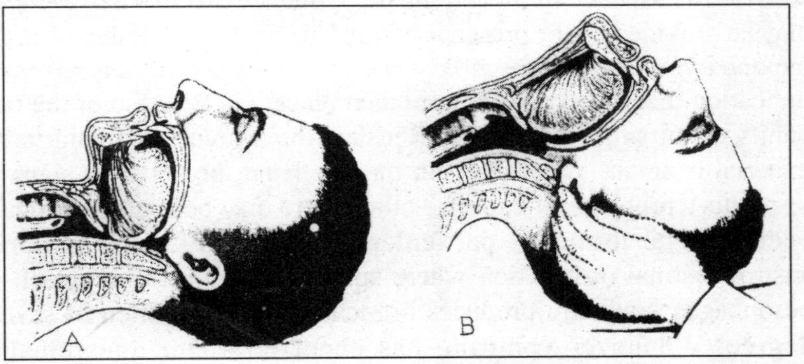

Fig. 6: Holding the jaw forward to maintain an airway. The same position of head and neck is adopted for bronchoscopy. A shows how the unextended jaw permits obstruction of the airway by the tongue. B illustrates (1) the forward displacement of the jaw by pressure at the angle and (2) the extension of the atlanto-occipital joint which permits direct access to the larynx for toilet or bronchoscopy.

Where simple methods do not suffice and total obstruction is present or impending, it is dramatic but unreliable to undertake emergency tracheostomy. In fact, in a dying patient with respiratory obstruction this may prove the *coup de grace,* as often an inexperienced surgeon struggles in the acutely congested neck to expose a wind-pipe that is gyrating in the storm of respiratory efforts. Better either:

1. To intubate the patient, overcoming trismus with a mouth gag. It should be the pride of every junior doctor to be able to intubate dextrously under direct vision, and the frequency with which endotracheal anaesthesia is used provides ample opportunity for him to acquire the technique. If there is any doubt in the mind as to effective intubation it is preferable to:

2. Plunge a 15 gauge needle through the thyroid membrane. This apparently fine pathway will maintain oxygenation until more effective measures can be set in hand.

Inhalation of Vomitus

The ill-managed surgical patient or the victim of some acute disaster such as accidental injury or drowning with loss of consciousness, may vomit and inhale. Evidence that this has occurred may be provided by the presence of vomitus on the bedclothes or in the hypopharynx. But the absence of such tell-tales are of themselves no indication that the event has not taken place: (1) Because of the tidy habits of nursing staff, or (2) Because the amount of regurgitated material is small. There may, on the one hand, be no overt signs of respiratory problems and, on the other, there may be acute pulmonary oedema. The former is particularly true of situations of upper gastrointestinal obstruction where spillover from a full stomach or oesophagus gradually produces bronchopneumonia, often of severe degree. Whenever vomiting has occurred under questionable circumstances, the hypopharynx and larynx should be viewed directly for signs of vomit and the former cleared by suction. If there is obvious respiratory difficulty, urgent bronchoscopy must be done or the trachea intubated so that suction can be applied through the endotracheal tube. While awaiting intubation or bronchoscopy, the patient is laid on his side or face, oxygen administered, and, if necessary, artificial respiration applied.

Re-establishment of an airway in acute respiratory obstruction from any cause is no guarantee that ventilation will ensue. Not infrequently, either some other respiratory condition is present which interferes with normal gas exchange, or hypoxia has been present for so long that partial or complete respiratory paralysis is already present. It is of the utmost importance to satisfy oneself that breathing is adequate once the airway has been restored.

Indications

1. Acute severe pulmonary collapse in the postoperative period which is diagnosed by fever, tachycardia, tracheal deviation, bronchial breathing and typical radiological appearances.

2. Retained tracheobronchial secretions in a patient too weak to cough where time may be gained to permit elective tracheostomy.
3. Aspiration of vomit, including blood.

Technique

An adolescent bronchoscope well lubricated with lignocaine (2%) jelly should be used combined with a large-bore suction tube. A venturi high-pressure oxygen source is attached so as to permit inflation of the lungs. The head is extended to a similar position for that of maintenance of the airway (Fig. 6) and the instrument gently inserted beside the tongue down to the cords. As the patient inspires and the cords open, it is slipped through the cords and down to the carina. Although uncomfortable, this method is preferable to sousing the cords with local anaesthetic which may then permit inhalation of oesophageal secretions or vomit before the cough reflex is recovered.

Once the instrument has reached the carina, the patient's head is inclined to either side, so permitting the tip to be slid into each main bronchus. Bronchial toilet is carried out with an oesophageal sucker of large bore and the instrument withdrawn. It requires considerable dexterity and sense of timing, but the results are well worthwhile. A chest film is obtained at the end of the procedure.

Fibreoptic bronchoscopes can also be used for this purpose but they are not so readily available.

Emergency Tracheostomy (Fig. 7)

Very occasionally emergency tracheostomy may be required. The technique used should be the simplest. The head is fully extended on a pillow placed under the shoulders. If necessary 1% lignocaine is infiltrated in the line of the incision from cricoid to manubrium, but the quantity should be kept at the absolute minimum for tissues much distended by liquid are not easy to dissect. A 6-cm vertical incision is made exactly in the mid-line downwards from just above the cricoid. It appears to lie fairly high in the neck which is extended (Fig. 7) but this is not so when a normal position is renewed. A horizontal incision is not recommended for urgent tracheostomy. The dissection is carried down to and through the investing fascia. Thereafter, blunt dissection

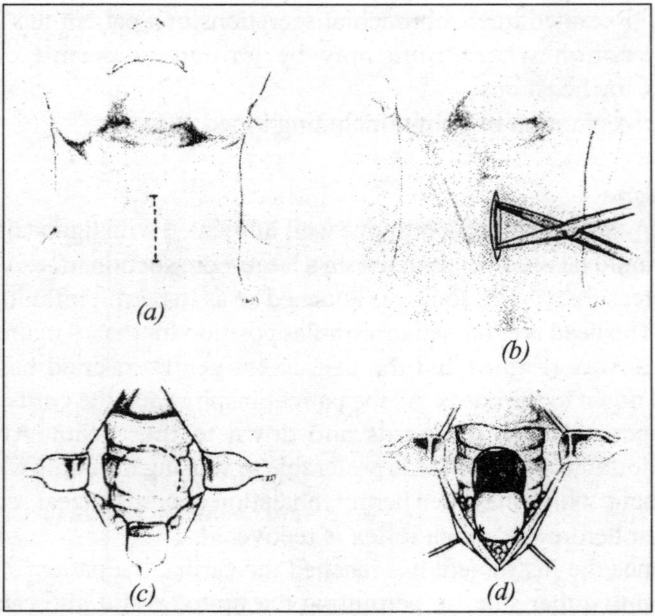

Fig. 7: The steps in 'burrowing' tracheostomy: (a) The incision; (b) Mid-line separation of pretracheal fascia; (c) Downward displacement of the thyroid isthmus; (d) Formation of distal flap of trachea.

spreads the fascia in relation to the thyroid isthmus which can usually be displaced downwards, and, by a combination of this and finger palpation, the upper ring of the trachea is palpated. The tube is held ready and a horizontal incision made at the level of the second ring. The lower lip of this incision is grasped and the cut converted into a semilune on either side. Use a trachae lumen opener. The tracheostomy tube is then slid over the resulting flap into the trachea while an

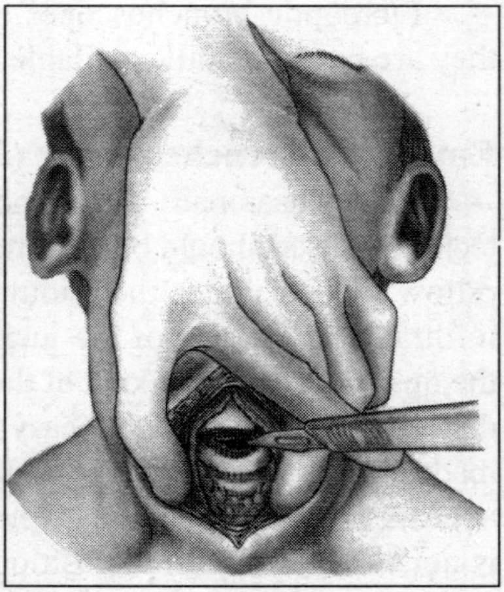

Fig. 8: Incision in a cricothyroidotomy.

attendant nurse inserts a sterile, soft, plastic catheter to suck out the blood and mucus that inevitably accumulate during the procedure. 'Burrowing' tracheostomy of this type is infinitely to be preferred to formal dissection, particularly in emergency situations. The thyroid isthmus need never be divided.

Choice of Tracheostomy Tubes

Use a disposable plastic tracheostomy tube. It comes in different sizes and has a side tube to inflate the bulb.

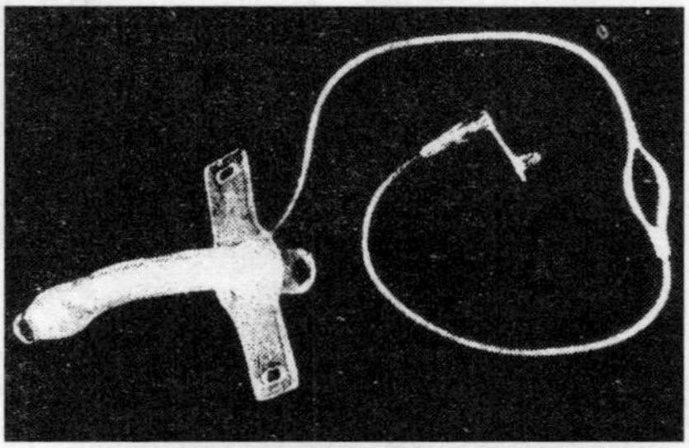

Fig. 9: A standard cuffed plastic tube for tracheostomy. Anaesthetic connections can be attached directly.

Management

The patient is not rendered safe by the relief of respiratory obstruction. Rather he is exposed to new dangers in that the humidifying and filtering mechanism of the nose is bypassed. The surgeon must ensure that:

1. The air or gas mixture supplied is clean. This can be achieved by drawing it from a line or cylinder rather than from the room. When air is entrained by a gas line, it should be filtered.
2. The tracheobronchial tree is kept moist. The simplest way of achieving this is by the regular hourly instillation of 2-3 ml of sodium bicarbonate, 1 mmol/ml. When equipment is available, all air supplied to the patient should be warmed to body heat and humidified. The gesture of bubbling air through water at room temperature is useless.
3. Careful repeated bacteriological control is kept on the tracheobronchial secretions and therapy promptly instituted as indicated.

Aspiration of Secretions

Aggressive high-vacuum suction will damage or even strip the mucosa from trachea and bronchi. The technique shown in Fig. 10 should be used. The soft, plastic catheter is inserted with the Y-piece open to the atmosphere. With the catheter *in situ* intermittent suction is applied by placing the thumb over the Y. Negative pressure should not exceed 20 cm water.

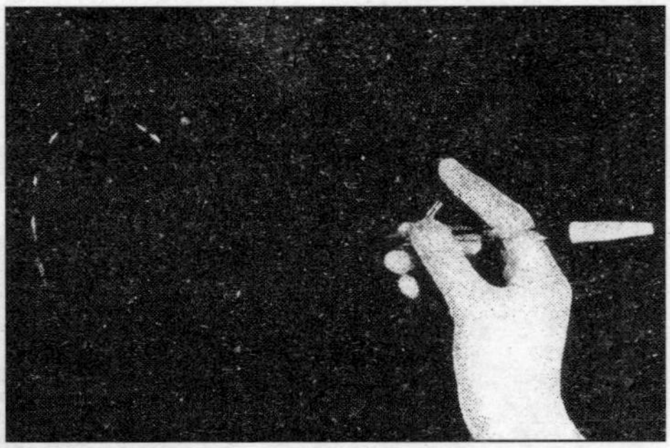

Fig. 10: A Y-catheler for tracheal suction. Negative pressure can be applied at will by a finger over the end of the Y.

Artificial Respiration

Complex methods of external artificial respiration have all been superseded by mouth-to-mouth breathing—Elisha's technique or as it is sometimes dramatically termed 'the kiss of life'. Mouth-to-mouth breathing (including mouth-to-mask, mouth-to-nose and mouth-to-tracheostomy opening) remains the most effective method of performing artificial respiration yet devised; there is evidence that in terms of maximum passive respiratory exchange mouth-to-mouth artificial respiration is superior to all other methods. Furthermore, the method is simple to learn and to carry out; it requires no apparatus; because it is not nearly so tiring as manual methods of artificial respiration, mouth-to-mouth breathing can be continued for more than an hour by most operators. An inadequate jaw-lift can be detected immediately by inability or difficulty in inflating the lungs—in no other method can the operator be sure that he is effecting respiratory exchange. Mouth-to-nose ventilation is aesthetically more acceptable to some people, and is becoming increasingly popular.

Technique

Rapidly check that the victim's tongue has not fallen back. Wipe away any vomitus from around the mouth. With one hand lift the lower jaw forwards; with the fingers of the other pinch the nostrils together (Fig. 11). After taking a deep breath, place the mouth over the victim's mouth and blow out strongly. Out of the corner of the eye it should be possible to see the patient's chest wall rise as his lungs are inflated. This forced inflation is continued at a rate of 16-20 breaths/min.

General Management of Respiratory Insufficiency

The greater part of the management of respiratory insufficiency in surgical patients seems to have passed to anaesthetists. Though they have detailed experience and skills appropriate to the task, the surgeon should maintain overall interest and often control. To do this he must understand general principles. These can best be addressed by looking at a series of questions.

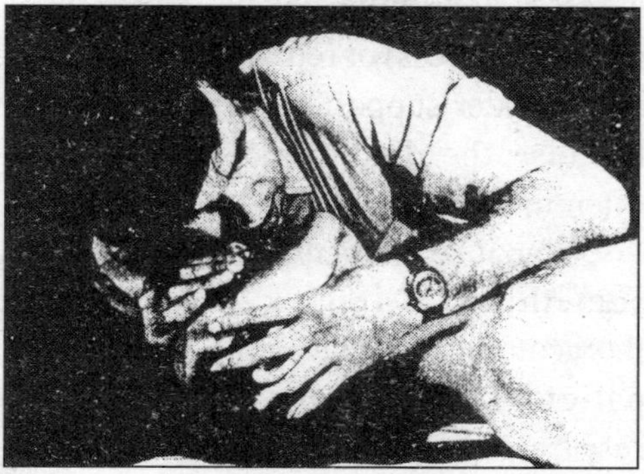

Fig. 11: Mouth-to-mouth artificial respiration in an adult. Note the position of the left hand of the resuscitator supporting the jaw. His eyes are watching the patient's chest; his right hand should be pinching the nostrils.

Is the cause of the problem likely to get worse, e.g. the first 2-3 days after an upper abdominal laparotomy or the progression over 10 days to two weeks of adult respiratory distress syndrome? If so, consideration should be given to the introduction of respiratory support early.

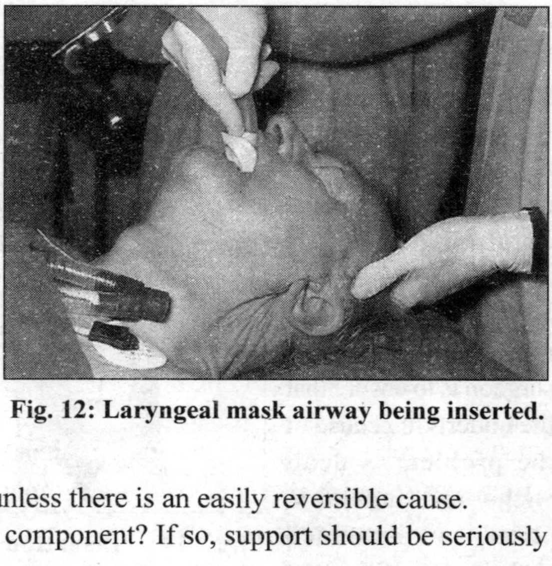

Fig. 12: Laryngeal mask airway being inserted.

Is the degree of fall in PO_2 such that the patient is already on the slippery slope? If so, respiratory support is mandatory unless there is an easily reversible cause.

Is fatigue a major component? If so, support should be seriously considered.

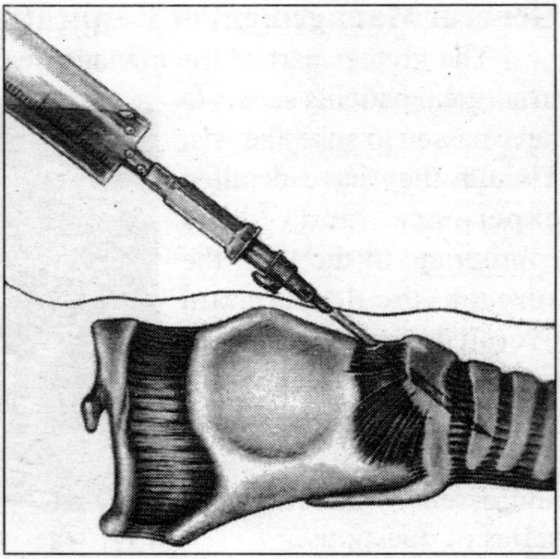

Fig. 13: Transtracheal needle introduction.

Is there another systems disturbance, e.g. cardiac, abdominal (ileus, residual abscess) or renal? If so, consider support earlier because the disturbances often interact.

Can it be predicted that something (e.g. a thoracotomy) will bring the patient to the verge of respiratory insufficiency, e.g. because vital capacity is less on tidal air or because there is obstructive airways disease? If so, respiratory support should be introduced prophylactically before the event.

By respiratory support is meant intermittent positive-pressure respiration (IPPR) through the endooral, endonasal or direct transtracheal route. Usually, the technique will be begun via the first two and tracheostomy undertaken only if the duration of IPPR is greater than 10 days.

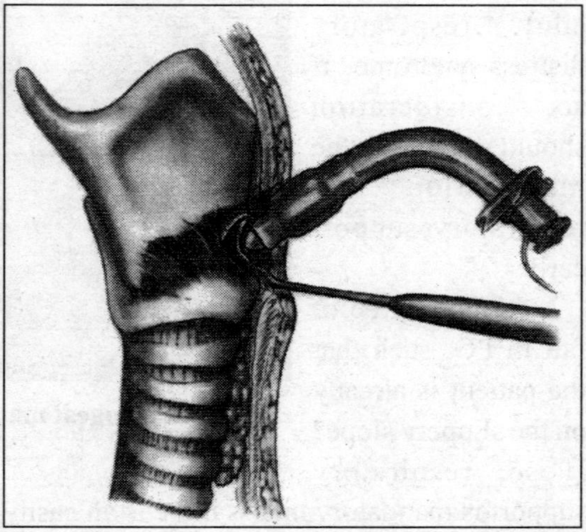

Fig. 14: Insertion of a tube after cricothyroidotomy.

During IPPR, the major role of the surgeon is to ensure that the underlying cause of the problem is dealt with—an unstable chest, a distended abdomen, a focus of sepsis. He should resist the urge to stop respiratory support just because things look better. Only complete resolution of the cause should be accepted as an indication to withdraw support.

A further role for the surgeon can be in ensuring adequate nutrition and normal water and electrolyte balance—matters often inadequately attended.

□

CHEST ASPIRATION AND INSERTION OF CHEST TUBE

Chest aspiration is a very important procedure. Before doing so one must have PA view of chest and lateral view of the chest of the side where there's fluid.

PA view will show you the level of the rib below which fluid is present and lateral view will show whether the fluid is in anterior, mid or posterior area.

Put the patient in sitting position with hands supported on a cardiac or food table. Count the ribs from Manubriosternal Joint anteriorly (second rib or space) and go downwards and count up to the level of fluid. Which you saw on the X-rays and then take the finger horizontally back in anterior or posterior area and put a mark there with needle or ink.

Now put one pair of sterile gloves and open the aspiration set. Take 5 ml of xylocaine and insert it in the skin, subcutaneous tissue, muscle and upto pleura. Wait for five minutes for the area to anesthetize.

If you suspect fluid then you can use an I.V. cannula about 2" long, size 18 F and connect to a 10 or 20 ml syringe.

You should always go in with one prick up to the rib and then slide the needle to upper border of rib and push it inside and aspirate. You should get fluid. If you fail, repeat the same process in one space below the previous one.

If you expect pus then use wide bore needle from the aspiration set and repeat the procedure.

The material obtained should be sent for cytology, Biochemistry and if needed then for AFB smear or malignant cells in a sterile container and immediately send it to laboratory.

Insertion of Chest Tube

Chest Tube in inserted for removal of either air or fluid from pleural cavity.

After aspiration if you get air or fluid, then remove the needle and with No. 15 blade—divide the skin for 1 cm up to subcutaneous tissue. Now use an artery forceps for splitting the muscles (intercostal) and using a proper size trocar catheter in (children size 4-size 10) and in adult (size 24-size 30) is put in the chest by pushing the catheter on the superior surface of rib below. The tube should be clamped, once you remove the trocar halfway and after clamping the tube remove the trocar. Now connect the distal end of tube to an under water seal bottle or chest drainage set.

In under-water seal bottle, there are two glass tube, one longone, which is to be connected to chest tube and lower end of this tube should be dipping in the water of the bottle and the other short tube exposed to air. It should not dip in water.

Now take a silk stich through the skin and tie it and then loop it 2-3 times around the tube and tie it around the tube. Fix the tube with a stich around the tube and fix it will dynaplast.

If large amount fluid is coming, it should be decompressed slowly 400-500 cc in on hour.

Never lift the bottle above the level of the insertion of chest tube. This will lead to putting in contents of the bottle in to the chest.

Should give mild analgesics and antibiotics.

A chest X-ray should be done in the evening or next morning in **sitting position**.

The chest tube should be immediately clamped before changing the chest bottle.

At times the chest bottle may break, then immediately clamp the tube with artery forceps and change the bottle rapidly. The organisms multiply rapidly, and bacterial toxins are absorbed giving toxaemia, which increases with rising tension. A progressive deposition of fibrin and cellular debris forms on the pleural surface, more marked on the parietal than the visceral pleura. In an acute infection with a free pleura, a total empyema usually results, but in some cases with previous adhesions or where the virulence of the organism has been suppressed by antibiotics, the infected area is walled off, giving a localised empyema. Further fluid may collect under pressure compressing the lung and deviating the mediastinum. In ruptured abscesses and staphylococcal tension cysts of lung, the situation is further complicated by an air leak from the bronchial tree, giving a tension pyopneumothorax. Rupture of the fluid back into the lung (broncho-pleural fistula) or to the skin surface (empyema necessitens) may result. After aspiration or drain-age, the inflammatory process usually settles, the thickened pleural surfaces approximate with the re-expansion of the lung, and obliteration of the pleural cavity occurs by adhesion. The fibrous layers of the thickened pleura gradually absorbs and in a few months time, the pleural membranes have returned almost to a normal consistency, although the original pleural space is permanently obliterated by adhesions. Persistence of pus between the two layers, however, will induce progressive thickening. The thick fibrous layer may be later peeled off in a virtually avascular layer from the pleural endo-thelium (decortication).

Clinical Recognition

There is usually a history of an acute illness, which is associated with pain in the chest on respiration, due to rubbing together of the inflamed pleural surfaces which may be audible. The pain passes off as fluid separates the visceral and parietal layers, but the toxaemia persists, with insomnia, poor appetite, anaemia, and a swinging temperature. As more fluid collects, lung compression and mediastinal deviation occurs with diminution of breath sounds and dullness. Empyema is, on occasion, bilateral.

The diagnosis is made by aspiration of a sample of fluid. A direct smear will show organisms with pus cells and cultures are made immediately for typing and antibiotic sensitivity.

Radiodiagnosis

A uniform opacity is seen over the whole of one side of the chest in the case of a total empyema. Where adhesions are present, a rounded localised opacity may be seen. Both PA and lateral views should be taken. Interlobar empyema is extremely rare, most cases so diagnosed are due to a super-imposition of a raised diaphragm over the heart shadow. It is important to study the chest films with great care to see if a cause for the empyema can be elucidated.

Indications for Surgical Treatment of Acute Empyema

Primary treatment is aspiration to relieve lung compression and toxaemia. Removal of 1,000-1,500 ml in the first instance, is usually adequate, and if the patient complains of tightness in the chest, the aspiration should be stopped. One gm of Neomycin can be inserted as a "broad-spectrum" antibiotic until the antibiotic sensitivity test results are available. Further aspiration can be performed daily and the appropriate antibiotic inserted. In about 75 per cent of cases, the empyema will be successfully treated by this method. If, however, it appears that this is inadequate, then an intercostal tube is inserted and connected to an under water seal bottle. If 10-14 days have elapsed since the known onset of the empyema, and aspiration or intercostal tube drainage is proving ineffective, a rib resection should be performed and a large drainage tube inserted, as by this time the empyema cavity is safely walled off and there is little likelihood of the lung separating away and producing paradoxical respiration. Many of the patients who have an intercostal tube inserted will require a subsequent rib-resection to obtain final obliteration of the cavity.

In children, aspiration should be persevered with, as drainage tubes are not tolerated in the chest for any length of time, and they may develop postural deformities associated with the discomfort of the tube.

Where underlying collapse of the lung is suspected, a bronchoscopy should be carried out at an early stage to exclude the presence of a carcinoma or foreign body.

When an empyema has supervened on a carcinoma, surgical treatment of the neoplasm is unlikely to be successful. Drainage of the empyema, however, should be avoided as it only increases the discomfort of the remaining weeks of life. As the organisms in these cases are relatively benign, treatment by occasional aspiration and antibiotic insertion is usually adequate.

Aspiration of Chest

As this may have to be repeated a number of times, it is important that a meticulous local anaesthetic technique is employed. Two per cent Procaine or 4 per cent Lignocaine should be used. An adequate selection of needles must be available and Luerlock fittings between syringes, needles, and taps will prevent spillage, ingress of air, and loss of temper!

In children, a small skin incision made at the first aspiration and used for subsequent procedures will save many tears.

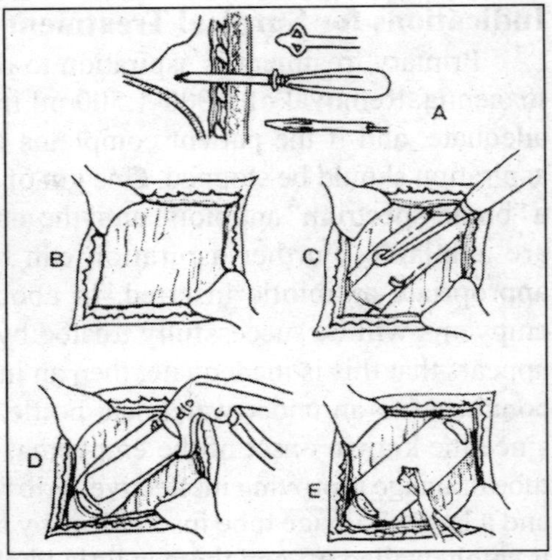

Fig. 1: Methods of draining the pleural cavity. A. Closed intercostal drainage using a Malecot's catheter. B-E. Rib resection. A tube is inserted through the opening made in the pleura and either connected to an under-water-seal bottle or drained into dressings. (After Eric L. Farquharson, Textbook of Operative Surgery.)

Over the proposed site of aspiration, a skin-wheal is raised with the finest hypodermic needle, fitted to a 2 ml syringe. This is withdrawn, a fine needle inserted through the wheal and advanced slowly towards and through the intercostal space to the pleura, injecting the anaesthetic solution all the time to separate the tissues. Some 7-10 ml should be used and then a three-minute halt is made so that anesthetisation can become perfect. A large needle fitted with a three-way tap and connected to a 20 ml syringe is then passed into the pleural cavity and the aspiration performed, the fluid being transferred to the receiver by turning the three-way tap.

Intercostal Drainage

Multi localize the space by aspirantion with a needle under sterile condition and only if fluid comes then put tube in this space.

Under local-anesthesia, the skin is incised, the trocar and cannula inserted through the inter-costal space into the pleural cavity gently. The catheter is filled with fluid clamp it with artery forceps and connect the catheter to an underwater-seal bottle. The catheter is strapped to the chest wall. It is liable to become uncomfortable in five to seven days' time due to infection in the sinus. A rib resection is then advisable in preference to maintaining the intercostal drain (Fig. 1).

Evidence of mal-drainage is shown by:

1. Increase or continuation of discharge. The daily discharge from a well-drained empyema rapidly decreases to a few ml and is without smell. An offensive discharge indicates a secondary infection (*B. subtilis, B. proteus,* or *B. pyocyaneus*) which signifies obstructed drainage and inefficient sterilisation, and is often associated with excessive vascular granulation tissue in the track. Daily wash outs with 1/1,000 proflavine or betadine solution, given by funnel and catheter, together with the re-establishment of adequate drainage are required.

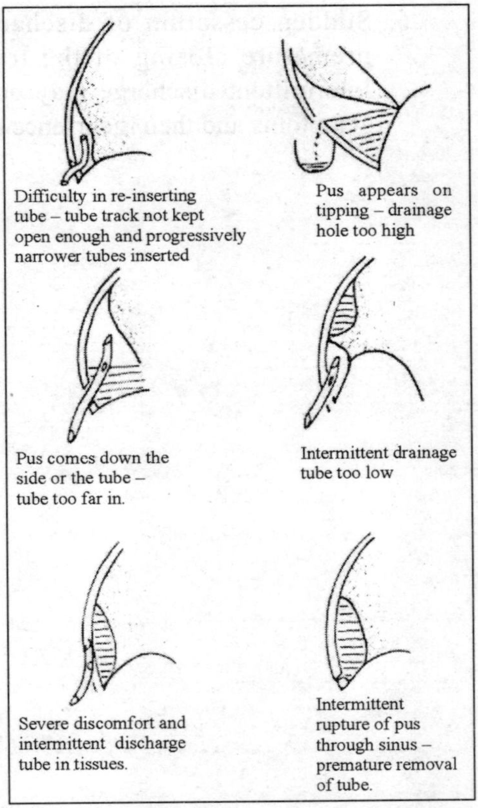

Fig. 2: Several forms of tube difficulty with drainage of an empyema.

2. When the tube is removed and the patient is tipped over, further pus comes out. This indicates that the cavity is not dependently drained. A new dependent drainage site must be instituted.
3. Pus comes down the side of the tube. This indicates that the tube is too far in and the pus is pooling around it. The tube must be pulled out for one or two cms.
4. Pain. The tube may be in the tissues superficial to a rib. Re-operation under general anaesthesia may be necessary.

5. Sudden cessation of discharge and toxaemia indicates premature closing of the track with pocketing above. Intermittent discharge may occur with complete relief of symptoms and then recurrence of the cycle.

□

PRINCIPLES OF WOUND MANAGEMENT

Pre-hospital Considerations

- Most lacerations are not life-threatening; however, other associated injuries must be excluded by performing a primary survey following the standard ABCs.
- Hemostasis should be achieved using direct manual pressure or pressure dressings.
- Elevation and splinting of the injured area will help stop bleeding and reduce patient discomfort.

The ultimate goals of wound management are to restore function and achieve an optimal cosmetic result. Infection, which develops in approximately 3% of wounds, adversely affects these goals. Therefore, meticulous care should be given to minimize this complication.

History

The following information should be obtained from all patients.

- **When did the injury occur?**—As more time elapses, the degree of bacterial contamination increases. It is commonly taught that if more than 6 to 12 hours have elapsed (the "golden period" of the wound), it is unwise to close the wound. In areas of good vasculature (e.g. face, scalp), however, the tissues' ability to resist infection is greater, and wounds can be closed up to 24 hours after the injury. Even in areas of good blood supply, if the wound appears highly contaminated, either excise the wound margins (thus creating a new wound if excess tissue is available) or defer wound closure for several days. (This is called *delayed primary closure.*)
- **What caused the injury?**—Injury with a dirty, potentially contaminated object increases the likelihood of infection. Mammalian bites (e.g. dogs, cats, humans) increase the risk also.

- **Is there any possibility of retained foreign bodies? PEARL: Always inquire about potential foreign bodies**—Foreign bodies are present in approximately 3% of wounds and increase the risk of infection. Regular soft tissue X-rays, ultrasound, CT scanning, or even MRI can help identify a foreign body. Probe all wounds manually for the presence of foreign bodies. (If sharp foreign bodies are likely, use an instrument to probe the wound.) Glass, the most common foreign body, usually is seen on regular X-rays regardless of its lead content. A skin marker and at least two views will help you to determine where the foreign body is.
- **Was the wound cleaned after the injury?**—What was used to clean the wound?
- **When did the patient last receive a tetanus shot?**—Table 1 presents the current recommendations concerning the need for both passive [tetanus immune globulin (TIG)] and active [tetanus-diphtheria toxoid (Td)] tetanus prophylaxis. **PEARL: Give TIG in inadequately immunized patients with 'tetanus-prone wounds.**
- **Does the patient have any underlying immuno-compromising conditions** (e.g. cancer, diabetes, steroid use, chemotherapy, AIDS)?
- **Is the patient allergic to antibiotics?** (This will affect your choice of antibiotics, if indicated.)
- **Is the patient allergic to local anesthetics?**
- **Is the patient allergic to latex products?** This is more common in health care workers and patients with spina bifida. If so, avoid all latex products.

Table 1: Recommendations for Tetanus Prophylaxis

	Clean Minor Wounds		*All Other Wounds*	
History of tetanus immunization	Td	TIG	Td	TIG
Doses, uncertain to < 3 yrs	Yes	No	Yes	Yes
Doses > 3 yrs	No*	No	No†	No

*Yes. if more than 10 years since last dose.
Td = tetanus-diphtheria toxoid; TIG = tetanus immune globulin.

Physical Examination

Adequate examination and management of a wound usually require local anesthesia. Always perform and document a complete neurovascular examination before giving an anesthetic. Evaluate pulses and capillary refill distal to the injury. In the hand, two-point discrimination (using a paper clip bent in two) is the best sensory modality to be examined. Elsewhere, evaluate pinprick sensation. **PEARL: Exclude nerve and tendon injuries in all extremity wounds.** Check range of motion to evaluate for tendon or ligament injury and muscle strength. An adequate examination requires good lighting and a relatively bloodless field. Temporary placement of tourniquets can be helpful in extremity lacerations.

Wound Preparation

The cornerstone of wound management includes mechanical debridement of devitalized tissue and copious irrigation with a balanced physiologic solution such as normal saline (NS).

Local Anesthesia

Local anesthetics (which stabilize cell membranes) are either esters or amides. An easy way to remember to which group a particular anesthetic belongs is to note that all amides have the letter "i" in their generic name before the prefix "caine" (e.g. lidocaine, mepivacaine). The importance of knowing the chemical class of a particular agent strains from the fact that most allergic reactions to local anesthetics are due to the esters or the methylparabate preservative used in lidocaine preparations. If a true allergy to lidocaine is present, you can use the parenteral form of diphenhydramine diluted 1:4 with NS or benzoyl alcohol (the preservative in multidose saline vials) as a local anesthetic. The most commonly used local anesthetics are lidocaine and bupivacaine. Their onset, duration, and toxic ranges are presented in Table 2. The addition of epinephrine to the local anesthetic causes vasoconstriction, resulting in improved hemostasis, decreased systemic absorption, and prolonged action. Epinephrine should be avoided in the digits, tip of nose, and tip of penis (think "nose, toes, fingers, hose").

PEARL: Topical anesthetics should be used to reduce the pain of infiltration. To decrease the pain caused by infiltrating a local anesthetic, take the following steps:

- Apply a topical anesthetic (lidocaine, epinephrine, and tetracaine) before injecting the anesthetic.
- Use a small needle, preferably #27 gauge.
- Inject as slowly as possible.
- Dilute lidocaine 10:1 with sodium bicarbonate 8.5% I.V. solution (this diluted product has a shelf life of at least one week).
- Warm the local anesthetic to body temperature.
- Pinch the skin adjacent to the wound just before injecting the local anesthetic.
- Inject the local anesthetic into the subcutaneous plane instead of the intradermal plane (this has a longer on-set but is much less painful).

Table 2: Characteristics of Lidocaine and Bupivacaine

Anesthetic Agent	*Onset (min)*	*Duration*	*Acceptable Safe Total Dose*
Lidocaine	2-5 min	30-120 min	4-5 mg/kg
Bupivacaine	5-10 min	4-8 h	2-3 mg/kg

- In clean wounds, insert the needle through the wound edges. (If the wound is contaminated, it is better to infiltrate the skin around the wound.) Enter at one end and slowly infiltrate the anesthetic around the wound in continuous circular advancements, so the patient will feel only one needle stick (Fig. 1).

Irrigation

Irrigation has been shown to be effective in removing both bacteria and infection-potentiating factors such as soil, from the wound. The efficiency of irrigation increases with higher pressures and volumes of fluid. **PEARL: Use a plastic shield when irrigating to minimize splatter.** We suggest using a 30- or 50-mL syringe with a plastic shield. A minimum of 100 mL of crystalloid per 1 cm of wound should be used.

After adequate irrigation, the wound and its surrounding edges should be scrubbed with a dilute 1% povidone iodine (Betadine) solution (do not use the scrub solution intended for propping operative fields in the operating room). Do not irrigate the wound with alcohol, hydrogen peroxide, or concentrated povidone iodine solution.

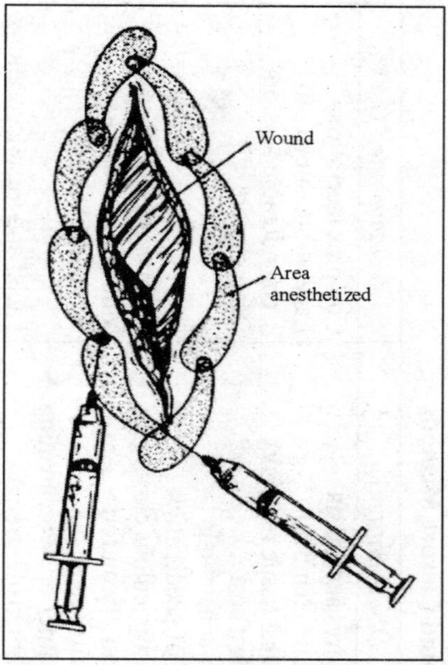

Fig. 1: Anesthetizing the wound. The wound is anæsthetized in a circular motion. With each successive injection, the needle enters a previously anesthetized area.

Debridement

Devitalized, crushed, avascular tissue forms an excellent medium for bacterial growth. **PEARL: Remove as much de-vitalized tissue as possible.** Adequate debridement some-times requires the use of local flaps or grafts for closure of the remaining defect. In these cases, it probably is best to consult the plastic surgeon. Vital tissues such as nerves and tendons, however, must be preserved.

Wound Closure

There are several options for wound closure, each with different advantages and disadvantages (Table 3). The most commonly used method for closing wounds is suturing. Choice of the appropriate suture material should be beted on the suture's characteristics and intended uses (Table 4). For facial lacerations, a 5/0 or 6/0 suture is appropriate; for most finger lacerations, use a 5/0 suture. For all other lacerations, a number 4/0 suture may be used.

PEARL: Appropriately used tissue adhesives save time and reduce discomfort. A new tissue adhesive, octylcyanoacry-late (Dermabond, Ethicon). It is an excellent choice for closure of non-

Table 3: Comparison of Wound Closure Methods

Method	*Advantages*	*Disadvantages*	*Recommended Uses*
Sutures	Considerable experience Allows most meticulous closure Greatest breaking strength Lowest dehiscence rate	Requires anesthesia Requires removal Greatest tissue reactivity Highest cost Time-consuming Risk of needle stick	Complex lacerations Lacerations subject to considerable tension Deep closure
Staples	Rapid application Ease of use Low tissue reactivity Reduced risk of needle stick	Less meticulous closure Patient discomfort Requires removal May interfere with imaging	Scalp and torso lacerations Multiple trauma Temporary closure
Tissue adhesives	Rapid application Ease of use May not require anesthesia Patient comfort No need for removal No risk of needle stick Resists bacterial infection	Lower tensile strength than sutures Higher initial cost Not good for hair-bearing areas	Facial and torso lacerations Extremity lacerations under minimal tension May be used in conjunction with deep sutures in lacerations subject to tension
Surgical tapes	Least tissue reactivity Lowest infection rates Patient comfort Low cost Rapid application Ease of use No risk of needle stick	Lowest tensile strength Highest dehiscence rate Use of toxic adjuncts to improve adhesiveness required Cannot be used in hair-bearing areas Must remain dry	Closure of superficial lacerations subject to no tension Usually in conjunction with deep sutures Good for reinforcing lacerations after suture or staple removal

Table 4: Suture Characteristics

Suture	*Knot Security*	*Tensile Strength*	*Duration of Wound Security (days)*	*Tissue Reactivity*	*Recommended Uses*
Non-absorbable					
Nylon (Ethilon)	Good	Good	NA	Minimal	Percutaneous closure Tendon repairs
Polypropylene (Prolene)	Fair	Excellent	NA	Minimal	Percutaneous closure Tendon repairs
Silk	Excellent	Fair	NA	Most	Percutaneous closure
Absorbable					
Surgical gut	Poor	Fair	5-7	Moderate	Mucous membranes
Chromic cut	Fair	Fair	10-14	Moderate	Mucous membranes
Polyglactin (Vicryl)	Good	Good	30	Minimal	Deep sutures
Irradiated polyglactin (Vicryl Rapide)	Good	Good	10-14	Minimal	Percutaneous or mucosal closure in children
Poliglecaprone (Monocryl)	Good	Good	30	Minimal	Deep sutures
Polyglycolic acid (Dexon)	Excellent	Good	30	Minimal	Deep closure
Polydioxanone (PDS)	Fair	Excellent	45-60	Slight	Deep closure under significant tension
Polyglyconate (Maxon)	Fair	Excellent	45-60	Slight	Deep closure under significant tension

contaminated wounds under minimal tension, particularly on the face and torso. Butylcyanoacrylate is an alternative for short superficial wounds, particularly on the face, but it is not yet FDA-approved. Compared with butylcyanoacry-late, octylcyanoacrylate is three times stronger, more flexible, and transparent (Fig. 2).

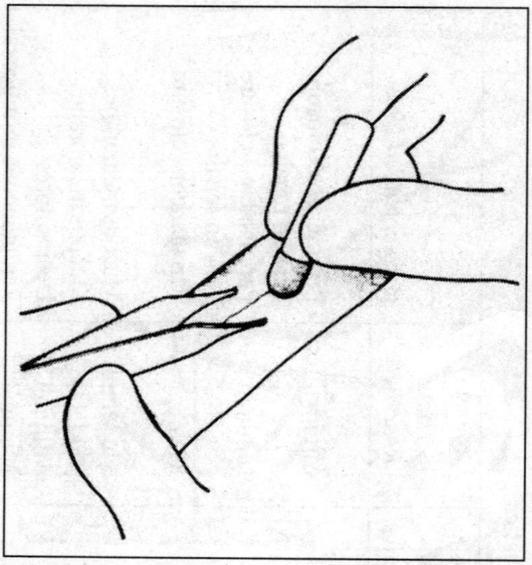

Fig. 2: Application technique for a tissue adhesive.

Tissue adhesives slough off after 7 to 14 days. Patients should not scrub or soak their wounds but may wet them. Don't place ointments and adhesive tapes on the adhesive. **Remember, just because you choose a tissue adhesive doesn't mean that a full wound evaluation and preparation are no longer required.**

Helpful Tips for Wound Closure

- Tie your knots just enough to approximate wound edges. **PEARL: Don't tie sutures too tightly; this will strangulate the tissues and cause necrosis and sloughing of the edges.** (Remember that tissue swelling will increase during the next 24 to 48 hours.)
- Take equal "bites" from both sides of the wound. More tissue should be taken at the depth of the wound than at the surface (Fig. 4).
- Try to evert the wound edges. If you have difficulty doing this, use a vertical mattress suture (Fig. 6). Sometimes, it is useful to alternate simple with mattress sutures to achieve eversion yet save time.
- If one side of the wound is longer than the other side, use wider spaces between adjacent sutures on the longer side. This may

prevent the formation of a "dog ear" at the end. The management of a dog ear is illustrated in Fig. 7.

- The length of the suture ends should be roughly equal to the distance between adjacent sutures. Don't cut the sutures too close to the end. This makes suture removal more difficult.
- Facilitate closure of scalp wounds by tying knots in the hair to keep wound edges together.
- **PEARL: Use deep sutures for all gaping wounds subject to tension to avoid dehiscence and wide scars (Fig. 8). Undermining of wounds may help closure.**

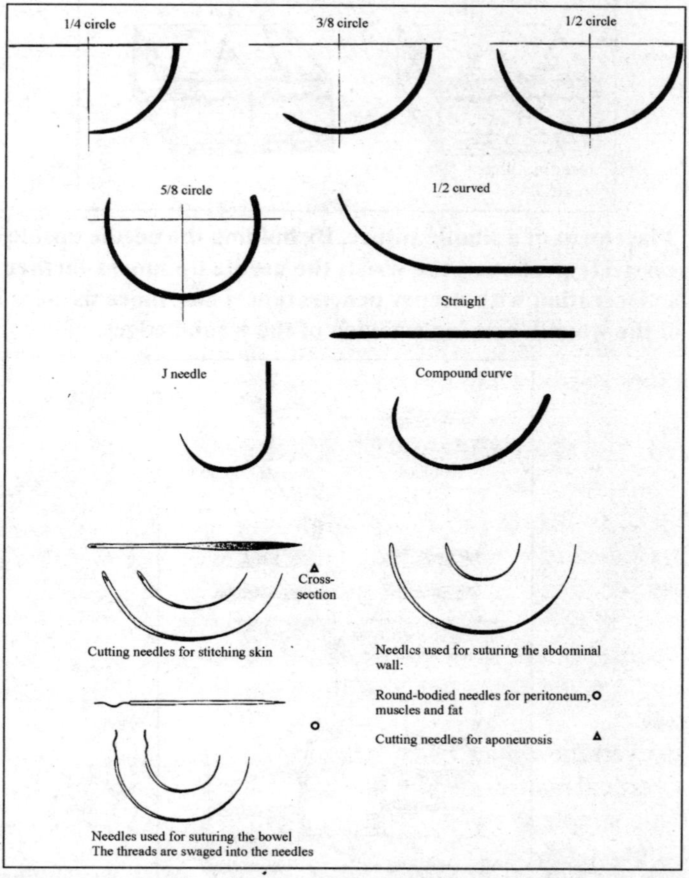

Fig. 3: Types of needles used for sutures. The sutures are swaged on to prevent a 'shoulder' and allow easy passage through tissues.

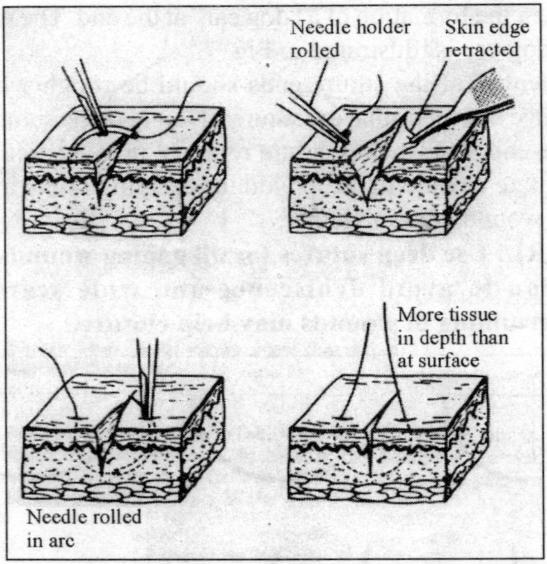

Fig. 4: Placement of a simple suture. By holding the needle upside down and excessively pronating the wrist; the needle tip moves farther away from the laceration with deeper penetration. Thus, more tissue is at the depth of the wound, causing eversion of the wound edges.

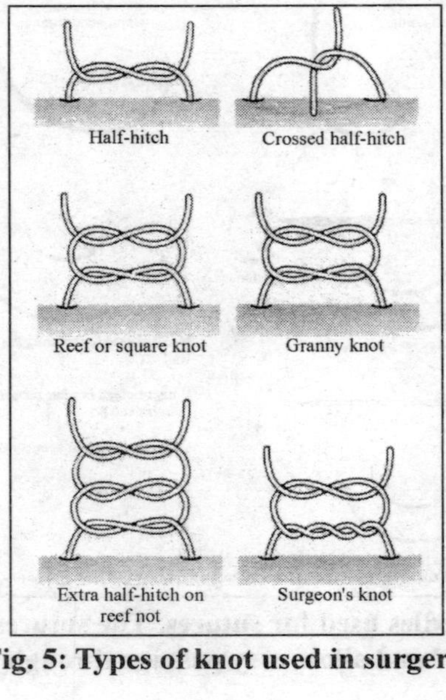

Fig. 5: Types of knot used in surgery.

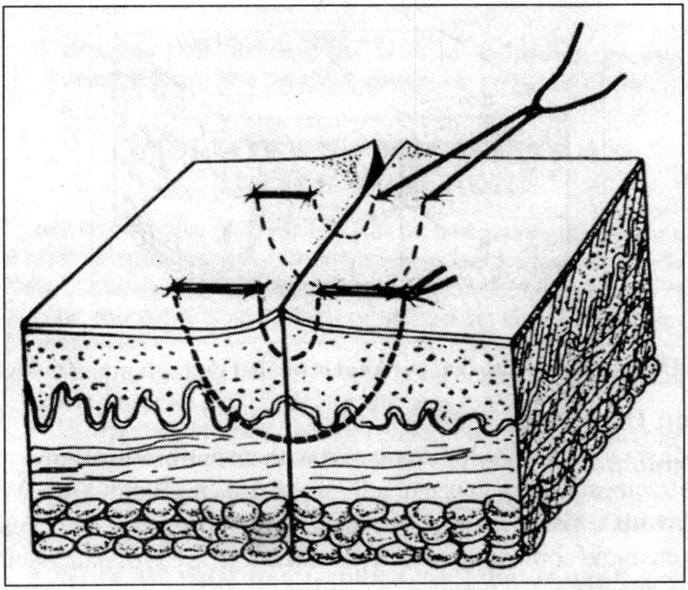

Fig. 6: Vertical mattress sutures for approximation and eversion of skin edges.

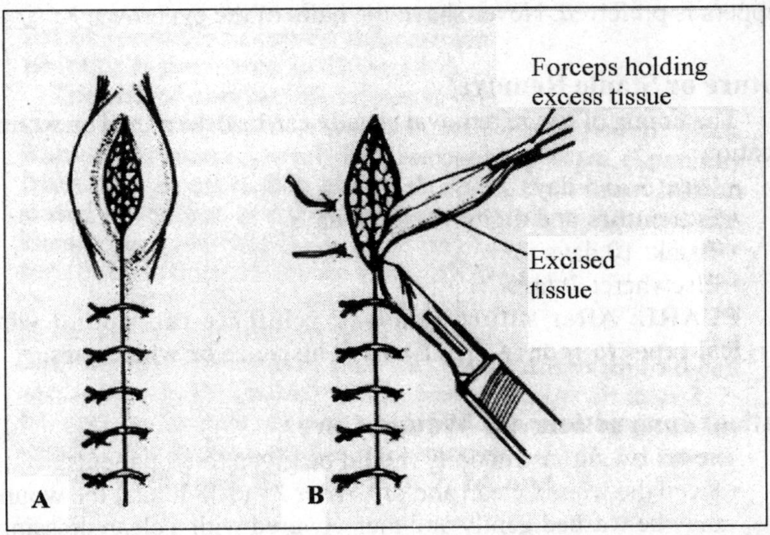

Fig. 7: Correction of a "dog ear." (A) Dog ear. (B) Excision of dog ear with closure of defect.

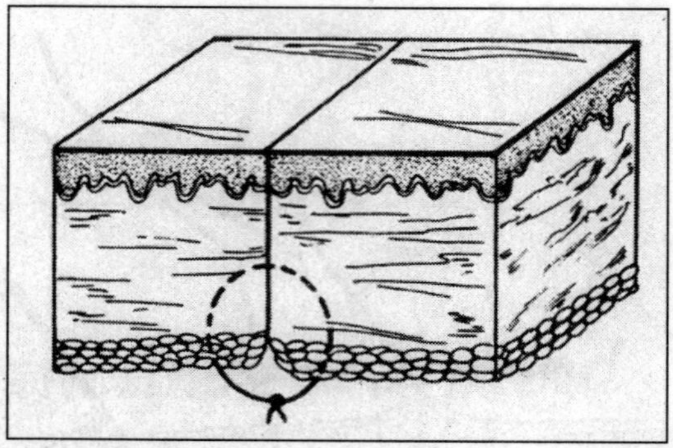

Fig. 8: Deep suture. Note that the knot is buried in the depth of the wound.

Wound Dressings

Most wounds should be covered with an antibiotic ointment such as bacitracin, and a dry gauze or adhesive bandage (Band-Aid). Wounds closed with a tissue adhesive can be covered with a dry dressing; however, avoid application of any ointments. In areas of hair, bacitracin alone is adequate. By the way, the purpose of shaving hair around the wound is to facilitate wound closure, not to reduce wound infection. In fact, it can increase the risk of wound infections. The use of hair clippers is preferred. Never shave the hairs of the eyebrow.

Suture or Staple Removal

The timing of suture removal usually can be determined by wound location:

- Face: 3 to 5 days
- Extremities and digits: 10 to 14 days
- Trunk: 10 days
- Elsewhere: 7 days

PEARL: After suture removal, reinforce the wound with surgical tapes to reduce the risk of dehiscence or wide scars.

Patient Instructions for Wound Care

The following instructions should be given to all patients:

- Keep the wound clean and dry. After 24 to 48 hours, the wound may be washed gently and then covered with a clean dressing.
- If the wound is on an extremity, elevate the extremity for 48 hours to reduce swelling.

- Return to the ED if there is increasing swelling, redness, or pain around the wound; yellow or green discharge from the wound; fever; or shaking chills.

Antibiotics

Prophylactic antibiotics are not routinely indicated.

The risk of contracting rabies is greatest in cases of raccoon, bat, and skunk bites. It is unlikely in rodent bites. Rabies has been reported with aerosol exposure, especially from bats. In cat or dog bites, ask about the immunization status of the pet. If the rabies immunization status is unknown, suggest that the animal be observed by the owner for 10 days. Contact the local health department for suspicious bites. In cases of exposure to an animal suspected to have rabies, give human rabies immune globulin 20 U/kg (half around the wound, half IM) plus human diploid cell vaccine 1 mL IM immediately, then 1 mL IM on days 3, 7, 14, and 28 days. Rabies vaccine absorbed can also be given instead of the human diploid cell vaccine—1 mL IM immediately, then 1 mL IM on days 3, 7, 14, and 28 days.

□

REMOVING SKIN SUTURES OR CLIPS

For Clips: There is a special clip remover which should be used. The lower blade of clip remover has to go horizontally under the flat portion of clip and after doing so, press with the top portion and the clip will open widely and you can remove it without causing any pain to the patient.

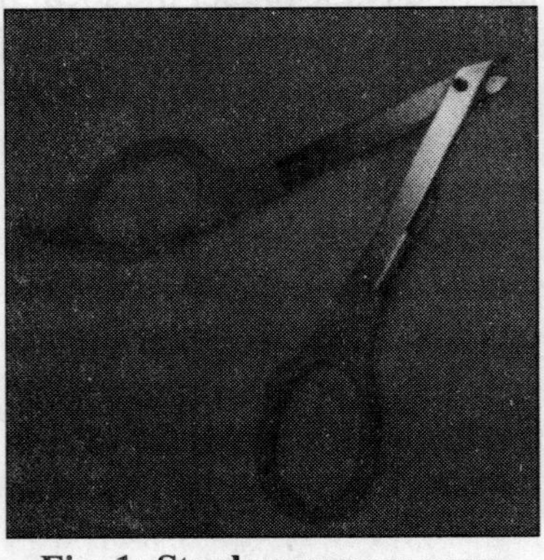

Fig. 1: Staple remover open.

For Sutures

☐ You should have a suture removing set with you which should have

(1) Straight artery forceps

(2) Straight or curved suture cutting scissors (fine)

(3) No 11 scalpel blade

With artery forceps catch hold of one of the edge of the stitch and gently pull it to opposite side. You will be able to see the loop on which knots is tied. With fine scissor you can cut this loop and easily pull the stitch out. Now we can remove other stitches after this one by one.

In abdomen: Please remove alternate stitches on one day and the remaining stitches can be removed

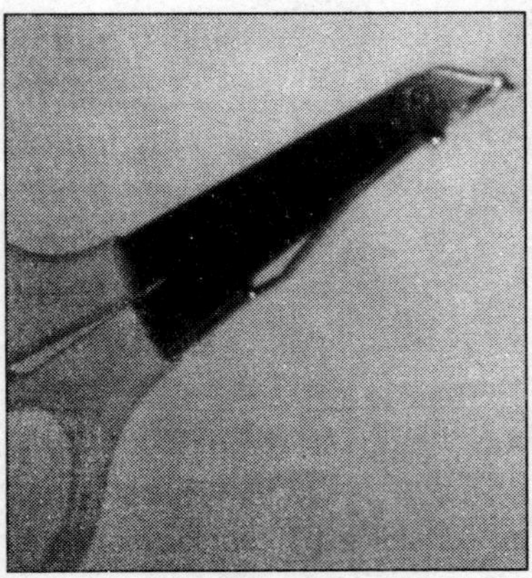

Fig. 2: Staple remover closed.

after 48 hrs. This will prevent against burst abdomen in obese, thin and malnourished patients and who are immunologically compromised.

After removing all the stiches, clean the wound with spirit and if need be apply a dry dressing on the wound and fix it with micropore.

How to Pullout a Drainage Tube

Once the drainage tube has done its job and no more discharge is coming out, then you can pull it by cutting the tube anchoring sutures around drainage tube and gently pull out the tube and apply a gauge on the site of the drain and put on adhesive micropore over the drainage site.

□

MINOR SURGICAL PROCEDURES

Cervical Lymph Node Biopsy

- Put on clean sterile towel.
- Apply a sandbag under the shoulder on the side where you wish to remove the node.
- Turn the head to the opposite side.
- Feel the node and apply local anesthesia, with a fine needle all around the node; avoid pushing the local anesthetic inside any vein nearby.
- With No. 20 or 21 blade, put one scalpel make on horizontal cut in the line of langer over the node.
- Cut the skin and then cut the platysma, before you will reach to the node.
- Many a time, one starts searching for the node before cutting the platysma. Nodes lie deep to platysma and until this is divided, the node will never come out.
- Once platysma is divided, you can feel the node with a finger and dissect all around it gently with artery forceps.
- Clear it from the base also with a artery forceps. If any vessel is found attached to node, apply artery forceps and tie the vessel with catgut or vicryl 3/0 and divide it now.
- The node will be free to come out.
- Take the node in a tray and divide it horizontally and see for any caseation.
- Put the specimen in a formaline bottle—one half of the node should be put in it.
- The other half of the node should be put in bottle of normal saine so the bacteriologist can do necessary tests.

- Now check for any bleeding in the wound. Most of the time the oozing gets controlled with pressure with a gauge piece.
- Now close the platysma, using catgut or vicryl 2/0 or 3/0 with round body needle.
- Now apply skin stiches.
- Put a clean dressing.
- Remove stitches after 6-7 days.
- Review the wound in 48 hrs and put on a light dressing after 48 hrs.
- Both the specimens should be sent to microbiology and histopathology labs.

Precaution: Cervical nodes are usually adhered to veins around them. Never try to pullout a node blindly after you feel it. Do dissection under vision. At time you can put a stiches with a linen thread through the node and leave it long to put traction on the node for better dissection of surrounding tissues under vision.

If you pullout the node blindly by putting a finger around it then at times you will have severe bleeding which will be uncontrollable. Please pack the wound and apply pressure on it and call senior to help you out.

Closure of Scalp Sound

The scalp wound can be:

(1) Superficial: Wounds of skin and subciliary subcutaneous tissue but do not include galea. These do not bleed severely.

(2) Deep: These wounds include galea also and bleed severely as the cut keeps the vessels open and they do not close.

Superficial wounds: After applying local anesthatic these can be closed using non-absorbable silk or cotton (linen) size 40 to 60 thread and take deep stitches using a cutting needle after putting on a sterile glove and removing all the dust and dirt from the wound. Put interrupted approximating stitches.

Deep wounds: While closing there wounds, after applying local anesthesia around the scalp wound, close these wounds either in two layers—first layer closing galae using absorbable vicryl sutures. This will stop major bleeding for this use around body tip needle. The next layer is superficial layer using catgut or vicryl suture using a taper cut needle. Apply interrupted stitches.

Remember that in deep wounds, until you close galea aponeurotica, the wound will keep bleeding in the subcutaneous tissues if you only apply skin stitches and there will be a hematomia. So one must close galea in such cases:

(a) Either take number 40-60 size linen suture using cutting tip needle and take deep bits including galea or

(b) Close in two layers as described above.

Removing of Sutures: The suture in face and head can be removed in 4-5 days as these heal well due to good supply of blood. After stitching, review the wound after 48 hrs and change dressing and then finally remove sutures on fifth day.

How to Put an Intravenous Cannula for Intravenous Infusion

- Apply a torniquet put above the anticubital region and ask the patient to fix his arm and release for 15-20 seconds.
- You will see a prominent vein either in cubital fossa or in the wrist area towards the radial side a prominent vein can be seen.
- The torniquet should be applied only tight enough to block the venous return but not to block the arterial flow.
- Apply antiseptic to the prominent vein area and for one inch distal to it.
- Put on a pair of gloves.
- Keep in fluid and I.V. set inserted into the bottle ready and remove air out of set by letting some fluid flow out in the bucket and now pinch the I.V. set tube.
- Take a proper size I.V. cannula (disposable size 20 or 18 or 22).
- Gradually, insert the cannula along with needle in the vein and once blood comes in the cannula, then gently pull the needle out of the cannula and if blood is still present in the cannula, then gently push the cannula in the vein. Remove the needle out completely. Now connect the end of cannula to the I.V. fluid set.
- Fix the cannula with a disposable cannula fixator pad.
- Adjust the rate of the drip depending on the speed with which you wish to give transfusion.

- Remove the torniquet, immediately after the cannula is in the vein.
- If I.V. fluid does not go in then gently pull the cannula for 1-2 mm and see if I.V. fluid goes in and if it goes in then refix the cannula.

Pulling Out the I.V. Cannule

- Stop the I.V. fluid.
- Remove the fixative for the cannula.
- Apply pressure at the site of vene puncture and remove and gently pull the cannula out.
- Press the puncture site for 3-5 minutes and apply gauge dressing on it.

□

HEAT STROKE

Heat stroke is a condition characterized by failure of central thermoregulation; patients present with a high temperature (usually defined as > 41°C) and an altered mental status. **PEARL: Consider heat stroke in all patients with an altered mental status, particularly after exertion.** In the past, it was believed that heat stroke was always associated with anhidrosis, but young patients with exertional heat stroke may present with diaphoresis.

Remember that the patient's temperature may have fallen spontaneously or because of cooling before arriving at the hospital. Therefore, do not exclude a heat stroke based on the initial hospital temperature reading. Also, it is very important to rule out other life-threatening causes of hyperthermia, including sepsis, meningitis, stroke, brain tumors, head injuries, and withdrawal from substances of abuse. Be wary of heat strokes especially during hot, humid weather and in patients who collapse after extreme physical exertion. **PEARL: A core temperature should be obtained early in all patients with an altered mental status.**

History

In obtaining the patient's history, ask the following questions:

- Did the symptoms follow strenuous physical activity?
- Were the symptoms concurrent with headaches, stiff neck, or vomiting?
- Does the patient have a history of any disorders that interfere with sweating and, therefore, heat loss (e.g. icthyosis, psoriasis)?
- Is the patient taking any medications that can predispose to heat stroke such as diuretics, beta-blockers, antiparkinsonian drugs, neuroleptic agents?

Assessment

- Begin by assessing the ABCs. Patients with heat stroke who are unconscious or lethargic may need to be intubated to protect their airway.
- Since patients with heat stroke often are dehydrated, establish I.V. access and start fluid resuscitation as required.
- Check bloodsugar with Glucometer and give $D_{50}W$ 50 mL by I.V. push if the glucose level is low, in addition to thiamine and naloxone, as you would for all patients with an altered mental status.
- Accurate measurement of the core temperature with a rectal probe is necessary for early recognition and treatment.
- Examine the patient for evidence of an infectious disease, head injury, or stroke.
- Draw blood for CBC, blood biochemistry, prothrombin time (PT), partial thromboplastin time (PTT), ABGs, creatine phosphokinase, and urinalysis.

Myoglobinuria is common and should be treated with alkalization of the urine and forced diuresis. **PEARL: The presence of dark urine may indicate myoglobinuria and rhabdomyolysis requiring aggressive diuresis and alkalinization.** Disseminated intravascular coagulation (DIC) can occur and should be treated with coagulation factors (i.e. fresh frozen plasma) and platelet replacements as necessary.

Treatment

Cooling the patient as quickly as possible forms the cornerstone of treatment. Patients who are alert and hemo-dynamically stable can be placed in a tub filled with cold water or ice. If a tub is unavailable or the patient is not stable, spray him or her with water mist and place the patient under a high-speed fan. Aggressive cooling should be continued until the patient's temperature falls to < 38.5°C (note: avoid overshooting and causing hypothermia). Fluid and electrolyte imbalance should be corrected as the clinical condition warrants. **PEARL: All patients with heat stroke need to be admitted.**

Heat Exhaustion

Patients with heat exhaustion present with dehydration, nausea and vomiting, muscle cramps, and sometimes confusion. Their temperature is only moderately elevated. I.V. replacement of fluid and salt repletion with a balanced isotonic solution often is required. This condition often is seen in poorly acclimatized patients who exert themselves in hot, humid climates. If severely dehydrated, these patients must be admitted.

Heat Cramps

Heat cramps are caused by depletion of sodium caused by extreme physical exertion and sweating. Patients can be afebrile and complain of muscle cramps. They should be treated with replacement of water and sodium losses, and most can be discharged. Patients should be encouraged to continue to consume large amounts of salt-enriched fluids at home.

□

FINGER ABCESS

The Operation

It is essential that a clear view is obtained into the depths of the abscess cavity and for this reason, the operation must be carried out in a bloodless field. In the case of a finger, this is secured by applying a fine rubber catheter tightly around the base of the finger and clipping it in place with a haemostat. This tourniquet is best applied before injecting the local anaesthetic. In the case of more proximal infections, the patient's arm is elevated above the patient's head for a minute, and is rendered ischaemic by inflating a sphygmomanometer cuff around the upper arm to a pressure above the systolic level. Because this soon causes pain it should be deferred until anesthesia is complete and the operation is about to commence.

The skin of the affected part is cleaned with a solution of 1% hibitane in spirit or betadine and the operation is planned. The aim is to provide drainage by the most direct route by an incision which will heal with the least possible scarring. The site of incision should be chosen before anesthetizing the part, as the position of maximum tenderness often has a good deal to do with the choice, and its direction should correspond with the tension lines (Langer's lines) of the skin. An incision which crosses the flexor creases is particularly to be avoided.

The instruments used in operating on the infected hand must be delicate, and a meticulous no-touch technique is followed. The operator's hands are gloved for the protection of his skin, but as they are not sterile, they must not be allowed to come into contact with any part of the patient's hand or any of the sterile dressings, and only the handles of the instruments are touched.

If *subcuticular pus is visible,* this may represent the superficial component of a collar-stud abscess (Fig. 1) and the operation is commenced by uncapping the superficial abscess, using a fine scalpel (No. 11 Bard-Parker). This accomplished, a deep extension is sought, and if such is present it is probed to determine its extent. The sinus is then enlarged by an incision through the dermis (in the direction of Langer's lines) to permit inspection of the walls of the deeper cavity. The edges of the incision are parted, and pus is mopped out with a pledget of cotton-wool. Any loose slough is picked out with fine forceps and obviously dead subcutaneous fat is cut away, care being taken not to remove any healthy tissue. During the removal of dead tissue the depths of the cavity are inspected frequently, to make sure that important adjacent structures, such as tendon sheaths or digital nerves, are not damaged.

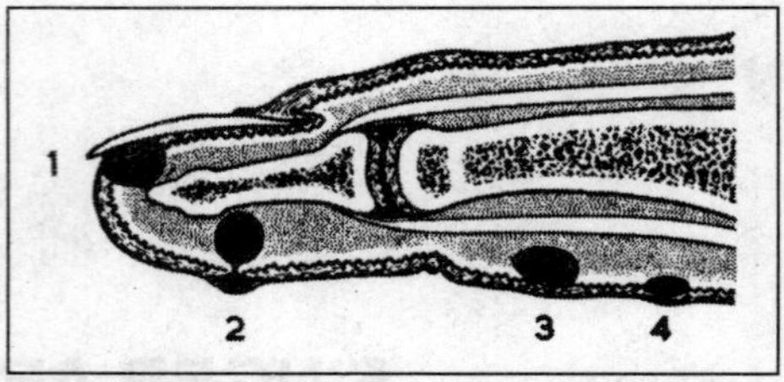

Fig. 1: Diagram of finger to show various types of abscess. 1. Apical abscess; 2. Pulp abscess with collar-stud extensions; 3. Subcutaneous abscess; 4. Intracutaneous abscess.

If *subcuticular pus is not visible,* the abscess is opened by an incision 0.5 cm in length placed immediately over it. When pus is located, if necessary the incision is extended to make it long enough to provide adequate drainage. The subsequent toilet of the abscess cavity is precisely similar to that described in the preceding paragraph.

Irrespective as to whether the abscess is superficial or deep, the edges of the skin incision are cut back with fine pointed scissors to form a narrow diamond-shaped opening (Fig. 6), and a dry gauze dressing is applied. No drains of any sort are used and the wound should never be plugged with a gauze wick. The dressing is bandaged into place. The tourniquet is then removed and the arm elevated in a sling.

After-care

The patient is instructed to keep the dressings dry. The first dressing should be carried out on the day following operation; as a rule the gauze dressing can be removed easily, but may need soaking off with a 1% solution of cetrimide.

The wound edges should be gently separated and the abscess cavity probed carefully to make certain that drainage remains adequate; if there is any doubt about this, the opening must be enlarged under anesthesia. Whether this step is necessary or not, a fresh dry gauze dressing is applied, and the part is bandaged. Subsequent dressings are carried out at intervals of 1-3 days until healing is complete. Antibiotics are not usually required after the first 24 h unless (1) the abscess is very large, (2) there are signs of bone infection, or (3) there is evidence of spreading infection. When there is much oedema or surrounding cellulitis, it is necessary to continue splinting and elevation of the hand for several days.

Specific Types of Infection

Paronychia

This is the commonest infection of the hand and occurs at the sides of the nail or superficial to its base. It begins as a cellulitis, but pus rapidly forms, and if left untreated, it may discharge spontaneously by separation of the cuticle from the surface of the nail, or, more often, extension occurs beneath the base of the nail so that the nail floats on a pool of pus.

Treatment

Antibiotic therapy is employed only if the infection is seen at a very early stage when there is a prospect of it being aborted completely. When pus has formed operation is required, and as a rule antibiotics are then unnecessary. To release the pus all that is necessary is to strip back the cuticle and lateral nail folds from the surface of the nail. This is carried out with the closed points of fine dissecting forceps (Fig. 2) and no cutting is required except to trim away loose portions of cuticle. No drains are used and it is unnecessary to tuck gauze between the edge of the nail fold and the nail. The base of the nail is resected (Fig. 3) only if it is undermined by pus, when it will be obviously loose and

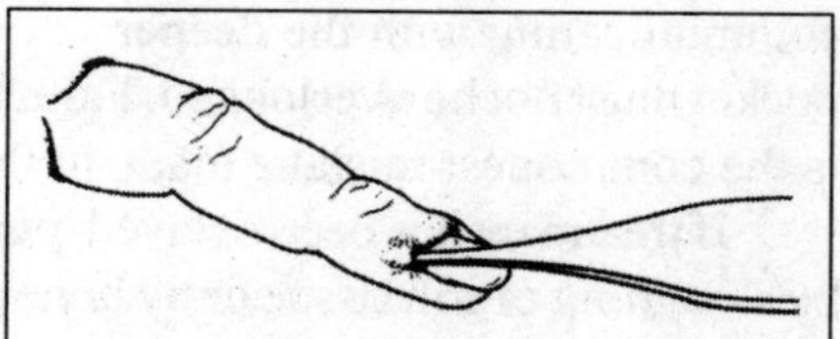

Fig. 2: Elevation of nail fold to drain a paronychia.

lacking its normal lustre. Care must be taken that no small fragments of dead nail remain.

In after-care, it is important to make sure that the stripped cuticle does not become adherent to the nail prematurely.

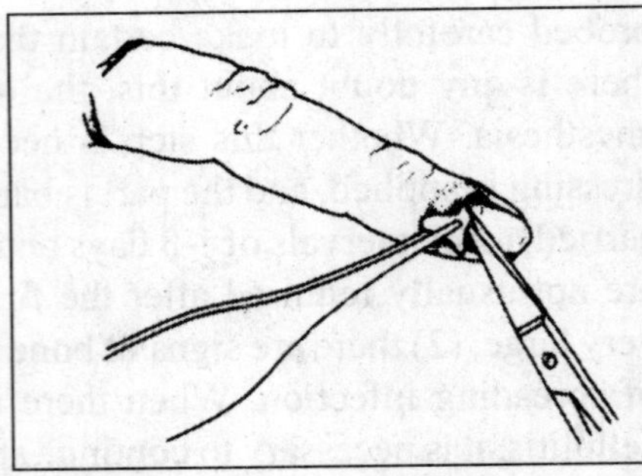

Fig. 3: Resection of base of nail when it is undermined by pus.

Pulp Abscess

Infection of the terminal pulp space is common and serious. When the patient is first seen pus may not be localized and it is a bad mistake to incise too early.

Treatment

In the stage of cellulitis, pulp infections are treated conservatively with rest and antibiotics. When there is clear evidence of localized pus, operation is required forthwith. The old 'hockey-stick' incision should not be used. Incisions must be placed directly over the abscess and should correspond in direction to Langer's lines (Fig. 4). A collar-stud abscess is common in the pulp and the sinus communicating with the deeper pocket must not be overlooked. Failure to recognize this deep extension is the commonest mistake made in the treatment of this condition.

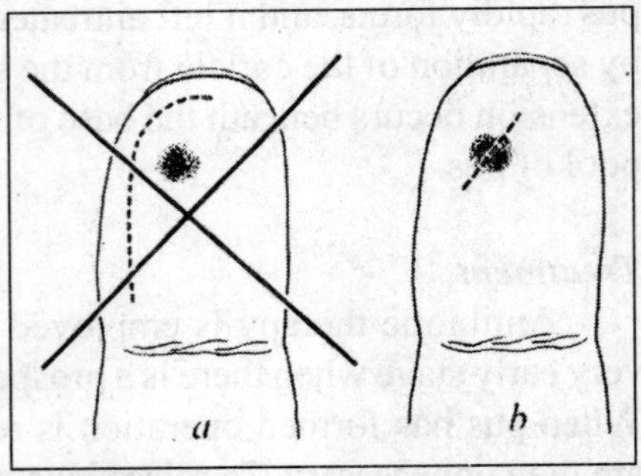

Fig. 4: Incision for pulp abscess, (a) Wrong; (b) Correct.

If treatment has been delayed, pulp abscesses are often complicated by sloughing of soft tissue or by bone infection. Necrosis of the terminal phalanx (a result of infective thrombosis and not of tension ischaemia) is best recognized by probing at the time of operation; the grating sensation of bare bone is characteristic. X-ray changes do not appear for at least 10 days. Recognition of bone infection is important, as it is a very strong indication for antibiotic therapy (which is not required in small uncomplicated pulp abscesses). Early osteitis may resolve with antibiotic treatment but in more severe cases, sequestration occurs which may involve the whole of the distal three-quarters of the terminal phalanx; the wound will not heal until the sequestrum has separated, which may take several weeks. Bone infection not only leads to prolonged disability but is responsible for scarring and deformity. It can be avoided only by adequate drainage at the right time.

Apical Abscess

The pus is situated at the extreme tip of the finger distal to the phalanx or just dorsal to its tip (Fig. 1). The main pulp space is not involved and the abscess points under the free edge of the nail. Tenderness is localized to the fingertip.

Treatment

Pus should be drained by a short transverse incision sited dorsally at the tip of the finger (Fig. 5(a)) and a V-wedge of nail is removed (Fig. 5(b)). Bone infection is rare and the prognosis is good.

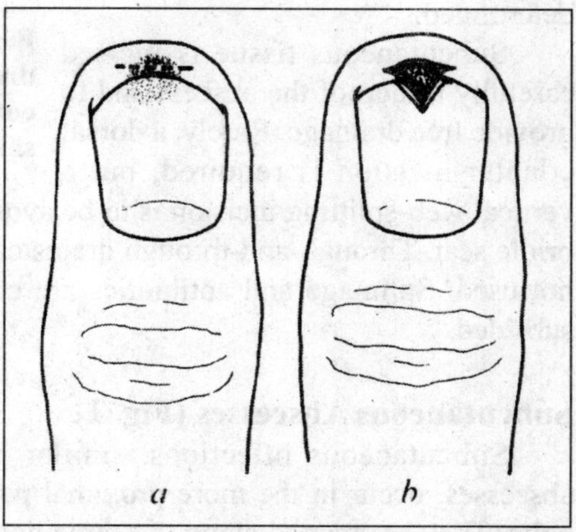

Fig. 5: Apical abscess, (a) Site for initial incision; (b) Excision of V-wedge of nail.

Web Abscess

Infection of the web spaces commonly follows blistering of the palmar skin. When first seen the patient's hand is often grossly oedematous, particularly on the dorsum, and exact localization of the pus may be difficult. A characteristic separation of the adjacent fingers is seen at a later stage.

Treatment

In nearly all cases, 24 h spent in conservative treatment is worth while. The hand is immobilized in a dorsal plaster-of-Paris splint, and is elevated. Antibiotics are given in full dosage to control spreading infection. When swelling has been reduced, the abscess is opened by a transverse incision on the palmar aspect, opposite the interdigital space and about 1 cm proximal to the free edge of the web (Fig. 6). Initially, the skin only is incised, to avoid damage to adjacent digital nerves. The abscess cavity is entered by blunt probing, and its extent determined.

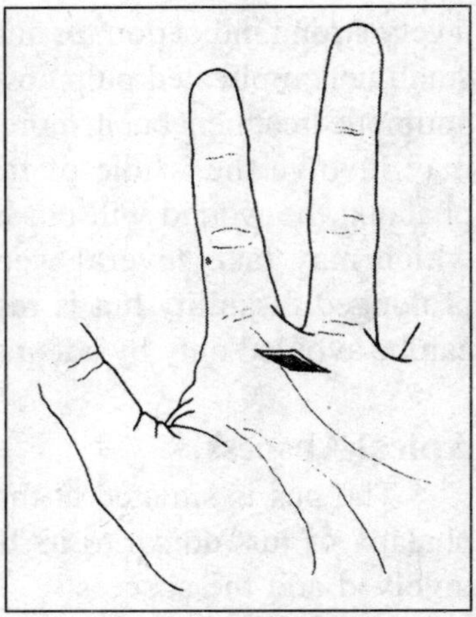

Fig. 6: Site of incision for drainage of a web space. Edges cut back to form a diamond-shaped opening.

Subcutaneous tissue is incised carefully to unroof the abscess and to provide free drainage. Rarely, a dorsal counter-incision is required, but a vertical web-splitting incision is to be avoided because this leads to a bridle scar. Through-and-through drains can only cause harm and are not used. Splintage and antibiotics are continued until oedema has subsided.

Subcutaneous Abscesses (Fig. 1)

Subcutaneous infections, similar in many respects to pulp abscesses, occur in the more proximal parts of the fingers or in the palm. They are treated along the same lines as a pulp abscess and no special comment is needed, except to give a warning that, in the case of a subcutaneous abscess on the anterior aspect of the finger, the floor of the abscess cavity lies very close to the flexor tendon sheath. If the depths of the abscess cavity are not clearly seen the tendon sheath may be opened with serious results.

Intracutaneous Abscesses (Fig. 1)

These abscesses, in which the pus lies actually *within* the dermis, are comparatively uncommon and even less commonly recognized. They are small but very painful. They are only certainly recognized at operation, when care must be taken not to trespass into the subcutaneous tissue.

Deep Palmar Abscess

This abscess, in which the pus is situated deep to the thick palmar fascia, is very uncommon and usually the infection follows a penetrating injury and extends along the tendon sheath.

□

TREATMENT OF ABSCESSES SUPERFICIAL AND DEEP

These remarks refer particularly to miscellaneous abscesses which are commonly encountered.

As a rule, to await the advent of fluctuation is to wait too long. As soon as pus has made its appearance manifest by softening or bogginess in an area of induration or, in some situations, by oedema of the overlying skin, no time must be lost in giving it exit. Those who wait for an abscess to point have allowed the subcutaneous tissue in the immediate vicinity of the area in question to become involved, and an incision at this stage is often followed by necrosis of the edges of the wound. **It is for this reason that operation is advised before pointing is allowed to occur.** Cultures made from pus obtained by incision of non-tuberculous closed abscesses unconnected with the intestine show that over 95 per cent are due to staphylococci, streptococci, or both. On the other hand, if through necrosis of the overlying skin a granulating wound is established, whether this occurs spontaneously or as a result of incision after waiting too long, secondary infection by coliform and other gram-negative organisms such as *E. coli* and *Ps. aeruginosa,* often occurs.

Once pus has formed it is useless and dangerous to rely on antibiotics alone. **'Where there is pus, let it out' is still the order of the day,** but under systemic antibiotic cover; mere incision and drainage is, with notable exceptions, insufficient, as will be explained immediately.

Surgical Pathology—An abscess increases in size in the following way: the innermost layer is killed by bacteria, while the outermost layer (provided the combined natural and acquired resistance of the host is adequate) becomes strengthened. As a rule the granulation

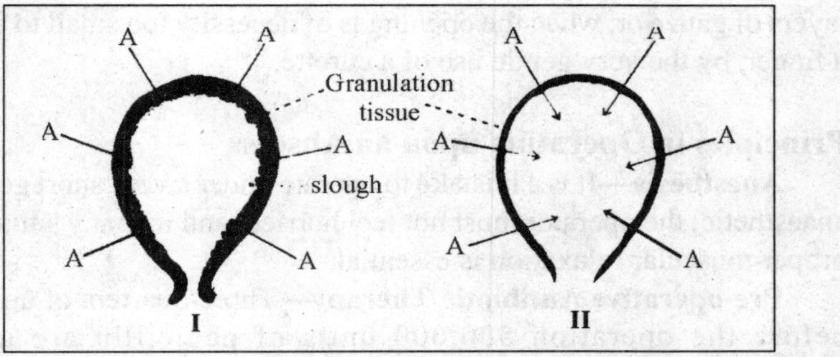

Fig. 1: 1. Abscess treated by simple incision. Antibiotic (A) cannot penetrate the granulation tissue-cum-slough barrier. II. Abscess treated by incision plus abrasion of the granulation tissue lining the cavity. Antibiotic (A) from the blood-stream enters the cavity.

tissue lining the walls of the cavity increases in thickness *pari passu* with the process of liquefaction. It is true that this lining is the chief barrier to bacterial onslaught, thrombophlebitis, and septicaemia. It is equally certain that, because of this barrier, but little circulating antibiotic can reach the abscess cavity, and none can enter when the inner layer has become a slough; slough is completely avascular (Fig. 1).

When, and when not, to remove the Lining Membrane (Granulation Tissue)—Removal of that part of the lining membrane that comes away easily is not new; in the nineties Sir Frederick Treves advocated such a procedure as part of the operative treatment of a psoas abscess. At the present time, from the point of view of treatment, abscesses can be divided into:

1. *Those where the Lining Membrane must be left undisturbed*—These comprise: (a) abscesses that are situated in juxtaposition to named blood-vessels; and (b) abscesses in the immediate vicinity of intestine.
2. *Those where there is no Contra-indication to removing the Lining Membrane*—The great majority of abscesses belong to this category.

A safe method of effecting the removal which, as will be shown, must be carried out under a high concentration of circulating antibiotic, is to wipe away the granulation tissue with a scrapper covered by two layers of gauze or, when the opening is of necessity too small to admit a finger, by the very gentle use of a curette.

Principles in Operating upon an Abscess

Anesthesia—It is a mistake to operate under a very short general anaesthetic; the operator must not feel hurried, and in many situations proper muscular relaxation is essential.

Pre-operative Antibiotic Therapy—Three-quarters of an hour before the operation 500,000 units of penicillin are given intramuscularly with the premedication for the anesthetic. If it is suspected that the infection may be caused by gram-negative as well as gram-positive organisms, triad spectrum antibodies are advised.

Obtaining a Specimen for Bacteriological Examination—Before commencing the operation, it is extremely important to have in readiness a sterile test-tube so that a sample of pus can be collected for bacteriological examination, including sensitivity of the causative bacteria to antibiotics.

Technique

Aseptic precautions must be as perfect as in a clean case. A scalpel with a standard blade is employed, except for superficial abscesses, when one with a fine-pointed blade is used in the manner depicted in Fig. 2. Usually, the incision follows Langer's lines or, when present, skin creases, but in the case of a deep-seated abscess situated in relation to important blood-vessels or nerves, the incision should lie parallel to, and not across, the direction of the structures which it is desired to avoid.

Hilton's Method—If important structures are likely to be encountered or injured, Hilton's method should be employed. This consists in incising the tissues down to the deep fascia and inserting a blunt-ended grooved director (Fig. 3) into the most prominent part of the swelling, or where, with a finger in the wound, softening is most obvious, until pus flows along the groove. Guided by the director, a hæmostat is passed into the cavity, its jaws are

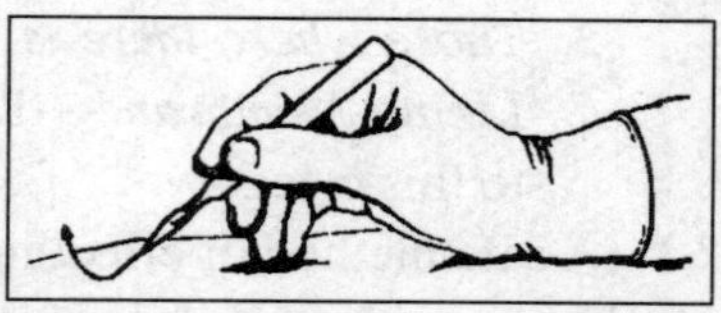

Fig. 2: Method of opening a superficial abscess.

opened, and with the jaws still open the hemostat is removed, thereby enlarging the opening.

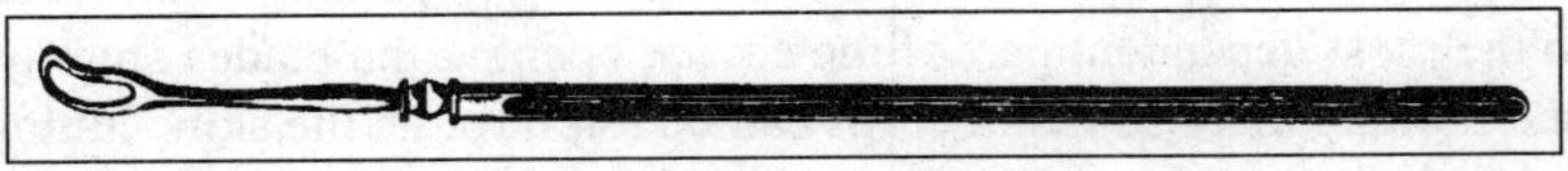

Fig. 3: Blunt-ended grooved director (Allen and Hanburys).

Standard Procedure—In most situations, the incision can be deepened with the scalpel until the abscess is opened, or deepened until it is judged that the wall of the abscess has been reached, and then plunging a closed haemostat into the cavity. The incision should be large enough to admit the index finger easily, or at any rate the little finger. A finger is introduced (Fig. 4) and all loculi are broken down so as to ensure that there is one cavity, and one cavity only. Unless there is a contra-indication for so doing, the lining membrane of granulation tissue is then abraded in the manner described already.

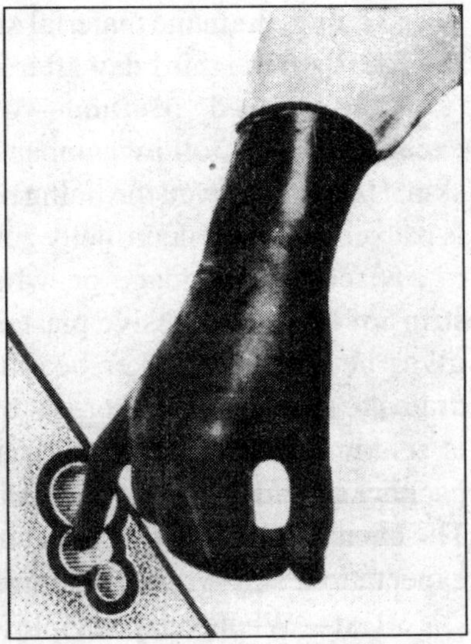

Fig. 4: The little finger is introduced into the abscess cavity and is used to explore and when necessary break down loculi.

Primary Suture—Although much discretion is required, provided the patient's general symptoms are mild and the abscess is situated where the cavity can be obliterated by a compression dressing, a number of surgeons recommend primary suture, with the main object of preventing secondary infection. Even if some blood-clot has to be evacuated at the first dressing, healing proceeds apace.

Drainage—As a rule when drainage is deemed necessary a soft rubber tube of fair size is employed. Should the location of the abscess be unsuitable for a drainage tube, e.g., it might cause pressure necrosis of an artery, corrugated rubber or a piece of rubber glove is substituted.

A Counter-opening—Often an abscess must be opened towards its centre, but sometimes this is not the site for dependent drainage. This may necessitate making a counter-opening by passing a haemostat to the most dependent part of the cavity, opening the blades slightly, and holding them so that the tips can be felt through the skin, cutting between them. After a drainage, tube has been inserted and anchored, the primary incision is closed. Unless there is some definite reason for not so doing, drainage material should be removed on the second, or at the latest, on the third day after its insertion.

The 'Closed' Method—When the overlying skin is involved, excellent results follow comparatively wide excision of the involved skin. Having removed the lining of granulation tissue, the abscess cavity is packed with petroleum-jelly gauze, the area being encased preferably in a viscopaste bandage or, when this is impracticable, covered by strips of flexible adhesive plaster (Fig. 5). This principle of treatment gives better and quicker healing than that obtained by bottleneck drainage (Fig. 6) with necrosis of the edges of the skin wound. There is seldom any need to disturb the dressing for a week, when fresh packing should be inserted, not in the ward, but in the operating theatre. The cavity soon fills in with healthy granulation tissue and contrary to expectation, skin-grafting is rarely necessary.

Rest—Whatever principle of operative treatment is employed, rest of the part concerned is a handmaiden that expedites healing. Neglect of this detail is a cause of a troublesome sinus. Whenever

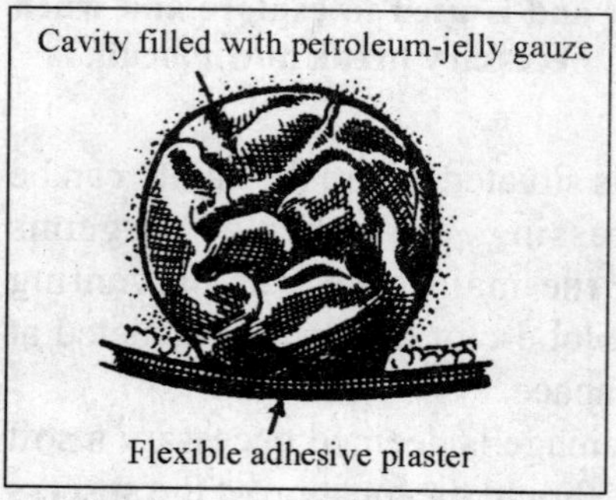

Fig. 5: Treatment of an abscess by excision of overlying skin and packing abscess cavity.

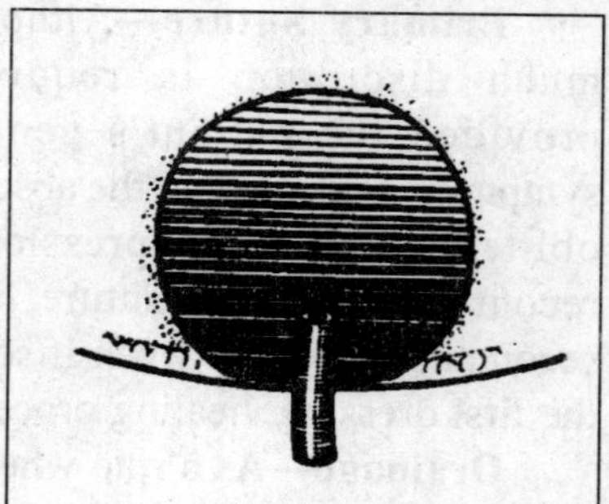

Fig. 6: Bottle-neck tube drainage.

possible the part should be immobilized by a bandage or a splint, a plaster slab being admirable, where applicable.

Abscess of the Breast

The highest incidence of acute mastitis is during the second week of the puerperium of a first pregnancy; a few cases occur before that time, but many are encountered when breast feeding has been prolonged unduly, often in the mistaken belief that continued lactation militates against conception. The predominating organism is the *Staphylococcus aureus.*

So common has infection by a penicillin-resistant staphylococcus become that it is wise to start treatment with broad spectrum antibiotic.

Methicillin therapy, combined with evacuation of milk and support to the breast with a firm many-tailed bandage over wool, if instituted early, relieves the pain remarkably and brings about resolution in not a few cases. On the other hand, the prolonged use of antibiotics after pus has formed leads to an increase in the surrounding induration and the production of a thick abscess wall that bleeds profusely when the abscess is incised, and delays healing. Therefore, the breast must be examined daily after the milk has been expressed. (*See* indications for operation below.)

To Wean or not to Wean is a question of great importance. Except when the patient has been suckling the child for over nine months, undoubtedly it is better not to wean. Feeding is continued from the uninfected breast, and the infected breast is emptied after each feed by manual expression, carried out by the patient herself; this is more effective than a breast pump, which does not always clear obstructed ducts.

In patients who have been suckling the child too long, weaning is advisable. To suppress lactation 5 mg of stilboestrol are given thrice daily for three days and then once daily for six days.

Indications for Operation—The breast should be incised when, after emptying, an area of tense induration is felt and/or when some oedema of the overlying skin is found. Usually, the area of induration is sector-shaped, and in early cases about one-quarter of the breast is involved; in many later cases the area is more extensive.

Incision—Since a neglected breast abscess tends to point at the areolar margin, or close to it, it is better to incise here (Fig. 8) rather than in the classical manner, radiating from the nipple. An incision following the cutaneo-areolar margin has also a high cosmetic value. The incision passes through the skin and the superficial fascia. A long haemostat is then driven into the abscess cavity. Every part of the

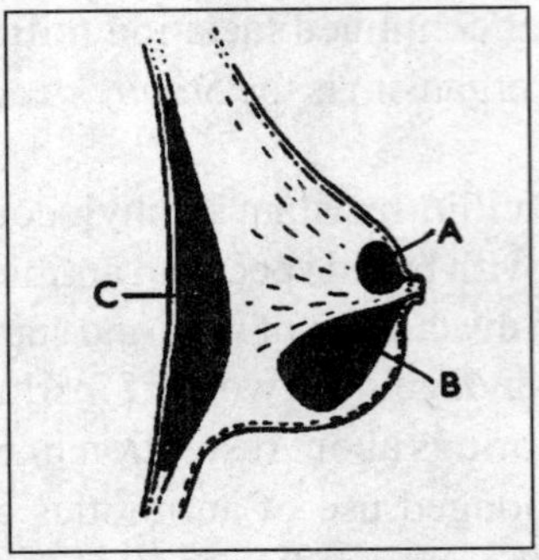

Fig. 7: Varieties of abscess of the breast. A. Subareolar; B. Intramammary; C. Retromammary.

Fig. 8: Incision exactly at the areolar margin.

abscess is palpated against the point of the haemostat, and its jaws are opened (Fig. 9). All loculi and 'lactoceles' that can be felt are entered. Finally, the haemostat having been withdrawn, a finger is introduced and any remaining septa are disrupted. Pus is sent to the laboratory for sensitivity tests. A drainage tube is inserted for 24 hours, and a dry dressing applied. In the case of a large abscess cavity, especially if it is

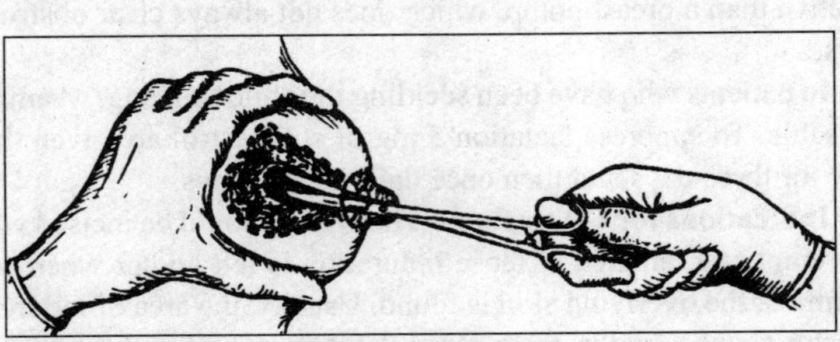

Fig. 9: Every part of the abscess should be palpated against the point of the hæmostat, and all loculi are entered and septa broken down.

occupying a lower quadrant of the breast, it is necessary to make a counter-incision at the most dependent part, and through this place the drainage tube. In this instance, the primary incision can be sutured.

After-treatment—Expression of milk is continued, as also is antibiotic therapy. In Canada, and elsewhere, several outbreaks of puerperal mastitis due to penicillin-resistant strains of staphylococci have occurred in maternity hospitals. In the past 20 years, there have been many reports of outbreaks of breast abscesses assuming epidemic proportions. In such cases, if penicillin has been prescribed, another antibiotic should be substituted as soon as penicillin insensitivity is suspected.

Subareolar Abscess shows a remarkable tendency to resist treatment, and to recur. If the infection is in a milk duct, the dilated ampulla, with its narrow duct, is likely to harbour organisms. In no less than 75 per cent of 64 patients with subareolar abscess studied by Kilgore and Fleming, recurrence or chronic sinus developed after the abscess had been opened or had burst spontaneously. Antibiotic therapy and irradiation were found to be ineffective. The most successful treatment was wide excision of the scar tissue and the underlying abscess cavity.

Retromammary Abscess is rare, and when it occurs it is a chronic abscess, sometimes due to tuberculosis of a rib or to an empyema necessitatis. It is best evacuated by a large incision following the inferior junction of the breast with the thoracic wall, similar to that used for submammary excision of the breast. In this way, the underlying pathology can be displayed and dealt with as necessary.

Follow-up—Out-patient supervision of patients with breast abscess is of the utmost importance. Recurrence, requiring a second operation, is not uncommon, and new abscesses may form later in the puerperium; 40 per cent of Wilson's cases required more than one operation.

Axillary Abscess

The majority of axillary abscesses are secondary to infection of hair follicles or sweat glands of the axilla. A rather frequent cause in females is the use of a chemical depilatory. The minority are due to suppurative axillary lymphadenitis. Although it is common for the lymph-nodes to become enlarged secondary to infections of the hand, because of antibiotic therapy for the primary lesion, it is unusual for the adenitis to proceed to pus formation.

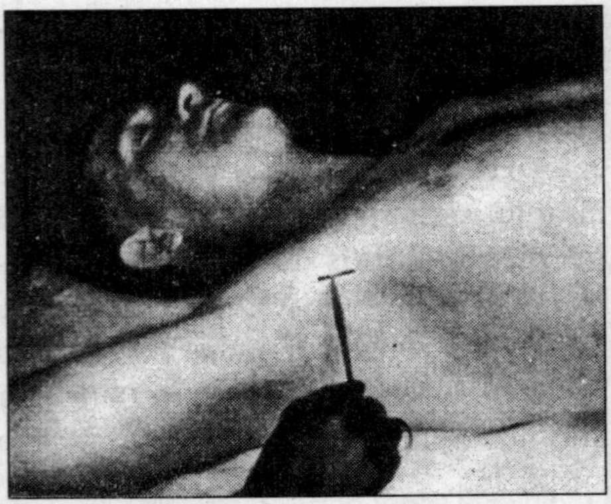

Fig. 10: Opening a deep-seated axillary abscess.

Abscesses of the axilla must be opened promptly, for the pus tends to extend along the path of the nerve-trunks into the neck. The site of the incision will depend upon the situation of the pus. *In acute abscesses pus usually lies under the pectoralis major.*

Fully abduct the arm. Make an incision quite 1 in. (2.5 cm.) long just below the fold of the pectoralis major (Fig. 10).

Hilton's Directions for opening a Deep Abscess in the Axilla— Cut through the skin, cellular tissue, and fascia of the axilla about half an inch behind the axillary edge of the great pectoral muscle. At that part we meet with no large blood-vessel. Then push a grooved director (Fig. 3) upwards into the swelling in the axilla; if you watch the groove in the director, a little stream of pus will show itself. Take a blunt pair of forceps and run the closed blades along the groove in the director into the swelling. Now open the handles and so tear open the abscess parallel to important structures. One can put a drain and connect it to a Romovac suction bag.

If the region of the axillary vessels is avoided studiously, there is no objection to abrading the granulation tissue lining the major portion of the cavity.

In late cases, when the whole axilla is merely a bag of pus, an incision into the lower part of the middle of the space will be found convenient. In such circumstances, a good means of drainage is the negative pressure method. After the pus has been evacuated, one end of drainage tube through a counter incision, which is closed tightly around the tube. The tube is anchored to the skin by a stout suture. The other end of the drainage tube is connected to Romovac vaccum drain.

Antibiotic Modification of Acute Abscesses

Modern methods have indeed revolutionized the treatment of abscesses. In so doing, they have profoundly altered many time-honoured aspects of suppuration:

(a) *The 'cold' abscess* was once an almost infallible sign that the abscess was tuberculous. After a few days of pre-operative antibiotic therapy even a florid infection can result in an abscess which is not only 'cold' but bacteriologically sterile.

(b) *Sterile pus,* like sterile pyuria, might still indicate tuberculosis, but nowadays it is much more frequently the result of a common pyogenic condition treated by the correct remedy. It is therefore important that information regarding the antibiotics a patient has received before admission should be forthcoming, and that when sending pus to the laboratory the bacteriologist should be informed of the therapeutic facts.

(c) Particularly noteworthy are the *reactivations of abscesses* after brief courses of antibiotics have been concluded. Following a dramatic initial response the patient is discharged, only to return in a short time with an acute recrudescence of his original infection. A veritable trap is the recently subsided appendix abscess, which 'flares up' soon after discontinuing antibiotics. For this reason, it is a good practice to see at least once in the Out-Patient Clinic, all short-stay hospital patients who have been admitted for suppurative lesions.

(d) The clinician must be on his guard for those thin effusions that, by reason of antibiotic therapy, sometimes form instead of pus. The serous fluid, when faintly blood-stained, appears more like the contents of a resolving haematoma than an abscess. When antibiotics have exerted their initial effects, so impressive is the relief of pain that these later effusions tend to progress insidiously. In aged and feeble subjects large collections of inert pus may develop indolently, especially in the thigh and buttocks, without the patient making any complaint whatsoever. Therefore, inspect the surrounding regions of all inflammatory lesions 'cured without operation' before sending the patient home.

Masking of signs of inflammation by antibiotics not infrequently leads to undue delay in opening a breast abscess, with a resulting excessive destruction of mammary tissue, sometimes amounting to a functional mastectomy. Now and then the excessive fibrosis thus induced and the absence of tenderness have caused the diagnosis to be revised in favour of carcinoma. Another disadvantage of undue delay is the deposition of a wealth of exuberant granulation tissue on the walls of the abscess: this has brought about profuse haemorrhage when the abscess is incised. To obviate these untoward possibilities, when in doubt as to the presence of pus, the indurated mass should be explored with a needle and syringe under general anesthesia, and incised if pus is found.

Carbuncle

The first consideration is to test the urine. If the patient is a diabetic, he must receive appropriate treatment for diabetes. It is important to realize that the toxaemia resulting from a carbuncle can give rise to glycosuria: should perplexity arise on this score, the blood-sugar level will provide the clue. When facilities exist a full blood-count should be ordered. The white-cell count will provide interesting and instructive data; the red-cell count and the haemoglobin estimation will ensure that unsuspected anaemia is not overlooked. The estimation of plasma-proteins is a help. Protein deficiency, if it exists, should be made good.

General Treatment—From the outset general treatment is of cardinal importance. A high fluid intake must be insisted upon.

When there is hypochromic anaemia, iron in one of the many available forms should be given. A light, but highly nutritious diet is an important detail. Mixed vitamins, abundant fresh air, and other common-sense means must be taken to build up the patient's resistance, for further carbuncles and boils are very prone to occur in what is termed 'the negative phase' which follows a seemingly encouraging early convalescence. In patients who tolerate it well, perhaps the most valuable of all general adjuvant treatment is natural sunlight. In its absence, local and general ultraviolet light is a good substitute.

Toilet of Surrounding Skin—If the surrounding area is hairy, wide atraumatic shaving is indicated. The area in question is washed with one per cent cetavlon. The object of this is to try to prevent satellite furunculosis—a common local complication.

Antibiotic Therapy—This is the sheet anchor of treatment. Pus from the carbuncle is secured as soon as possible and sent for sensitivity tests. While awaiting the results antibiotics are started, commencing with penicillin (500,000 units 6-hourly). If the patient has previously received penicillin, or when the carbuncle has developed in hospital, it is quite likely that the staphylococcus is penicillin-resistant. Under these circumstances, methicillin 1 g 6-hourly is advised.

Local Treatment—This consists of mopping the part gently with cetavlon solution; then dry gauze is applied and over that adhesive plaster. The dressing is changed only when sodden.

In the majority of cases, a slough forms in the centre of the carbuncle and in due course this can be lifted off with dissecting forceps painlessly and without an anesthetic. If the slough is slow to separate, proteolytic debridement can be used with advantage. The clean underlying ulcer is covered with tulle gras dressings. Healing is usually rapid and complete. If the raw area is large, as soon as the clean, red, and flat granulation tissue is present, healing can be expedited by skin-grafting.

Operative Treatment—The relative inactivity just described is surprisingly successful in the majority of cases. Provided there is not a contra-indication to a general anesthetic, there should not be undue reluctance to resort to the operative measures when, after several days of treatment, the pain remains severe and there are signs of toxaemia associated with softening in the centre of the carbuncle.

The operative procedure consists of three phases. The important detail is that good access to the part is essential, as so often a carbuncle is situated on the nape of the neck, the back, or the buttocks. A few moments spent in consultation with the anesthetist as to the patient's position during the operation is time well spent.

1. *Cruciate incision*: A large cruciate incision is made into the whole of the carbuncle, well into the red skin at the periphery. On no account is any scraping performed; loose slough can be removed by wiping it firmly with a gauze swab.

2. *Excision of carbunculous skin*: The four flaps resulting from the incision are dissected up and their apices are removed, erring on the side of liberality.
3. *Application of a closed dressing*: The wound is lightly packed with petroleum-jelly gauze. A viscopaste bandage or strips of flexible adhesive plaster complete the dressing, which is not disturbed for a week unless there is some indication.

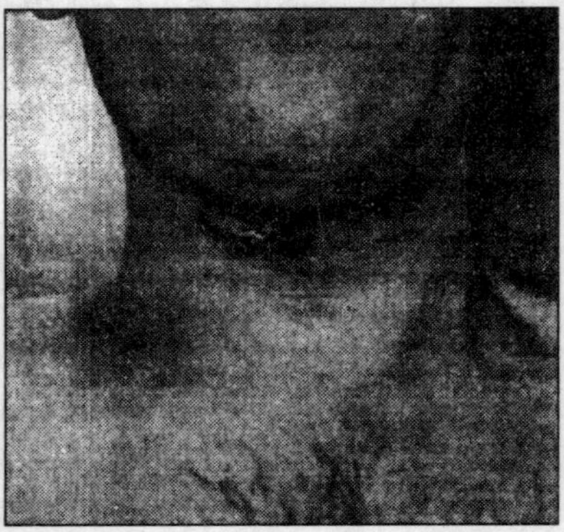

Fig. 11: Suppurating supraclavicular adenitis secondary to a boil over the Adam's apple. Abscess drained by Hilton's method.

Uncomplicated Cervical Abscess

(Suppurating Cervical Lymph-nodes)

In dealing with this common condition, one can delay operation with safety and advantage until the centre of the swelling is soft, or until the overlying subcutaneous tissue becomes (Edematous and reddened (Fig. 11). A comparatively small incision is made, and a blunt-nosed laemostat is inserted gently with due regard to the great vessels; its jaws are opened cautiously to enlarge the opening. Tube drainage is employed.

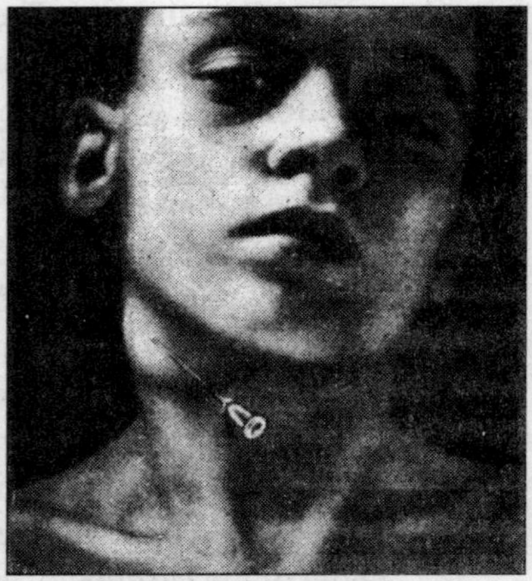

Fig. 12: Aspirating a tuberculous collar-stud abscess by the oblique method of Calot.

Conditions which Simulate Cervical Abscess—Inflammation may complicate a *branchial cyst.* Such inflammation almost always subsides with expectant treatment, after which the cyst should be enucleated. The diagnosis of branchial cyst may be confirmed by aspirating a little of the contents of the cyst. The substance withdrawn looks like pus, but if a drop is examined under the microscope an abundance of cholesterol crystals will be seen.

Inflammation also complicates *cystic hygroma,* which is usually found in the lower third of the neck, and nearly always in childhood. The diagnosis can be clinched by the translucency of the swelling.

Tuberculous Cervical 'Collar-stud' Abscess—A tuberculous collar-stud abscess sometimes requires aspiration as a quasi-emergency measure. By timely aspiration skin involvement, fistula formation, and secondary infection can be prevented. Such abscesses should always be aspirated by the oblique method of Calot (Fig. 12). A small quantity of local analgesic is injected into healthy skin about 1½ in (3.8 cm) from the periphery of the swelling.

Anorectal Abscesses

Fistula-in-ano is a common condition. Because most of these fistulae are an aftermath of inadequate treatment of anorectal suppuration, anorectal abscess is a subject that demands close attention by the emergency surgeon. In this instance, inadequate operations are the result of neither lack of experience nor want of manual dexterity; on the contrary, they are the direct outcome of sheer lack of knowledge. Too much reliance on antibiotics, fomentations—waiting for the abscess to 'ripen'—a short incision—more fomentations; this is the unholy sequence of events that invites fistula formation. The most reprehensible practice is to open an ischiorectal abscess by Hilton's method.

So much for what should *not* be done.

Bacteriology—The presence of stinking pus usually indicates the presence of *Bact. E. coli.* Bacteriological examination of the pus, however, shows that *Staphylococcus aureus* is present in about three out of five abscesses (M. Ellis).

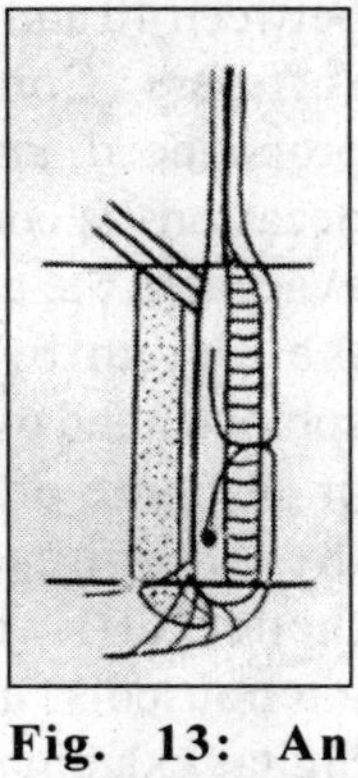

Fig. 13: An anorectal gland. The upper branch is usually a simple tube.

Varieties of Anorectal Abscesses

In a high percentage of cases (some estimate it at no less than 90 per cent) the abscess commences as an infection of an anal gland. Because the upper branch (there is often only one upper and one lower branch (Fig. 13)) of the anal gland is tubular, it does not become the seat of an abscess so readily as the bulbous-ended inferior branch.

S. Kisenhammer has revised the classification of anorectal abscesses (Fig. 14). Special attention is directed to (1) high and (2) low intermuscular abscess; (1) has not been described as such before, but as a submucous abscess (which most certainly it is not), while (2) was known as a perianal abscess.

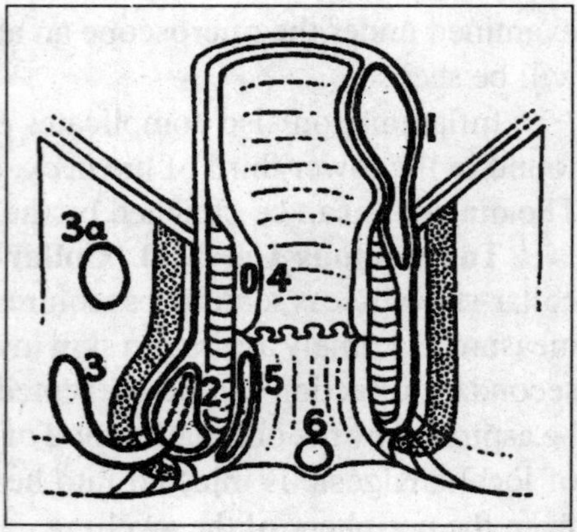

Fig. 14: Anorectal abscesses: 1. High intermuscular; 2. Low intermuscular; 3. Ischiorectal from an extension of (2); 3a. Blood-borne ischiorectal abscess; 4. Submucous abscess; 5. Abscess beneath anal canal skin; 6. Subcutaneous abscess.

High Intermuscular Anorectal Abscess (10 per cent) is situated deep to the internal sphincter and occupies the upper part of the intermuscular space. Men between 40 and 55 years of age are the usual sufferers. Constitutional symptoms are pronounced, and the pain that the abscess occasions is considerable. If the pus is not evacuated the abscess either (a) bursts into the rectum by penetrating the internal sphincter and overlying mucous membrane, or (ft) more often spreads to the whole of the intermuscular space (Fig. 15), thenceforth to behave like a low intermuscular abscess'. The diagnosis is made in the early stages by digital examination of the rectum, when an acutely tender, rounded cystic lump about the size of a walnut is felt above the level of the dentate line, generally in the posterior quadrant.

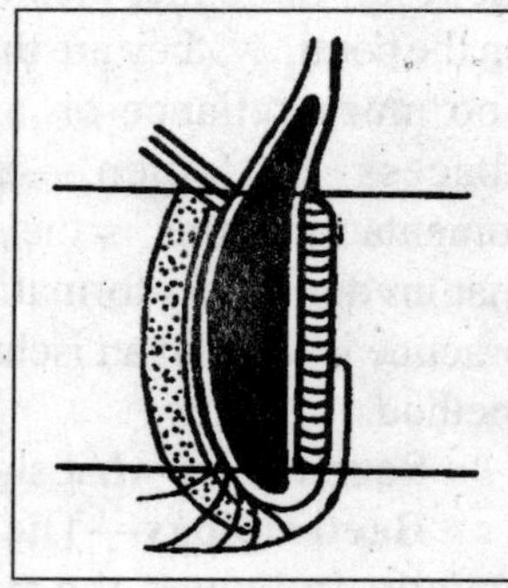

Fig. 15: Total infection of the intermuscular space.

Low Intermuscular Abscess (80 per cent)—This, the most common abscess of the region, affects persons of all ages. Constitutional symptoms are less pronounced than in the high variety, and the pain is less severe. Untreated, frequently the abscess presents subcutaneously near the anal margin.

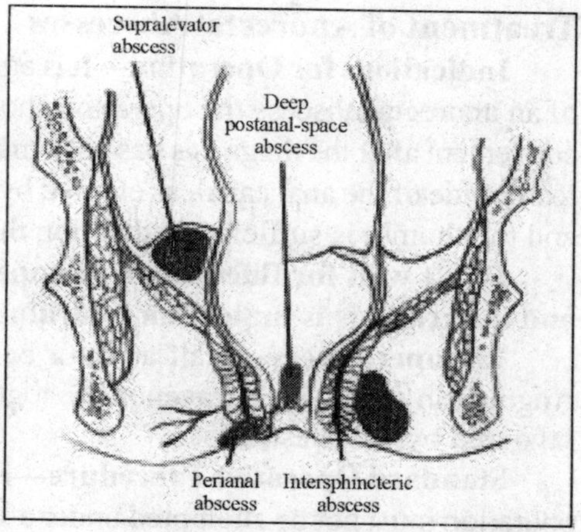

Anorectal abscess

Ischiorectal Abscess occupies the ischiorectal fossa. The ischiorectal space communicates with that of the opposite side via the post-sphincteric space. The constitutional symptoms of an ischiorectal abscess are more pronounced than in other varieties of anorectal suppuration. In comparatively early cases there is no redness of the skin.

Post-sphincteric Abscess is often small, but if it is allowed to spread it does so into both ischiorectal fossae, with which it is anatomically continuous. The post-sphincteric abscess lies rather deeply between the coccygeal attachments of the levator ani above and the coccygeal attachments of the superficial part of the external sphincter below.

Submucous Abscess—Doubtless a submucous abscess often bursts spontaneously. When present, it presents as a tender swelling of the anal canal extending downwards to the anal groove, and often to well beyond the anorectal ring. Occasionally, it extends into the perianal space, giving rise to an L-shaped bilocular abscess (Fig. 16).

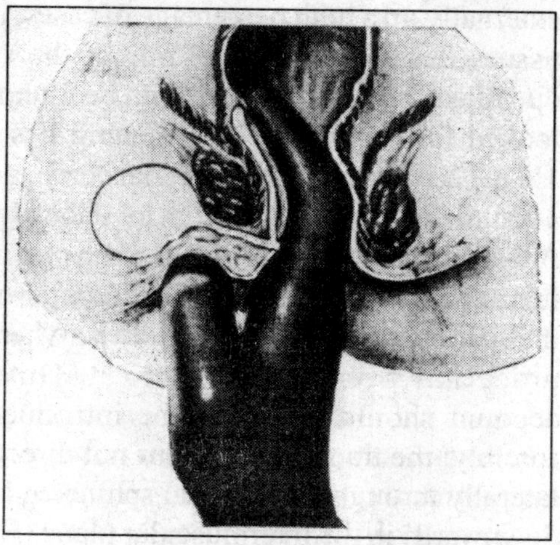

Fig. 16: An upward extension of the suppuration under the mucosa feels like a pencil.

Treatment of Anorectal Abscesses

Indications for Operation—It is agreed generally that in the case of an anorectal abscess the operation should be undertaken as soon as convenient after the diagnosis has been made. A tender, brawny swelling to one side of the anal canal, as elicited by palpation between the finger and the thumb, is sufficient indication that operation is necessary.

Don't wait for fluctuation to appear in the area tenderness and indurations is indication to drain the abscess.

Pre-operativery—Half an hour before the operation 1.2 gm of Augmentin are given intravenously, together with the premedication favoured by the anesthetist.

Standard Operative Procedure—Full anesthesia is required: the operation must not be attempted under a short-acting anesthetic, which causes the operator to feel hurried. The patient is placed in the lithotomy position, and if, as is often the case (because of tenderness of the parts), shaving has been inadequately performed, this is remedied before other skin preparation receives attention. The seated surgeon then examines the region with the object of not only evacuating pus, but of preventing a fistula.

The situation of the abscess (induration) can be defined by palpation between the finger within the rectum and the thumb externally. In a high percentage of cases, infection reaches the perianal tissues through a lesion of one of the valves of Ball, and a minute opening in the mucosa can often be found if looked for especially. The opening lies 1-1½ in (2.5-3.8 cm) from the anal verge, and a common mistake is to search for it too high. A teaspoon is a useful retractor when making this examination. If pus is not exuding from the tiny opening, often it will do so when a probe has been inserted into it. On no account should the probe be introduced forcibly; the track usually runs not directly laterally through the external sphincter, but downwards in the intermuscular plane (Fig. 13). The end of the probe, therefore, must be bent at an acute angle (Fig. 17) if the track

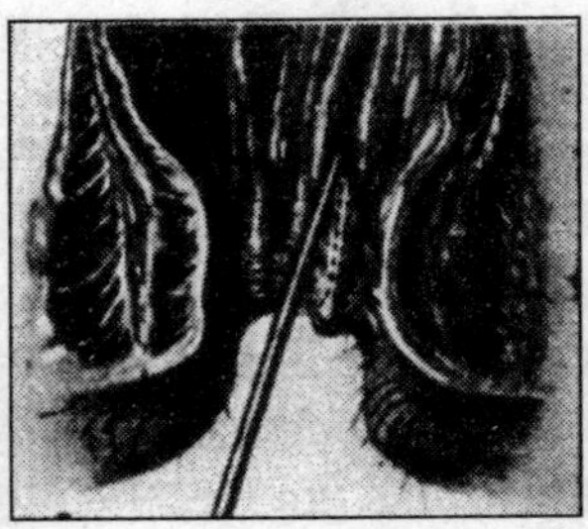

Fig. 17: The track leading from the tiny opening in the mucous membrane usually first of all passes downwards at an acute angle.

is to be followed. From time to time an indurated vertical ridge which feels like a pencil can be palpated. This is an *upward* extension of the suppuration under the mucosa, and it ends blindly at varying distances up to one inch (2.5 cm) or more above the internal sphincter (Fig. 16). If a very troublesome form of fistula is to be prevented it is just as important to drain this extension adequately as to attend to the ischiorectal abscess proper. Fortified with exact data, the surgeon now changes his gloves, for this is not an occasion for haste. A liberal crucial shaped incision is made into the abscess. The length of the incisions should be at least twice the depth of the abscess (W.F. Gillespie). An adequate portion of skin, that includes most, if not all, of the floor of the abscess, is excised (Fig. 18 inset). The cavity is explored, and if septa exist they should be broken down gently with the finger, and what is most important is that the granulation tissue lining its walls is removed by a finger wrapped in gauze. If this is not done, antibiotics administered systemically cannot reach the abscess cavity. In cases where an internal opening is located, *and the opening is below the anorectal ring* (i.e. the upper margin of the internal sphincter), the bridge of tissue intervening between the opening and the perianal skin

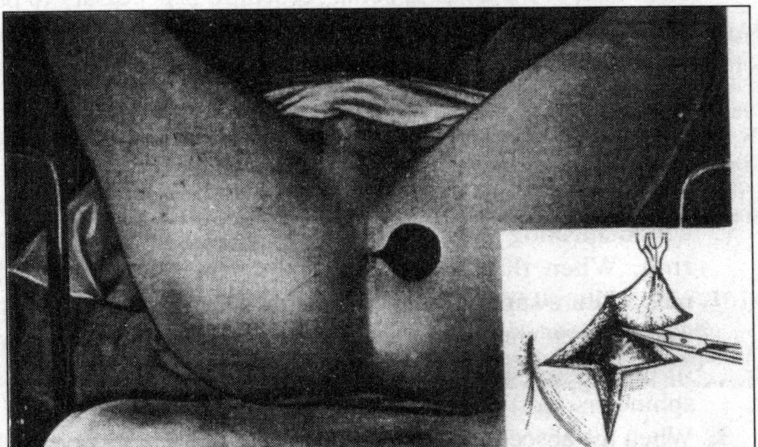

Fig. 18: Excising the skin overlying the floor of the ischiorectal fossa. The four flaps resulting from a cruciform incision are dissected free and removed. The completed operation leaves a pear-like deficiency. The body of the pear is represented by the skin deficiency while the stalk is the slit-up mucous membrane.

is severed. The resulting operative cavity may then be likened to a pear; the body of the pear is represented by the excised skin and the stalk of the pear by the slit-up mucous membrane (Fig. 18). Under no circumstances should the incision be extended through the full height of the internal sphincter, i.e. above the anorectal ring, or incontinence will follow. *The anorectal ring must be left intact.*

Poet-operative Dressing—The whole cavity is very lightly packed with gauze wrung out in betadine solution; if neither of these is available, acriflavine emulsion is suitable. A T-bandage is applied.

After-treatment—Antibiotic treatment is continued for a week or longer, if necessary. The cavity is irrigated daily preferably with eusol solution, and a flat, moist dressing, or very light packing, is renewed. Antiseptic sitz baths can be commenced on the third day in most instances. After a week the cavity is usually lined with healthy granulation tissue. Healing is rather slow. When the cavity is filled with granulation tissue skin-grafting expedites final epithelialization.

Variations in Operative Procedure to meet Special Circumstances—

1. In the somewhat unusual event of a pencil-like submucosal extension of the abscess being present, it is necessary to pass a director along the track and to lay it open. Brisk haemorrhage is to be expected, and it is difficult to apply ligatures. In cases of difficulty, haemostats having been applied, they should be left *in situ* for 48 hours rather than persist in ineffectual attempts to ligate inaccessible bleeding vessels.
2. On still rarer occasions an internal opening will be found communicating with the ischiorectal fossa above the anorectal ring. When this is the case on no account should the musculature superficial to the fistula be divided at this stage. The surgeon should restrict the operation to simple drainage from below—a recurrent fistula may later follow but the sphincters must not be sacrificed on this account.
3. When the abscess is bilateral, both sides should be opened by the technique described. The communicating track, which invariably runs posterior to the anus, is laid open.
4. In the rare event of the case proving to be one of a pelvirectal abscess, and pus being found coming from above the levator

ani, the opening in the apex of the ischio-rectal fossa is enlarged with a finger, and a drainage tube inserted. Otherwise a drainage tube is not employed.

5. When a high intermuscular abscess is encountered, no time should be lost in evacuating pus in the following manner: when the abscess is still high, access to it is obtained by inserting a Sims's speculum into the anal canal. A short longitudinal incision is made over the lower border of the internal sphincter (Fig. 13) extending upwards for ½ in (1.3 cm). A blunt-pointed director is passed deep to the internal sphincter into the abscess cavity, and pus flows. The opening is enlarged sufficiently to allow digital exploration. This accom-plished, the anoderm is freed bluntly from the internal sphincter, which is divided from below upwards under direct vision on to the director. The division is extended to the uppermost limit of the abscess cavity. Bleeding-points, which are not numerous, are controlled. No drainage tube is employed.

□

FISTULA IN ANO

The most important thing one should explain the patient has to have proper dressing for 3-4 weeks till the wound has completely healed. The excision of fistula has to be complete and then the healing has to befrom the base of the wound and daily dressing after sitz bath has to be done with proper packing so that no residual fistula is left and give trouble in future.

□

HAEMORRHOIDS

Piles are seen with a proctoscope these can be

1st Degree: Prolapse of mucera of anal canal.

2nd Degree: Buldge in the lumen of the anal canal.

3rd Degree: It prolapse in anal canal but goes inside with removal of proctoscope.

4th Degree: When the piles remain Prolapsed outside always.

Symptoms

— Bleeding.

— Itching in anal region case of prolapsed piles.

— Pain is more seen in case of thrombosed piles.

Management

1. Injection of sclerosants sodium tetradecyl sulphate 1% is used with special gabriel syringe and needle and injected in 1st and early second degree pile 2-5 ml solutions injected till when the covered mucore becomes pale.

2. Banding the pile with a special equipment in 3rd and 4th degree pile or late second degree piles.

3. Haemorrhoidectomy surgical excision of piles after ligating the base of piles.

4. Stapled Haemorrhoidectomy.

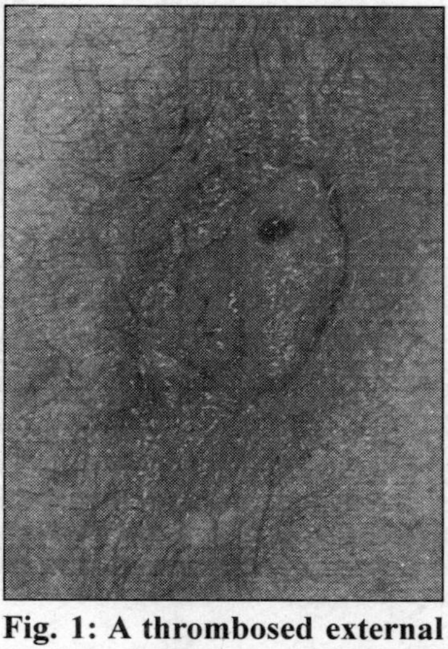

Fig. 1: A thrombosed external haemorrhoid that has. There is also a mucosal prolapse, which is separate from the cutting lesion.

Indication for Haemorrhoidectomy

1. 3rd and 4th degree piles.
2. Second degree piles where injection and banding have failed.
3. Thrombosed piles.
4. Interno external piles.

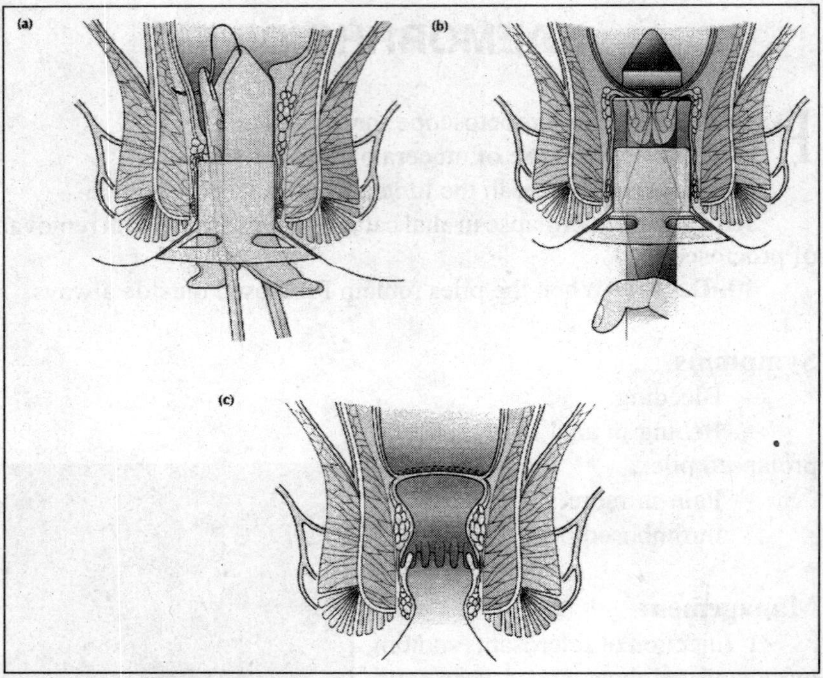

Fig. 2: Stapled haemorrhoidectomy, (a) The purse-string suture is placed several centimetres above the dentate line. (b) The anvil of the fully opened stapling gun is inserted endoanally so that it is above the purse-string suture, which is then tied around the shaft of the gun. The gun is closed and fired. (c) After firing, a 3-4 cm strip of mucosa and submucosa containing the haemorrhoids is excised and the mucosal edges are simultaneously stapled together.

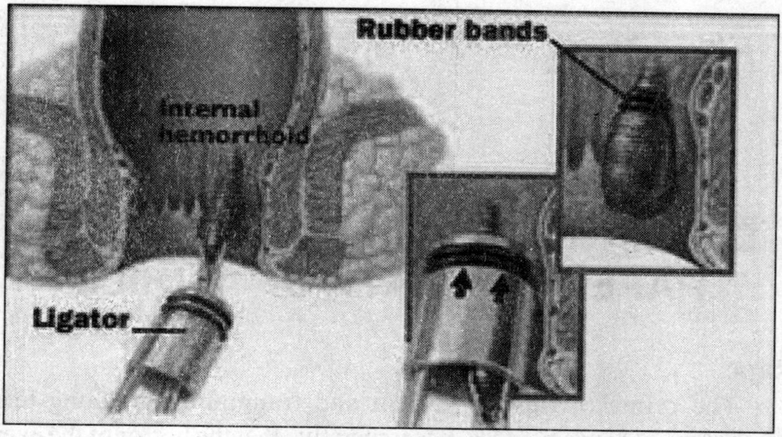

Hemorrhoids

□

DEALING WITH SPECIAL CASES OF RAPE AND DEATH OF A CHILD

Rape

The crime of rape is violent and traumatic with long-term psychological consequences. It is imperative that the horror of the event doesn't include the victim's treatment in the ED. Have a social worker or a community ED companion immediately available to help the patient get through the medical evaluation.

The initial evaluation must be directed to the patient's physical well-being. Injuries must be treated as for those of any other patient. Approach the patient in a non-threatening and reassuring manner. Always have an assistant present who is of the same sex as the victim. Once immediate physical problems are dealt with, get a brief history of the attack. Document the general appearance and the patient's demeanor and physical findings appropriately on the chart, with particular attention to bruises and marks. Use a body map to describe the bruises. Obtain permission and take photographs of any marks or bruises, especially if the patient hasn't involved the police yet. Ask the patient if he or she wishes to involve the police. Using a rape evidence kit facilitates the physical examination. Follow local protocols for its use. The patient should receive STD prophylaxis, hepatitis virus vaccination, HIV prophylaxis, and postcoital contraception according to CDC recommendations (Table 1).

Although not all experts agree, most patients probably benefit from prophylaxis because (1) follow-up of patients who have been sexually assaulted can be difficult and (2) patients may be reassured if offered treatment or prophylaxis for possible infection. Make appropriate referral for counseling and follow-up.

Assault

In the case of a victim of assault, again, the medical care of the patient is paramount. Because of the legal issues, the history and physical should be documented meticulously. As with rape cases, ascertain if the victim wants the police to be involved, and make any such arrangements. Certain states require EDs to report felony assaults (e.g., gunshot wounds, knife wounds). Patients should be referred for counseling as well.

Abuse

In the ED, always maintain a high degree of suspicion of abuse. **PEARL: Screen all women for risk of domestic violence.**

Table 1: STD Prophylaxis and Postcoital contraception in Rape Cases

Drug	*Dosage*
STD prophylaxis	
Ciprofloxacin	500 mg PO once
Plus	
Azithromycin	1 g PO once
Plus	
Metronidazole	2 g PO once
HIV prophylaxis	
Combivir (zidovudine 300 mg and lamivudine 150 mg)	1 tablet PO BID for 4 weeks
Plus	
Indinavir	800 mg PO TID for 4 weeks
Postcoital contraception (within 72 hours of coitus only if pregnancy test currently negative)	
Norgestrel (Oral)	2 tablets PO [or (Lo/Ovral) 4 tablets PO]; repeat dose in 12 hours

All ages are susceptible to being abused, although children, women, and the elderly are more likely to be victims. As always, medical care is paramount. Whenever you do suspect abuse, you should notify the appropriate agencies; this usually is a legal requirement for physicians. Often, if not always, the hospital's social work department should be involved. Although many women who are victims of abuse will not volunteer any information, they will discuss it if asked simple, direct questions in a non-judgmental way and in a confidential setting. **PEARL: Ask every woman if anyone has hurt her or hit her or if she is afraid to go home because of violence.** You may want to offer a statement such as: "Because violence is so common in many women's lives, I've begun to ask about it routinely." Then, you can ask a direct question such as: "At any time, has your partner hit, kicked, or otherwise hurt or frightened you?" *If the patient answers yes, the following steps are suggested:*

1. Encourage her to talk about it.
2. Listen non-judgmentally.

The Death of a Patient

One of the hardest psycho-social situations you will face in the hospital is informing a family of a patient's death, especially the death of a child. In general, you should have the family members placed in a separate and quiet room, preferably with a phone available. Have someone go in with you such as a nurse, social worker, or member of the clergy. Usually, the attending physician should be with you as well for at least part of the discussion. Be direct but supportive. Use the word "dead"; euphemisms such as "passed away" or "didn't make it" may not get the message across. Always tell the family that you did everything you could. If possible, assure them that the death was painless and that their relative didn't suffer. After you have told them, stay in the room as long as needed to answer their questions.

If the family is not present, it is best not to tell them over the telephone. Instead, tell them that their relative is critically ill and that they ought to come in. Tell them to drive safely and make sure they know how to get to the hospital.

Finally, remember to deal with your own feelings about the death. Don't hesitate to talk to coworkers, friends, social workers, clergy, or counselors if you are troubled. Many resources exist to help you deal with the legal, social, and ethical difficulties that crop up in the hospital. Clergy often are on call for patients who need or request them. They can help a family to deal with the stress of a death or serious illness.

The social work service of your hospital may have a full-time or on-call social worker; this person should be involved in all cases of possible abuse or neglect and can be an additional support for families facing the stress of illness. Consider them also for patients with primarily social problems such as the homeless. Also consider them for patients who may have psycho-social difficulties in addition to their medical problems such as the elderly, patients with subtance abuse problems, or patients with financial trouble that may compromise their care (e.g. preventing them from filling prescriptions). Keep in mind that you are not alone, and use the help available to you.

□

PROCTOSCOPY

The proctoscope (Fig. 1) is designed to examine the lower rectum and anal canal only. An ordinary tubular instrument is satisfactory for general work but the Graeme Anderson pattern with an oblique end is useful for inspecting the side wall of the anal canal, e.g. when examining the internal opening of an anal fistula. Lighting is supplied by a fitted fibreoptic light attachment or by an adjustable Anglepoise-type light behind the examiner's head.

The instrument is inserted to the full distance in the direction of the umbilicus and the obturator is withdrawn. Any stool or mucus is swabbed away and the mucosa of the lower rectum examined. The instrument is then slowly withdrawn. This will reveal in turn the anorectal junction (marked by the point at which the mucosa closes at

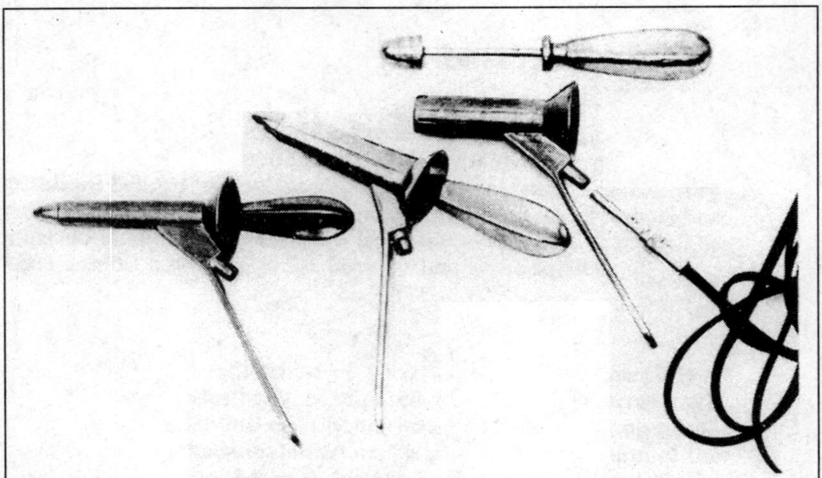

Fig. 1: Tubular proctoscopes, with interchangeable illumination. The longest one shown is that normally used for the examination of adults.

Skin staple remover in open posture

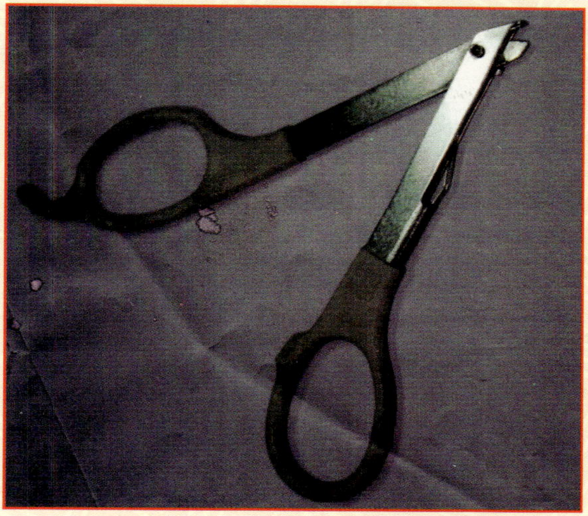

Skin staple remover in closed posture

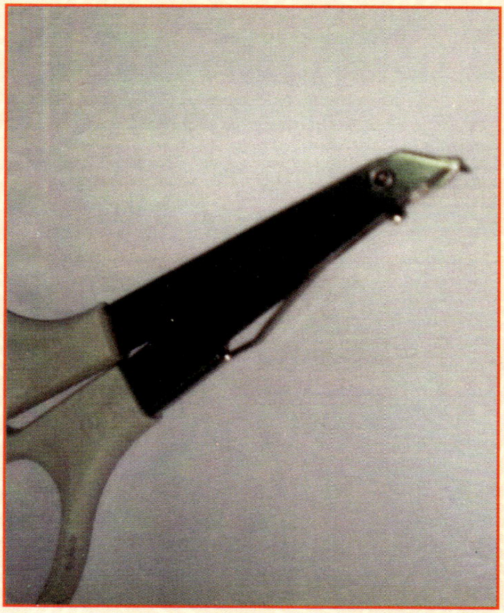

Memingitis

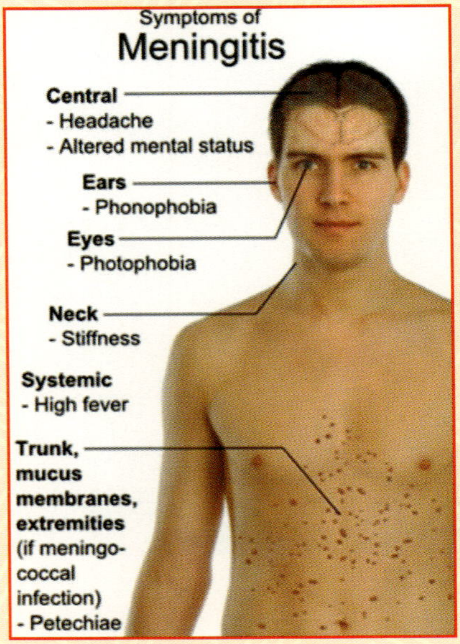

Ptosis

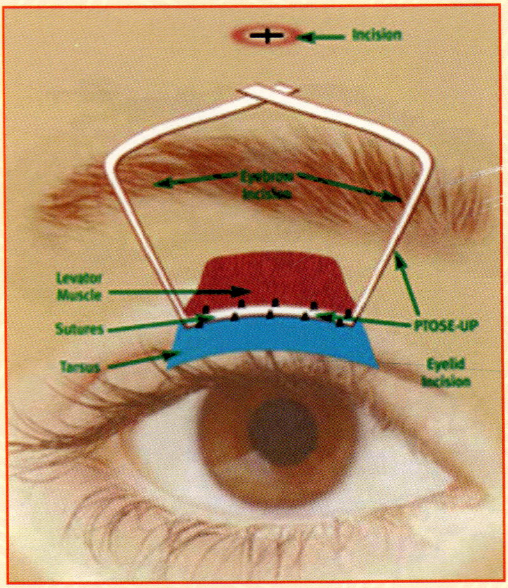

Polio Patient

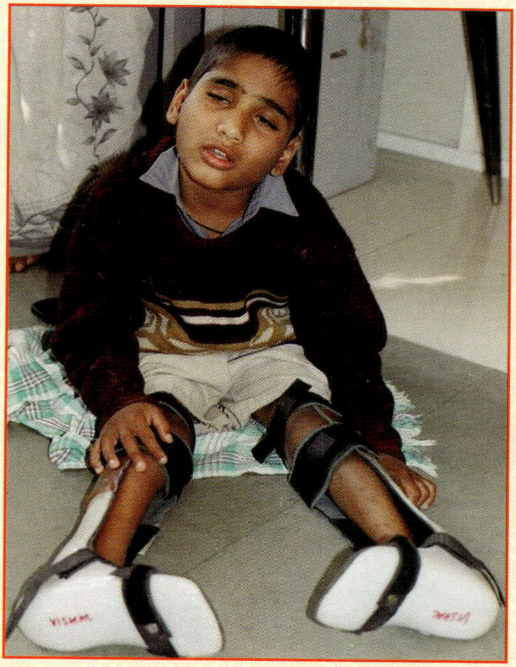

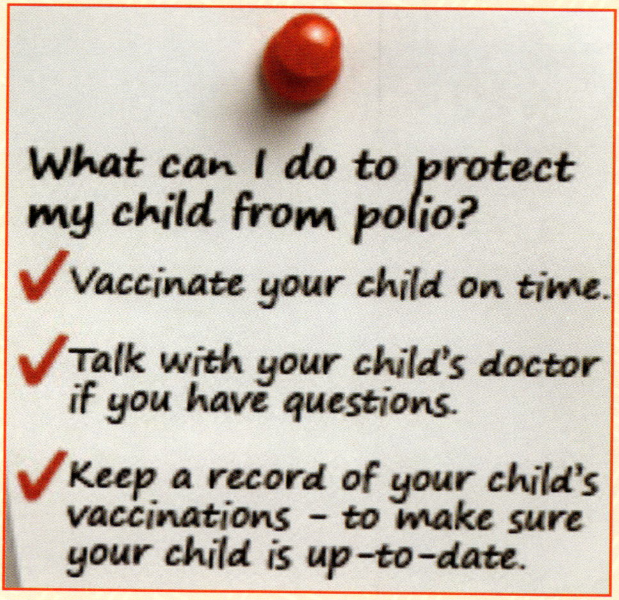

Kernig's Sign

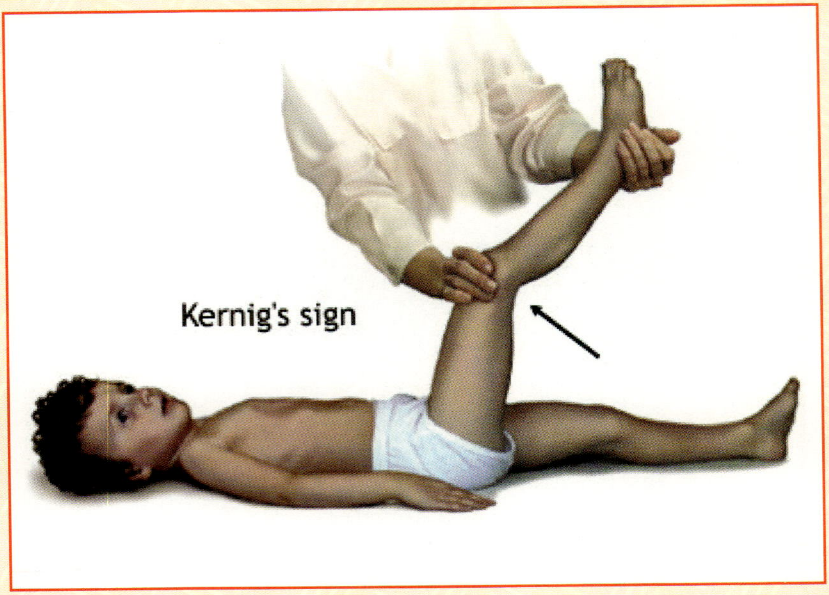

Palpation of Liver

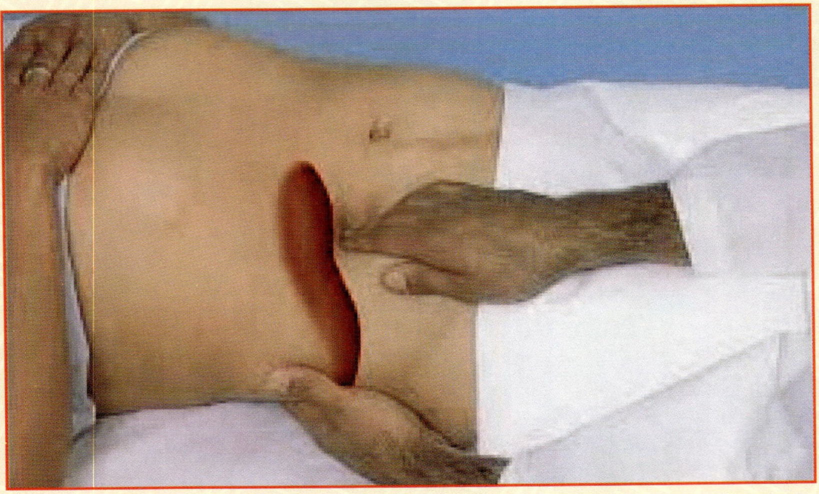

Enlarged nodes in neck

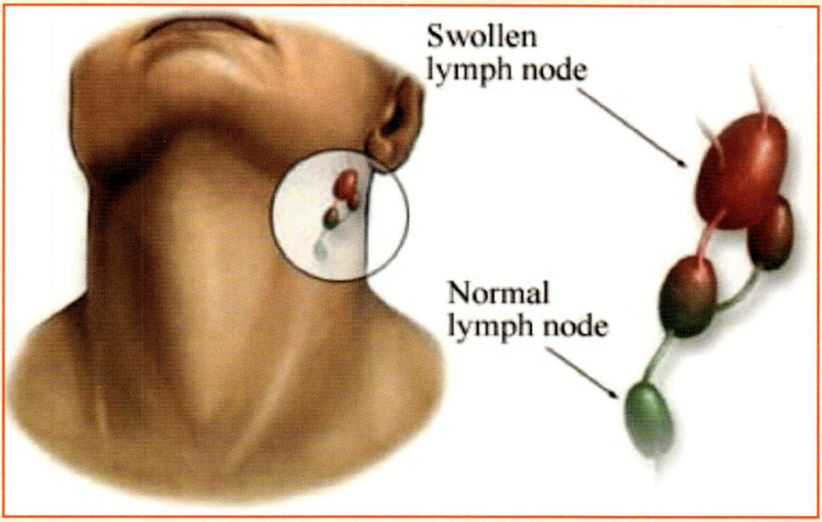

Mongolism

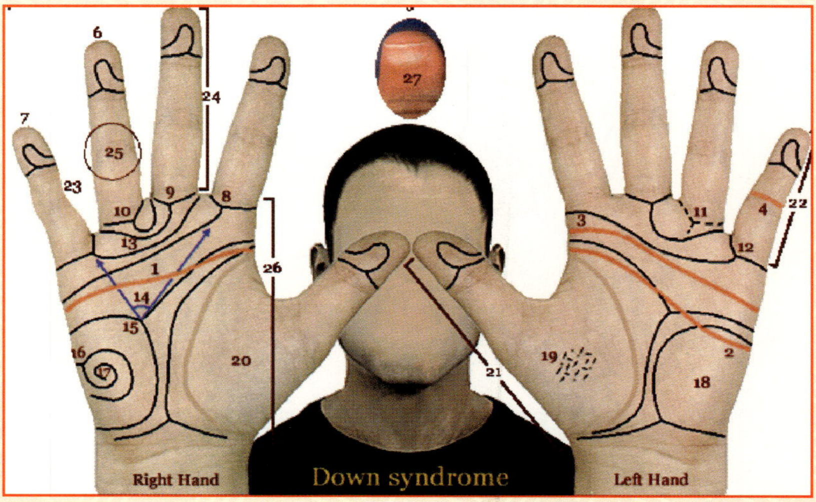

Spastic Diplegia

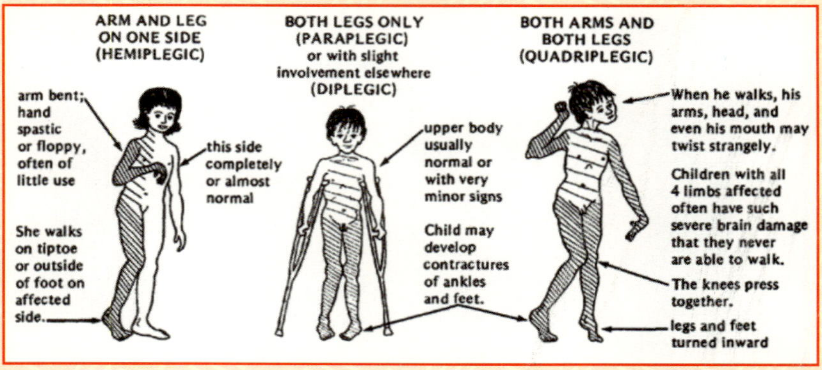

Rickets

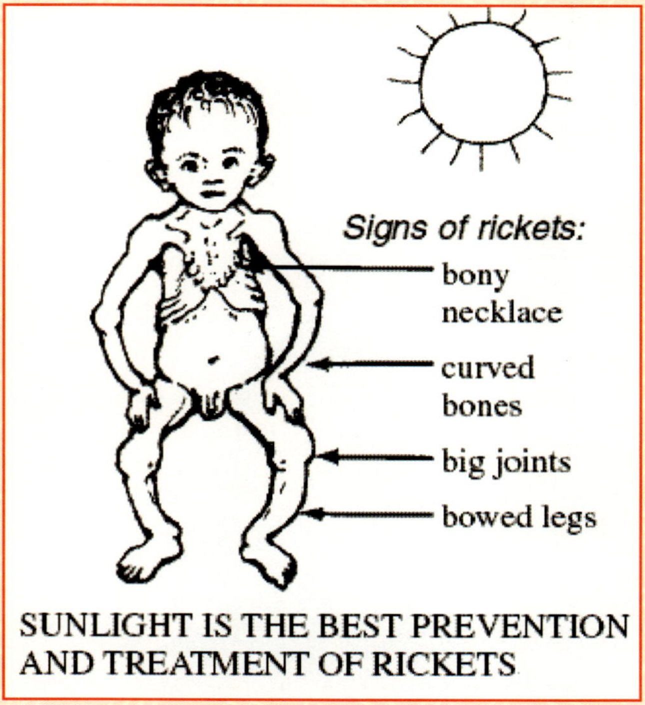

Spastic Diplegia

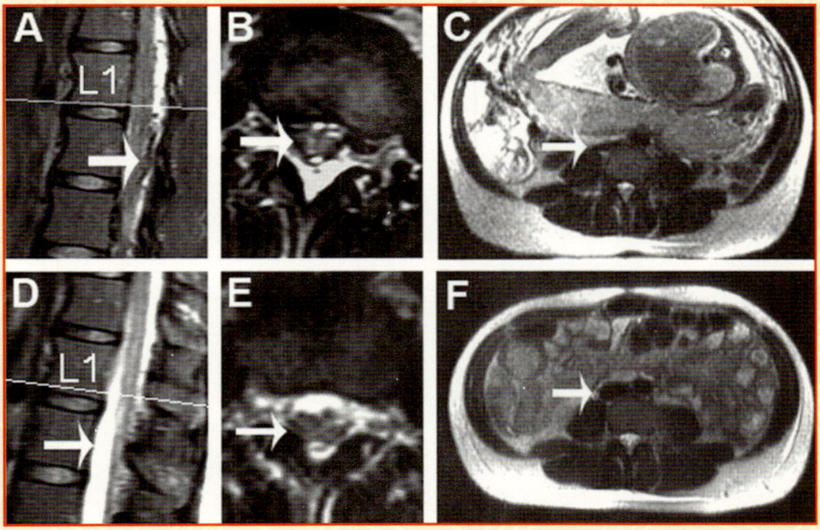

Rheumatoid nodules

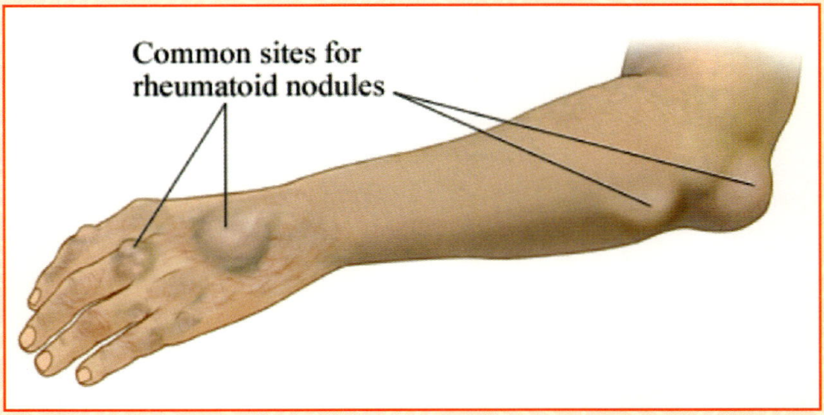

Palpation of cardiac impulse

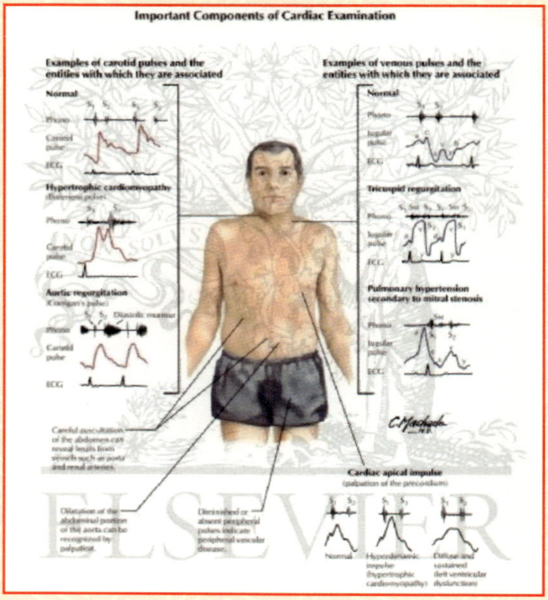

Distended superficial veins

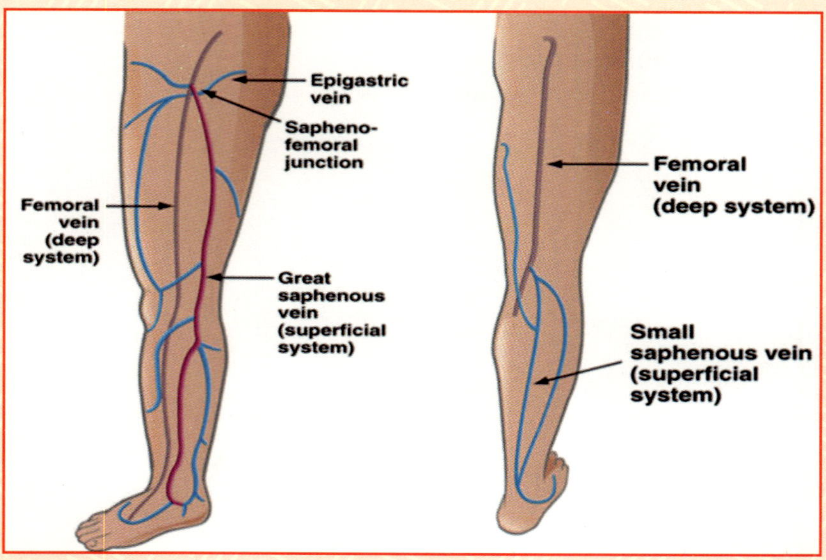

Ascites

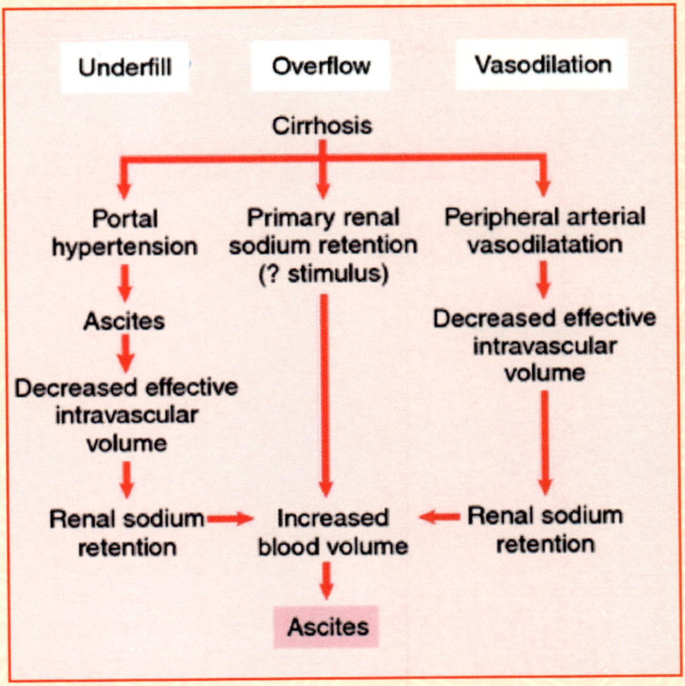

Palpation of kidney

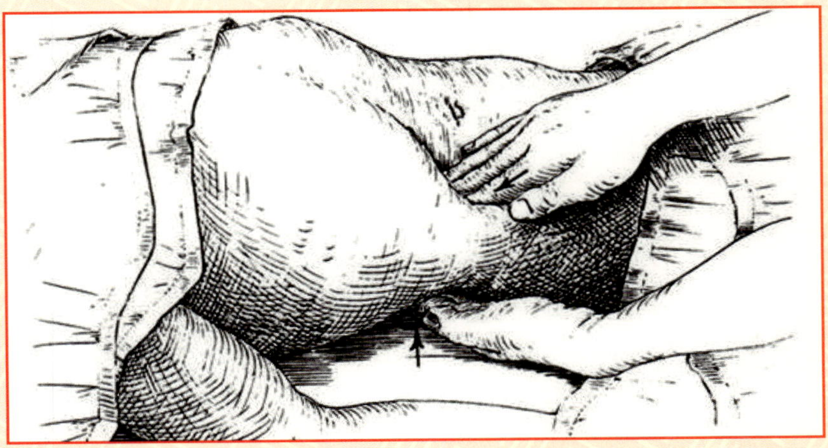

Meningitis

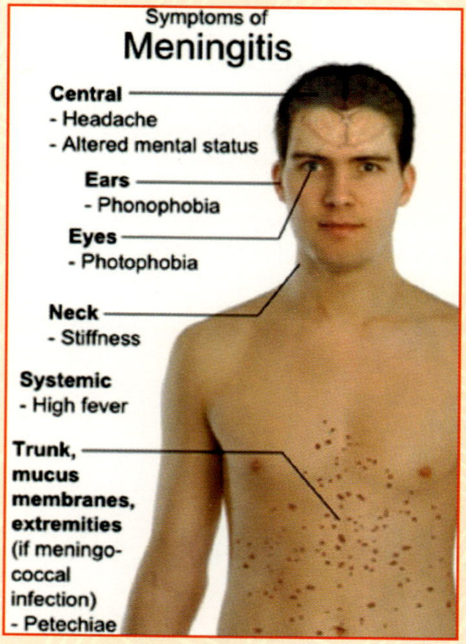

Rheumatoid rash

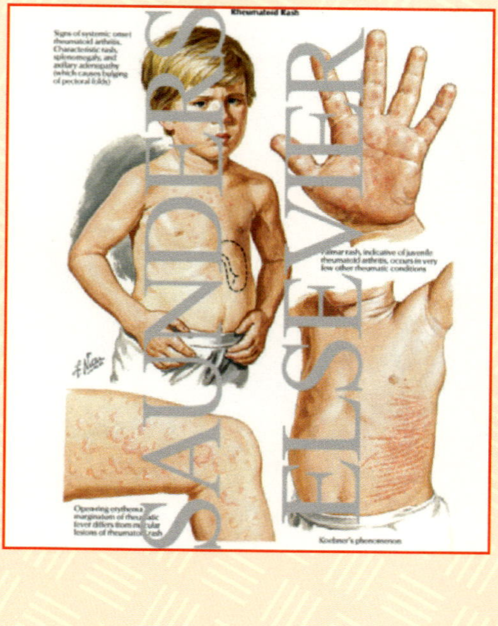

Cretinism

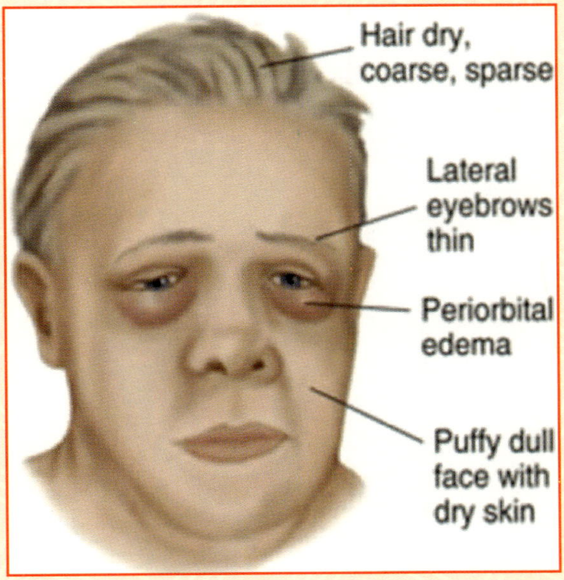

Exophthalmos

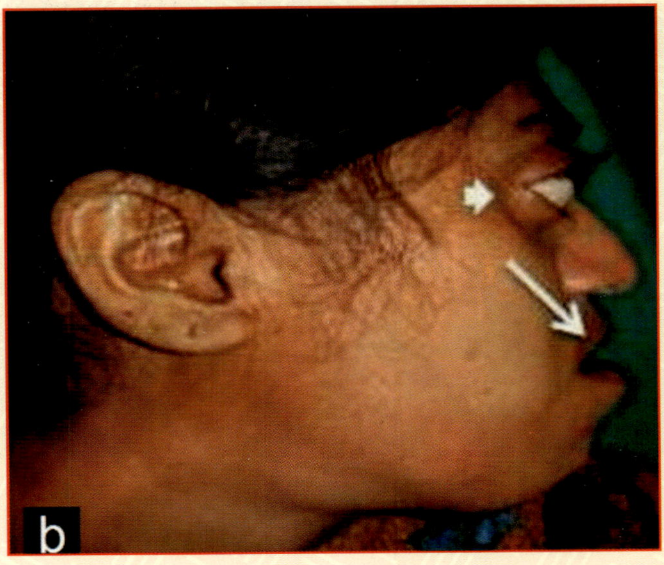

Palpation of abdomen

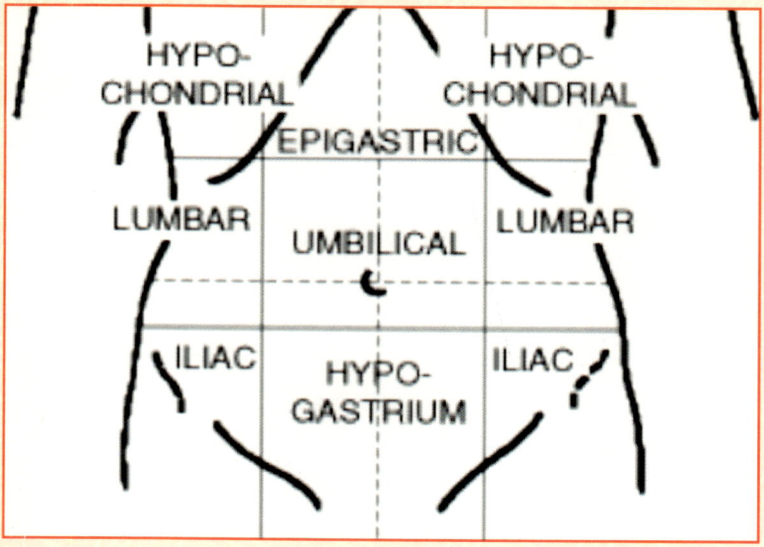

Meuro fibro mitosis

Hemorrhoids

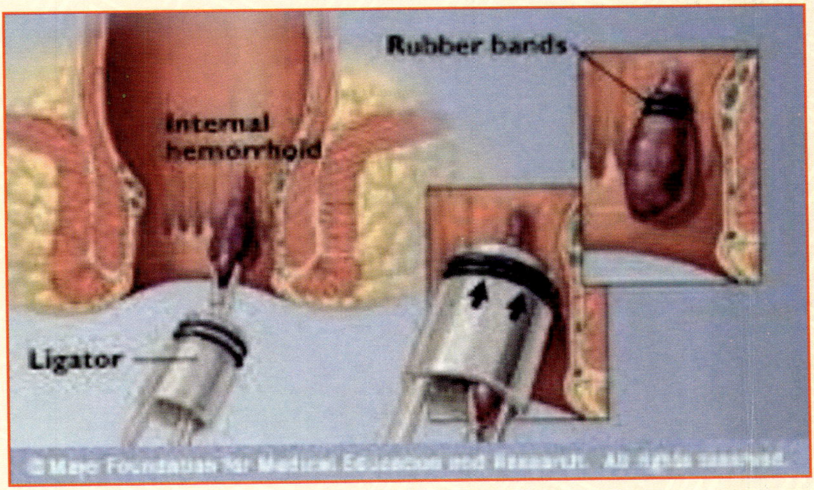

Central vein catheterization

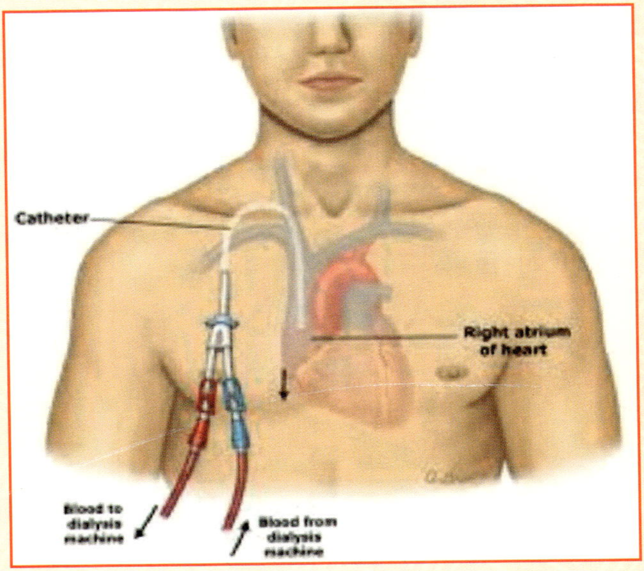

Paraphimosis

Figure 5. Paraphimosis Reduction

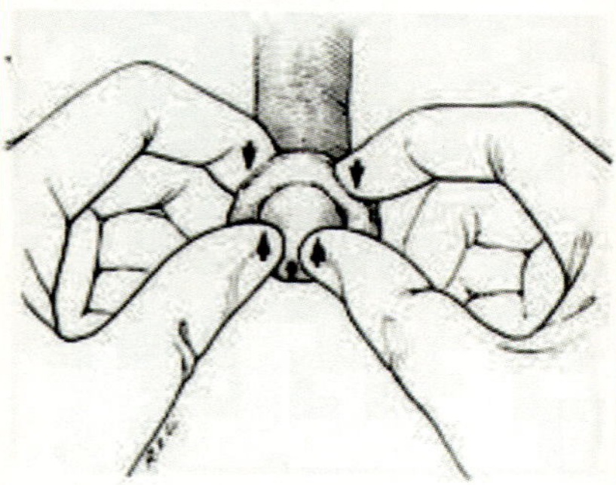

Reprinted with permission from Barone JG, Fleisher MH. Ped Emerg Care 1993;9:5:299. © 1993 Lippincott Williams & Wilkins.

Foleys catheterization

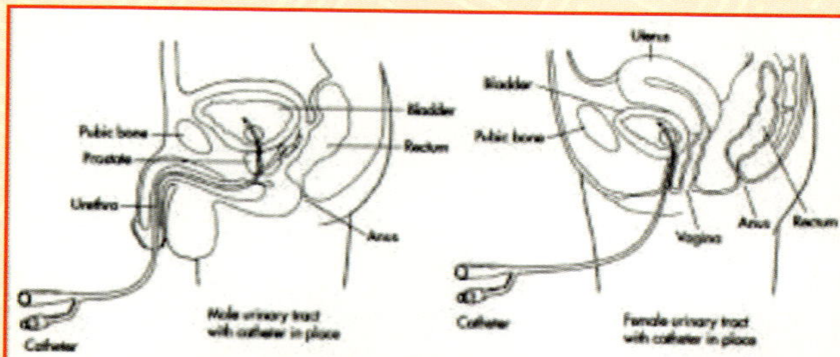

Anorectal abscess

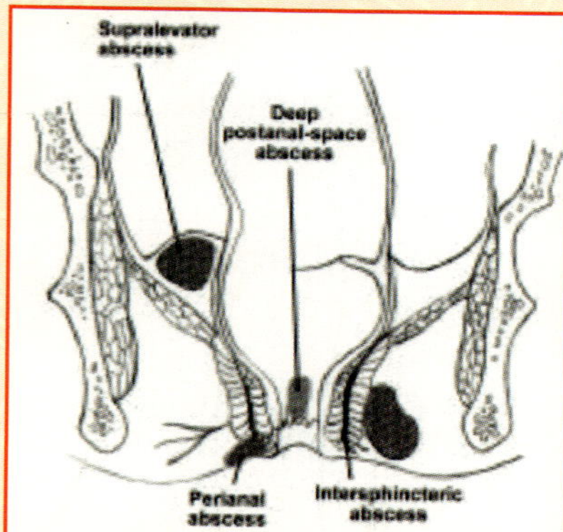

Bronchial spasm

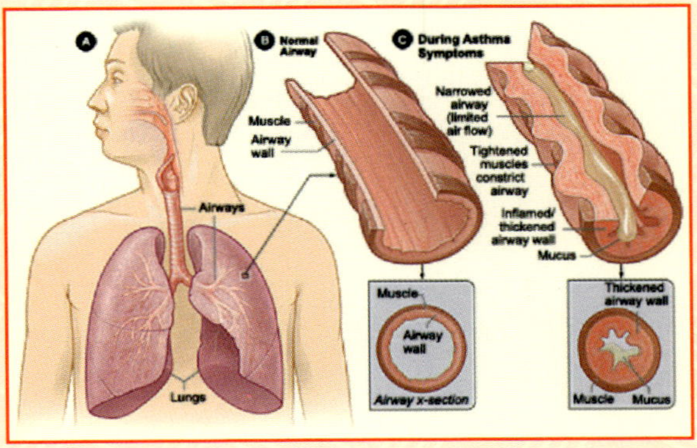

Prominent neck veins

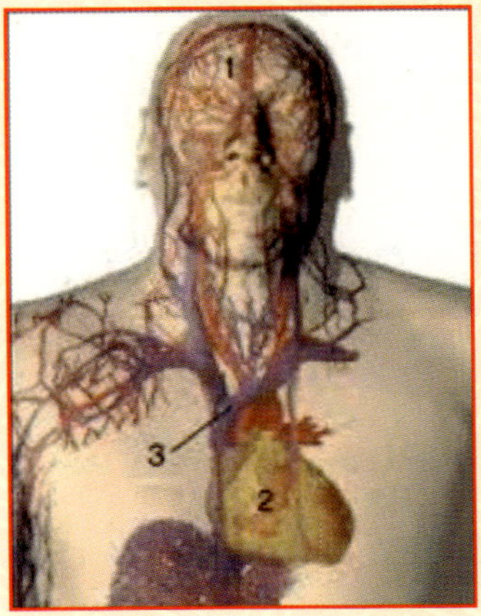

Acromegaly

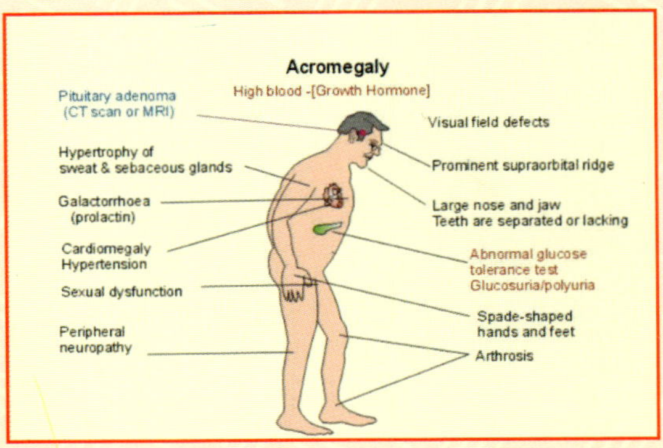

Parkinsonism

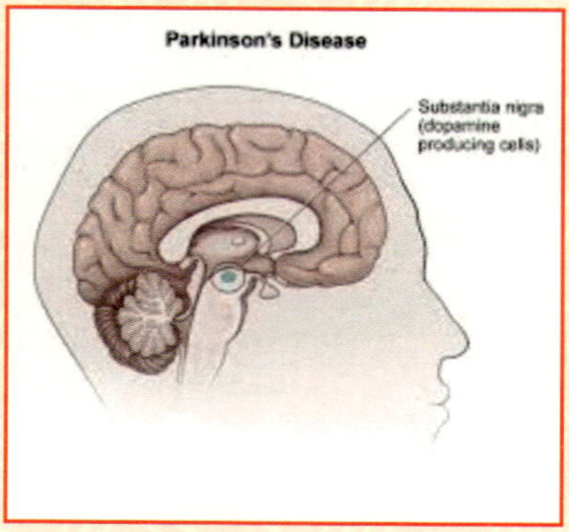

Rheuaatoid arthritis

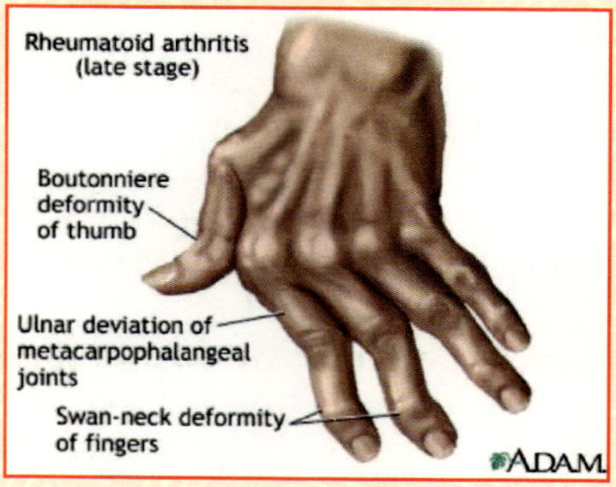

Clubbing of fingers

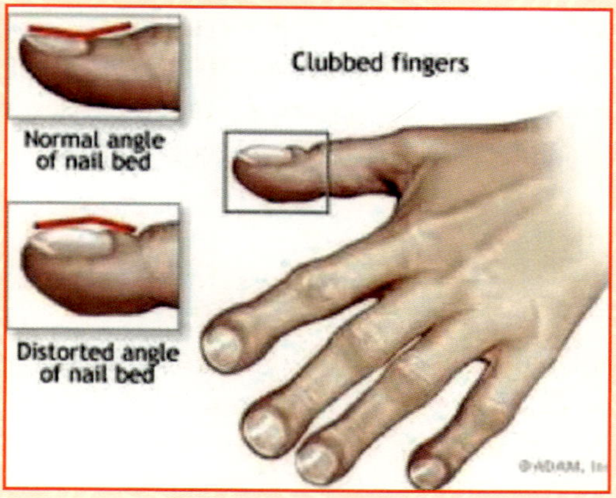

the tip of the proctoscope), the normal anal cushions and the dentate line. The proctoscope is reinserted and the examination repeated with the patient straining downwards. Haemorrhoids are seen as enlargements of the normal anal cushions in the anterior, left lateral and right posterior positions. Internal openings of fistula tracks, anal polyps, fissures and ulceration may also be identified by proctoscopy.

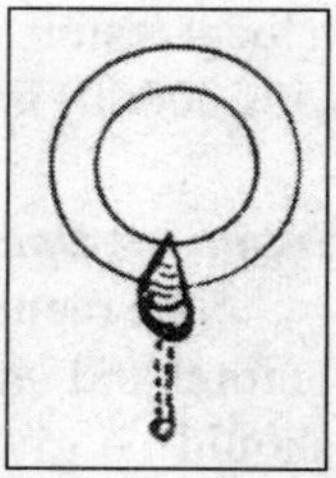

Fig. 2: Facsimile record of the findings in a case of a chronic posterior fissure with a short direct fistula.

Recording of Findings

The results of the anal examination are conveniently recorded on a rubber stamp diagram (Fig. 2). The outer circle represents the anal margin, the inner the anorectal junction. Lesions can be shown graphically and the same system can be used for recording operative procedures. If the circles represent a clock face, the position of any lesion can be given with reference to the mid-line anterior point of 12 o'clock.

Surgical Management of Minor Anorectal Cases

Outpatient Operations

No particular bowel preparation is required. Procedures above the dentate line (e.g. injection or rubber band ligation of haemorrhoids) do not require anaesthesia. Operations below this level do so and local anesthesia is satisfactory for most. For these, the skin should be cleaned with aqueous chlorhexidine or betadine. **Under no circumstances should a spirit-based solution be used.** The left lateral position is most comfortable for both patient and surgeon.

Local Anesthesia

For small perianal lesions local infiltration of about 5 ml of lignocaine (1%) is sufficient. If more extensive anesthesia is required (e.g. for sphincterotomy), 5-10 ml of lignocaine are injected into each ischiorectal fossa using a long spinal needle. This blocks the inferior haemorrhoidal nerves producing relaxation of the lower sphincter and perianal anesthesia. A further 1-2 ml of anesthetic can be placed around a local lesion. Bleeding is reduced if lignocaine containing adrenaline (1: 200000) is used.

Inpatient Operations

The rectum should be emptied by a phosphate enema given 1-2 h beforehand unless the anal lesion is very painful when no preparation should be given. General anesthesia is quick and reliable but some surgeons prefer spinal or caudal block. If either is contraindicated, local anesthesia is sufficient for many procedures. The anal region can be shaved at the start of the operation and the skin prepared as above. Shaving on the ward is not necessary. The lithotomy position is used by most surgeons in this country.

Postoperative Care

Outpatient Operations

A mild laxative should be prescribed. Wounds should be dressed with gauze soaked in Eusol or Milton's (2.5%) solution and overlaid by a gauze pad (20 × 10 cm). The dressing is held in place by disposable underpants or adhesive tape. Over the next few days, this is changed at home twice daily after a bath and the wound is then reviewed in the outpatient department.

Inpatient Operations

General

Normal feeding is resumed on recovery from the anesthetic and mobilization started as soon as possible, depending on the degree of discomfort of the wound. A limited number of opiate injections (e.g. tramadol) should be prescribed and constipating analgesics (e.g. codeine) avoided.

Bowels

After most anal operations, patients should receive an aperient (e.g. cremaffin, 15 ml b.d.) from the first postoperative day until the bowels are open (usually within 3-4 days). A bulk laxative for 1-2 weeks helps to maintain a soft stool. After a pelvic floor repair for incontinence higher doses of aperient (e.g. magnesium sulphate, 20 ml t.d.s.) are given for a few days to produce diarrhoea, thus avoiding straining which might damage the repair. Only occasionally with very extensive wounds, e.g. after some fistula operations, should the bowels be confined. The patient takes a liquid or elemental diet.

Wound

At the end of the operation, a gauze dressing soaked in Eusol solution is laid onto the wound. Packing or drains placed in the anal canal are painful and unnecessary. The dressing is overlaid with a gauze pad which is held in place by a T-bandage. The T-bandage is tied to produce some pressure on the dressing. The dressing is removed after a warm bath on the first postoperative day. Closed wounds, e.g. after sphincterotomy, usually require no more than twice-daily baths at home applying surface gauze dressings for a week.

Large open wounds should be irrigated and dressed with Eusol-soaked gauze. Some large fistula wounds may require redressing under anesthetic on one or two occasions. With deep wounds, the dressing should be tucked into the apex of the cavity with sinus forceps. The wound should not be forcibly packed. During irrigation, the patient lies in the left lateral position on a waterproof sheet draped into a bucket. A reservoir containing normal saline on an infusion stand is connected by tubing to a nozzle. This is introduced into the wound and the flow of liquid controlled by a tap on the nozzle. Debris and pus are washed from the wound in this manner. Irrigations and twice-daily dressings should be continued until the wound is small enough for the patient to be managed at home.

Complications

The common complications after anal operations are bleeding, urinary retention and faecal impaction.

1. Bleeding

Reactionary bleeding occurs during the first few hours postoperatively and the dressing should be checked during this time. Bleeding from a small vessel at a wound edge may be stopped by pressure or by the application of gauze soaked in topical adrenaline solution (1: 1000), a method which can also be applied to rectal wounds via a proctoscope or sigmoidoscope. If local measures fail, the patient should be taken back to the operating theatre to secure haemostasis under direct vision.

Secondary haemorrhage occurs in 2-5% of cases with open wounds, usually on the ninth to tenth postoperative day and can be brisk. The pulse and blood pressure should be monitored and blood taken for cross-matching. The foot of the bed is elevated, the patient sedated and an intravenous infusion started if there is evidence of shock. Local pressure is then applied to the bleeding site. With bleeding from within the anal, canal, this can be achieved by two methods. A large balloon catheter (30°F gauge, 30 ml balloon) is inserted into the rectum and the balloon inflated. Traction is applied to the catheter to bring the balloon against the bleeding site and the catheter is strapped under tension to the thigh. Alternatively, a large rubber tube with a thick coat of paraffin gauze wrapped around it is inserted into the anal canal via a proctoscope. The proctoscope is withdrawn, leaving the tube in place with the gauze surround pressing against the bleeding site. The tube is transfixed with a safety pin on the outside and held in place by gauze dressings and adhesive strapping. It is removed after 24-48 h, after when it is most unusual for bleeding to recur. This method is more reliable since, with the first, the catheter is liable to slip out of the anus. If these measures fail, the patient should be examined under anesthetic and control of bleeding directly established. Nowadays, one can use anal gelsponge which comes in a cylindrical shape. It is inserted in anal canal. Nowadays, reg lag bolule is used. It is drink with water 3-4 hours before the operation.

2. Urinary Retention

Retention is more likely if there is pre-existing bladder outflow obstruction or where the anal wound is large. The patient should be catheterized and the catheter removed after 1-2 days. The advice of all patients above age 60 yrs should be put on Vetlam F Tab daily.

3. Faecal Impaction

Impaction is uncommon if aperients are given, but is a likely sequel to confining the bowels. It often presents as the frequent passage of small amounts of liquid faeces. The diagnosis is made by digital examination per rectum. Olive oil retention enemas and aperients should be given. Occasionally, disimpaction under general anaesthetic is necessary.

Digital Examination

It is unnecessary to perform digital examination in the early postoperative period unless there is an indication, e.g. suspected faecal impaction or bridging of wounds. After haemorrhoidectomy this can be done on the first outpatient visit provided the bowels are working satisfactorily, the aim being to establish that there is no stricture. After fistula operations digital examination should be performed to ensure that bridging of the wound is not taking place. This can be done a few days after the operation to be repeated if necessary at regular intervals (e.g. every two days) until the wound is healing satisfactorily. Analgesics may be necessary shortly after operation.

Major Rectal Cases

Preoperative Preparation

Investigations

These include: Haemoglobin
Blood for cross-match (3-4 units)
Urea and electrolytes
ECG
Chest X-ray
Barium enema examination
±IV urogram if a growth is possibly involving the urinary tract

Bowel Preparation (also used for Colectomy and Hemicolectomy)

It is important to obtain physical clearance of the bowel. Four satisfactory regimens are shown in Table 1. *All are contraindicated in complete intestinal obstruction* and with partial obstruction castor oil should not be used, as there is a danger of perforation as a result of induced gut contraction. One litre of mannitol (10%) by mouth will give a clear bowel in 3-4 h. Fermentation by gut bacteria produces hydrogen and methane and there is a danger of explosion if diathermy is used within the lumen (e.g. endoscopic polypectomy). Whole gut irrigation produces excellent results in the unobstructed bowel. The patient can be admitted as little as one day before operation, A nasogastric tube is passed and the patient placed on a commode. An isotonic electrolyte solution is then delivered down the tube at a rate of 3-4 litres/h. The bowels begin to open after 30 min and washings are clear in 2-3 h. One to two litres are absorbed into the circulation during the procedure and the patient should be carefully observed for signs of fluid overload. Particular care is needed in elderly, cardiac and in already exhausted patients.

Table 1: Mechanical Bowel Preparation Regime

Day before operation	*1*	*2*	*3*	*4*
4,3	ADMISSION Low-residue diet	ADMISSION Low-residue diet	Low-residue diet	Low-residue diet
2	Evacuol 30 ml	Magnesium sulphate, 15 ml t.d.s.		
1	Evacuol 30 ml Oxyphenisatin enema (Veripaque)	Oxyphenisatin enema (Veripaque)	ADMISSION Oral mannitol (10%) 1 litre Oxyphenisatin enema (Veripaque)	ADMISSION Whole gut irrigation
0				

Antibacterial Agents

The postoperative wound infection rate is reduced by intravenous antibacterial agents; giving them for 24 h during and around the time of surgery is as effective as any other regimen. Any combination of agents should include metronidazole (Flagyl) which is active against anaerobic bacteria. Metronidazole (500 mg IV) is given on induction of anesthesia and repeated at 8 and 16 h postoperatively. Many surgeons add an antibiotic such as an aminoglycocide (e.g. tobramycin, gentamicin) or a cephalosporin to metronidazole giving it at the same frequency and for the same duration. Further advances in antibiotic prophylaxis can be expected.

Sexual Function

A high proportion of male patients (20-50%) having rectal operations for carcinoma become impotent or have failure of ejaculation owing to operative damage to autonomic nerves. They should be warned in advance about this possibility. Impotence after intersphincteric excision of the rectum as used in inflammatory bowel disease is very uncommon since pelvic nerves are avoided by the close rectal dissection.

Postoperative Management

The postoperative care of patients having major rectal surgery is similar to that following any abdominal operation. Almost all will have an intravenous infusion and urinary catheter and many an abdominal or perineal drain. A nasogastric tube is not needed routinely since in most cases bowel function recovers satisfactorily without it. Occasionally, a nasogastric tube has to be passed postoperatively, e.g. if paralytic ileus develops.

The First Few Hours

The house-surgeon should check the following:

Pulse (rate, volume)
Blood pressure
Respiration
Urine (output, colour)
Stoma (colour, viability)
Drains (patency, volume drained)
Dressings (blood)

After operation on the rectum, there is often temporary bloodstaining of urine. It is most important to inspect the colour and assess the viability of the stoma. Drains and dressings should be checked for blood loss and soaked dressings should be changed.

The First Few Days

The house-surgeon should attend to the following:

Mobilization
Oral fluids
Urinary catheter
Wounds
Intravenous fluids

The patient should be mobilized and given energetic chest physiotherapy. Recovery of normal bowel motility is indicated by the passage of flatus and the appearance of gut sounds along with a soft, non-distended abdomen.

Oral fluids can then be started and the intravenous infusion removed when oral intake is well established.

The urinary catheter should be left on open drainage for at least 5-6 days until the patient is reasonably mobile. In patients with a large perineal wound or preoperative symptoms of prostatic obstruction, it should be left longer. The catheter is removed in the morning and the patient encouraged to pass urine. If, after several hours, there are symptoms or signs of retention, the catheter should be re-inserted and left for a few more days before withdrawing it again. If retention occurs on the second occasion, a urological opinion should be obtained. The frequent passage of small volumes of urine with an enlarged bladder indicates incomplete emptying and is an indication to re-insert the catheter.

Urinary continence may be disturbed after rectal operations but is usually regained during the first few postoperative weeks. The urologist should advise if symptoms persist.

Perineal Wound

At operation the perineal wound can be left open or closed by primary suture. *Open perineal wound*: The pack or drain is removed at 48 h and the wound is dressed twice daily. It is irrigated and a finger is inserted daily to check for pockets or loculi. The edge of a large gauze dressing is tucked into the wound gently to hold the wound surfaces apart. On no account should small pieces of gauze or cotton wool be used as they may easily become lost within the wound.

Where the posterior vaginal wall has been excised, the perineal wound is in effect open, even if the skin has been sutured. The wound is drained by a suction or corrugated drain brought out through the posterior vaginal wall. This is removed on the second to third day and the skin sutures on the fourteenth day. *Closed perineal wound*: Primary suture is now widely practised, both after intersphincteric excision of the rectum where a small wound is produced and after rectal excision for cancer. It is contraindicated where there has been gross contamination of the wound. Suction drainage is provided by a vacuum drain or sump suction system, the drain being brought out to the side and away from the wound suture line. This should be checked daily to ensure it is not blocked and a note made of the volume of blood draining in the previous 24 h. A satisfactory system using a three-channel sump drain is shown in Fig. 3. The wound can be irrigated by a slow infusion of normal saline down one channel. The drain should be removed on the fifth postoperative day, and the sutures on the tenth to fourteenth day.

The management of the abdominal wound is described.

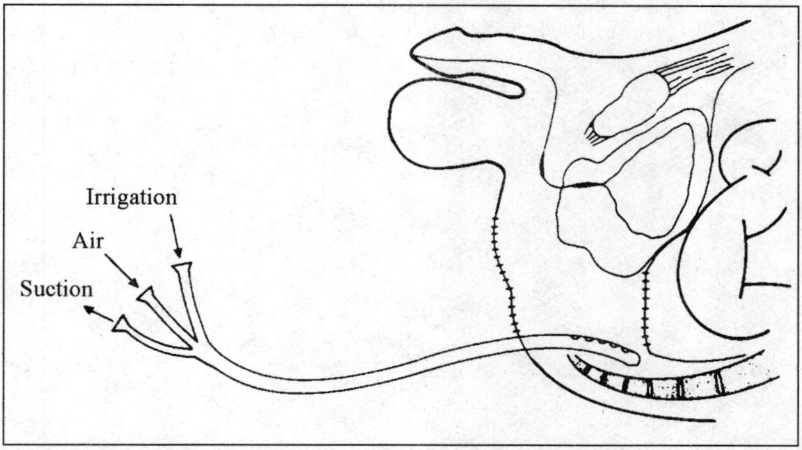

Fig. 3: Three-way catheter providing drainage for the presacral space after excision of the rectum.

Anastomosis

There is no special management of a colorectal or coloanal anastomosis. Early digital examination can be damaging and should be avoided. It may be desirable, however, to know whether the anastomosis has healed satisfactorily. Radiological and digital examination of colorectal anastomoses are unlikely to cause harm beyond the tenth postoperative day. A water-soluble contrast medium (e.g. Gastrografin) should be used. A coloanal anastomosis should be assessed at about two weeks by digital examination and very gentle sigmoidoscopy or proctoscopy.

MANAGEMENT OF STOMAS

Life for patients with intestinal stomas has improved in the past 20 years for two chief reasons. First, the development of disposable adhesive appliances has made daily management easier, and secondly, the availability of specially trained stoma therapists has helped both the practical and psychological difficulties of the patient. The stoma therapist should counsel the patient *before* operation, and her advice and assistance afterwards are invaluable.

There has been a tendency for the number of stomas to fail with the increasing application of sphincter-preserving operations.

Stoma Care Nurses

Stoma care nurses are now employed in many general hospitals and all patients should, if possible, be seen preoperatively. In collaboration with the medical team, she will be able to help with the following:

Preoperative Counselling

Explanation, reassurance and advice to the patient are essential. A stoma is compatible with a normal life. The help of ileostomy or colostomy associations is also available and members are ready to meet patients.

Siting of the Stoma

The success of the stoma depends greatly on its site and this should be decided preoperatively. The stoma should be well away from skin creases, scars, including the umbilicus, and previous surgical wounds and bony prominences. It must be visible to the patient and easily accessible for fitting appliances. The site should be marked preoperatively with waterproof ink with the patient standing and a disposable appliance fitted immediately. The patient can then spend several hours finding out whether the site is satisfactory. He can try sitting, bending, walking, etc. to get the feel of the appliance. An unsatisfactory position can be changed.

Appliances

All stoma appliances consist of a bag and a flange which attaches to the skin surrounding the stoma. These are inseparable in a one-piece appliance but can be detached from each other in a two-piece appliance. With the former, the flange is backed by a non-irritant adhesive and is penetrated in its middle by a hole which fits round the stoma. The hole may be bounded by a polyethylene ring or gasket between bag and flange onto which a belt can be fitted. In some one-piece models, there is a ring of karaya gum on the skin side of the gasket. Bags are available in gasket sizes ranging from 25 to 100 mm diameter. With a two-piece appliance, the separable flange is usually backed by a sheet of Stomahesive (*see below*) in which a hole can be cut with scissors to the size of the stoma. A protruding polythene ring on the flange forms a joint with a slightly larger ring on the bag. The bag can thus be removed without disturbing the flange.

Disposable bags have largely replaced non-disposable appliances made of rubber or latex, but these may be preferred by some patients.

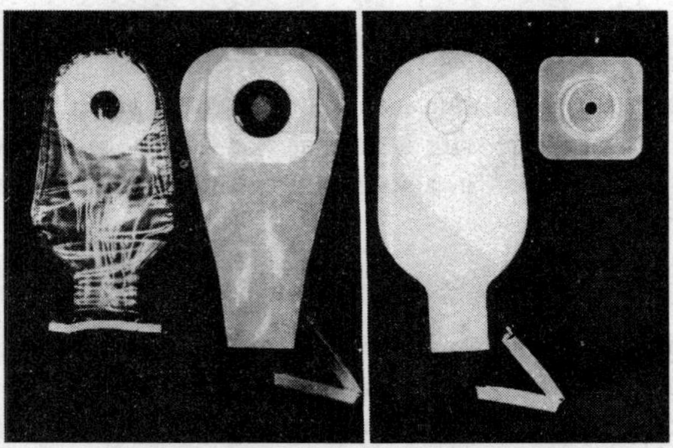

Fig. 1: Draining types of disposable ileostomy bugs, the one on the left sticking directly to the skin and that on the right having a separate adhesive flange.

Fig. 2: Colostomy bags.

Appliances may be drainable or non-drainable, both being available as one-or two-piece units. A drainable appliance (Fig. 1) must be used for an ileostomy where the stool is fluid whereas for a sigmoid colostomy producing solid faeces a non-drainable bag is more suitable (Fig. 2).

Plastic caps with belt attachments or adhesive covers are available for patients who have adopted the natural method of colostomy evacuation or use irrigation.

Accessories

A variety of accessories are available (Fig. 3). Karaya and Stomahesive paste are useful in filling small defects between stoma and flange, especially where there is irregularity of skin contour. Several barrier creams to protect the skin are marketed and deodorants can be obtained. Gas in the bag may cause unsightly bulging or lead to detachment of the flange. It can be released by puncturing the bag with a needle and covering the site with a charcoal filter which allows gas to continue to escape while trapping its odoriferous elements. Adhesive sheeting (Stomahesive (Squibb), Hollister) is incorporated into the flange of some appliances but can also be obtained separately. The sheets are 10-cm square and are made of material consisting of sodium carboxymethyl cellulose polyisobutylene, gelatin and pectin.

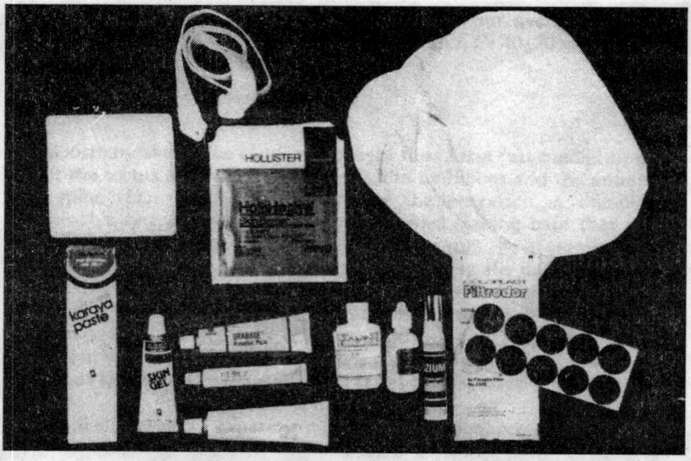

Fig. 3: Accessories for stoma care, including cover bags (top right) to hide disposable bag, waist belt for greater security (top), skin barrier mini-blankets (centre), karaya paste (bottom left) and odour filter (bottom right).

The substance is non-reactive to skin and can stick to moist surfaces; it can be moulded to skin contour and easily cut with scissors.

Ileostomy

An ileostomy may be permanent or temporary. A permanent ileostomy results after proctocolectomy where the anal sphincter mechanism has been removed and is therefore an end ileostomy. A temporary ileostomy is usually fashioned as a loop. Either should be constructed to form a spout about 2-3 cm long to allow the effluent to pass directly into the bag. The postoperative management is similar for both.

Physiology

The daily output is about 500 ml and volumes over 1000 ml are abnormally large. The effluent contains proteolytic enzymes which will digest skin. The electrolyte composition is very variable among different individuals but average concentrations are as follows: Na 110-120 mmol/1, K 6-12 mmol/l, Cl 40-70 mmol/l and HCO 30-40 mmol/1.

Management

A permanent ileostomy should be sited in the right iliac fossa just medial to the outer border of the rectus abdominis, away from the umbilicus and the anterior superior iliac spine (Fig. 4). At the end of the operation, a one-piece translucent drainable bag of the correct size is applied, taking care that it is properly fixed. This may be satisfactory for several days and the absence of any leakage in the early postoperative period gives confidence to the patient.

In the first 1-2 days, the stoma should be inspected through the translucent bag for necrosis, bleeding and retraction. Most ileostomies act within 48 h and for the first few days may produce volumes of over 1000 ml/24 h. This high output gradually settles but water and electrolyte balance must be maintained until it does so. Mucocutaneous sutures (even if absorbable) should be removed after the tenth day.

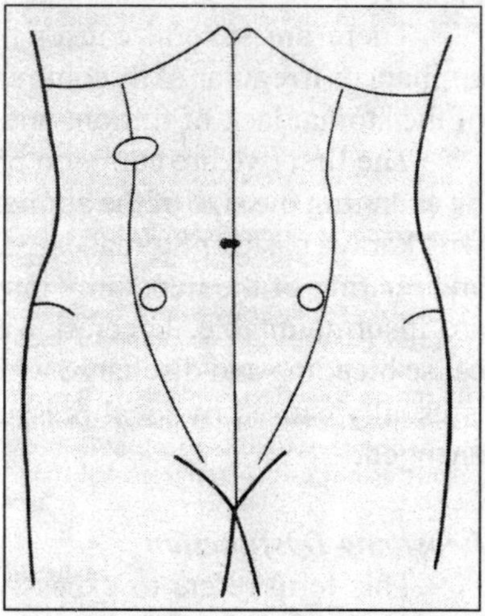

Fig. 4: Sites for ileostomy (lower) just medial to lateral border of rectus muscle, and for a transverse colostomy (upper right).

The patient will discover by experimentation which appliance is most satisfactory. With time, the ileostomy becomes smaller and a smaller appliance will be necessary. The aim is to change the flange as infrequently as possible, and most ileostomists do so every 4-5 days. The bag should be emptied when half-full, since it can detach the flange if it becomes too heavy.

Complications of Ileostomy

Skin Problems

Skin problems may arise from too vigorous cleansing, allergy or contact of effluent with the skin, due either to leakage or to an appliance too large for the stoma. Secondary fungal infection may occur.

Allergy

The skin may be allergic to substances within the adhesive, although this is uncommon. Allergy should be suspected if the area of involved skin corresponds with the area of the appliance in contact. The appliance should be removed, the skin gently cleaned and Stomahesive or a karaya sheet should be placed on the skin before reapplying the bag. Steroid creams may be necessary.

Leakage

There are several causes of leakage, including: poorly fitting appliance; irregular skin contour; retraction of the stoma; ulceration of the stoma; lack of tuition; and lack of manual dexterity.

The first two are common problems which may be solved simply by changing the size of the appliance or overcoming skin irregularities with karaya paste or Stomahesive. Retraction will require refreshioning and resiting of the ileostomy may be necessary if contour difficulties are insurmountable. Ulceration at the mucocutaneous junction may cause bleeding and discharge which can lift the flange from the skin. It is usually caused by local pressure of the appliance which should be changed.

Ileostomy Dysfunction

This term refers to excessive output from the ileostomy which may produce water and electrolyte (especially sodium) depletion and increases the likelihood of calculus formation (renal, biliary). A persistently high output (> 1000 ml/24 h) may be due to: subacute small bowel obstruction; non-obstructing small bowel disease; pancreatic disease; drugs; diet.

Mechanical obstruction may be caused by adhesions, strictures (e.g. ischaemic, Crohn's disease), food bolus or stenosis of the stoma. Non-obstructing small bowel disease includes inflammation (e.g. Crohn's disease) and the short bowel syndrome. Common drugs producing diarrhoea include laxatives and antibiotics, and certain foods, e.g. vegetables especially onions, fruits and alcohol may be responsible. Often, no cause is found when symptomatic treatment should be tried. Bulk laxatives thicken the stool but increase sodium and water output. Codeine, loperamide and diphenoxylate with atropine (Lomotil) may slow transit and reduce volume.

Other Complications

Prolapse occasionally occurs and may require refreshioning. Parastomal hernia is uncommon. Lateral space obstruction, also rare, occurs when small bowel loops pass between the terminal ileum and parietal wall and become obstructed. Many surgeons close this space in an attempt to avoid this complication. Stenosis may be due to ischaemia or recurrent Crohn's disease of the terminal ileum. It may be manageable by dilatation but refreshioning is often necessary.

Colostomy

A colostomy may be permanent or temporary. The two commonest types are: (1) a permanent end colostomy, and (2) a temporary loop colostomy. A permanent colostomy results after excision of the rectum and anal canal, usually for cancer, and is formed by the sigmoid colon. A temporary loop colostomy is used to defunction the distal bowel and is usually sited in the proximal transverse colon or in the sigmoid colon.

Physiology

The effluent from a transverse colon colostomy resembles that from an ileostomy, being fluid and discharging more or less continuously. It contains proteolytic enzymes and can therefore damage skin and excessive output may cause water and electrolyte depletion. A colostomy in the left side of the colon usually produces 1-3 actions of formed faeces/24 h.

Management

The practice of delayed opening of a colostomy has now been superseded by immediate opening at the end of the operation, the edge of the bowel being sutured to the skin directly after (mucocutaneous suture).

Permanent End Colostomy

An end colostomy in the sigmoid colon should be sited in the left iliac fossa about half-way between the umbilicus and anterior superior iliac spine centred just medial to the outer border of the rectus abdominis muscle (Fig. 4). As with an ileostomy, the appliance should be translucent to enable the stoma to be inspected postoperatively for viability and retraction. It should also be drainable as the effluent is usually liquid in the early postoperative period. A viable stoma will bleed when pricked with a needle. Occasionally, some necrosis occurs and its proximal extent can be assessed by introducing a paediatric sigmoidoscope gently into the stoma. If the distal 1-2 cm only are affected the patient should be kept under careful observation. If more is necrotic, revision of the stoma is necessary. Digital examination should not be performed in the early postoperative period. The colostomy usually acts within 3-5 days, producing some flatus before faeces appear. Some oedema of the stoma is common during the first week but this settles spontaneously.

Long-term Management

There are three methods of long-term management.

Natural Method

Occasionally, the colostomy can be relied upon to act at a predictable time each day, often in response to a stimulus such as tea. Between actions a covering such as a plastic cap supported by a belt may be all that is required to maintain cleanliness. Dietary adjustments and antimotility drugs, e.g. codeine, loperamide or Lomotil, may help to establish this method.

Appliance Method

More often, however, the action is not predictable and many patients find a permanent appliance satisfactory. One- or two-piece non-drainable bags are most commonly used, being disposed and changed after each action. One-piece appliances may be applied to a Stomahesive base which stays in place for several days.

Irrigation Method

The distal colon is emptied by irrigation every 24-48 h. Advantages include freedom from an appliance between irrigations, and perhaps some saving in time and cost. Irrigation should start 2-4 weeks postoperatively under the supervision of a stoma therapist. Kits are commercially available (Hollister, Coloplast) including a short plastic cone, and long plastic sleeve backed by an adhesive flange which fits around the stoma. With the cones now available perforation is no longer a hazard. The technique is as follows: the patients sits on the lavatory and connects the cone to a plastic reservoir suspended at the level of his head. The cone is gently inserted into the stoma and 750-1000 ml of water at room temperature are run in from the reservoir. A sleeve is then applied to the stoma and its open end is directed into the lavatory bowl. The colon acts after 10-30 min. The sleeve is then folded and clipped, enabling the patient to walk around carrying on normal activities during which time a little more effluent is evacuated. The sleeve can then be removed, the stoma cleaned and an adhesive stoma seal applied.

Complications

Severe skin problems are less likely than with ileostomy but allergy and maceration by moisture resulting from leakage may occur. The remedies are similar to those given for ileostomy. The commonest late complications are paracolostomy hernia, prolapse and stenosis. Hernia is very common and repair is often followed by recurrence. Usually, however, symptoms are minimal and no specific treatment is required. An abdominal support may be necessary if bulging is causing discomfort. Occasionally, strangulation occurs when operation is obligatory. Stenosis and prolapse may require refashioning of the stoma.

Temporary Loop Colostomy

The site for a sigmoid loop colostomy is identical to that for an end colostomy. A transverse loop colostomy should be made through the rectus abdominis muscle away from the costal margin and the abdominal wound (Fig. 4). The loop is supported by a rod placed through the mesentery adjacent to the bowel.

□

THE PEDIATRIC AIRWAY MANAGEMENT

Adults tend to die cardiac deaths; children tend to die respiratory deaths. **PEARL: The common pathway to cardio-pulmonary collapse in most children is respiratory failure and/or shock.**

Supporting a child's respiratory status often is the deciding factor in saving his or her life. Intubation of a child—essentially the same procedure as in an adult—has some quirks. Tube size depends on the age of the child; use the following formula to estimate it.

$$\text{Tube size (mm)} = 4 + \frac{\text{Child's age}}{4}$$

Children's tubes (up to size 6, about age 5) are uncuffed, because, unlike in an adult, the tightest area of the airway is subglottic. A straight (Miller) laryngoscope blade may be easier to use because a child's

Table 1: Pediatric Immunization Schedule

Age	*Immunizations*
Birth	HBV
2 months	DTP, HbCV, OPV, HBV
4 months	DTP. HbCV, OPV
6 months	DTP, HbCV, HBV
15 months	MMR, HbCV
15-18 months	DTP, OPV
4-6 years	DTP, OPV
4-12 years	MMR
14-16 years	Td

DTP = diphtheria, tetanus, and pertussis vaccine; HbCV = *Haemophilus influenzae* conjugate vaccine; HBV = hepatitis B vaccine; MMR = measles, mumps, and rubella vaccine; OPV = oral polio vaccine; Td = tetanus and diphtheria adult formulation vaccine.

Table 2: Common Pediatric Oral Drug Doses

Generic Name (Brand Name)	*Formulation*	*Dose*
Acetaminophen (Tylenol)	80 mg/0.8 mL 160 mg/5 mL 80-mg chewtab	15 mg/kg q 4 hours
Ibuprofen (Pediaprofen)	100 mg/5 mL	10 mg/kg q 6 hours
Albuterol (Preventil)	2 mg/5 mL	2-5 years: 0.1 mg/kg tid 6-11 years: 2 mg tid 12+ years: 2 mg tid-qid
Prednisone (Pediapred)	5 or 25 mg/5 mL	2 mg/kg/day
Amoxicillin (Amoxil)	125 mg/5 mL 250 mg/5 mL	10 mg/kg tid
Penicillin V potassium (Pen Vee K)	125 mg/5 mL 250 mg/5 mL	10 mg/kg qid
Cephalexin (Keflex)	125 mg/5 mL 250 mg/5 mL	10 mg/kg qid
Trimethoprim-sulfamethoxazole (Bactrim, Septra)	TMP 40 mg and SMX 200 mg/5 mL	Based on TMP as TMP 4 mg/kg bid
Erythromycin-sulfamethoxazole (Pediazole)	200 mg EM and 600 mg SMX/5 mL	By weight: 8 kg: 2.5 mL qid 16 kg: 5 mL qid 24 kg: 7.5 mL qid >45 kg: 10 mL qid
Clarithromycin (Biaxin)	125-250 mg/5 mL	7.5 mg/kg bid
Azithromycin (Zithromax)	100-200 mg/5 mL	10 mg/kg single dose, followed by 5 mg daily for 4 more days

EM = erythromycin; SMX = sulfamethoxazole; TMP = trimethoprim epiglottis is longer, floppier, and more anterior than an adult's. Also, because of a child's smaller size, it's easier to intubate the right mainstem bronchus, so be wary of this and try to avoid passing the tube too deep. The distance from the teeth to the carina can be estimated by the following formula.

$$\text{Distance (cm)} = 12 + \frac{\text{Child's age}}{2}$$

Try not to hyperextend the child's neck because this brings the larynx even more anterior and complicates the intubation. At the end of the endotracheal tube are two black stripes. The first stripe should be passed beyond the vocal cords; leave the second stripe above the cords, which will ensure that the tube is always in place. The hardest part of intubation is ensuring that the tube stays in place—holding it and securing it with tape is essential! If you're having difficulty with intubation, consider doing a digital intubation after visualizing or palpating the epiglottis.

□

ACUTE BREATHLESSNESS

A doctor is often called to see patients in the throes of respiratory distress. Even the examination of such a patient, who is certainly too ill to be questioned much, is fraught with difficulties. He cannot undress himself and attempting to do this for him may make him even more distressed; he is restless; and he grunts and groans frequently, so that inspection and auscultation of the chest are done under very trying conditions. It is true that, as a student, you would probably see little of such a patient. In hospital he would be seen and diagnosed on admission by the resident officer; students would be warned not to examine him in the acute stage lest the exertion which that would entail should jeopardize his condition.

General observation of the patient's behaviour and breathing is at least as important in diagnosis as a more systematic examination of the body. You can, therefore, begin to train yourself by watching such patients, and, in preparation for the day when you yourself will be faced with the urgent problem of diagnosis, rehearse the methodical steps you will then have to take in their examination. Ideally, to find out the cause of acute breathlessness it is necessary to obtain as full a history as possible from the patient or his relative, and to follow this with a most thorough examination of the chest, cardiovascular system, and the rest of the body. Overshadowing this ideal, however, lies the fact that unnecessary exertions are harmful for the patient; it would be absurd to test the muscular power and co-ordination of his arms after examination of his chest had already revealed the presence of heart failure. In practice, therefore, the patient is both questioned and examined with a view to establishing a practical diagnosis as soon as possible, the finding of any one clue possibly altering the course of the subsequent examination. Always, as in most acute disease, the general observation of the patient and his behaviour is vital. A clear mind, a knowledge of probabilities, and the capacity to be certain about physical signs will be your chief weapons.

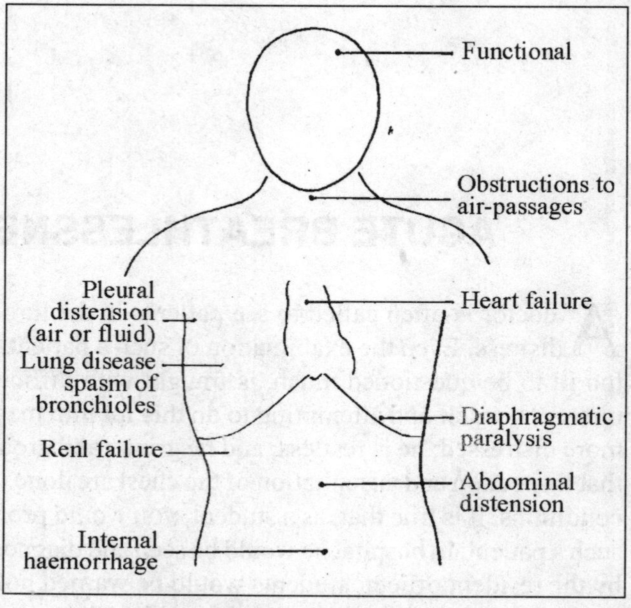

Fig. 1: Some causes of dyspnoea.

If you look at the diagram (Fig. 1) you will see illustrated some of the chief causes of respiratory distress. The dyspnoea in each case is produced by varying mechanisms, sometimes a mixture of several.

(a) **Mechanical**—An impediment to air entry and flow within the lungs, which reduces the vital capacity, and is produced by obstructions to air-passages, spasm of bronchioles, paralysis of muscles of respiration, or loss of lung elasticity (emphysema).

(b) **Chemical**—Cerebral anoxaemia such as occurs after severe haemorrhage. Acidosis, as in renal failure.

(c) **Reflex**—Disturbances in the pulmonary circulation which produce an exaggerated vagal respiratory reflex, as in heart failure and pulmonary embolism.

(d) **Functional**—Anxiety in psychological disturbances, which causes an interference with the normal respiratory rhythm.

Scheme of Examination

History—You may not be able to obtain a full history from such a very ill and distressed patient, and the relatives will probably be vague about details. But in making your inquiry, try to determine a few essential facts. Particularly important is the knowledge that the attack of dyspnoea is one of the following:

(a) A new event never experienced by the patient before.
(b) The worst of a series of attacks similar to the one from which the patient is suffering.
(c) The culmination of a gradually increasing dyspnoea.

The natural history of certain diseases is such that they are much more likely to fall into one or other of these categories. For example, the subject of emphysema or mitral stenosis is likely to complain of *gradually increasing breathlessness* culminating in the acute attack observed. A *sudden attack* of breathlessness would suggest respiratory paralysis, pneumonia, or oedema of the glottis, whereas *repeated attacks* would lead you to think of asthma, paroxysmal rapid heart action, or hypertensive heart failure. Find out as much as you can about the onset of the breathlessness, whether it was sudden, slow, or insidious, and whether it was brought on by any factor such as exertion, trauma, or an infection.

If the patient complains of pain, inquire about its character; and severity, its position, duration, and relation to respiration.

Inquire about the patient's previous health, his occupation, his working capacity, and his previous illnesses.

You may not be able to obtain as much information as this, but try to. After making sure of the essential points, you can postpone the taking of more detailed history and proceed to examine the patient without worrying him about things he is too ill to remember.

Colour—Pallor, associated with breathlessness, suggests some disease which by virtue of great pain or blood-loss causes a state of shock (coronary thrombosis or haemothorax), Cyanosis is often most intense in conditions which prevent the proper ventilation of the alveoli in the lungs, but also occurs in lung infections and heart failure (owing to a mixture of various factors). Never decide that a patient is cyanosed after seeing him in a poor light. Blue venules on the cheeks do not mean cyanosis.

Bearing—The patient may be alert and anxious, confused and apathetic, or even comatose. Pay particular attention to his general condition and bearing, as these will affect the prognosis as well as the diagnosis.

Character of Respirations—Count the respiratory rate, note the depth of the respirations, and watch for irregularities in the depth and rate of respiration such as Cheyne-Stokes' breathing (periods of apnoea followed by hyperpnoea). The respirations may be sighing or hissing in character, as in 'chemical dyspnoea'; or they may be quick, short, sharp, and accompanied by grunting, as in 'reflex dyspnoea'. Watch the patient's face for signs of pain at any phase of respiration.

Inspiratory or Expiratory Dyspnoea?—You may notice inspiratory difficulty and an audible stridor in inspiration, or, on the other hand, you may find the patient struggling to expire, his efforts being rewarded by a feeble wheeze rather than a good blow out. Look carefully at the chest to see in which position it tends to be fixed, the over-expanded position or the collapsed position. When the patient breathes, look at the intercostal muscles to see whether they are sucked in on inspiration or even completely paralysed; and look at the upper abdomen to see whether the epigastrium is pushed out on inspiration as it should be by an active diaphragm, or whether it is sucked in on one side or the other, by the uplift of a paralysed diaphragm. Look at the root of the neck; inspiratory obstruction leads to increased negative pressure within the thorax and sucking in of the tissues above the clavicle at each 'inspiration.'

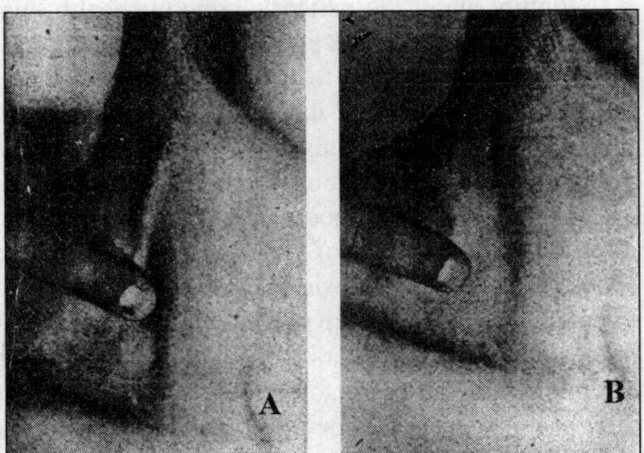

Fig. 2: Emptying of neck veins. A. Finger obstructing external jugular vein; B. Vein empties when finger removed.

It is a strange fact that even though a patient's chief difficulty is to *expire,* he will, in response to the feeling of breathlessness which this provokes, attempt to *inspire* even more forcibly than before. Thus, a patient with asthma and spasm of his bronchioles will attempt to expand his chest even further by contracting the accessory muscles of respiration—the shoulder-girdle and neck muscles—at each inspiration.

Inspection and Palpation of the Mouth and Neck—Look at the lips; herpes simplex often accompanies inflammatory conditions of the lungs. Smell the breath and inspect the tongue. Frothy fluid in the mouth or throat may be found in patients with pulmonary oedema. Take the temperature, always remembering when you read the result that absence of pyrexia, especially in very old or very young people, does not exclude inflammatory conditions. While the thermometer is in the patient's mouth, look carefully at his neck: if it is at all possible, let it be in a good light. If the patient is thin enough for you to see his external jugular vein, place the tip of your forefinger on its lowest visible part so that it fills from above (Fig. 2A). Remove your finger, and if the vein empties well into the great vessels below you can safely say that there is no venous distension in the neck (Fig. 2B). The importance of this manoeuvre lies in the fact that it is easy to be deceived by a visible vein into saying that it is distended, whereas, when your finger obstructs its lowest part, you will see at once that not only is it capable of much greater distension, but it empties freely when you remove your finger. If the veins are truly distended, gauge the vertical distance above the sternal notch to which the level of distension rises.

Examine both sides of the neck for enlarged glands or pulsatile masses, and determine the position of the trachea. Look at the fingers while feeling the pulse. The presence of finger clubbing suggests some long-standing pulmonary disease leading up to the attack of dyspnoea.

Examination of the Chest and Heart—Inspection, as always, is of paramount importance. A fixed, rigid, barrel-shaped chest suggests that bronchial spasm complicating bronchitis and emphysema may be the cause of the patient's breathlessness (Fig. 3), but the presence of such a chest deformity, so common in the general population, should not make you exclude other diseases from your mind. Look for bulging of the intercostal spaces and diminished movement on one side, which would suggest air or fluid in a pleural cavity, and look for generalized or local inspiratory in drawing of the intercostal spaces which would suggest laryngeal obstruction or collapse of a lung.

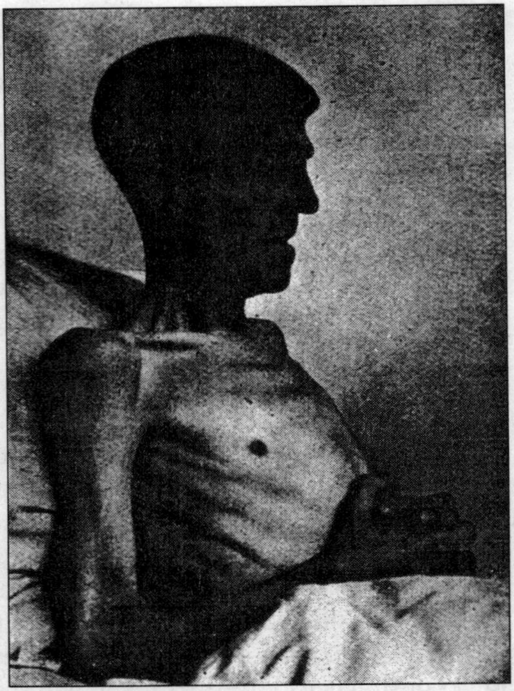

Fig. 3: Bronchial spasm, chronic bronchitis, and emphysema.

Determine the position of the apex beat, count the cardiac rate, and note the exact abnormalities of cardiac rhythm if such are present. If irregularity of rhythm is present, has that irregularity a rhythm of its own or is it totally irregular, as in auricular fibrillation? Compare the cardiac rate and rhythm with the pulse-rate and rhythm, noting at the same time any abnormalities of the pulse wave itself. If tachycardia is present, make several observations of the cardiac rate to see whether it varies from moment to moment. Thoroughly palpate the precordia and then percuss out the cardiac outline. Never forget to percuss the right border of the heart if the apex beat is found to the left of its normal position; otherwise you may think a heart is enlarged when in reality it is only displaced to the left by some pulmonary condition—a mistake which might have serious consequences. Nevertheless, such mistakes are often made through carelessness and failure to visualize the organs beneath the chest wall.

When auscultating the heart, listen carefully to the heart-sounds themselves, asking yourself if they are as loud as they should be, if the first sound is louder than the second sound, as it should be at the apex, and if there are any extra sounds producing a triple rhythm.

Palpate, percuss, and auscultate over the lung fields at the front of the chest. If adventitious sounds are present, determine whether they are heard in inspiration or expiration, and whether they are generalized or confined to one area.

Sit the patient forward, getting him to clasp his hands around his bent knees. If he is very ill, you must get someone to hold him; a bed table or pillow for him to lean forward upon may be very useful. First look for oedema over the sacral region; this may not be obvious, so press gently with a finger over the sacrum for a few seconds and then stroke the area which has been pressed to see if you have left a depression there. Look at the movements of the lower chest from above so that you can see the full posterior curve of the ribs, and test the relative expansion of the two sides by the method shown in Fig. 3. Percuss the back of the chest lightly at first, to detect slight impairments of resonance, and then more firmly towards the bases to define exactly the lower limits of the lung resonance on each side. Auscultate over the back of the chest with some care and elicit vocal resonance over the bases as a routine step, since aegophony in that region may be the only sign of a small pleural effusion.

The Abdomen—Inspect and palpate it. Gross abdominal distension may itself cause severe dyspnoea. Always feel carefully for enlargement or tenderness of the liver, since this is such a valuable sign of congestive heart failure.

The Blood-pressure—When taking the blood-pressure, let the column of mercury drop very slowly past the point at which the first sounds come through. If the rhythm is regular and yet you find that half of the heart-sounds come through at a greater pressure than the rest, you are observing an alternating pulse (pulsus alternans), which is a very important sign, of heart failure caused by the inability of the ventricle to beat with equal force at each systole.

The Sputum—Always try to look at the sputum. Anyone with severe breathlessness is liable to cough. A light frothy sputum suggests pulmonary oedema; if the froth is tinged pink, blood as well as plasma has exuded into the alveoli to discolour the oedema fluid. Scanty, sticky, mucoid sputum is coughed up by asthmatics, whereas those with bronchitis often bring up a purulent or mucopurulent sputum. The sputum of a patient with pneumonia is often scanty, purulent, and rusty-coloured, due to the presence of altered blood.

The Urine—Pink urine, due to a heavy concentration of urates, is often passed by patients with heart failure. Slight or moderate albuminuria also often occurs in patients suffering from acute respiratory distress, and should not be regarded as indicating renal disease. Pale urine, of low specific gravity, on the other hand, passed by one in such a condition is very suggestive of renal failure.

C.N.S—If there is any indication of respiratory paralysis, the nervous system must be examined.

Summary

Consider the possible causes of acute breathlessness.

Try to find whether your patient's acute breathlessness is a new event, one of a series of similar attacks, or the culmination of gradually increasing dyspnoea.

Study the patient's colour, bearing, and respiratory activity.

Look at his mouth, neck, and fingers.

Make a routine examination of the chest and heart, sitting the patient up only once to examine his back, and making certain to look for lumbar oedema at this time.

Find out all you can about any abnormalities of cardiac rhythm and take the blood-pressure.

Examine the abdomen, the sputum, and the urine. Examine the C.N.S. if there is respiratory paralysis.

Oxygen can be delivered in the following ways:

1. **Face Mask:** Oxygen can be given by face mask. There mask as disposable nowadays. The tube is connected to oxygen cylinder or a central oxygen delivery line 2-5 litre per minute oxygen can be given with it. The flow of oxygen can be controlled with the flow meter which is attached with the cylinder.
2. **Red Rubber Catheter:** Use a sterile catheter and check if that it is patent lubricate distal 4" the catheter and insert it in nostril and atleast 4"-6" in the nostril. So that the catheter lies in the Nasopharynx and oxygen is delivered in the nasopharynx. This can also be give 2-5 litres per minute.

Nasal Prongs: Use nasal prongs in both nostril and give O_2 2-5 litres/minute.

□

FITS

Very frequently, patients consult a doctor because of attacks in which they lose consciousness. These attacks may be called by various fanciful names—'black-outs', 'faints', 'queer turns', 'coming all over queer'—and only rarely 'fits'. Diagnosis has often to be based on the story of a relative, for only rarely does the doctor himself witness an attack. For this reason you must pay even more attention than usual to the history, taking care to separate the important details from the irrelevancies.

If the description obtained is vague it is worth while giving the patient or relative a short questionnaire, embodying the essential inquiries to enable you to make a diagnosis, and which should be answered after the next attack.

Both your history-taking and your examination are based on probabilities, which cannot be disentangled from the problem of differential diagnosis. A good way in which to start is to make sure you know the characteristics which enable you to recognize a major or a minor epileptiform attack.

The first question you must attempt to answer is: *Is the attack a genuine 'fit' or 'convulsion'*?

Major Epileptic Attacks

A 'Jacksonian attack' starts by localized twitching of one group of muscles, with a definite sequence of progression to other muscles. The site at which it commences indicates irritation Of the part of the cerebral cortex which controls movements in that area.

As a rule, the common major epileptiform attack proceeds as follows:—

1. The Aura—An adult often recognizes that a fit is about to occur, because of a preliminary sensation or aura which tends to be constant for the individual. It may take the form of numbness or tingling in a limb, or giddiness, or a characteristic flavour, smell, or noise, or flashes of light or complete visual hallucinations. It is extremely brief, lasting only a few seconds as a rule.

The aura is quickly succeeded by the next stage.

2. The Tonic Stage—This may be immediately preceded by a cry, either of conscious terror, or the unearthly sound produced by inspiratory spasm drawing air over the vocal cords before they, too, go into spasm.

The patient falls to the ground, wherever he may be, and the voluntary muscles may be seen and felt in tonic contraction. The face sets rigidly with firmly closed jaws, the eyes turn up and out, the arms are flexed with the fists clenched, and the legs are stiffly extended. Since respiration has ceased, cyanosis quickly develops.

The duration of this stage is usually up to half a minute.

3. The Clonic Stage—The muscles alternately relax and contract, so that whole limbs may flex and extend or the body move violently. The intensity of the movements tends to increase quickly, then more slowly to diminish. While the jaws are alternately clenching and unclenching, the tongue may be extended and bitten. The patient may 'foam at the mouth' because saliva is extruded by the movements of the jaws. The involuntary passage of urine, and more rarely of fæces, may occur.

This stage may last from a few seconds to one or two minutes.

4. The Sleepy Stage—As a rule, the patient passes into a stage of apparently natural sleep which lasts some hours, or he may merely feel sleepy, or complain of headache, or appear dazed and unreceptive. Occasionally, 'post-epileptic automatism' may occur, in which he may undress or behave viciously or queerly, without apparent volition or recollection.

In most cases, all the deep reflexes are temporarily abolished and the plantar responses are extensor. These signs are of great importance as confirmatory evidence.

Minor Epileptiform Attacks

A minor epileptic attack is essentially a sudden break of a few moments in the continuity of consciousness. It may or may not be noticed by the patient himself. Without warning, the patient becomes suddenly still, though he does not fall. His expression is Vacant, his face pale, and his eyes seem fixed. After a few moments he may proceed with what he was doing previously, apparently oblivious to what has occurred, though sometimes he may be confused or hysterical for a 'short time'.

Other Conditions

Fits and 'fainting' occur mainly in two main groups of conditions—*cardiovascular* and *cerebral.* Let us consider some common conditions which resemble epileptiform attacks, to try to bring out the important points in which they differ. Without this preliminary knowledge it is impossible to work out a rational scheme of history-taking or examination.

1. Fainting (Syncope)—This may be due to postural or nervous causes, anaemia, or severe heart disease (e.g. aortic incompetence). You should remember that: (a) Fainting does not occur in a patient who is lying down; (b) Profuse sweating is constant; (c) Pallor is constant; (d) Nausea and vomiting frequently follow; (e) Occasionally there are clonic movements, but they are never more than a mild twitching, and tongue-biting does not occur.

All these points can be elicited from the history. In addition, if you see the patient during an attack you will—observe that the pulse becomes very slow and may be so weak as to be imperceptible.

2. Stokes-Adams Attacks—Repeated 'Stokes-Adams attacks' almost always develop on a basis of chronic heart-block. Momentary loss of consciousness or major epileptiform attacks may occur, with cyanosis and convulsive movements. Sweating, tongue-biting, and incontinence of urine very rarely occur. The main diagnostic feature is extreme slowness or absence of the pulse, a finding which should be confirmed by auscultation of the heart.

3. Hysterical Attacks—The keystone of differential diagnosis is that an hysterical attack simulates the convulsive but not the other features of epilepsy. There may be violent movements, but there is no cyanosis, tongue-biting, or involuntary micturition. During the attack the eyelids may be forcibly closed and tenaciously resist opening. A preceding aura and subsequent sleepy stage are absent. The reflexes remain unaffected throughout. Hysterical attacks are often brought about in dramatic circumstances, frequently in the doctor's presence, and between attacks the patient's personality may provide clues as to the condition.

4. Feigned Fits—These occur almost exclusively in unwilling Service personnel. To add verisimilitude to an artistic performance the patient may bite his tongue deliberately, foam at the mouth by dint of chewing soap, and even ungratefully soil the trousers temporarily.

5. Meniere's Syndrome—Momentary collapse and unconsciousness may occur in this condition, but they are preceded by a buzzing noise in the ears and intense giddiness, and vomiting is common. There are no convulsions.

6. Intracranial Conditions—Disturbances of brain function may be accompanied by fits. Some of the conditions causing such a disturbance are: asphyxia, trauma, neoplasm, meningitis, encephalitis, vascular disease (as with hypertension), syphilis. Uraemia may also give rise to convulsions. Such 'secondary' epilepsy is usually indistinguishable from 'idio-pathic' epilepsy. An important point in differentiation from cardiovascular causes is that the pulse remains strong in all these intracranial conditions. Examination of the patient, and particularly the central nervous system, may reveal the underlying condition.

Infants and Young Children

For some unknown reason fits are relatively commoner in early life. Most of the causes already described in the case of adults apply also to young children, but some others deserve special mention.

1. Fevers—At the start of any feverish illness a child may throw a fit or a series of fits. This group of causes probably accounts for more fits than all other causes together in the first few years of life. The fits fall into the group of major epileptiform attacks. Your first task is, therefore, to attempt to demonstrate an underlying inflammatory lesion such as tonsillitis, pneumonia, otitis media, or cerebrospinal fever.

2. Brain Damage—In the first few weeks of life fits, of the major epileptiform type, are usually due to birth trauma.

3. Hypocalcemia—Rickety children, generally between the ages of 6 and 16 months, with a low blood-calcium, may develop fits which are indistinguishable from epilepsy. Only in very severe cases do signs of tetany such as carpopedal spasms and laryngospasm, also become evident.

4. Pyknolepsy—In this condition, a large number of minor epileptic attacks occur in children who are otherwise healthy. A single attack is indistinguishable from 'petit mal', but the tendency to mental 'degeneration which may accompany frequent attacks of true petit mal does not occur.

5. Breath-holding—This is seen in uncontrollable young children. Breathing suddenly stops, usually after a bout of screaming, the body becomes rigid, and cyanosis develops. In a severe case, the child loses consciousness and may twitch convulsively before finally becoming pale and relaxed.

6. Masturbation—The flushed face and fixed, staring expression associated with the act of masturbation, and the pallor, exhaustion, and sleepiness manifest afterwards, may suggest epilepsy in infancy. It is unusual for the doctor to be able to observe an attack, but the thighs and genitalia may show evidence of friction, and sometimes the child is mentally retarded or neurotic.

Diagnosis

We have now considered the important, commoner causes of fits and similar attacks. Any individual case must be considered from two aspects: (a) *During the attack*—what type of attack is it?—epileptiform or otherwise; (b) *Between the attacks*—what is the cause of the attack?

(a) **During the Attack**—Details obtained from the history may, of necessity, have to replace those obtained by your own direct observation. The information you should seek may be set out: as a series of questions.

1. Warning of attack? If so, what sensation and in what area of the body?
2. Onset of attack—sudden or gradual? Was there a localized twitching which became widespread?
3. Circumstances of onset—lying down or standing?
4. Presence of convulsions? Type and distribution.

5. Tongue-biting or other injury?
6. Incontinence of urine or faeces?
7. Colour of patient during attack? Pale, cyanosed, or plethoric.
8. Perspiration?
9. Pulse-rate and tension?
10. Duration of attack?
11. Sequelae of attack? Sleepiness, headaches, automatism.

(b) **Between Attacks**—Your aim is, in essence, to determine the *cause* of the attacks, having already obtained a description of the type of attacks.

1. *Personality*—Try to assess the patient's personality. The patient who has suffered from idiopathic epilepsy for years may have a peculiar, hang-dog mentality, some part of which may be due to persistent drug-taking. Mental deterioration, which may become apparent in epilepsy, occurs also in general paralysis of the insane or slow-growing intracranial tumours. The hysterical patient may present a mild compliance which alternates with violent dramatization.
2. *General Observation*—This is particularly important in children. Take the *temperature,* and estimate the *pulse* and *respiration-rates*; they may provide valuable evidence of infection. Also be on the look-out for evidence of anaemia and of rickets.

Examine the *skin* and mucosa closely for the prodromal signs of specific fevers and for suppurative foci.

□

USE OF HEAT OR COLD THERAPY AFTER INJURY

On Metabolic Rate

The principal effect of cooling living tissues will be to reduce its metabolic rate in accordance with van't Hoff's predictions. (The rate of any chemical action that can be affected is increased by a temperature rise.)

Swelling would increase the distance of cells from their usual supply vessels and possibly occlude some smaller ones.

Most evident will be the reduced oxygen uptake; in fact the erythma due to cold induced vasodilatation is distinguished from that due to heating, due to its 'pinkness' because it contains less reduced Hb. Thus cooling does not benefit healing process.

On the Peripheral Nervous System

Cold may be used therapeutically in the suppression of pain and treatment of hypertonicity. Primary sensation of cold is produced by activation of cold receptor, which generate activity in small diameter, mylinated A—DELTA fibers.

Synaptic transmission can also be delayed. All nerve fibers are not equally affected by cooling. A – Delta fibers are most susceptible to cold.

On the Motor System

Can increase muscle strength and endurance

Muscle strength is diminished by cooling the limb in water at 10-15° Celsius, probably because of its effects on viscosity and metabolic rate, but there is evidence that the strength increases over the original value.

Can reduce motor activity and fine skill performance.

General Effects of Cooling

Extreme cold is experienced as pain, involving pair receptor. Both pain and temperature neurons synapse in posterior horn of the spinal cord; the subsequent neuron ascend in the spinothalamic tract of the opposite side.

Apart from synapse in thalamus with a neuron to the sensory cortex, giving awareness of cold there are many collateral paths, particularly to hypothalamus.

Effects of Cooling

Temperature changes in the tissues will depends on:

1. Temperature difference between the coolant and the tissues; the colder the application the greater the heat loss from the tissues.
2. The thermal conductivity of tissues: This differs from one area to another. In general, water filled tissues such as muscle; have a high thermal conductivity compared to fat or skin. Thus, cooling of deep tissue depends on nature of overlying tissue.
3. The length of time for which the cold is applied.
4. The size of area that is being cooled.

Physiological Changes Due to Cooling the Skin

Effect of Cooling the Skin

Cooling the body surface is simply the transfer of energy away from tissues.

Local Effects

On Cutaneous Blood Vessels

There is immediate vasoconstriction of cutaneous blood vessels, shown by the blanching that occurs this restricts the blood flow in the skin so that heat loss is minimized. This speed with which vasoconstriction occurs indicates that it is a reflex in the autonomic nervous system, which is triggered by stimulation of thermal receptors in skin. This vasoconstriction leads to a decrease in blood flow through skin, hence limits the conduction of heat to the body surface. The increased blood viscosity due to cooling, will slow blood flow.

After some time, the vasoconstriction may give way to a marked vasodilatation which itself may last some 15 min before being replaced by another episode of vasoconstriction. This alternation of constriction and dilatation is called the 'LEWIS HUNTING REACTION'.

On Muscle Blood Flow

The response of muscle blood flow to cooling is less dramatic. It seems likely that cooling provokes vasoconstriction in all vascular smooth muscle and the increased viscosity certainly reduces the blood flow.

Physiological Effects of Heat

Lehman stated that temperature increase up to 1°C reduce mild inflammation and increase metabolism.

Up to 2°C-3°C decrease pain and muscle spasm

Up to 3° C-4°C increase tissue extensibility

Thermal Effects

Effects on Metabolism

- Metabolism is accelerated, both anabolism and is catabolism is enhanced
- 02 supply to tissues is increased
- Removal of waste products is increased
- Nutritional supply to tissues is increased
- Healing is accelerated

Effects Due to Increased Blood Supply

- Increased filtration and diffusion
- Fasten transport of enzymes
- Reduces viscosity of blood
- Reduces peripheral resistance, lowers blood pressure

Effects on Nervous Tissue

- Alters conduction in nervous tissue, perception of pain reduces
- Sensation of sedation
- Increases pain threshold
- Does not stimulate motor and sensory nerve, no muscle contraction is produced

Effects on the Muscular System

- Efficacy of muscles to contract is increased
- Induces muscle relaxation due to faster removal of waste products

Effects on Sweat Glands

- Stimulates centers for regulation of sweat glands
- Production of sweat is increased
- Increased elimination of waste products

Increases Extensibility of Fibrous Tissue like Tendons, Joint Capsules and Scars

Non-Thermal Effects

- Altered cell membrane function and cellular activity
- Electromagnetic field can affect ion binding to cell membrane
- Growth factor activation in fibroblast and changes in myosin phosphorylation
- Regulation of cell cycle by binding of Ca ion
- Stimulation of ATP and protein synthesis
- Na ion tends to accumulate in cell during inflammation process, thus creating a negative charged environment
- When magnetic field is induced Na ion pump is reactivated, allowing cell to regain normal ionic balance

Therapeutic Effects

Effects on inflammation

- Acute inflammation: should be used with caution

- Sub acute stage: stronger doses are applied
- Chronic stage: thermal dose of fairly long duration should be used

Relief of Pain

- Effective in relieving pain because of sedative effect
- Removal of waste products
- Strong superficial heating relieve pain by counter irritation

Muscle Spasm

- Induces MS relaxation
- Increases efficacy of muscle action

Ice Treatment

Ice treatment is most commonly used for acute injuries. If you have a recent injury (within the last 48 hours) where swelling is a problem, using ice treatment. Ice packs can help minimize swelling around the injury.

Ice packs are often used after injuries such as an ankle sprain have occurred. Applying an ice pack early and often for the first 48 hours will help minimize swelling. Decreasing swelling around an injury will help to control the pain.

Ice treatments may also be used for chronic conditions such as overuse injuries in athletes. In this case, ice the injured area *after activity* to help control inflammation. **Never ice a chronic injury before activity.**

Heat Treatment

Heat treatments should be used for chronic conditions to help relax and loosen tissues, and to stimulate blood flow to the area. **Use heat treatments for chronic conditions such as overuse injuries, before participating in activities.**

Do not use heat treatments after activity, and do not use heat after an acute injury. Heating tissues can be accomplished using a heating pad, or even a hot, wet towel. When using heat treatments, be very careful to use a moderate heat for a limited time to avoid burns. Never leave heating pads or towels on for extended periods of time, or while sleeping.

Ice or Heat?

Table 1: Ice or Heat?

	Ice	*Heat*
When to Use	Use ice after an acute injury such as an ankle sprain, or after activities that irritate a chronic injury such as Shin splints.	Use heat before activities that irritate chronic injuries such as muscle strains. Heat can help loosen tissues and relax injured areas.
How To Do It	Read through the information on how to ice an injury. There are several ways to ice an injury.	Heating pads or hot wet towels are both excellent methods. Place a washcloth under hot tap water and then apply to the injured area.
For How Long	Apply ice treatments for no longer than 20 minutes at a time. Too much ice can do harm, even cause frostbite; more ice application does not mean more relief	It is not necessary to apply a heat treatment for more than about 20 minutes at a time. Never apply heat while sleeping.

Complications of Cryotherapy

Caution must be exercised when applying cryotherapy in the vicinity of superficial nerves, especially if cold is combined with compression. Peroneal neuropathy as well as ulnar, axillary, and lateral femoral cutaneous nerve injury after cryotherapy has been documented in the literature. Other reported side effects of cryotherapy include cardiovascular effects (bradycardia), Raynaud's phenomenon, cold urticaria, frostbite, and slowed wound healing secondary to decreased metabolic activity.

Thermotherapy

Thermotherapy is the therapeutic application of any substance to the body that adds heat to the body resulting in increased tissue temperature. Characteristics of various thermal modalities are listed in Table 2. Heat therapy, which can be either superficial or deep, is like cryotherapy in that it provides analgesia and decreased muscle tonicity. Unlike cryotherapy, thermotherapy increases tissue temperature, blood flow, metabolism, and connective tissue extensibility (Table 1). Heat therapy is delivered by three mechanisms: conduction, convection, or conversion.

Table 2

	Method of Application	*Indications*	*Precautions*	*Adverse Treatment Effects*
Cryotherapy	Ice pack Vapo-coolant spray Ice massage Cold whirlpool	Acute injury/trauma Chronic pain Muscle spasm Delayed onset muscle soreness Inflammation	Circulatory insufficiency Cold allergy Advanced diabetes	Cardiovascular effects (bradycardia) Raynaud's phenomenon Cold urticaria Nerve and tissue damage Slowed wound healing Frostbite
Thermotherapy	Conduction Hydrocollator pack Low-level heat wrap Paraffin bath	Acute muscular pain Delayed onset muscle soreness Menstrual pain	Diabetes mellitus Multiple sclerosis Peripheral vascular disease Spinal cord injuries Rheumatoid disease	Bums
Thermotherapy (continued)	**Convection** Fluidotherapy Hydrotherapy	Wound debridement		Infections Cardiovascular issues
	Conversion Ultrasound Heat lamp Diathermy	Tendonitis Joint contractures Muscle spasms Osteoarthritis	Pregnancy Laminectomy sites Spinal cord Malignancy Vascular insufficiency	Bums Increased pain Increased inflammation

			Eye, testes, heart Growth plates Anesthetic area Joint prosthesis Total hip replacement	
Contrast Therapy	Alternating cryotherapy and thermotherapy	Complex reflex sympathetic dystrophy Desensrazation of skin		Burns Frostbite Cold urticaria Raynaud's phenomenon

Increased blood flow facilitates tissue healing by supplying protein, nutrients, and oxygen at the site of injury. A 1°C increase in tissue temperature is associated with a 10% to 15% increase in local tissue metabolism. This increase in metabolism aids the healing process by increasing both catabolic and anabolic reactions needed to degrade and remove metabolic by-products of tissue damage and provides the milieu for tissue repair.

Some of the benefits provided by topical heat therapy may be mediated directly in the brain. Functional brain imaging research has revealed central effects of non-noxious skin warming with increased activation of the thalamus and posterior insula of the brain. In addition, innocuous tactile stimulation of the skin activates the thalamus and S2 region of the cerebral cortex. These direct effects on the brain may mitigate the sensation of pain in the brain, thereby providing pain relief.

Topical heat treatment applied directly on the skin increases both deep tissue temperature and blood flow. Mujkern et al. found that heating pad treatment on the skin of the lower back region at 40°C increased deep muscle tissue temperature 5°C, 3.5°C, and 2°C at muscle tissue depths of 19 mm, 28 mm, and 38 mm below the surface of the skin, respectively. Conductive topical heat treatment of the knees of healthy subjects increased popliteal artery blood flow by 29%, 94%, and 200% after 35 minutes of treatment with heating pad temperatures of 38°C, 40°C, and 43°C respectively it was demonstrated that deep tissue blood flow was found to increase 27%, 77%, and 144% in the trapezius muscle of healthy volunteers with heating pad treatments, resulting in skin temperature increases of 38°C, 40°C, and 42°C, respectively. The latter two studies show a two- to threefold increase in deep tissue blood flow with moderate levels of conductive the skin. In addition, it was recently reported that a significant increase in trapezius muscle conduction velocity, most likely due to increased tissue blood flow, occurred with hot pack treatment at moderate temperatures.

Although the differences between moist and dry heat are commonly referred to in clinical practice, scientific data supporting the alleged differences are lacking. This belief began with a 1946 study that showed moist (hot baths) heat warms tissue faster than dry (infrared lamp) heat. Moisture increases the rate of heat energy transfer and tissue warming. Although these findings support the use of moist heat when rapid tissue warming is desired (such as during an office visit when time is limited), the results do not show that moist heat is therapeutically superior to dry heat. In fact, no therapeutic outcomes were measured during the study. Furthermore, dry heat (infrared lamp treatment) is rarely used anymore as a topical heat modality.

Continuous low-level heat therapy directly on the skin has been shown to be safe and therapeutically effective in treating musculoskeletal disorders. A randomized controlled clinical trial evaluating the effects of a wearable medical device that provided eight hours of continuous low-level heat therapy for the treatment of delayed onset muscle soreness of the quadriceps muscles was reported. The results showed significant increases in pain relief after eight hours of heated knee wrap wear at temperatures of 38°C and 40°C compared with a control group that wore unheated control wraps on both knees.

Continuous low-level heat therapy directly on the skin has also been found to be effective for treating acute muscular low back pain and menstrual pain. Steiner et al. in a randomized controlled trial showed a significant increase in pain relief with continuous low-level heat therapy for eight hours per day over three con-secutive days compared to an unheated control treatment. The significant increase in pain relief persisted in the heat-treated group 24 hours after all treatments were stopped. Akin et al demonstrated that continuous low-level heat therapy with a wearable medical device applied directly on the skin of the lower abdomen for 12 hours per day for two days, provided significant pain relief in patients with control group wearing an unheated device. The pain relief was similar to that obtained with the maximum over-the-counter dose of oral ibuprofen.

Additionally, a recent prospective randomized study showed that topical heat applied directly to the skin was superior to both acetaminophen and ibuprofen in the treatment of acute low back pain for all therapeutic measurements, including pain relief, muscle stiffness, lateral trunk flexibility, and disability. Pain relief was greater with the heat wrap than with either acetaminophen (>52%) or ibuprofen (>33%). Two days after treatment was discontinued, extended pain relief was significantly greater for the heat wrap than for either acetaminophen (>34 %) or ibuprofen (>56%).

Continuous low-level heat therapy is also effective for the treatment of wrist pain associated with strains, sprains, and osteoarthritis. Michlovitz et al. showed incremental pain relief with eight continuous hours of topical heat treatment for three consecutive days compared with placebo treatment. Pain relief progressively increased with each successive day of therapy and persisted in the heat-treated group on the fourth and fifth day after all treatments were stopped. The therapeutic benefit of heat therapy in subjects with wrist pain included a significant increase in grip strength after three consecutive days of low-level heat therapy, which remained two days after all treatment had stopped. Similar therapeutic benefits were observed in subjects with carpal tunnel syndrome.

Complications of Thermotherapy

Thermotherapy should be used with caution in patients with diabetes mellitus, multiple sclerosis, poor circulation, spinal cord injuries, and rheumatoid arthritis because it may cause disease progression, burns, skin ulceration, and increased inflammation. When using thermo therapy, skin should be protected in heat-sensitive or high-risk patients, especially over regions with sensory deficits. Caution should be used with products generating high intensity heat (greater than 45°C) such as with Hydrocollator packs or electric heating pads. Infections of the skin, urinary tract, and pulmonary system have been associated.

Complications of ultrasound include altered cellular function, plasma membrane damage, acceleration of metabolic processes, and temporary stoppage of blood flow. Ultrasound is contraindicated over the eye, testes, heart, pregnant uterus, spinal cord injuries, laminectomy sites, anesthetic areas, malignancy, and growth plates, and in vascular insufficiency.

Additionally, ultrasound should not be used in patients with joint prostheses. Ultrasound therapy may cause overheating, cracking, and melting of the prosthetic joint due to a greater absorption of energy in the prosthesis than in overlying soft tissue. Loosening of cement in total hip replacement is the most common joint prosthesis effect with ultrasound therapy.

Contrast Therapy

Contrast therapy (treatment that alternates between cryotherapy and thermotherapy) is commonly used in rheumatic conditions and regional pain syndrome. Two well-controlled studies have shown that contrast therapy has no effect on muscle tissue temperature. The first was conducted with whirlpool contrast treatments of healthy subjects over a 20-minute time period at a ratio of 4:1 minutes for heat and cold exposure of the lower leg, respectively. Calf muscle temperatures increased significantly in the heated control group, but no change in muscle temperature was detected in the contrast therapy group. Similar findings were reported in a second study that involved alternating hot and cold pack treatments over a 20-minute period of time at a ratio of 1:1 (five-minute exposures). Calf muscle temperatures decreased significantly in the ice-treated control group. No significant changes in overall muscle temperature with contrast therapy were observed.

The therapeutic benefits of whirlpool contrast therapy in the biceps delayed-onset-muscle-soreness model were studied. Contrast, cold and heated whirlpool treatments were administered at 24, 48, 72, and 96 hours after the inciting novel exercise. Contrast therapy decreased pain intensity at 72 and 96 hours after exercise compared with an untreated control group, but this response was similar to that observed with cold whirlpool therapy alone.

□

ANAPHYLAXIS

Patients with anaphylaxis usually have a history of allergy to some substance known to them to trigger these attacks such as bee stings or foods such as peanuts. They can present with severe facial swelling, stridor, wheezing, and hypotension. If treated rapidly, they can recover quickly. If the patient at any point requires intubation or develops hypotension, ICU admission is mandatory. The most common cause of true anaphylaxis is still penicillin.

A usual course is to begin therapy for early anaphylaxis with epinephrine 1:1,000 solution 0.3 to 0.5 mL SC (0.01 mg/kg SC in children). Follow this with 50 mg I.V. diphenhydramine (1.0 mg/kg in children). Patients with wheezing can benefit from nebulized beta-agonists. Be cautious with epinephrine in any patient with suspected coronary artery disease, but remember that anaphylaxis can kill, so be prepared to use epinephrine.

Any patient who has no history of hypotension and no dyspnea or stridor following treatment may be given one dose of IV corticosteroids. In addition, the patient may be discharged on oral corticosteroids (such as prednisone as outlined previously for asthma in adults) and diphenhydramine (often 25 to 50 mg every six hours for adults) for several days. Observe such patients for about four to six hours before discharge to ensure that they do not relapse before the steroids begin to take effect. All other patients should receive I.V. corticosteroids and be admitted. An H_2-blocker such as cimetidine 300 mg I.V., may have additional benefit.

Hypotensive patients require epinephrine 1:10,000 solution 1 to 10 mL slow I.V. push to reverse life-threatening shock. They also require fluids, such as up to six liters of Ringer's lactate can be required. □

PULMONARY EDEMA

The treatment modalities for pulmonary edema can be summarized by the mnemonic LMNOP:

- **L** Lasix (frusemide) I.V. one or two times the patient's usual dose, or 40 mg if the patient is not usually on the drug.
- **M** morphine, given in doses of 2 to 4 mg I.V. Avoid respiratory depression.
- **N** nitroglycerin, often given I.V.; may be given sublingually every two minutes while the drip is being prepared. Start with 5 to 10 μg/minute IV and increase by 5 μg/minute every 3 to 5 minutes. Hypotension should be avoided.
- **O** oxygen; 100% O_2 should be given to all patients with pulmonary edema.
- **P** position. The patient should be, and will want to be, sitting up.

In general, start therapy with the patient in an upright position with O_2, nitroglycerin and I.V. frusemide. If the patient does not improve, start IV nitroglycerin at a rate of 10 μg/min, titrating to a 10% to 30% decrease in the mean arterial pressure. Give small doses of morphine to anxious patients. Throughout the treatment, follow the patient's pulmonary status (e.g. by pulse oximeter), and urine output (which may require bladder catheterization). Get ABG values, ECG, and chest X-ray early.

Consider intubation if the patient is worsening clinically, has deteriorating mental status, or remains hypoxic, acidotic, or hypercarbic despite aggressive therapy. **PEARL: Before intubating, consider non-invasive positive-pressure ventilation methods. BIPAP (bilevel positive airway pressure) or CPAP (continuous positive airway pressure) masks are effective treatments, which may prevent intubation.** Most patients with PE are admitted to the ICU. Some may go to a monitored step-down unit, a few may be able to go to an unmonitored bed, and only stable, chronic patients are discharged home. □

APPENDIX
THE ART OF CLINICAL EXAMINATION

THE CLINICAL APPRENTICE

CHAPTER I

INTRODUCTION

Standing by the bedside, watching your chief at work, is a thrilling yet humbling experience. He is deft with tongue, ears, and hands; impressively direct with questioning and examining. He seems to sense what he is after. He may go through the routine which you are labouring to acquire, or he may take short cuts; but either way he appears to be achieving something definite, even if it is only the Nirvana of a confident—"Nothing abnormal detected".

As an apprentice, you would do well if you could take over your chief's methods *in toto,* and you should start by attempting to do this. You may find, in time, that some of these methods are unsuitable for you, but at least you have given yourself the chance to learn that one of the most deeply satisfying advances you can make is to modify a standard technique to suit your own needs. Do not, however, depart from the well-worn paths merely for the sake of novelty, or as a concession to laziness, or in a misguided attempt to save time. Remember that your chief represents the hard-won experience of many generations; yet all the time progress is being made, and it should encourage you to realize that apprenticeship is more than mere imitation.

You must first of all learn to examine and to assess your cases at leisure. For these purposes chronic cases are ideal. They allow you time to re-examine when you are uncertain, and you will often be in doubt at first; they allow time to think, to read, and to question—not only your chief and your books, but yourself. The first part of this Appendix is accordingly devoted to the technique of examination of non-acute medical cases, as a foundation on which to build.

Acute cases present very different problems: you cannot be expected to tackle them until you have learned the basic technique on chronic cases. Watch your chief dealing with an acutely ill-patient such as a man in coma, and you will observe that his approach differs greatly from that with a patient presenting, say, chronic wasting or premature greying of the hair. He is examining with a view to immediate diagnosis; diagnosing with a view to urgent treatment. The ability to do this is a hallmark of medical maturity. The difference in approach is difficult to describe and slow to acquire, yet it remains vital.

Above all, however, remember that it is essential to know the normal before you can appreciate what is abnormal. The more you know about what constitutes good health the easier you will find it to recognize the patient with early signs of disease. Throughout this book you will find us emphasizing the maxim—"Know the normal". Begin by examining your own friends; it is a good test of friendship. Examine the hearts of abdominal cases and the abdomens of cardiac cases.

Important as it is to recognize the earliest signs of ill-health, it is usually unwise to base a diagnosis on a single abnormal physical sign. Such a finding will put you on your guard, but you should continue to search for further confirmation or disproof, and remain sceptical until one or other is found. Finally, may we remind you that a patient is a person not a case illustrating a disease.

This introduction ends with a warning. If you believe unquestioningly all that is told you, we shall have failed you and you will have failed yourself. The essence of all learning is to ask—'Why?'.

□

CHAPTER II

THE APPROACH TO A PATIENT

When you are allotted your first 'case', and find yourself confronted with a patient who is perhaps hostile, perhaps over-talkative, or perhaps just amused by your efforts, you are to be forgiven for feeling embarrassed, confused, and lost. When the years have rolled by and you look back upon that day it will not be easy for you to define just what you have gained in the intervening years to make an interview with a patient, once so difficult, become a stimulating adventure. Experience of disease, certainly, you will have gained, and confidence too; but perhaps most important of all you will have learned how to deal with people. You will have learned how to coax a history out of a taciturn man, to persuade a sullen child to co-operate, to calm the fears of an anxious woman so that she can tell her story coherently, and to be patient with a garrulous man, knowing that in the midst of all his verbosity he will quietly let drop the facts you have been waiting for. Even your chief, with all his experience, may find it difficult to fit together the jig-saw puzzle of which the patient has presented you with only a few random pieces; but to you at the beginning of your career it seems a hopeless task. It is not hopeless; every doctor has gone through this stage, though some take longer than others.

Do not start with the idea that taking a history will ever be an easy process. The more you will learn the more will the horizon widen for you and the more difficult will it seem to be to fulfil your dream of the 'perfect history'. The perfect history lies in the imagination, an ideal always impossible of complete attainment. So **the *first principle* is the principle of humility—try for all that you can, but do not expect the stars.**

The *second principle* concerns you and your patient, and will govern the relationship between you, whether you see him for five minutes or whether he remains under your care for twenty years. It is this: not only must you want sincerely to help your patient, but you must let him see that you are on his side. It is easy to be irritated by a talkative man who wastes your precious time, to speak sharply to someone you know to be exaggerating, and to resent the patronizing manner of one who thinks herself a great lady; but if you show hostility, the patient will sense it at once and will fail to come out into the open or to speak the truth as nearly as he can. You must not allow this to happen.

Let the patient talk. This is the *third principle.* When he is talking, he will be happy, he will feel that you are on his side because you are listening so peacefully, he will overcome his initial shyness and become more coherent. The time you may lose by listening to a few minutes of irrelevant gossip will be repaid to you later in the ease with which you can extract the essential facts you have to know. Besides, from amidst the confusion of talk you may suddenly hear the sweet sound of a brilliant description of a symptom—"like someone squeezing the inside of my chest every time I gets a move on".

You must be friendly, therefore, to all your patients. When you know what sort of person you are dealing with, you can afford to vary your manner somewhat. With a nervous or anxious patient you must be completely confident and yet essentially sympathetic. With a patient who is overacting and overdescribing his symptoms you can afford to be firm. With the rather hostile patient who doesn't "think there's much the matter", "has never had a day's illness", and "never held with doctors", you could perhaps meet him half-way, building up a lighthearted atmosphere in which he loses the fear of ill-health which is making him hostile and difficult to deal with. In the case of a child, let the mother talk. Meanwhile, get the child to play, gradually joining in yourself later. Unlike adults, children become reticent and withdrawn if you take an immediate and direct interest in them. They respond and become co-operative if you demonstrate that you are on good terms with the parent, and attempt to gain their confidence only when that first objective has been achieved.

The *fourth principle* governing your interview is that you must extract from the patient's talk and by your own questions this fundamental piece of information: *the real reason* why he is consulting you. It may be a simple catastrophe such as a broken wrist or a haematemesis, which has just befallen him; all is then plain sailing.

But perhaps he comes complaining of a pain which has been present in the shoulder for two years. There are innumerable reasons why he should consult you. The pain may have become gradually worse so that he cannot sleep, it may be preventing him from moving his shoulder so that he cannot work, it may have been very severe on one particular day so that he became alarmed, or his wife may have sent him because he was becoming more and more irritable. It is up to you to sort out these things and discover the real reason. By doing so you gain a most valuable insight into your patient's mentality, his work and background, and his disease; without doing so you cannot take a satisfactory history.

Let us take another example, one common enough in ordinary practice. A patient complains that: "All the food I eat comes up again at once". Looking at the patient you may know that his statement cannot be exactly true because he is fat and the symptoms have been present for six months. It is essential for you to find out the real reason why he is consulting you. The so-called vomiting, obviously little more than eructation, is not likely to be the real reason, but merely a manifestation of some other disturbance, physical or mental, which makes him fear, or need help. While searching for this, try to discover how much the symptom interferes with his work and normal life, and for how long it has been present. This will bring you to the important question of the onset of the symptom.

The Onset of Symptoms—You will find that most sufferers from chronic disease are very vague on this point, whereas those with acute symptoms can usually give the day and the hour when they began to feel ill. Seize on this information, and don't let it escape from your mind or your patient's while you make him trace for you the progression of his symptoms between their onset and the time of the interview. When more than one symptom is present you must carefully elucidate the order of their appearance and their relative severity, for this information is often vital to diagnosis.

Another very important fact to know is whether the symptoms have varied in intensity since they began. For instance, dyspepsia which is severe for about a week and then easier for about two weeks is suggestive of peptic ulceration, whereas progressively worsening dyspepsia is more typical of carcinoma of the stomach.

If pain is present anywhere you should make ten distinct inquiries: you should want to know two things about the pain itself (its character and severity); three things about its location (site of maximum intensity, area of maximum spread, and its radiations to other areas); three things about its time relations (date of onset, length and time of attacks, and periods of freedom); and, lastly, what makes the pain worse and what makes it better. Let us apply this plan to an ordinary case of headache.

A young man, aged 19, complains of headache which is a very throbbing and severe ache. It is maximal over the right eye, extends over the right side of the head and sometimes shoots down the back of the neck. He has suffered from attacks of such pain since he was 14 years old. They usually begin first thing in the morning and last about seven hours; they occur about once in every three weeks, but more frequently when he is working for an examination, or when he is over-tired or worried; and they are partially relieved by rest and aspirin.

A history such as this would suggest the common malady of migraine. Unless you are prepared to obtain such a thorough history of the pain, it will be impossible for you to diagnose the condition, since you are not likely to find any abnormal signs on physical examination.

You must be just as thorough in your elucidation of other symptoms. For instance, you will want to know whether a patient's cough is severe or slight, moist or dry, how long it has lasted, whether it is worse in summer or winter, whether it occurs in paroxysms or singly and at what time in the twenty-four hours, what brings it on, and what relieves it.

You must shape your inquiry according to the patient's symptoms. If he complains of pain in the chest, you must ask about his weight, and whether he has a cough or breathlessness or has ever coughed up blood; if he complains of abdominal symptoms you must ask about his weight, appetite, and bowel and urinary functions as a matter of course. The exact form your history should take cannot be told at the onset of the interview. As you go along you will mentally sort information and decide on the next stage of inquiry.

There is, therefore, much about symptomatic inquiry that can only be learned by experience, and it would not be profitable to you to read more about the details, but we would like before leaving the subject to ask you always to remember to inquire about the patient's weight and weight changes. The knowledge will always be valuable. Remember, too, that loss of weight can occur in mental as well as physical illness.

The Past History—When you have built in your own mind a picture of what the patient's real symptoms are, when they began, and how they have affected his life, you should turn the patient's mind back to his past history: his childhood, usual health, education, marriage the vitally important question of occupation his habits and life generally.

Family History—Then you should inquire about the stock from which he was born, the health or disease of its members, their longevity and character. The past history and family history should not be just a catalogue of childish ailments from which the patient has suffered, and the dis-eases from which his parents died. A good past history is an expression of your estimate of the man, his past (and the stock he sprang from) for example: "This farm labourer, of 36, was born of healthy stock into a large family. His childhood was marred by two long illnesses (probably rheumatic fever) at 7 years and 14 years of age respectively. His education was, therefore, much interrupted and on leaving school he was unable to take up more than unskilled employment. After working as an errand boy for four years, he obtained steady employment on a farm. He married at the age of 28 and has had three children. His present symptoms, cough and breathlessness, he has noticed occasionally since the age of 30, but the breathlessness has been so severe recently that he has not been able to carry on his work for three months".

When you have finished 'receiving' the history—it must always be 'received' never 'taken'—you should know a good deal about the man you are dealing with, whether he is a moderate man or a murderer, a moron or a magnificent liar. You should also know something about the disease which has attacked him and how he has responded to it. Lastly, you should know whether he is very ill or merely mildly inconvenienced.

Summary

There are four overriding principles. When receiving a history:

1. Adopt an attitude of humility towards the problem presented.
2. Let the patient see you want to help him.
3. Let the patient talk.
4. Find out the real reason why the patient came to you.

Your inquiry must start with the onset of the chief symptom, then develop along lines which can be determined only as you go along, and end with a general survey of the patient's past, his life and work and stock.

□

CHAPTER III
GENERAL SURVEY

The Adult

Comparatively, few patients show those interesting physical signs which are so attractive and striking when demonstrated in the wards or pictured in a book. So, if you rely merely on an unimaginative overhaul of your patient, system by system, you may be at a loss for a diagnosis when some important clue stares you in the face; you will be in the humiliating position of the man who turns his house upside down in a search for spectacles which all the time are on his own head. Therefore, attune yourself, like Sherlock Holmes, to observe minutely from the moment you see your patient and to be ever on the watch for details as well as to obtain a general impression.

Approach your patient with your eyes wide open. Much that is described in the following pages can be noticed while you are hearing the patient's story. After listening to his main complaint, it is a good plan to feel his pulse and look at his tongue, making the other general observations while the patient talks to you.

Just as in your studies of histology, you have learnt to look first with your naked eye at the slide and only later with the low- and high-power objectives, so in the practice of medicine you must first survey your patient as a whole, and then later focus your attention on particular parts of his body. To make a spot diagnosis is not a sign of clinical laziness but of superior powers of observation. To leave that spot diagnosis unconfirmed is, however, most culpable negligence.

First Stage: General Observation

The Mentality—The good clinician during every moment spent with his patient is absorbing a general impression of his mentality. Is this within the range of normal? (The measuring sticks must be the clinician's own mind and his experience of human beings.) If abnormal, does the patient under-react or over-react to his illness? One man's agony is another man's ache; you must know what sort of man you are dealing with. This is imperative, since on this assessment depends how much importance you can attach to his feelings and symptoms as he describes them. Is his intelligence normal? A patient may lack intelligence, or he may appear slow-witted because of some emotional disturbance.

The two most common emotional reactions of patients are anxiety and depression, sometimes a combination of both. Many patients show some anxiety in the presence of a doctor: their hearts beat rapidly and they sweat and tremble; but do not attach too much importance to these unless you find other evidence of more long-standing anxiety such as heavily bitten finger-nails, rapid self-conscious breathing, clenching of the bands, talkativeness, jerkiness of movement, and a hunted look such as is seen in students before their 'Finals'.

It is most important to recognize the depressed patient, for he may not always have enough insight into his condition to tell you he is depressed, and yet may be so ill that after leaving you he may hang himself on the tree nearest to your consulting room. A depressed patient appears emotionally flat and dull; you cannot penetrate the blank wall which he presents to you. Although he may talk, you feel you are not really understanding, and, conversely, what you tell him appears not to sink in.

Physique and Nutrition—When observing the patient in front of you, try to assess his general physical condition. By looking carefully you may learn not only about his present nutrition but also something of the body he was born with and the imprint that time has made upon him.

First, guess the patient's *weight,* and compare your estimate with the expected weight for age. With practice, this becomes almost an intuitive step, and certainly should not occupy your mind for more than a few moments.

Then consider the *subcutaneous tissues.* If the patient has been fat for a long time the skin hangs in baggy folds with well-marked creases between them; swelling due to oedema, however, looks quite different—the skin is tense, sometimes shiny, and, although the hair follicles may be unduly obvious, the skin creases tend to be ironed out. A fat person who has lost weight looks just as you would expect, like someone whose skin, as well as his clothes, are too large for him. The subcutaneous scars called *lineae atrophicae* provide evidence of stretching of the skin; if the scars are purple, the stretching has been recent, but with age they become pale.

Generalized *muscular wasting* is usually obvious; but you may be in doubt as to whether the patient was always poorly developed or has recently lost some of his muscle weight. Flickering, or fibrillation of muscle-fibres when you touch them, testifies to recent wasting. Common sense and a consideration of the patient's occupation will help you; puny biceps are less remarkable in a clerk than in a miner.

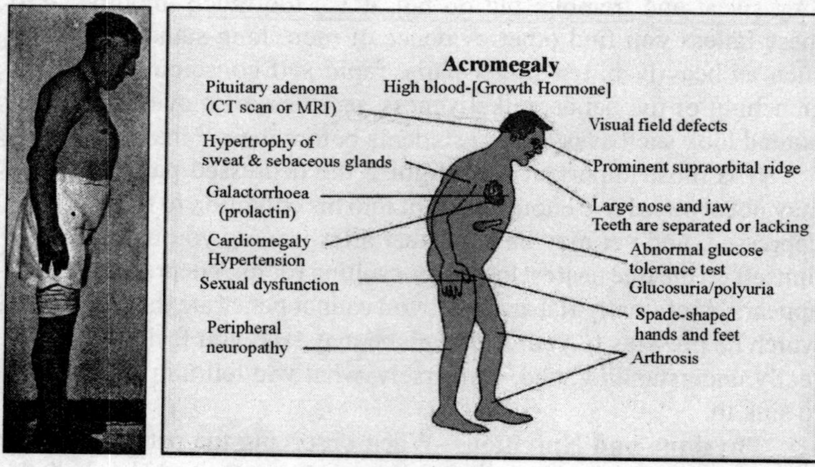

Fig. 1: Acromegaly.

A patient's muscular development often bears witness to his occupation, and his *skeletal development* to his heredity, early nutrition, and the balance of his endocrine glands. The well-built young man with big bones probably inherited these admirable characteristics from his forebears and was well-fed as a child. If, however, his size is disproportionate, his arms long, his hands heavy and coarse, his lower jaw massive, he may be a victim of over-activity of his anterior pituitary glands—an acromegalic (Fig. 1). In the same way, smallness of stature is often inherited, but is sometimes due to malnutrition, either from a deficient intake of the right food or inability to utilize it. Dwarfism with marked disproportions—very short arms and legs—is probably

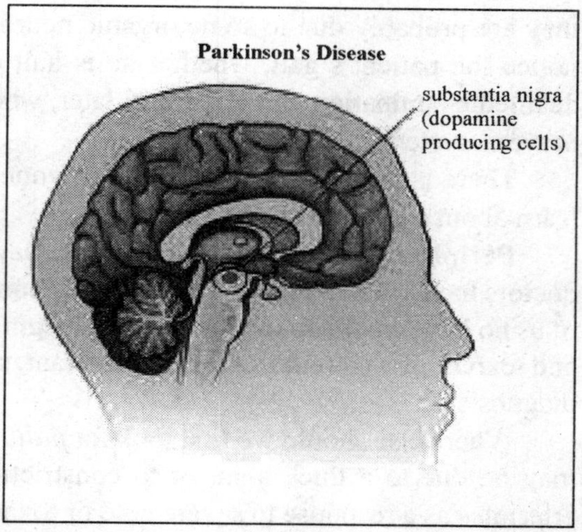

Fig. 2: Parkinsonism.

due to more specific diseases of bone and cartilage formation, or endocrine disorders.

Lastly, human beings tend to be built according to two main plans—these are the broad-chested, thick-set individuals, and the narrow-chested, tall, thin individuals. There are many between those two extremes, but since we can associate certain habits of mind and activity with each type of build, it is worthwhile noting if your patient is clearly one or the other. Thus, the broad-chested, thick-set man tends to be over-active, energetic, and an extrovert. The tall, thin person tends to be a thinker rather than a doer. In this, as in so many ways, the observation of structure may give you a clue as to function, and be invaluable in determining your attitude to the patient.

Bodily Activity—Observe your patient's actions. The droopy asthenic youth with hypotonic muscles, excessive curvature of the spine, and flat feet is heir to one set of ills; the plethoric, talkative young man to another. Quick jerky movements, rapid speech, and behaviour may be a clue to thyrotoxicosis. On the other hand, incoordinated movements, clumsiness, grimaces, and excessive fidgetiness, will make you think of chorea. Poverty of movement, an expressionless face, and dragging feet are signs of Parkinsonism which you can also notice at once (Fig. 2). Tremors, if fine and generalized, are usually due either to thyro-toxicosis or to an anxiety state; if coarse or localizect, they are probably due to some organic neurological lesion. You will notice the patient's gait, whether he is halt or lame, but may defer detailed examination and tests until later, when you can consider the nervous system as a whole.

There is much, therefore, which in your general survey you can learn about a patient's bodily activity.

Peripheral Circulation—Since the days of Galen and before, doctors have tried to learn from a study of complexions. Though most of us no longer believe in sanguine or phlegmatic humours, the colour and texture of a patient's face are important, sometimes vital, clues in diagnosis.

Where else should we first look for *pallors* but in the face? Pallor may be due to a thick skin, or to constriction of the subcutaneous arterioles as a response to severe cold or toxaemia. It may also be due to a small amount of blood travelling through the skin, as in traumatic shock, or to a low haemoglobin concentration in the circulatory blood—anaemia, in other words. Having observed pallor, you must be very careful not to diagnose anaemia; anaemia can only be confidently predicted after you have looked at a drop of the patient's blood; but you are less likely to err in clinical judgement if you look at the mucous membrane, the palate, the tongue, the palpebral conjunctivae, or the palms of the hands, preferably all five. The outward appearance of anaemia in infants is even more unreliable than in adults.

A pink *flushed face* caused by dilated cutaneous arterioles may be found in emotional states, after exercise, or with raised metabolism or fever. In fever, the flushed cheeks often throw into prominence the dead-white skin around the lips. This circumoral pallor was at one time thought to be a diagnostic sign of scarlet fever, but it may occur in anyone with a pyrexia, particularly in the very young.

The complexions of the old often bear the imprint of their past. The thickened, weather-beaten countenance of the sailor and farm-hand may, nevertheless, be difficult to distinguish from that of an alcoholic. A peculiar bluish-red flush high on the cheek bones, associated with some blueness of the lips, occurs extremely frequently in advanced mitral stenosis. This is one of those curious empirical facts abounding in the study of medicine, and invaluable in practice, but for which no adequate explanation can yet be given. Its companion is the fact that sufferers from aortic valvular disease are nearly always pale in countenance.

Cyanosis, meaning blueness, is an exact term. Its presence suggests that the haemoglobin of the blood beneath the area of skin observed has been reduced. Local cyanosis of the face may then mean nothing more than that the peripheral capillaries and venules are dilated due to cold, and that the blood stagnating in them has become blue. If, however, the cyanosis or blueness is universal; if, in fact, the lips, mouthy and forehead are as blue as the most exposed parts such as the ears,—nose, and cheeks, then you may infer either that more than a third of the total haemoglobin of your patient is in the reduced form, or that there is some delay in return of blood from head to heart. Such an inference, if soundly drawn, is of immense value to you. But *don't* say a patient is cyanosed just because he has dilated blue venules on his cheeks, or has an expensive alcoholic nose.

The Hands—Surely, the next thing you must do is to feel his pulse. This is both customary and convenient. Thereby a bond is established between you, a hush falls upon the scene, and you have unrivalled opportunities both for thought and careful observation of his hands. A man's *hands* (Fig. 3) are as informative as his face, and often more truthful than his tongue. Consider one finger alone: it is covered by about 5 sq in of skin, all of which you may observe, and it contains three joints, several tendons, one fingernail, and the richest supply of blood-vessels. You continue your study of the patient's circulation, therefore. Are the fingers warm; what colour are they; do the finger-tips pulsate abnormally? Observe the colour of the nail-bed and any capillary pulsation there. Are there any petechial spots in the pulp of the finger or beneath the nail?

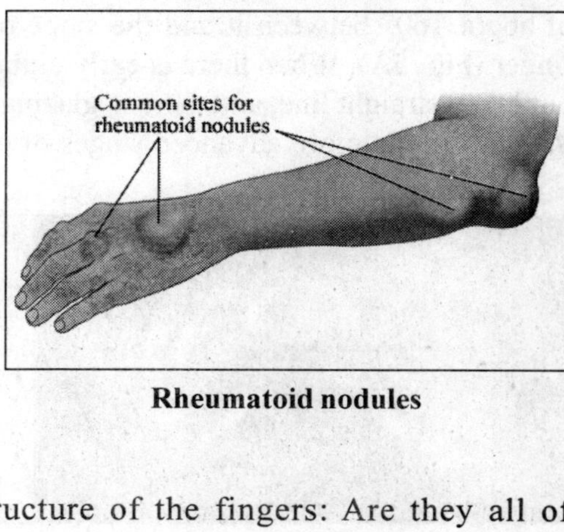

Rheumatoid nodules

Next look at the structure of the fingers: Are they all of proportionate length; are the joints fully mobile, are they swollen or

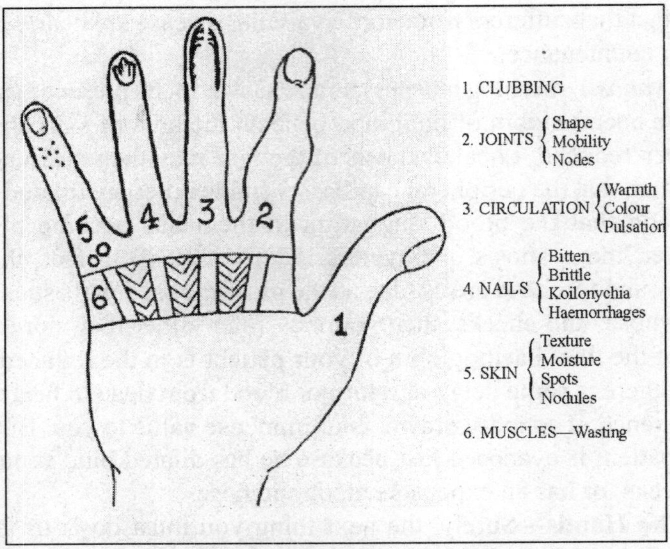

Fig. 3: What to learn from the hand.

deformed; are there any swellings around the joints? (Fig. 4). Look at the tips of the fingers; is there any finger clubbing? (Figs. 5 and 6). The earliest stage of *finger clubbing* which you will be able to recognize is a filling in of the normal depression between the terminal interphalangeal joint and the root of the nail (Fig. 5B). Normally, the nail springs from the finger in such a way as to leave an obtuse angle of about 160° between it and the slope of the dorsal surface of the finger (Fig. 5A). When there is early clubbing, this angle is flattened out into a straight line, and there is glazing of the skin over the root of the nail. In the more advanced stages of clubbing, there is a gradual

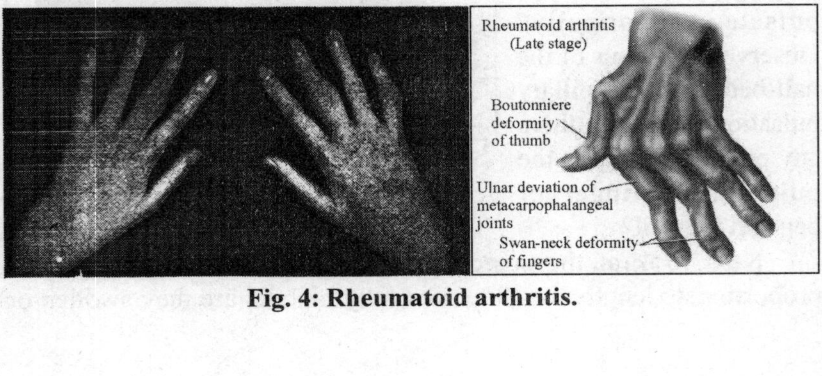

Fig. 4: Rheumatoid arthritis.

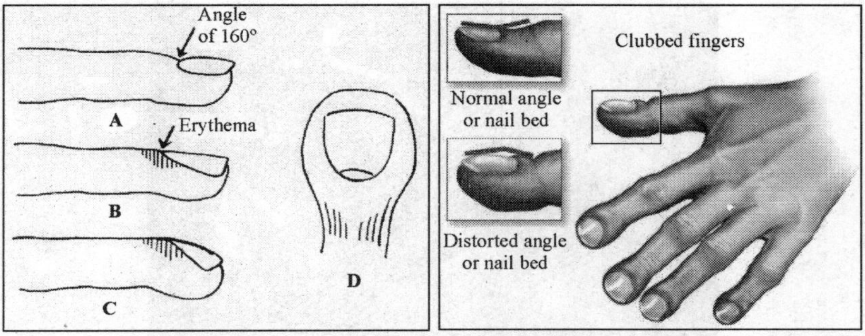

Fig. 5: Finger clubbing. A. Normal finger-tip; B. First stage of clubbing; C. Second stage; D, Third stage ('drumstick' fingers).

convex curve from the terminal joint right on to the tip of the nail (Fig. 5C).

In the most marked degrees of clubbing, you will also find, when the hand is held up, that the tips of the fingers are expanded to look like drumsticks or the spores at the ends of tetanus bacilli (Fig. 5D).

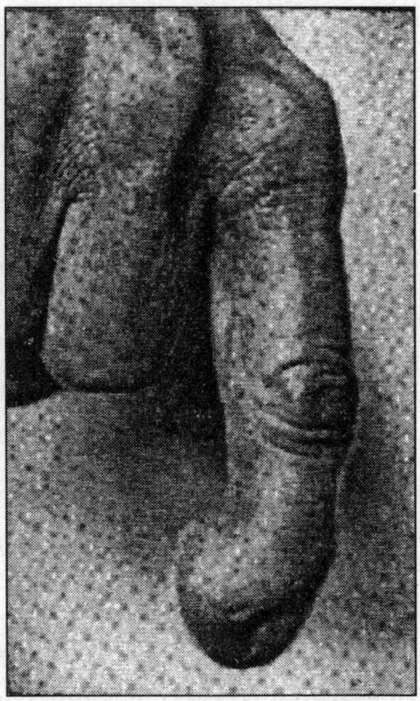

Fig. 6: Osteoma of index finger.

Lastly, consider the *fingernails* themselves: Are they shiny and well formed, or brittle and lifeless; is there koilo-nychia (spooning of the nails)? (Fig. 9). If you find evidence of severe nail biting, that may help you in building up a picture of the patient's mental state; but remember it may be, like nicotine staining, just a manifestation of a habit. The nails may also show evidence of a man's occupation.

The Skin and Hair—When looking at a patient's complexion and his hands you must, of course, pay attention to the skin itself, as thereby you will be able to learn something about the patient's metabolism. For example, the skin of a thyrotoxic patient appears thin, shiny, warm, and moist, whereas the skin of a myxædematous patient

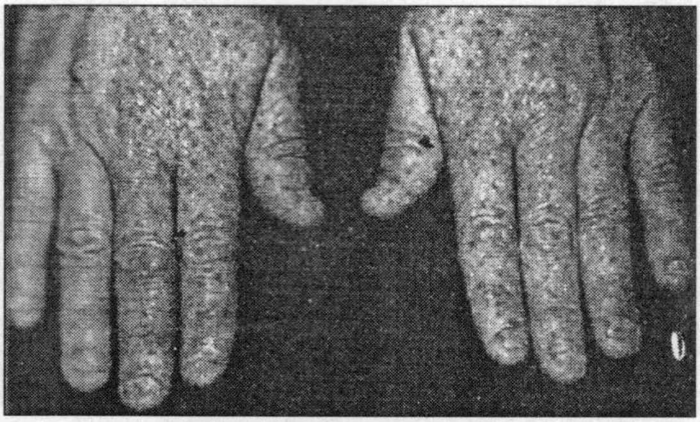

Fig. 7: Short fingernails as a result of bring them.

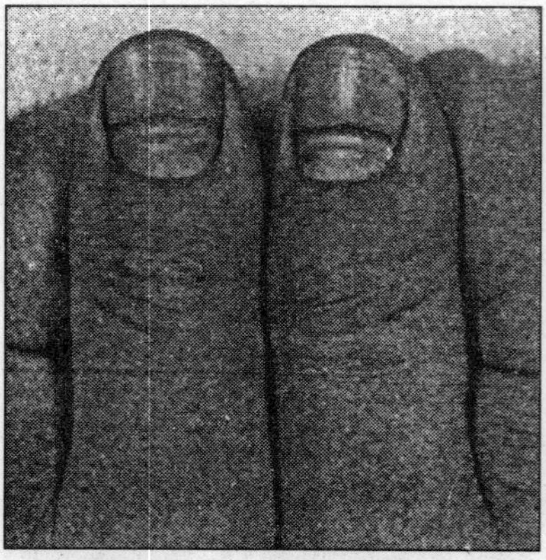

Fig. 8: Furrows in fingernails after

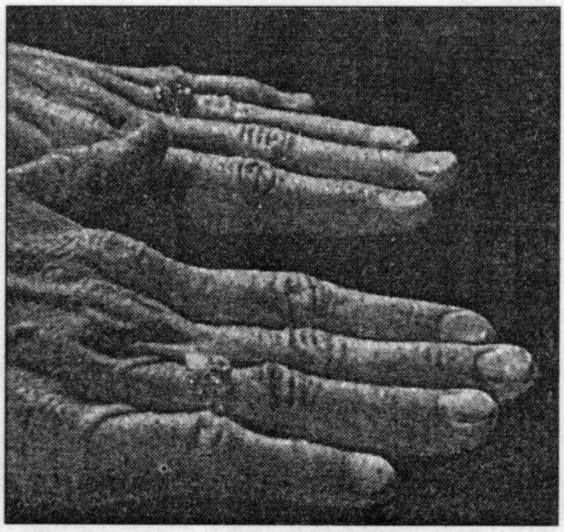

Fig. 9: Spoon nails.

appears thick, coarse, opaque, and dry. *Pigmentation* of the face may be due to heredity, sunburn, or some pathological cause. Yellowness of the skin may be due to race, to fading sunburn, to drugs, or to jaundice. You should notice a generalized rash or the presence of spots; if spots are present, do they fade on pressure, or are they true petechial spots—that is, small haemorrhages beneath the skin?

The hair, like the skin, is coarse and dry in myxaedema and also grows thinly. When you see the hair growing out irregularly, so as to give a moth-eaten appearance, it is as well to think of syphilis. Deficient pubic and axillary hair, or lack of facial hair in a man, suggests infantilism or destructive changes in the pituitary gland. So *don't* forget to look at the hair as well as the skin.

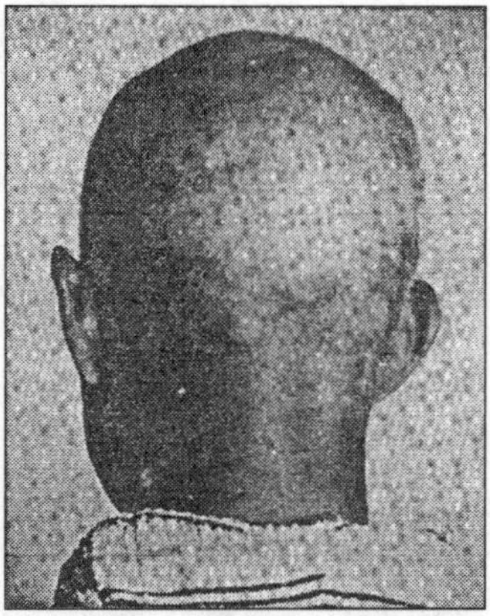

Fig. 10: Alopecia in diabetes.

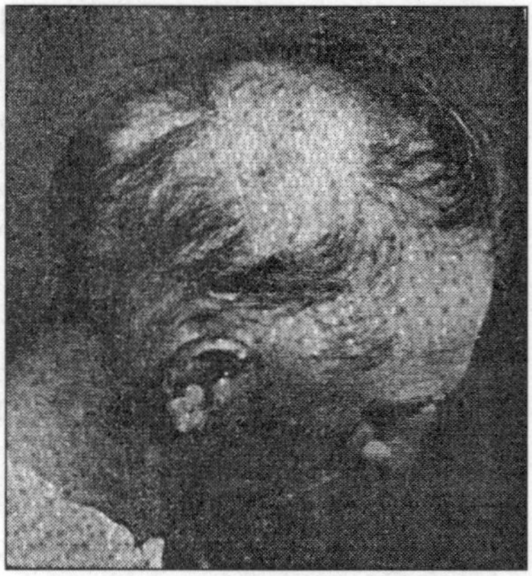

Fig. 11: Alopecia.

Swellings on Skin

In some patients, you may see nodule on the skin, some sessile, some pendunculated over the skin in various places. This is generalised neurofibromatosis or von recklinghausen's disease.

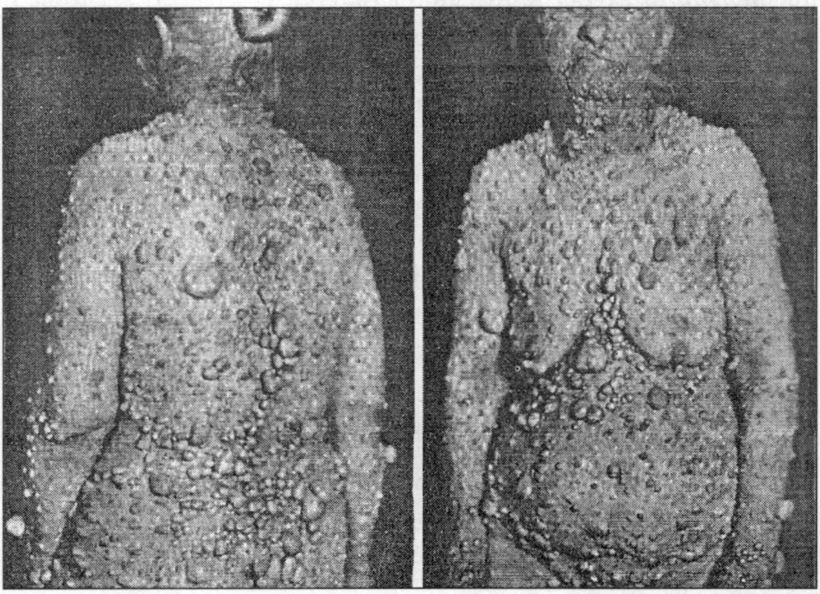

Fig. 12: Von Recklinghausen's disease—multiple neurofibromatosis.

The Eyes—You will probably have to look closely into the structure and functions of your patient's eyes if his chief disability is neurological, but you must also train yourself to notice many things during your first few minutes with him (Fig. 14). Notice ptosis, prominence (Fig. 15), or sinking in of the eyes, and notice oedema of the eyelids. Look for signs of jaundice in the conjunctiva, squint, or abnormalities of eye movements. Lastly, look at the pupils, their size and shape.

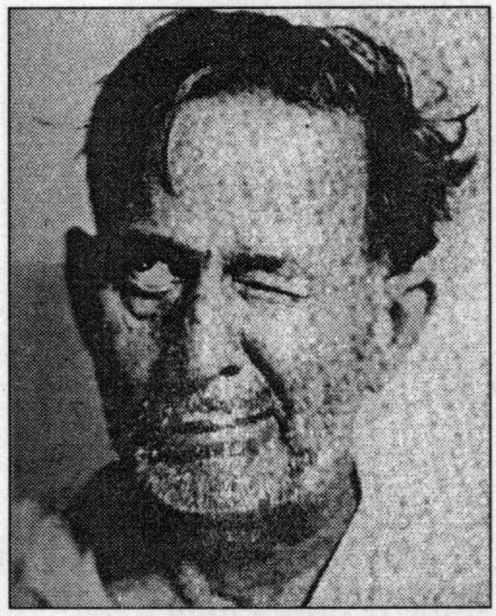

Fig. 13: Paralysis of the right facial nerve Belll's palsy.

The Tongue—Examination of the tongue is essential in acute disease, but no less important in the diagnosis of chronic disease. The tongue, which may show important neurological signs, is also said to be the mirror of the stomach. Perhaps the most important aspect of examination of the tongue lies in the information you may-obtain from it about the *hydration* of the body, about the *anaemias,* and about *toxaemia.* Something will be said later on about the tongue in acute emergencies and about the tongue in digestive and neurological disease, but here are some guiding principles for its examination. The first rule is—never forget to look at it. The second rule is—look at it carefully. Look at the size of the tongue and see if it is in proportion to the face. Is it wasted and wrinkled? Observe any tremors or weakness of tongue movements. Consider the colour of the tongue, together with the colour of the inside of the cheeks, and try to

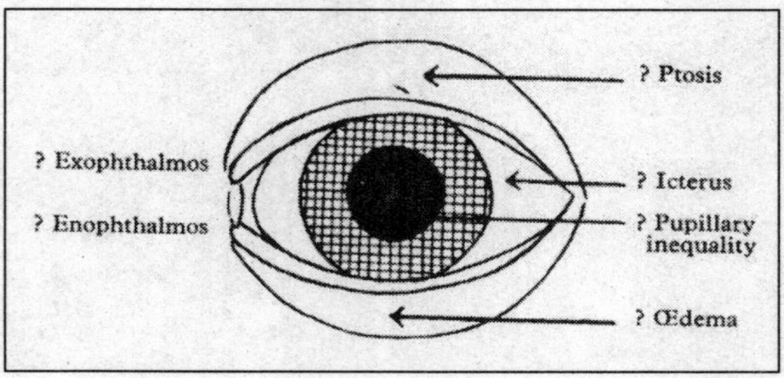

Fig. 14: What to learn from the eyes.

make an estimate of the haemoglobin concentration in the blood. Look at the surface of the tongue: is it dry or moist? A dry tongue, like the symptom of thirst, usually means dehydration and water depletion, but excessive panting, talking, or breathing with the mouth open may cause a temporary dryness. If the tongue is coated, note the colour and distribution of the 'fur'. See if the tongue has the normal quota of

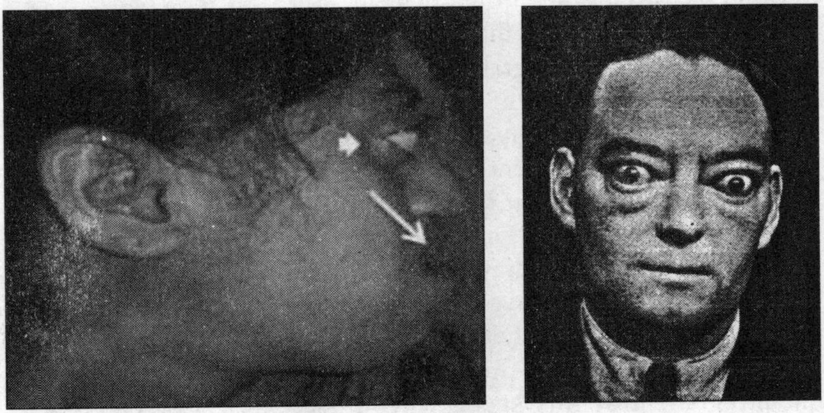

Fig. 15: Exophthalmos.

papillae which give it a rough appearance, or whether it is smooth and shiny due to loss of papillae. Lastly, look for disease of the epithelium, for ulcers, fissures, or cancer.

When you realize that, by so examining the tongue, such widely different conditions as uraemia, dehydration, and secondary syphilis may all be tentatively diagnosed, perhaps you will learn to remember it and to make the patient put out his tongue as you finish your observations oh his pulse and hands.

Second Stage: Undressing the Patient

Throughout your hearing of the patient's history, you will have been busy with your eyes and ears. You will also have felt the patient's pulse and asked him to put out his tongue. But you will not have made any attempt to examine him systematically. Before you do this you must try to make one more general survey of the patient, this time when he is undressed. Later, in a busy practice, you will not find it possible to examine every patient stripped, but by that time you will have gained sufficient medical insight to know which of many patients needs to be undressed. As a student you should examine all your patients undressed, except the acutely ill. This is a difficult thing to do if you yourself are shy about it. Don't be. Be clear and firm. Let them gather from your remarks that complete undressing is taken for granted. If the symptoms point to disease of the nervous system or locomotor system, it is probably best for the patient to leave on only a single upper garment, shirt or vest; in all other cases it is best for the patient to strip down to a pair of drawers. In the case of women, try to have a nurse or female friend to help them; the old particularly need help and encouragement at this stage. If you examine your patient as a whole, stripped or nearly stripped, you will have an incomparable advantage over the doctor who tries to fumble for clues amidst a maze of under-garments. (These remarks apply chiefly to chronic disease; in acute emergencies it may be quite against the patient's interest to undress him completely, but we will return to this later.)

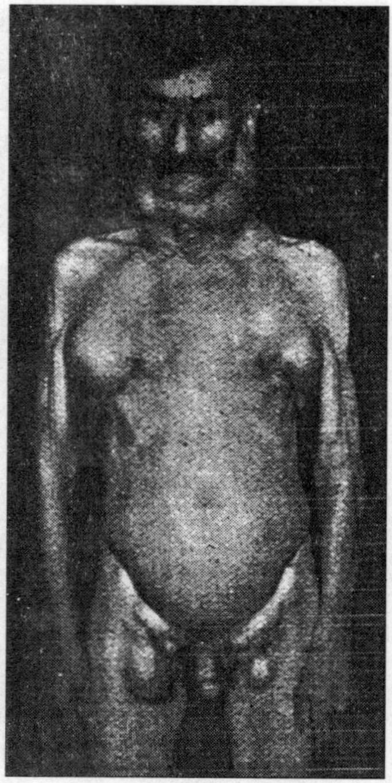

Fig. 16: Lymphatic leukæmia.

Once the patient is undressed, if he is an outpatient, try to examine him standing or walking while undressed. In this way you may notice all sorts of things—scoliosis, wasting of muscles, shortening of limbs, asymmetry of the chest, for

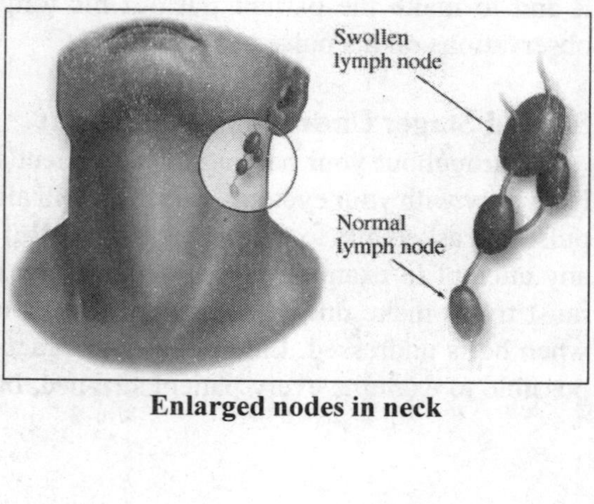

Enlarged nodes in neck

example—which might have escaped you had you tried to examine him piece by piece. If the patient is in bed, stand at the bottom of the bed and look at his body as a whole. Once you have examined a patient thoroughly, stripped, there will probably be no need for you to do so again during his illness. A limited field of observation will suffice for further examinations.

The Lymphatic Glands and the Joints (Fig. 16)—We ourselves have found it useful to examine the mobility of a patient, his joints, and his lymphatic glands at this early stage of examination. Others, no doubt, would do these things later. In defence of our system, we would say that unless you make these routine observations at the beginning, you tend to forget them at the end. So watch the patient's movements; examine his main joints carefully, if necessary flex the elbows and the knees to see if you can observe rheumatic nodules, but do this in a good light.

Next palpate the occipital region, both sides of the neck, the axillae, the supratrochlear region, and the inguinal region for enlarged lymphatic glands. Remember that small bunches of inguinal glands occur in most normal people, and they may be quite numerous in a patient who has had repeated injuries or septic places on the legs or feet. Small soft glands in the posterior cervical region and axillae are often palpable, too, in normal people, especially children. Even the diagnostic significance of enlarged epitrochlear glands has been doubted of late, since these are also found in a proportion of normal people. Where there is extensive skin disease or sepsis, you should expect to find a generalized lymphadenopathy, and the same is true for many conditions in early childhood. In an adult, generalized glandular enlargement with a palpable spleen is always of significance. Large, firm, hard, or tender glands are naturally more likely to be important than small, soft, painless glands.

Summary

In the first few minutes, try to sum up your patient—his mentality, nutrition, and bodily activity. As you feel his pulse, study his complexion and the circulation in his finger-tips. Notice any abnormality of the hands, the nails, the hair, or the skin.

Next look down the patient's face, paying particular attention to the eyes. Ask him to put out his tongue, and inspect it carefully.

If it has not been done already, your patient must undress almost completely. When he has undressed, you can examine his bones, joints, and lymphatic glands (Fig. 17).

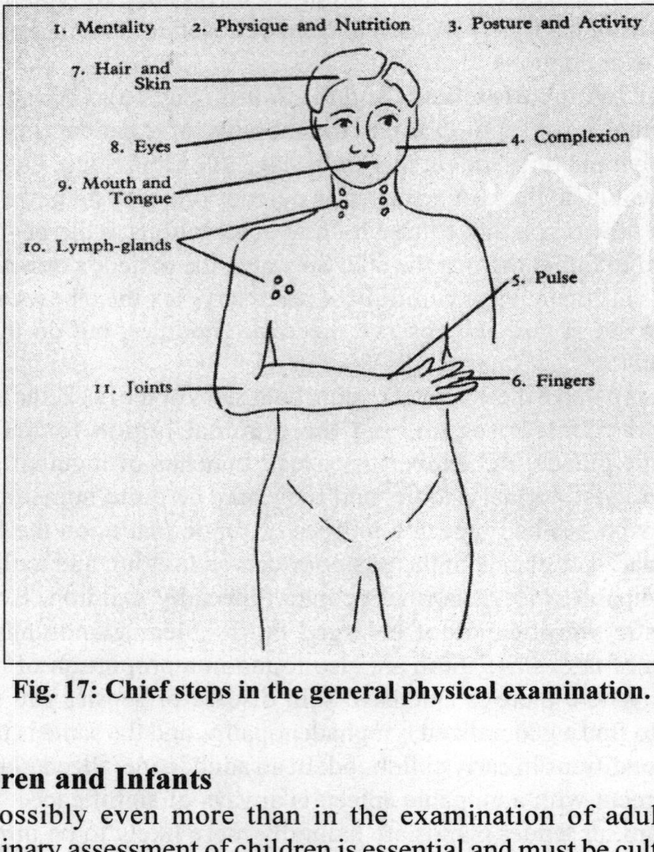

Fig. 17: Chief steps in the general physical examination.

Children and Infants

Possibly even more than in the examination of adults, the preliminary assessment of children is essential and must be cultivated. If, in your preliminary survey, you fail to observe that a child is seriously ill, perhaps even almost dying, you may never realize the fact until it is too late.

Children differ in many ways from adults: the child is *not* merely a miniature man. If you expect to find exactly the same manifestations of disease in the child, and, therefore, attempt to examine him in the same way, you will in many cases be completely misled. A few essential principles will help you in your approach to children.

The outstanding difference between patients in the pediatric age group and others is simply expressed by the one word—'growth'; the child is growing anatomically, physiologically, mentally, and morally. To understand the disorders of childhood, you must, therefore, know something about the harmony of normal growth. The child's total personality is made up of characteristics which are in a state of flux; new features are constantly being added and old ones lost, and the relative proportions are always changing. Though children differ among themselves even more than adults, you can, on the basis of certain 'milestones' which represent average achievements, make a useful assessment. Your first step, then, is to learn these milestones, the more important of which are summarized here:

Weight—At birth, 7 lb.; doubled in five months, trebled in one year, quadrupled in two years; 33 lb. at three years, 49 lb. at seven years.

Height—At birth, 20 in.; doubled in four years, then 2 in. added each year.

Skull Circumference—At birth, 13½ in.; at one year, 18 in.; at three years, 19 in.

General—By six months, sits up and first teeth appear; by one year, has four teeth, stands up, speaks a few words and obviously experiences emotions; by 15 to 18 months, walks and speaks perhaps a dozen words, and the anterior fontanelle is closed; by two years, speaks sentences of a few words and recognizes colours; by three years, is continent of urine, and all 24 teeth of the first dentition have erupted.

The method of examining a child differs from that which you follow for adults. For success you need to combine the qualities of *patience* and *opportunism*. You will be unable, as a rule, to examine young children in an orderly sequence, and must learn to adapt yourself according to circumstances, yet without sacrificing thoroughness. The doctor who "gets on well with children" does so by seeming able to imagine himself in the same position as the child, to feel as the child does in the difficult situation of being examined, and by the understanding and sympathy which develop is enabled to put the child at its ease.

A young child is not an entity which can be isolated; in the problems which affect the child the mother is intimately concerned.

Your examination must, therefore, include the mother in its ambit, and to win confidence you must try to build up the **'paediatric trinity'**, which may be expressed by a diagram:

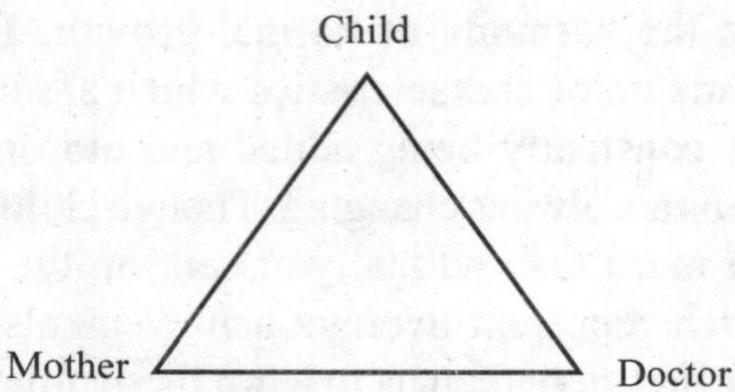

Older Children—Your best plan is to ignore the child at first, until it has become accustomed to your presence and your voice. Adults expect and appreciate a direct approach, but a child feels insecure and frightened if a stranger intrudes by looking and speaking directly at him. Let the child play with a toy while you talk to the mother. In a short time, you will have obtained the history, and then both you and the mother can unobtrusively join in her child's play. The mother can now start to undress the child (or encourage an older child to undress itself) and you should not attempt to help. All this time you are absorbing impressions, not only of the child but also of the mother and of their relationship, the one to the other.

You will notice whether the child is unduly dependent on its mother, for many childhood disorders arise from this cause. Thus, an overdependent child may develop anorexia or enuresis when a new

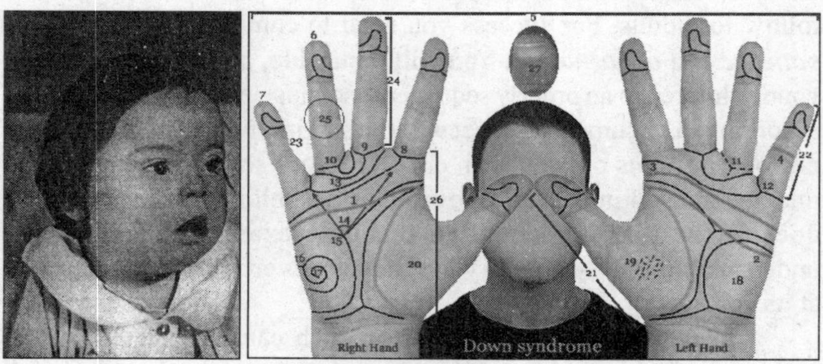

Fig. 18: Mongolism.

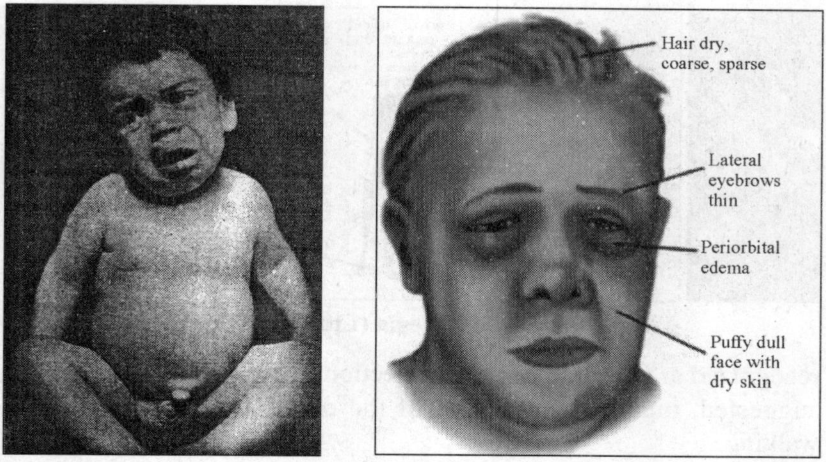

Fig. 19: Cretinism.

child is born into the family and its own security appears to it to be endangered. On the other hand, a child may appear irresponsive and withdrawn if it is not receiving its due share of affection.

A single glance will usually enable you to recognize a *mongol* (Fig. 18), by its slanting eyes set in a small round head, and its cheerfulness associated with mental retardation, and you can often confirm the diagnosis by finding accompanying congenital defects such as a congenital heart lesion, and queerly shaped ears and fingers. A *cretin* (Fig. 19) may also be recognized at a glance; mentality, metabolism, and development are all retarded, so that the child is dull and backward, with a thickened, cold skin and scanty hair, and is slow in everything he does. In both these conditions, more complete examination may reveal nothing of diagnostic importance; the diagnosis is made on the first impression. *Mental deficiency* can also be recognized at a glance by the trained observer. It is sometimes difficult to define, especially in the absence of such gross lesions as microcephaly, but may be characterized by a vacant look in the eyes, lack of attention and concentration, and sometimes by the presence of physical stigmata (such as poorly-developed ears, a high arched palate, etc.). The diagnosis, however, depends mainly on a history of marked slowness in passing the normal milestones.

Physical defects such as spastic diplegia (Fig. 20) are also quickly

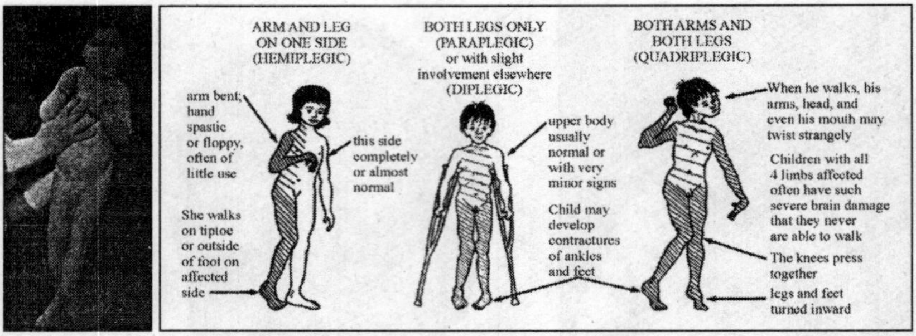

Fig. 20: Spastic diplegia (Little's disease).

recognized at your preliminary inspection, which should, as we have suggested, include observation of the child at play, moving, and walking.

Infants—Infants present even more distinct problems. A baby can be within a few hours of death, yet the severity of the condition may pass un-recognized by those unaccustomed to dealing with infants. The only satisfactory way of getting over this sort of difficulty is to see as many infants as possible, in their homes or in hospital, to inquire what is wrong with them and to find out what happens to them.

When you set about the examination of an infant, try to profit from the experience of your chief. In the first few months of life, when the child cannot sit up, you will find it is best examined lying on its mother's lap, after she has undressed it. By the age of a year, when it has learnt to sit up well, the child may cry if you make it lie down, and it is then often necessary to carry out some part of your examination with the infant sitting up on the mother's lap.

If you are fortunate enough to see the child when it is asleep, do not wake it—a considerable part of your examination can be carried out very well in this state. For example, you can observe the pulse-rate in young infants by palpating the anterior fontanelle. The rate of respiration may also be estimated and provides extremely valuable information; a rate higher than 60 in a minute is almost certainly due to pulmonary infection, and is the more important because abnormal physical signs in the infant's chest may be difficult to elicit. The heart may be briefly examined before the child starts to cry on waking up. The abdomen may often be completely palpated if your hands are warm and gentle; in this way, during sleep, the sausage-shaped mass of an intussusception may sometimes be felt without recourse to an anaesthetic. Even the optic fundi may be examined without waking the child.

When the baby is awake deal gently with him still. Sudden, violent movements are disturbing; instead, move and speak deliberately, and slide the hands or the stethoscope equally deliberately and gently from one part to another.

General Assessment—Train yourself, as for adults, to estimate the weight by the child's appearance, though an accurate weight is to be obtained whenever possible. The state of *nutrition* is very important; learn to estimate it by comparison with other children, and learn to estimate it both by the appearance and by feel. The feel of a wasted child is different from that of a healthy one. The greatly wasted, marasmic child, is readily recognized; it is listless, shrivelled, with sunken eyes and grey appearance, and a depressed fontanelle and inelastic skin. The less-marked forms require more practice for their recognition.

Dehydration presents a similar picture in the advanced stages—marasmus is only an end-result, which may be reached by various routes—but in the early stages, so important for treatment, it is best recognized by careful observation for dryness of the tongue and skin, loss of tension in the fontanelle, and diminution of urinary output.

While you are making your general assessment, observe the infant's alertness and activity, both mental and physical.

Scheme of Detailed Examination—It should be repeated that in the examination of infants and children, you may not be able to follow a set routine, but your examination must, nevertheless, be thorough.

Look at the *face,* but beware of diagnosing anaemia merely because the face is pale. Many normal young babies have a flat nose, but after the first few months it may be due to syphilis or achondroplasia—A hare-lip is not to be missed, and the palate should be inspected later, when you come to view the throat.

Note the size and shape of the *skull*; rickets (Fig. 21), for example, is 'manifest' and can be diagnosed earliest in the skull*;* at the age of three or four months soft areas can be indented by the examining finger. The *anterior fontanelle* is a most important source of information, and must always be palpated in the examination of any infant. The

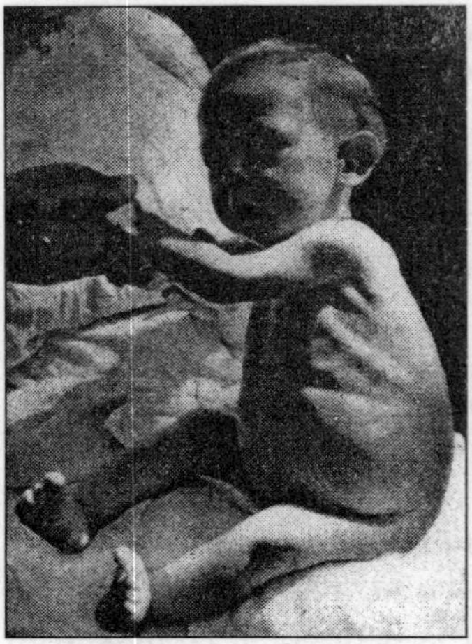

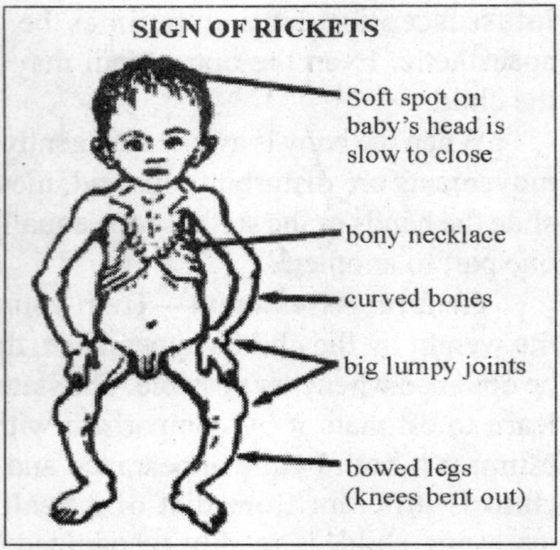

Fig. 21: Rickets. Note bossed head, rickety rosary on ribs, and distended abdomen.

accompanying diagrams (Fig. 22) illustrate the conditions which this examination will help you to recognize—once you have excluded crying as a cause of bulging.

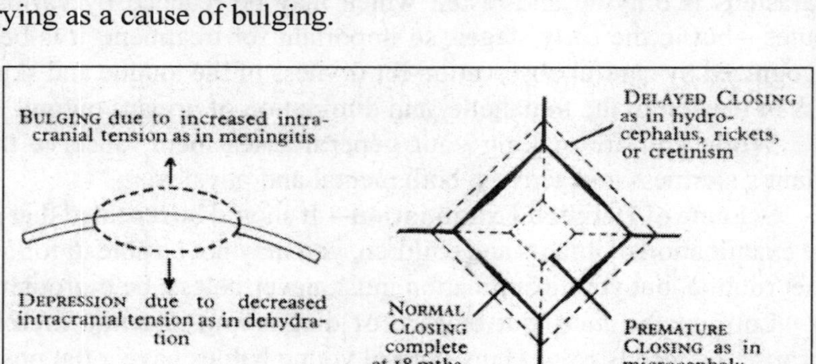

Fig. 22: The anterior fontanelle.

Having dealt so far with the head, test for *neck rigidity,* but postpone inspecting the throat and ears until the end of your examination, because the ungrateful patient will resent your thoroughness violently and vociferously.

Now examine the *trunk* and *limbs* superficially, noting in particular any skin lesions, especially of the umbilicus, or superficial congenital anomalies. Next examine the *heart* and *lungs,* remembering that percussion is not only of limited value in the infant or small child, but is also frightening for your patient. Thorough palpation of the *abdomen* is followed by movement and palpation of the *limbs.*

When your examination is otherwise complete, you must invariably end by examining the *mouth* and *throat* and both *tympanic membranes,* and, at some convenient moment, by collecting a sample of *urine* for examination. You will recognize the experienced pediatrician by the protective towel draped over his knees and the convenient receptacle modestly hidden under his chair.

□

CHAPTER IV

EXAMINATION OF HEART

In any leisurely examination, it is a sound rule to attend last to the organ probably at fault. Consequently, in suspected heart disease, the heart should be left until the remainder of the body has been examined. The most culpable, though probably the most popular 'method', is to smack a stethoscope over one or two vague areas of the precordia and proceed at once to make a diagnosis. This is unforgivable.

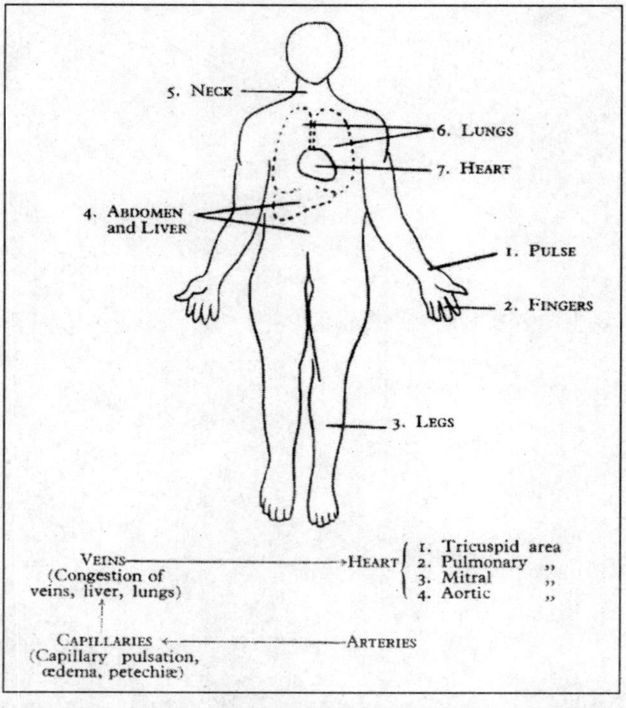

Fig. 1: The 'circulatory tour'. A scheme for orderly examination of the cardiovascular system.

On the other hand, even experts may have no fixed and logical order of examination, although it must make for simplicity and completeness to follow some orderly routine of examination.

An attractively simple scheme is to conduct the examination of the cardiovascular system by following the direction of flow of the blood. This is an extremely helpful method of training yourself to examine not only the heart, but the whole circulation really thoroughly, and we propose to impress it on you by calling it **'the circulatory tour'.**

Going with the blood-stream, we suggest you start by examining the arterial tree, as exemplified by the radial artery; next, the capillaries and peripheral circulation, as seen in the face, fingernails, and skin in general; then the venous system, including the neck veins and liver. After that, logically, you come to the right side of the heart, and examine the tricuspid and pulmonary valves. Still following the bloodstream, you next examine the lungs, then finally pass on to the mitral and aortic valves of the left side of the heart. At the end of your examination, you can have omitted nothing of importance in the cardiovascular system and your thoroughness will have carried you a long way to a complete diagnosis.

It is reasonable to alter the scheme slightly, by examining the lungs before the heart; in this way the heart is examined as one entity, though still in the order suggested.

The accompanying diagram (Fig. 1), illustrates 'the circulatory tour'. It will be described in essential detail after symptoms have been described, since that is the order in which you will, in practice, consider the patient.

Symptoms

It goes almost without saying that you should learn as much as possible from the patient's symptoms before starting your examination. It would be desirable to consider symptoms, too, in the same logical order as already described for physical signs. It is unfortunate, however, that they do not lend themselves to such precise marshalling, and for this reason we shall describe them instead, as far as possible, in the order in which they appear chronologically.

Before proceeding to consider the symptoms of cardiovascular disease two warnings are necessary: (1) Even in the presence of disease there may be *no* symptoms if an efficient circulation is being maintained. (2) If symptoms *are* present they may appear unconnected with the cardiovascular system, e.g. faintness, due to cerebral anaemia; or dyspepsia, due to engorgement of the intestinal tract.

1. *Dyspnaea*—Difficulty in breathing is a symptom not of any specific cardiac lesion but of some forms of heart failure. The sequence of increasing deterioration is: Shortness of breath with moderate exercise → with slight exercise → at rest → on lying down (orthopnaea). Dyspnoea develops because increasing distension of the pulmonary veins is accompanied by increasing rigidity of the lung tissue, with a resulting disturbance of the Hering-Breuer reflex.

Dyspnoea is the commonest symptom of heart failure, but this must not be diagnosed without supporting evidence.

In the natural history of mitral stenosis, dyspnoea may occur very early, long before other symptoms become evident. On the other hand, in aortic regurgitation or hypertension it is usually a late symptom.

In the late stages of cardiac failure other respiratory symptoms such as cough and haemoptysis, may occur; but, apart from dyspnoea, respiratory symptoms are generally due to respiratory disease and not to heart disease.

2. *Palpitation*—This may be simply defined as consciousness of the beating of the heart. In most cases, it has nothing to do with heart disease: the more the heart is felt, the less abnormal is there to feel in it. In most instances, the complaint of palpitation suggests nervousness, but it may be due to many other causes. Palpitation may sometimes occur with organic heart disease, as in advanced aortic regurgitation with an enlarged left ventricle. If it occurs in bouts, with a definite and sharp beginning and end, it suggests one of the paroxysmal tachycardias. Commoner than all these is the sensation of a 'missed beat', which is usually due to an extrasystole, but which is also referred to by the patient as a palpitation.

3. *Precordial Pain*—The only well-recognized cardiac pain is due to ischaemia of the heart muscle; this is one of the occasions when anaemia really hurts. The local anaemia may be permanent (coronary

thrombosis) or temporary (angina of effort), but in both cases the pain is characteristic in many ways. *Type*: Gripping, aching, or pressing. *Severity*: Mild to agonizing. *Variation*: There is no fluctuation, though it may slowly wax or wane. *Site:* Usually beginning under the middle or upper part of the sternum, though occasionally under the lower sternum or in the epigastrium. *Spread* (if severe): Usually to left arm, less often to the neck, occasionally to the jaw or abdomen.

These features are common to cardiac ischaemia, but as the diagnosis is an ominous one you must be most meticulous in eliciting all the features of the pain, to enable you to distinguish it from less serious pains such as those of neurosis, pleurisy, or indigestion.

4. *Gastrointestinal Symptoms*—Cardiac failure may lead to congestion of the abdominal viscera, with the production of anorexia, nausea, a sense of fullness, pain over the liver (more marked with effort), and occasional vomiting. Without more definite evidence these are of only imprecise diagnostic value.

5. *Cerebral Symptoms*—Mental confusion, due to cerebral anoxaemia, may be the first symptom of heart failure. It is worth remembering this, and examining your patients carefully in the casualty department before packing them off to the asylum. Symptoms such as headache, dizziness, and fainting also occur with heart disease, but they are more commonly due to emotional disturbances.

6. *Malnutrition*—When the degree of cardiac failure becomes marked the patient may waste or fail to thrive; often, however, even gross wasting is masked by the simultaneous occurrences of aedema. Severe congenital heart lesions are quite frequently the cause of stunted growth and infantilism.

Physical Examination

The Circulatory Tour

It is easier to go with the stream than against it, and some of the energy you save can be used to observe the vegetation and landmarks on the banks. As we have already emphasized, it is logical to start your examination at the pulse, to proceed by assessing the capillary and then the venous circulation, and to end up at the heart. By this orderly procedure nothing of importance is likely to be omitted, and you can train yourself to look, *en route,* for additional clues such as cyanosis, nodules, clubbing, petechiae, oedema, rheumatic rashes, and thyroid enlargement.

The Pulse—

How to feel—It is essential to feel with the sensitive tips of the fingers. Customarily, it is taught that three fingers are placed on the patient's radial artery, but two are sufficient for nearly every purpose.

What are you feeling for?—Know *consciously* what you are feeling for, or your examination will degenerate into a gesture with no significance.

1. Gauge the *vessel* you are feeling, i.e. its calibre and the condition of its wall.

2. Gauge the factors dependent on the *heart,* i.e. the rate and the rhythm.

3. Gauge the factors dependent on *both,* i.e., the volume of the pulse-wave and the form and shape of the wave. You may also, with more practice, estimate the blood-pressure at the height of the beat (systolic pressure) and between beats (diastolic pressure).

The Artery Wall—You may feel undue hardness or sinuosity of the artery wall, as in arteriosclerosis. If in doubt, compare with the feel of your own radial artery, palpated with your free hand placed on your examining hand; but if you are in doubt, the artery is likely to be normal. The normal artery, rolled under your first and second fingers, seems to merge into the surrounding soft tissues. This feature tends to be lost in middle age, and in old age the artery feels like a hard cord under the fingers; but beware of any diagnosis made on this finding alone. At the same time as you are feeling for hardness and sinuosity you will be able to form some idea of the comparative elasticity of the artery wall.

Rate—The average adult rate is 72 in a minute, but it varies from individual to individual, and with posture and many other factors. In the newborn, the rate is almost twice as fast as, and in old age is slower than, in the prime of life. If there is any marked divergence repeat your count after a few minutes, when such factors as excitement will have abated. In doubt, or with any unusual figure, compare the pulse-rate with the heart-rate; in this way you may detect dropped beats, for example.

Rhythm—The commonest irregularity in *children* is **sinus arrhythmia,** in which the rate increases with inspiration and decreases with expiration. Getting the patient to take slow, deep breaths markedly accentuates this irregularity; any cause leading to a rapid pulse-rate tends to abolish it. In *adults,* the commonest irregularity is caused by extrasystoles, which may give rise to a missed beat or a beat earlier than expected at the wrist. With extrasystoles the irregularity tends to be only occasional; with auricular fibrillation, on the contrary, it is an uninterrupted or irregular irregularity. To distinguish between these two conditions try the effect of exercise on the rhythm; with rapid rates of beating extrasystoles disappear but auricular fibrillation becomes more evident. But, whatever you suspect, make no final decision about abnormal rhythms until you have examined the heart itself.

Volume—With your two fingers practice repeatedly to distinguish between the normal, moderately full pulse of health, the bounding pulse of fever, and the thin, therapy pulse of shock.

Form and Shape—With even a little experience you can recognize the different forms of pulse. The common type is the regular 'up-and-down' wave of the normal subject.

Another type is the very steep wave which occurs in conditions where there is a considerable difference between the systolic and diastolic blood-pressure (as in aortic regurgitation or thyrotoxicosis). Such a pulse, which flicks momentarily against the examining fingers, is known as a 'Corrigan' or 'water-hammer' pulse. It is misleading to call it a 'collapsing' pulse, as is often done, because the characteristic flick which is felt is produced by abnormally rapid filling of the artery, and the rate of emptying or 'collapse' is less marked and less easily recognized. The flick of the pulse against the finger is much more easily felt if the patient's wrist is held up while you palpate; the position is that which is taken if you tell the patient to keep his elbow on the table while holding the hand as high as possible.

At the opposite extreme from the Corrigan pulse is the uncommon 'anacrotic' pulse, observed characteristically, in aortic stenosis, in which the pulse-wave falls and rises very gradually.

Types of Pulse

Extrasystoles Note the 'regular irregularity'.	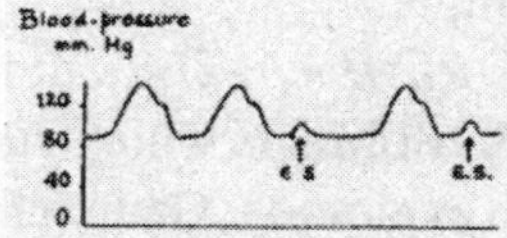
Auricular Fibrillation Note 'irregular irregularity', with variation in depth and frequency of beats.	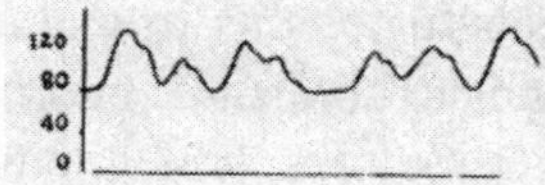
Corrigan Pulse Note the excessive pulse-pressure, and the steep ascent which produces the characteristic 'flick' against the finger.	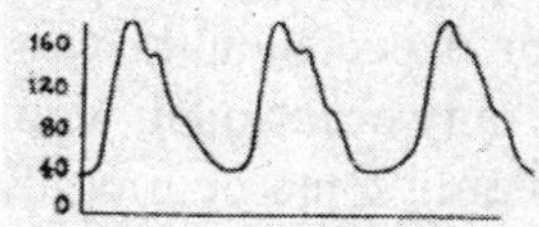
Anacrotic Pulse. Note how it contrasts with the Corrigan pulse, so that it feels 'sustained' against the examining finger.	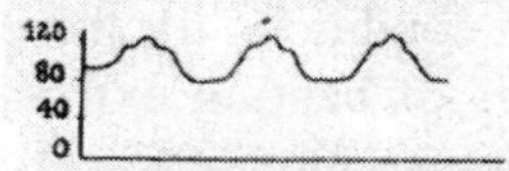

With any unusual pulse shape, and particularly if the pulse-wave appears flat, train yourself to pass on automatically to palpating *both* radial pulses at the same time and in the same position. In this way, you may get an early clue to unilateral pressure on some part of the arterial tree, for instance, by an aneurysm pressing on a subclavian artery.

Blood-pressure—With only a little practice you can gain for yourself a reputation as a 'human sphygmomanometer'. Feel the pulse, first with light, then firm, pressure. A pulse which can be felt best with light pressure suggests a low blood-pressure; a pulse felt best with firm pressure suggests a high blood-pressure.

Sphygmomanometry—Measuring the blood-pressure is an essential part of any examination of the cardiovascular system. Nevertheless, it is only too easy to be 'blinded by science'; the sight of a delicate mercury column and precise figures marked on the 'instrument may very easily lead you to attach quite a fictitious importance to minute deviations, and to regard the instrument as an infallible index instead of merely one weapon in your armamentarium. Remember that even the 'normal' figures are not sharply definable; thus, for life insurance purposes the common practice in England is to take 160 mmHg as the maximal systolic pressure, while in the U.S.A. 145 mm is the maximum. With the following precautions, and bearing clearly in mind the fallacy of any rigid adherence to set figures, blood-pressure estimations can, however, help you considerably.

First, wrap the armlet neatly round the upper arm. Then make sure that both the patient and his arm are comfortably relaxed. Feel the radial pulse, as a preliminary, and read the pressure level at which it can no longer be felt. It is important to carry out this preliminary reading as a guide to the more accurate auscultatory method, which you now proceed to. Feel with your fingers for the brachial artery in the cubital fossa, and place your stethoscope over it. Now you are ready, but the patient still is not. The excitement of this applied science will produce an abnormal reading, so distract his attention for a little while to give it time to abate. Now inflate the armlet rapidly, while you listen over the brachial artery. When the sound disappears continue to inflate the armlet for a time; if you stop at that point you will frequently obtain fallacious readings. Now let the air in the armlet escape slowly, and listen carefully. **The *systolic* pressure is taken as that point at which the sound first becomes audible again. Deflation is continued, and the sound becomes louder; suddenly it is replaced by a weak sound, soon to disappear.** The *diastolic* pressure is taken as the point where this sudden replacement occurs. If no sudden change occurs the diastolic pressure cannot be accurately determined, but the point at which all sounds disappear should be recorded.

A single determination may be extremely misleading. Always determine the pressure at least twice, with an interval between the readings during which you put the patient at his ease.

Other Arteries—The radial artery has been very conveniently placed by a beneficent Nature having due regard both for convenience and modesty. Nevertheless, there are other arteries with a palpable pulse which are of importance in clinical examination. The *femoral* artery should be palpated in all cases of suspected congenital heart disease or of high blood-pressure in children; if you cannot feel it consider, seriously the possibility of coarctation of the aorta. The *tibial* arteries, palpable just anterior and posterior to the internal malleolus, should be felt for in patients of middle or advanced age with symptoms referable to the legs, as in intermittent claudication or diabetic gangrene. The *retinal* arteries are the only arteries which may actually be inspected, and in hypertension in particular you should always examine the optic fundi.

If you do not look at the fingers now you probably never will. Examine them for *clubbing* and for *abnormalities of the nails* such as

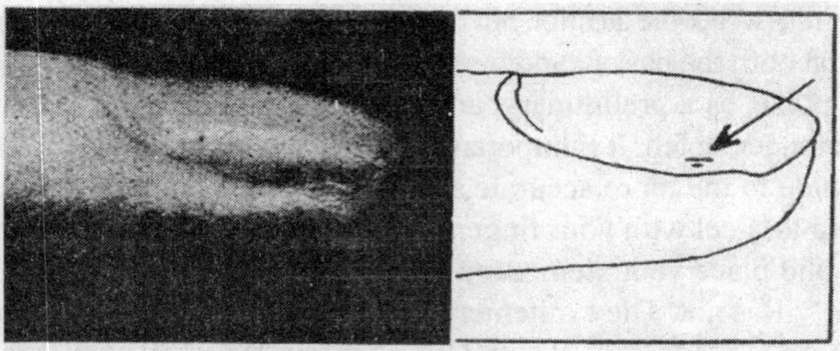

Fig. 2: Linear haemorrhages beneath nail.

the spoon-shaped nails of microcytic anaemias. Look also for *petechia,* and for the *linear haemorrhages* (Fig. 2) under the nails seen in bacterial endocarditis. In suspected acute rheumatism and in chorea look very carefully for *nodules* over the wrists, backs of the fingers, elbows, and ankles (Fig. 3). If present, these nodules are an infallible index of active rheumatic infection. They are much better seen than felt; if the skin over the joints is put on the stretch they can readily be seen in a good light, and the skin is freely movable over them.

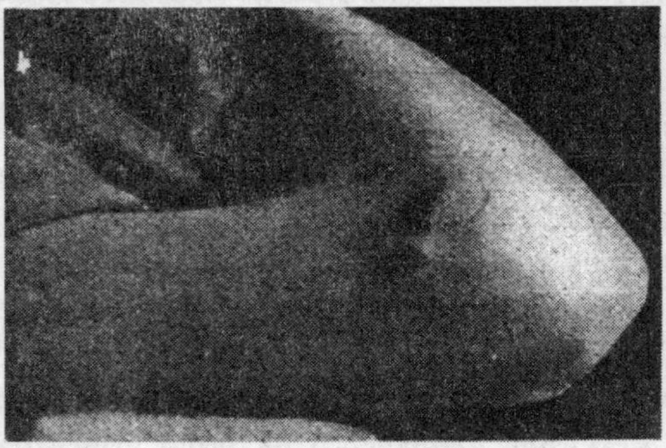

A

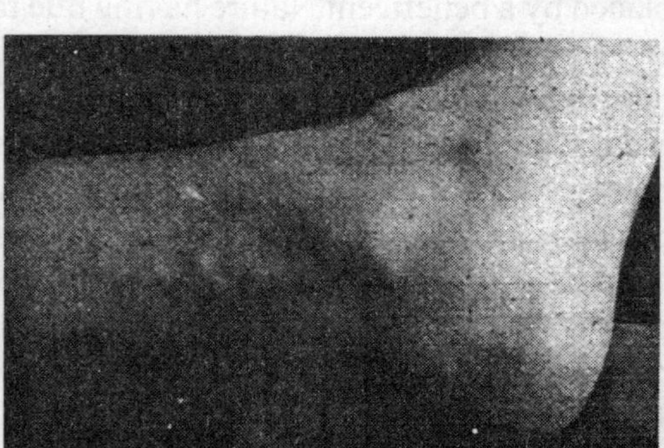

B

Fig. 3: Rheumatic nodules. A. At elbow; B. At ankle.

The Capillaries—The important *direct* observation is that of *capillary pulsation.* Elicit this sign by pressure on the finger-nail sufficient, but only just sufficient, to cause blanching. If the blanched area becomes alternately red then blanched again with each heart-beat, the test is positive. Another way of detecting capillary pulsation is to press a glass slide against your patient's lip until blanching is produced. Do not fall into the elementary error of attributing pulsation of the capillaries to excessive pulsation of the aorta. The capillary pulsation test is positive in any condition where there is excessive vasodilatetion, as in hyperthyroidism for example. But it is most marked where the pulse pressure (the difference between systolic and diastolic pressure) is also high, and is thus best seen with aortic regurgitation. The most obvious *indirect* effect of capillary dysfunction is *oedema,* due to stasis in the peripheral circulation. Edema is late in appearing in the natural history of heart failure. It should be sought in the dependent parts of the body, where the fluid accumulates because of the force of gravity (Fig. 4). In the ambulant patient, look and test for it (pressure over a bone, maintained for several seconds, produces 'pitting') round the ankles, **in a bed-ridden patient examine the sacral area,** which is the most dependent part.

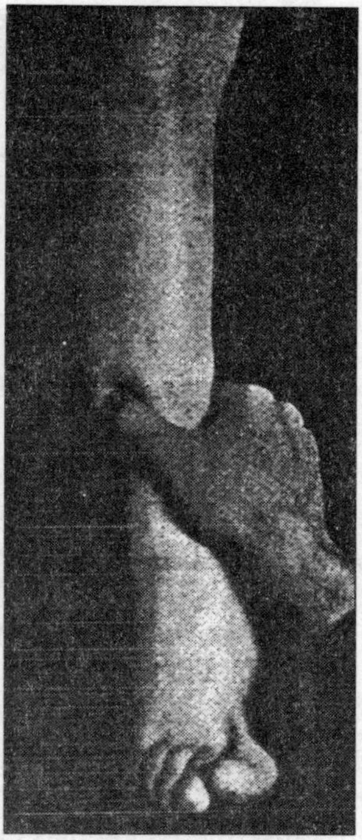

Fig. 4: Oedema.

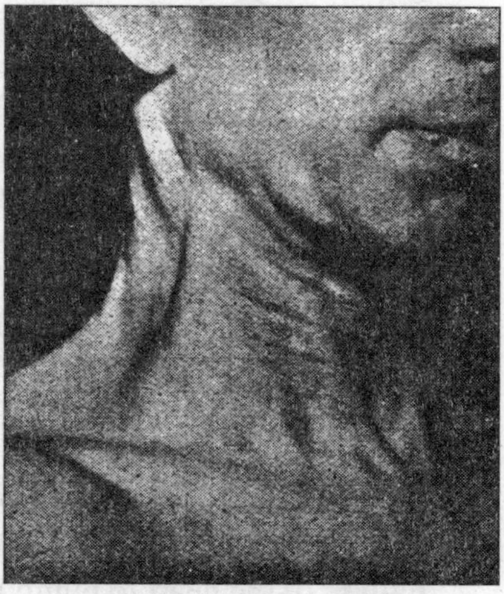

Fig. 5: Venous engorgement.

Veins—Bear clearly in your mind that *zero level* for the venous system is at the right auricle! Above this level veins should normally be partially collapsed; below it, more or less filled. Consider the upper edge of the manubrium sterni as indicating the position of the auricles; distension of any vein, above the level of the manubrium sterni indicates abnormal filling of that vein. This distension may be due to local pressure; but it it is bilateral, and if it pulsates markedly, it can safely be attributed to heart failure. (There is one important proviso: do not be deceived by the effects of a tight collar.)

Venous engorgement is most easily seen in the neck, where the jugular veins are readily observed (Fig. 5). Whatever the position of the patient, jugular distension above the level of the rnanubrium sterni is significant. In the upright position, it is never normal; in severe cardiac failure the distension may even reach up as far as the angle of the jaw.

The point about pulsation, in addition to engorgement, is important. In contradistinction to cardiac failure, the engorgement due to mediastinal obstruction (by tumours, etc.) is not accompanied by pulsation.

At the same time as you look for venous engorgement in the neck examine also the thyroid, because *thyrotoxicosis* is a common cause of cardiac disease in the middle-aged. While examining the neck look also at the lips and face, and try to come to a definite decision about the presence or absence of *cyanosis*: look at the *inside* of the lips, because there cyanosis cannot be produced by cold.

Portal and Pulmonary Circulations—*Ascites* and *liver enlargement* may occur in advanced cardiac failure, and oedema of the lung bases may also occur. Examination of the liver, for example, is so important in cardiovascular disease because the hepatic veins empty almost directly into the right auricle, and increased venous pressure quickly results in enlargement of the liver. Such a congested liver may be very tender, and the abdominal muscles over it take up a protective rigidity, so that the blunt liver edge is very difficult to feel. Armed with this knowledge, you will suspect congestion of the liver whenever you find tenderness of the right hypochondrium in a cardiac case.

The Heart

Now at last you come to the examination of the heart, but your tour of the circulatory system will by no means have been wasted.

Failure of the heart to pump blood adequately is manifest chiefly at the periphery, by distension of veins and oedema. For this reason, it

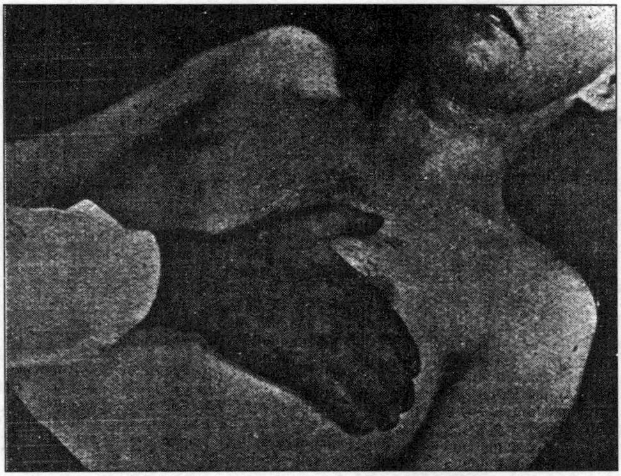

Fig. 6: Palpation of cardiac impulse.

is advisable to commence your examination by a survey of the periphery; by so doing you preserve an integrated view of the whole circulatory system, and you—have started to answer the fundamental question: "What can the heart do?"

In the same way, when you examine the heart itself remember clearly that it is one single muscular organ; what matters most is the

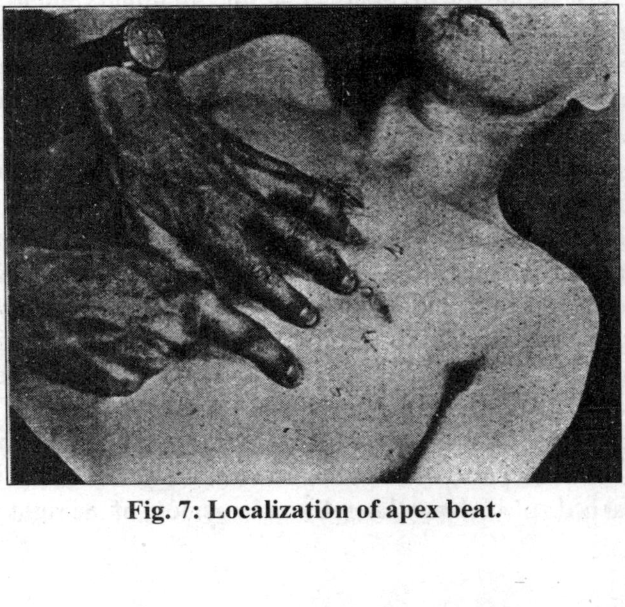

Fig. 7: Localization of apex beat.

state of this muscle, and only secondarily that of the valves. The division of the precordia into 'mitral', 'aortic', and other areas is no mere than a temporary convenience. What you should aim at is to build in your mind a working model of the heart you are assessing.

The Apex Beat—*The most important single physical sign in the chest is the position of the apex beat.* Use it as the foundation Stone on which to build your model, then go on to the usual four methods of examination—inspection, palpation, percussion, and auscultation.

The position of the apex beat can usually be seen, can nearly always be felt, and can be confirmed by medium percussion. The apex beat **is that part of the impulse which is farthest down and out,** yet is still strong enough to be felt distinctly by the palpating finger. But before you turn to defining it so precisely, get all the other information you can from it. First, place the *palm* of vour hand over the area where you see the impulse (Fig. 6). Now note its general character; it may be forceful and heaving as in left ventricular "hypertrophy; or slapping, as in right ventricular enlargement; or it may give the impression of being double. At the same tune, generally with a lighter touch, you may feel a thrill *in* this area.. Now, but only now, change to the more precise method of localizing with your forefinger (Fig. 7).

In a healthy adult, whether standing up or lying down, the cardiac impulse is usually in the 5th intercostal space, 3 to 4 in from the mid-line, i.e. just within the mid-clavicular line. In infants and in children, because the heart is relatively larger than in adults and because the belly seems a more important region and takes up more space, the maximal impulse is more usually in the 4th space ana very often reaches the mid-clavicular line.

In an adult, if the outer border of the maximal impulse is clearly 4½ in or more to the left of the midline, or well outside mid-clavicular line, it denotes a pathological condition, in one of two groups. The cause may lie *outside the heart*: (1) The heart may be pulled over, e.g. by collapse of the lung on the same side; (2) The heart may be pushed over, e.g. by pleural effusion of pneumothorax on the opposite side; or more rarely, (3) The heart may be displaced by malformation of the chest wall. Alternatively, the cause may lie *in the heart:* (1) If the apex beat is displaced both downward and outward, enlargement of the left ventricle is often present, as with disease of the aortic valve; (2) If the apex beat is displaced only laterally, enlargement of the right ventricle is often present, as m advanced mitral stenosis or pulmonary stenosis (Fig. 8).

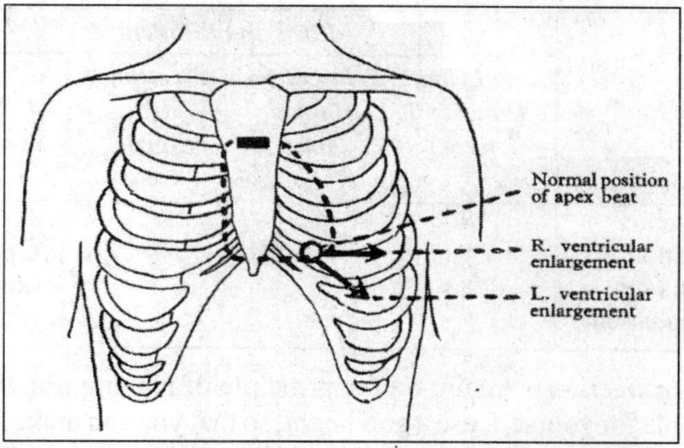

Fig. 8: Position of apex beat with ventricular enlargement.

On these findings, which you can determine for yourself quite clearly, you may begin to build up your model and your diagnosis.

Four Methods and Four Applications—You now pass on to the well-tested methods of inspection, palpation, percussion, and auscultation. But for a thorough examination they must be applied in four ways, and though this is by no means always necessary the essentials should never be omitted, if there is any doubt whatsoever. The four applications are:

1. The four routine methods, with the patient lying down.
2. Palpation and auscultation only, *at the apex* with the patient in the left lateral position.
3. Palpation and auscultation only, *at the base,* with the patient in the upright position and leaning forward.
4. Repeat (2) and (3) *after exercising the patient,* according to where the lesion is suspected.

This looks a great deal, but in practice it takes very little time. Each of the four methods and each of the four applications is calculated to bring out some individual lesion which may be completely missed without it. If you see your chief omit some of them you may envy—but do not emulate. These methods make diagnosis easier and more certain, and at your stage you need to learn the easy and not the hard way. What has just been said is summarized below:

	Position of Patient			
	1. Lying Down (All Areas)	*2. L. Lateral (Mitral Area)*	*3. Sitting Up (Aortic Area)*	*4. After Exercise*
1. Inspection	×			
2. Palpation	×	×	×	Repeat 2 and 3
3. Percussion	×			
4. Auscultation	×	×	×	

1. *Inspection*—Again, on the principle of making things as easy as possible for yourself, use a good light, so that you can make a definite decision about what you see. You will note any deformity of the precordia, often due to congenital enlargement of the heart. Look deliberately for the cardiac impulse. Look also for other pulsations such as those due to aneurysm of the aorta. You may observe that the ribs are indrawn with each systole, usually over the region of the apex beat, as occurs with some forms of adherent pericarditis.

2. *Palpation*—We have dealt already with the apex beat. Having palpated its position do not forget it, or just remember it vaguely. It should move to the left by ½ to ¾ in when the patient turns into the left lateral position, and you will need to follow it round in the left lateral position before auscultating.

Now feel at the apex, at the base of the heart, and over the sternum for a *thrill.* A thrill is a murmur, only more so. A thrill is a definite evidence of organic heart disease, with only rare exceptions. You may miss a thrill through having cold hands, through not feeling very gently with the whole hand, and above all through not positioning the patient correctly. For apical thrills, turn the patient into the left lateral position; for basal thrills, sit the patient up, get him to lean well forward, and if necessary get him to hold his breath in expiration while in this position. You may mistake a forceful or reduplicated heart sound for a thrill, but not if you remember that a thrill is definitely sustained in time. It is exactly like the sensation produced when the hand is placed on the back of a purring cat. You can try to time the thrill, but the murmur of which it is part is more easily timed through your stethoscope.

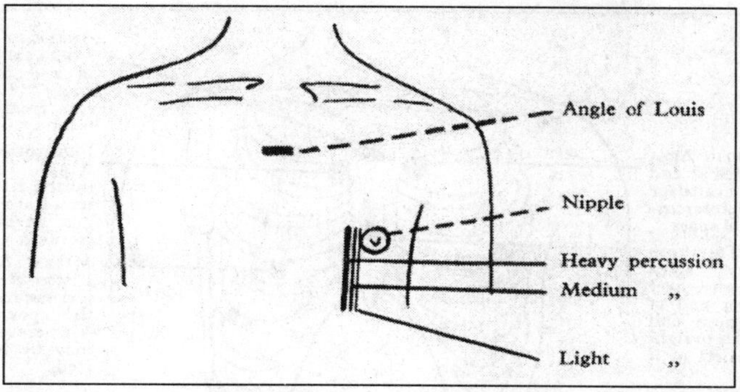

Fig. 9: Percussion of cardiac dullness, illustrating apparent variation in position of apex according to strength of percussion.

3. *Percussion*—There are three useful rules about percussion of the heart:

1. Use *medium* percussion, because this gives the most accurate estimate of the size of the heart (Fig. 9).
2. **Percuss from resonant to dull,** and not in the opposite direction.
3. Keep your pleximeter finger parallel with the border you are percussing (it is unnecessary to percuss the left border of the heart when the apex beat has been defined).

Dullness to the right of the sternum indicates considerable cardiac enlargement (if the heart is not displaced). *Dullness over the manubrium sterni* suggests aneurysm, pericarditis, or a tumour (retrosternal goitre is the commonest tumour). *To the left of the lower part of the sternum* it is resonance which is pathological.

4. *Auscultation*—At long last you are going to use your stethoscope—but still not to listen for murmurs. They must still wait. They are, after all, adventitia, and you must first listen to the heart-sounds themselves. In the same way, when auscultating the lungs you must listen first to the breath-sounds, and only afterwards for adventitious sounds.

Where to listen (Fig. 10)—Listen precisely over the correct place, not somewhere near it. In particular, you will miss the diastolic murmur of mitral stenosis if you do not listen exactly over, and just medial to the apex beat which you have previously located and remembered so carefully. So listen at the *exact* site for the appropriate valve sounds;

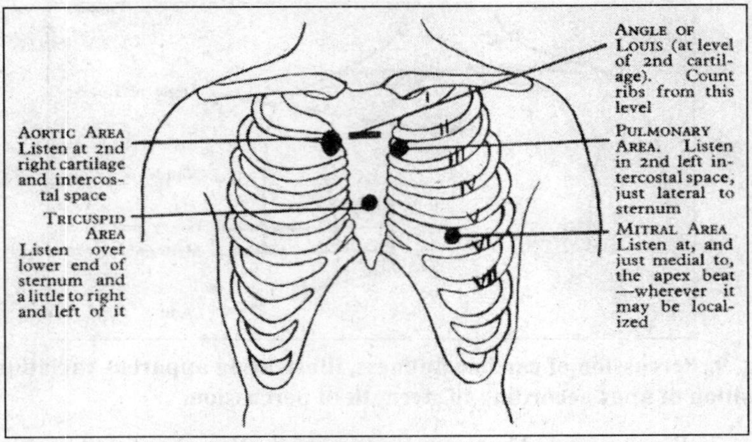

Fig. 10: Sites for auscultation.

for mitral sounds at and just medial to the apex beat, even when it shifts as you move the patient, and for the other valves at the sites marked in the diagram.

What to listen for—Here is an invaluable rule: First listen *to* the sounds; then listen *between* the sounds.

1. *Listening to the sounds:* The normal lub-dup may sound distant. This is usually due to causes *outside* the heart, e.g. obesity or emphysema. Only rarely is it due to causes *in,* the heart such as severe carditis, and is then of comparatively sudden onset in an acutely ill patient.

The sounds may all be unusually loud, seeming to come through your stethoscope with a violent thud. If *all* are equally exaggerated the cause is usually extracardiac. Nervous overaction of the heart is by far the commonest underlying factor.

It is more significant if only *one* sound is accentuated, and in that case you may well find some cardiac cause for the alteration. Before you even consider the possibilities, however, go over the normals in your mind. The first sound is normally louder than the second at the apex, and the second louder than the first at the base of the heart. In children, the pulmonary sounds are louder than the aortic; in old age the aortic become the louder of the two, while in adult life they are approximately equal. Having learnt these, you can then recognize genuine abnormalities. The first sound at the apex may be accentuated, as with cardiac hypertrophy or mitral stenosis. A sharply accentuated 'slapping' first sound should be taken as a warning to listen particularly carefully for the diastolic murmur of mitral stenosis. The second sound at the pulmonary area tends to sound loud and sharp with any cause of congestion in the pulmonary veins such as occurs in mitral stenosis. With hypertension or aortic atheroma the second aortic sound assumes a sharp, exaggerated tone.

Instead of two heart-sounds you may hear three. The *third heart-sound,* which occurs quickly after the normal second sound and is heard as a short thud, is rarely important. It may be heard with careful listening in perhaps a third of normal children. Its frequency grows less with advancing age, so that over 40 years of age it is practically never heard in normal hearts. A third sound which fits in with this description can be considered as normal. Not so another type of extra sound. The triple cadence known as '*gallop rhythm*' is not uncommon in failing hearts, with hyper-tension for example, where there is no evidence of valvular disease. This ominous rhythm is best heard at the apex when the heart is beating at about 100 beats a minute. The extra sound is of intensity almost equal to that of the other two, and it usually occurs a little before the normal first sound.

Listening still *to* the sounds, you may detect an irregularity in rhythm or in force. In that event put your hand on the pulse and feel it at the same time as you listen to the heart. In this way you will recognize 'dropped beats'. They are ventricular contractions which are too weak to propagate a pulse-wave.

2. *Listening between the sounds—murmurs (see below).*

Murmurs

Do you realize that this chapter on cardiovascular disease is almost completed—that you should already be in a position to determine a good many important facts, and make some accurate diagnoses, even though murmurs have been almost entirely ignored? Murmurs are by no means the be-all and end-all of cardiac examination; they are no more than a part of the evidence on which to assess the cardiovascular system and the patient.

Train yourself, once you have listened to the heart-sounds, to shut them out from your perception, so that you can concentrate on the intervals between them. With conscious attention to this point you will find yourself listening intently from the end of one sound to the beginning of the next. The importance of this training lies not only in the comparative ease with which it will enable you to pick up murmurs, but also in the confidence with which you can satisfy yourself that there is *no* murmur present.

Some General Rules for Listening to Murmurs:

1. Listen exactly over the correct site for the individual murmur.
2. Listen in the logical sequence suggested in 'the circulatory tour', then listen down the sternum.
3. Listen consciously *to* the heart-sounds, then *between* the heart-sounds.
4. When you hear a murmur, proceed first to time it, i.e. ask yourself whether it occurs in systole or diastole. To help, feel the apex beat with your finger at the same time as you are listening. The heave of the apex times the beginning of systole, and should leave you in no doubt.
5. Next, note where the murmur is loudest, by following it in various directions.
6. At the same time you will have observed the direction of transmission, if any.
7. The character of the murmur will also have impressed itself by now. You should be able to say whether it is harsh or soft, of high or low pitch, blowing or rumbling or squeaking. In general, in trying to find an apt description of what you hear, use simple adjectives. Such phrases as 'the shriek of a hungry sea-gull' or 'a borborygmous murmur' are misplaced.
8. Observe what happens to the murmur when you alter the patient's position or after exercise (re-read the important suggestions at the beginning of this section).
9. Keep in mind the physiological principles you have for so long laboured to acquire. Fig. 11 illustrates schematically how they form the basis of your understanding of cardiac murmurs. Only the quality of the sound could not be deduced by you from physiological principles, and that is added empirically, as the result of observation of cases in practice.

These features are co-ordinated in the accompanying diagram (Fig. 12).

	Normally open in	*Therefore Stenosis produces Murmur in*	*Normally closed in*	*Therefore Regurgitation produces Murmur in*
Mitral Valve	Diastole	Diastole	Systole	Systole
Aortic Valve	Systole	Systole	Diastole	Diastole

Blowing sound. Rough sound.

Very rough, or rumbling sound.

Fig. 11: The production of murmurs.

Characters of Murmurs—Now you have gone over the necessary business of determining murmurs it is profitable to consider them individually and, as individuals, to learn to know their idiosyncracies.

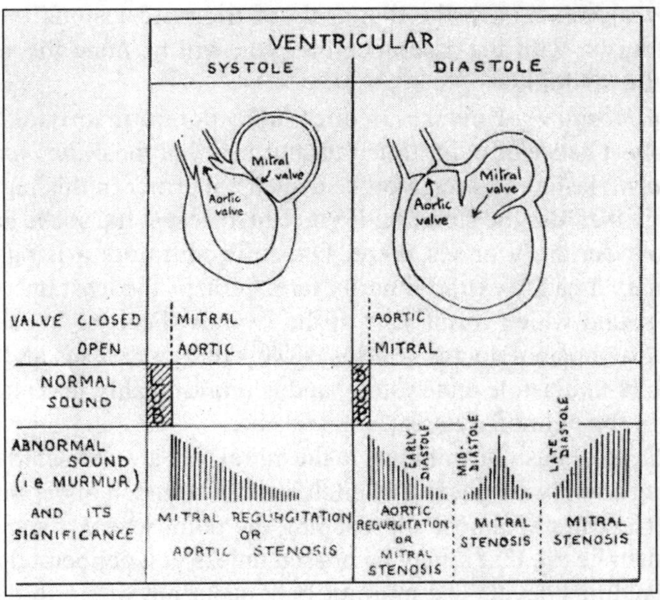

Fig. 12: The relationships of heart-sounds. (The left side alone is shown.)

At the different sites murmurs have different characteristics. Just as you can learn to recognize a dog by its bark, so you will learn to confirm your timing of a murmur by its characters. Sooner or later you wIll be able to reverse the order: you will automatically recognize a murmur by its character, and time it only for confirmation, but it will need a little experience before you can trust your ear sufficiently for that.

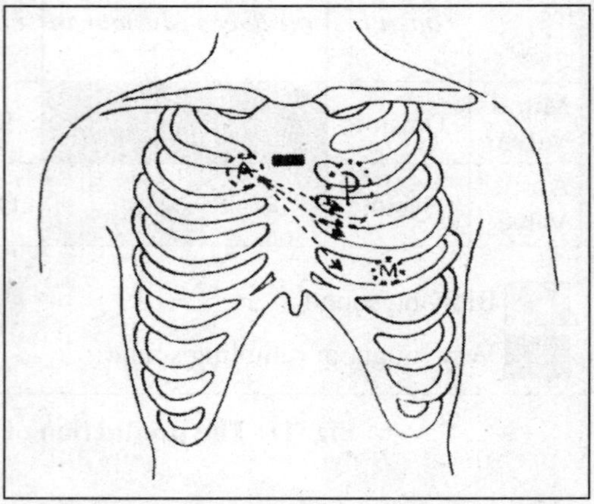

Fig. 13: Diastolic murmurs. Areas of audibility and direction of conduction. A, Aortic; P, Pulmonary; M, Mitral.

1. Diastolic Murmurs (Fig. 13)—Diastolic murmurs are always pathological.

Tricuspid—Leave the diagnosis of tricuspid lesions to expert cardiologists, with the assurance that you will be none the worse a doctor for so doing.

Pulmonary—Beware at once of a common mistake. The commonest cause of a diastolic murmur heard at the *pulmonary* area is an *aortic* lesion. If, then, you hear such a murmur in this region try to follow it across the sternum; if you can hear it at the aortic area too it almost certainly arises there. Diastolic murmurs arising at the pulmonary area are extraordinarily rare. Perhaps the least uncommon is that sound which forms part of the 'water-wheel' or 'machinery' murmur of a patent ductus arteriosus. This murmur waxes and wanes through both diastole and systole, and is unmistakably maximal at or lateral to the pulmonary area.

Mitral—Diastolic murmurs in the mitral area are characteristically rumbling and low in pitch. The pitch is often so much lower than that of other murmurs, almost approaching the point where it can be felt rather than heard, that it may be missed unless you deliberately listen at this auditory level. The murmur may occur anywhere in diastole, but if it is truly pre-systolic (i.e. in the short interval immediately preceding the first sound) it seems to be crescendo in character and ends in a first sound which is sharp and slapping. Note again, in difficult cases, the necessity for listening for a mitral diastolic murmur with the patient in the left lateral position, in the few beats just after exercise, and exactly over or just within the area of the maximal impulse to which it may be exclusively confined.

Aortic—A diastolic murmur at the aortic area is missed by students and by doctors more often than any other cardiac murmur. The reasons are many, and understandable. It is described as a blowing murmur, but is often extremely distant and faint. It may be missed because of the noisiness of the breath-sounds in this region, or because it is heard at its loudest with the patient upright. To make sure of hearing such a murmur, therefore, listen while the patient leans well forward in the upright position, and if necessary holds his breath in expiration while maintaining this position.

2. Systolic Murmurs (Fig. 14)—Considered alone, a systolic murmur is of no significance. Considered together with other evidence it is often of help, but the diagnosis of an organic lesion based solely on a systolic murmur is unforgivable.

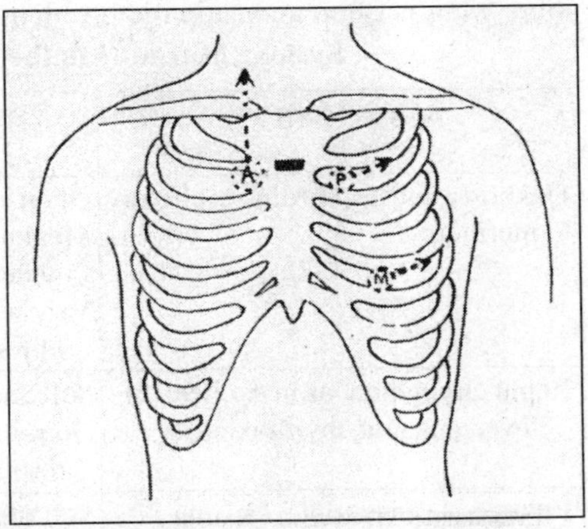

Fig. 14: Systolic murmurs. Area of audibility and direction of conduction. A, Aortic; P, Pulmonary; M, Mitral.

Tricuspid—Systolic murmurs in the tricuspid area are of no practical significance.

Pulmonary—In the pulmonary area, either alone or as part of a widespread murmur at the base of the heart, systolic murmurs are heard in a large number of normal subjects. They tend then to be soft and blowing in character, and to vary with position, respiration, and exercise. If, however, the murmur is loud and rough, and if it is accompanied by a thrill, the diagnosis of pulmonary stenosis is possible. A systolic murmur may be the most audible part of the 'machinery' murmur of patent ductus arteriosus, already described.

Mitral—Systolic murmurs at the mitral area have given rise to more controversy than any other noise known to Medicine. Though they rarely mean anything serious, this does not help you in any individual case. Without other evidence they must be flatly ignored as a basis for the diagnosis of cardiac lesions. Suggestive supporting evidence would be enlargement of the heart, or the onset of the murmur in acute rheumatism where no murmur was previously audible. If the murmur is harsh and is propagated far out into the axilla an organic basis becomes more probable, but no more than that. **It is safest to consider a mitral systolic murmur as a warning**—a warning to intensify your search for the truly diagnostic diastolic murmur. In the long run you will do much less harm by ignoring all apical systolic murmurs than by making your patient worry about his heart while you solve what is often an academic problem (*see* table).

Systolic Murmurs in the Mitral Area

May be due to	*Possess these Characteristics as a Rule*
Unknown causes, cardio-respiratory murmurs	Often soft or squeaking in character Maximal in pulmonary area, but often widespread Vary with position. Vary with phases of respiration
Rapid circulation, as in excitement, fever, anæmia, thyrotoxicosis	Soft and usually widespread Do not vary greatly with position or respiration
Enlarged left ventricle, causing relative mitral incompetence	Soft or moderate blowing murmur Maximal in mitral area Not varying with respiration
Organic disease of mitral valve, as in acute rheumatism or sequel of bacterial endocarditis	Soft to loud blowing murmur Maximal in mitral area Made louder with patient in left lateral position Not affected by phase of respiration

Aortic—A soft aortic systolic murmur is nearly always unimportant, and is certainly common in healthy subjects. Even harshness is a most unreliable guide, and harshness is no more than a warning to examine for a thrill. A systolic aortic murmur may be heard when the heart is beating fast, and sometimes when it is slow, even in healthy subjects, in the presence of anaemia, atheroma of the aortic valves, aneurysm, or aortic stenosis. It should be accompanied by a thrill for the diagnosis of stenosis to be permissible, a diagnosis which you will already have considered when you found a 'flat' anacrotic pulse at the beginning of your tour.

The accompanying table summarizes the important facts about the significance of systolic murmurs heard in the mitral area. Work out for yourself a similar one for aortic systolic murmurs.

3. Other Murmurs—

Congenital Heart Disease—The murmurs of congenital heart disease have several helpful features in common. They nearly always sound rough, and they occur centrally or at the base of the heart. Quite frequently they are accompanied by a thrill. There may be other supporting evidence such as clubbing of the fingers, stunting of growth, cyanosis, or enlargement of the heart. Without the thrill or other supporting evidence a definite diagnosis is not permissible.

Remember that congenital heart disease may remain symptomless even into adult life. Murmurs which in position, character, and transmission do not correspond with those of acquired heart disease should suggest the possibility of congenital heart disease.

Pericarditis—Pericardial friction sounds may cause confusion with valvular murmurs, especially with the to-and-fro murmur of aortic valve disease. Loud pericardial friction resembles the leathery grating of pleural friction and is easily recognized. The less obvious sounds may be extremely soft, and the student who hears them without being shown may be proud of his achievement. They may be confined to a very small area, generally at the base of the heart, and the site may change quite quickly, but usually it does not correspond exactly with the sites at which valve sounds are best heard. Nor do the friction sounds correspond exactly in time with the sounds of the heart-beat. Often the murmur caused by pericarditis is extremely superficial, sounding almost like an echo, and it may vary according to the pressure you exert with your stethoscope. If friction sounds are heard and to vary with the phases of respiration they are called 'pleuro-pericardial', and are then commonly due to inflammation of that part of the pleura which is in contact with the pericardium.

Exercise Tolerance Test—You will by now have most of the data on which to build your medical working model, but you need one more item of information—you want to know how the patient's heart works under stress. *If the heart is already beating fast, or if the patient is breathless after undressing or at rest, additional testing is obviously unnecessary; the heart has very little in reserve,* and it would be dangerous to put it under an increased strain. In fact, the patient's history will often give more information than any test you can devise, and no test can be relied on to separate mental from physical limitations to exercise. For these reasons exercise tolerance tests are frequently omitted, but the use of the same test with all your patients will often give you some help. A simple one is to get your patient to place one foot on a chair, then raise himself on it to the upright position twenty times in one minute. Count his pulse, and observe the depth of respiration, when he is standing quietly at rest before starting to exercise, and again immediately after the test and after an interval of one minute. Do not draw any conclusions until you have carried this out on normal subjects of different ages and made a 'norm 'for yourself.

Summary

1. Obtain a complete history.
2. Look at the patient as a whole.
3. Carry out 'the circulatory tour'. Start by examining the arteries, then proceed to the capillaries, the veins, and finally end with the heart.
4. During this process of 'going with the stream', look for additional evidence such as clubbing, petechiae, oedema, liver enlargement, lung engorgement, cyanosis, and thyroid enlargement.
5. The heart should be examined last, in the orderly manner suggested, using the four methods of inspection, palpation, percussion, and auscultation and their four applications.
6. Your ultimate object is to ascertain what the heart can do. To do this try to build up in your mind a working model of the cardiovascular system by using not one but every possible item of information.

□

CHAPTER V

EXAMINATION OF RESPIRATORY SYSTEM

"Chests are so difficult". How often does one hear that complaint from students! It is true that the diagnosis of chest disease may derive from the history alone or from radiography, but physical examination is nonetheless important. There are many facts which can only be known after you have used your eyes, your hands, and your stethoscope upon the chest. You are no doctor until you have mastered the art.

First Principles

While examining a patient's chest, try to bear two pictures in your mind at the same time—one is a still picture of the underlying lung, its gross anatomy and finer structure, and the other is a moving picture of the mechanism by which the physical signs you seek to elicit are produced.

Wherever your eye or your hand or your stethoscope rests, picture beneath that spot the bronchi, vessels, alveoli, and pleurae. Whenever you elicit a physical sign, try to under-stand just how that physical sign is produced. By thinking thus in terms of anatomy and physics you can often build up a picture of any pathological process within the chest.

Remember that chest examination at first is difficult and that the art is not easy to acquire; so, until you are really familiar with what normal chests look like, feel like, and sound like, hesitate to attach any importance to isolated 'abnormal' physical signs.

Symptoms

In the diagnosis of respiratory disease, few things are so important as a knowledge of the patient's normal environment and work, his past illnesses, and his general health. So many chest diseases begin with general symptoms such as loss of appetite and weight, sweating, malaise, and lassitude. So many chest diseases have their roots in a past illness or an industrial hazard. Your history of the patient must be very full, and precise about dates of onset. Luckily, local chest symptoms are relatively few and easy to interpret. You should, therefore, in every case inquire whether the patient suffers or does not suffer from one or other of the three primary chest symptoms—pain, cough, or breathlessness. If *pain* is present, make the usual inquiries about the pain. If *cough* is present, find out whether it is dry or productive of sputum. The daily amount and character of the sputum must be discussed with the patient. Haemoptysis, the spitting of blood, may mean either a slight staining or streaking of the sputum or the product of a severe pulmonary haemorrhage. You must try to find out which sort the patient means, and whether the blood came from the mouth, the pharynx, or the lungs. *Breathlessness* should be considered against a back-ground of the patient's normal activities, sleeping, walking, or running—and you should try to find out exactly when and where it hampers him.

Breathing

Respiratory Behaviour—Breathing is a process which, since man first recorded his thoughts, has been regarded as synonymous with life itself. There is much to learn by watching it. Emotion, organic brain disease, and abnormalities of the blood, of metabolism, of excretion, of the circulation, or of the lungs themselves, may all interfere with normal respiration.

First, notice whether your patient's breathing is easy, so that he is not consciously aware of doing it. Uncomfortable, laboured breathing—*dyspnoea*—may merely mean that the patient has, for deep-seated emotional reasons, become aware of the normal subconscious movements of respiration and, by a conscious effort to breathe, is actively interfering with the mechanism. Such dyspnoea is most obvious when the patient's attention is directed to it and is absent during sleep. On the other hand, dyspnoea may mean very serious organic disease. But whether dyspnoea is present or not, count the respiratory rate, estimate the depth of breathing, and watch for irregularities or variations in its rate and depth over a short space of time (such as Cheyne-Stokes breathing). Dyspnaea, if it is marked, will bring the 'accessory muscles' of respiration, the scaleni, sternomastoid, and nasal muscles into play. The latter cause the wings of the nose (alas nasi) to expand with inspiration, a movement which provides valuable objective evidence of respiratory distress. Again, severe dyspnoea will usually cause your patient to sit upright (*orthopnaea*), particularly if the dyspnoea happens to be of cardiac origin.

Inspiratory Dyspnaea—This is the name given to painful breathing due to obstruction to the inflow of air into the lungs, as by a narrowing of the laryngeal inlet. Its characteristics are prolonged difficult inspiration, accompanied by sucking in towards the mediastinum of the soft tissues of the neck, and of the intercostal spaces and ribs, particularly the 6th, 7th, 8th, and 9th, between the anterior axillary line and the sternum.

Expiratory Dyspnaea—This is either due to bronchial spasm or inflammation, or due to loss of contractibility in the lung tissues, so that expiration, normally almost a passive process, becomes an active muscular effort. Its characteristics are prolonged difficult expiration, but with contraction of the accessory muscles during inspiration.

Interruptions to Breathing—Notice whether the patient's inspiration is suddenly checked by pain so that he grunts, or coughs, or moves at the same phase of each respiration. This phenomenon is due to disease either of the pleurae or overlying muscles.

Adventitious Noises—While watching your patient breathe, you must also keep your ears open. You may hear a sighing or crowing noise at each inspiration—*stridor*—which indicates some obstruction high up in the respiratory tract, or you may hear wheezy noises arising deeper in the chest. If these occur both in inspiration and expiration, they are more likely to indicate some organic obstruction in a main bronchus. If they occur only in expiration they are probably caused by bronchial spasm or mucus in the smaller bronchi.

Voice—Hoarseness and loss of voice are usually due to organic or functional disease of the larynx, but may be due especially in children, to secretions from the nasopharynx obstructing the movements of the vocal cords.

Grunting—Patients who are breathing rapidly and shallowly often grunt at the start of expiration. This usually indicates painful respiration, as in pneumonia or acute inflammation of the pleura.

Cough—It is useful to be able to know by its sound whether a cough is due to irritation of the pharynx or to mucus in the bronchi, whether it is due to disease of the larynx or the pleura. Though it is difficult to reach this ideal, there is a good deal to learn from the character of the cough. A dry, hacking cough, repeated every few minutes, is usually due to inflammation or secretion in the pharynx; in children with enlarged tonsils this type of cough may sound thicker. A harsh cough is often associated with a hoarse voice, and suggests laryngitis. If the vocal cords are paralysed the cough becomes brassy or bovine. Pleural pain may produce a dry sharp cough, which characteristically occurs at the same phase of each respiration, and is very distressing to the patient. Cough due to secretions in the chest irritating the sensitive spots at the bifurcation of the bronchi is often paroxysmal and moist. The cough starts explosively, sounds dry at first, but with each successive volley becomes moister, until a blob of mucus is cast up into the pharynx and the patient is relieved. If a patient has advanced bronchiectasis, a sudden movement or a cough may fling some of the mucus from the insensitive dilated bronchi on to undamaged sensitive mucosa, so that a veritable storm of moist coughing ensues, and ends only when the patient has coughed up a large quantity of sputum. It is a poor prospect when a patient cannot laugh without this happening to him. If the patient's respirations are weak, then there is no force behind the cough, secretion accumulates, and the cough becomes very moist.

Inspection

During the earlier stages of your examination you will have been absorbed in watching the patient's respiratory behaviour and keeping your eyes and your ears, open for any clues. Next you should proceed to make a more systematic inspection of his chest. It is all-important for you to obtain a *good view of the chest,* therefore do not hesitate to ask the patient to strip right down to the waist. Later in the examination, if the weather is cold, you can arrange to cover those parts of the chest which are not actually being examined, but don't deny yourself the first good look at the chest as a whole. With an out-patient it is convenient to inspect the chest of the patient standing and then let him turn round so that you can see the back. When the patient is in bed let him lie down flat while you stand at the foot of the bed. If the light is good you will then be able to make out the general shape of the chest; asymmetry may be obvious, and you can see the pattern of the ribs clearly. For instance, from that vantage point you might see quite clearly that the muscles over the left apex were wasted and the ribs crowded together in that region, whereas had you looked from close by you would have been beset by doubt. You might see obvious flattening of one side of the chest. You might see a slight, but nonetheless definite, bulging of the intercostal spaces all down one side; if this was on the right side and you could, at the same time, see the apex beat displaced to the left of its normal position, you would be in the enviable position of being able to make a diagnosis of right pleural effusion or pneumothorax, without having laid a hand upon the patient. This sort of opportunity occurs quite frequently. The importance of inspection of the chest cannot be over-rated.

See *what sort of chest* your patient has: is it symmetrical and flattened anteroposteriorly as it should be, or is it blown out into a barrel-shaped cylinder as happens with the all-too-common emphysema of advancing age? Such a chest is bounded by widely-separated ribs, which, instead of sloping downwards, tend to run forward in the transverse plane.

Next, *watch the chest movements* deliberately: does the cheat expansion look full, or is it restricted? Particularly watch for any inequality of movement between the two sides. If you think there might be, tell the patient to take deep breaths and watch again; try to make up your mind there and then. You are more likely to find the answer by the use of your eyes than you are by palpation or any other means, so it is no good putting off your decision. We would stress the importance of this observation, because by failing to make it avoidable mistakes occur, and because so much can be deduced from the finding of diminished movement on one or other side. After all, if there is diminished movement and you are certain of it, it must mean disease on that side, or chiefly on that side. This knowledge will be a guide to you throughout the rest of the examination. Other observations, perhaps difficult of interpretation, will then have to be made to tally with the undoubted fact that side X is the diseased or the more diseased side of the chest.

Palpation and Inspection Combined

It is not right to insist upon a rigid plan of examination which, in the first place, involves difficulty and labour for patient and examiner, and which anyway will probably later be abandoned by the student. Thus, it is wasteful to make your bed-patient sit up more than once in the course of a chest examination. Provided that you have not skimped the first good long look at your patient's naked chest from the foot of the bed, you should then proceed to palpate the chest, watching as you go.

First, satisfy yourself about *three priorities—finger clubbing,* the *apex beat,* and the *trachea.* Pick up your patient's hand and look at the fingers for evidence of clubbing. This should become an automatic action as you approach a patient's chest.

Secondly, if inspection hasn't helped you to do this, determine the *position of the apex beat* by palpation. The site of maximum intensity of the cardiac impulse should be sought for first by laying the palm of the right hand across the left anterior chest. After estimating the position of the apex beat in this way, proceed to localize it exactly with a finger-tip, then both measure the distance from the mid-sternal line *and* estimate its position in relation to the mid-clavicular line. Because of the wide variations in chest shapes it is always as well to have two cross-bearings on this most important point. The position of the apex beat is vital to the diagnosis of respiratory as well as cardiovascular disease, so make no mistake about it. But two words of warning: if the heart is dilated or diseased, the apex beat should be localized at the farthest point from the mid-sternal line at which a cardiac impulse can be felt distinctly. If the apex beat is difficult to feel, owing to a thick chest wall or underlying emphysema, try getting the patient to expire and hold his breath for a few seconds, as this will often enable you to feel the beat.

Thirdly, determine the *position of the trachea.* Here again, you should use two or more methods to try for a sure answer. Look to see if the clavicular insertion of one sternomaatoid is more obvious than the other, as it is when the trachea is deviated to that side. Next, run the tip of your right index finger up and down the front of the trachea from the cricoid cartilage to the sternal notch, to appreciate the general trend of the trachea. Next, try inserting your finger down between the trachea and the sternomastoid insertion on each side. If it slips in easily on one side but not on the other, then the trachea is deviated away from the side into which your finger slips easily.

The next step in a routine chest examination is to look at the *nose, mouth*, and *throat.* This doesn't mean a complicated examination—just inspection of the shape of the nose, of the interior of the mouth, and of the fauces. With a good light, a tongue depressor may not be necessary, but if it is, take care not to place its blade too far back on the tongue where it will irritate a sensitive area which makes the patient 'gag'. If the patient has false teeth, make him remove them before the examination. After looking at the throat, palpate both sides of the neck for enlarged glands or other abnormality.

Next, lay your hands on the front of the chest, one below each clavicle, to check on the movements of the apices. When you have done this, get the patient to say "one, one, one" or "ninety-nine". Then move the hands lower down, so as to grasp the chest between the axillae and nipples, and repeat the manoeuvre.

Tactile Fremitus—A word must here be said about this method of examination. The voice sets up vibrations in the alveoli of the chest which are normally conducted outwards to the chest wall and are there palpable. There are great variations in the degree of conduction and palpability of these vibrations in normal chests, and you must not attach importance to minor variations. The method is more useful in certain circumstances than in others. Though a child's chest conducts vocal vibrations well, the high-pitched female voice is not deep enough to make easily palpable vibrations come through the thicker chest wall. Thus, tactile fremitus in adult females is often very difficult to elicit and consequently of doubtful value. You should ask your patient to say in a deep voice "one, one, one" rather than "ninety-nine", because the former words can be pitched deeper and "come through the chest" more easily. Do not be misled by minor variations in tactile fremitus, and remember that the only real alteration which matters is their absence or marked decrease in a certain area of the chest. This occurs most markedly with pleural effusions, pneumothorax, and pleural thickening (which cut the path of the vibrations from the lung to the chest wall), and it is in the diagnosis of these conditions that the elicitation of tactile fremitus is of most value. Apart from this, tactile fremitus plays only a very minor role in chest examinations, so do not lose your sense of proportion about it because it seems to be a novel method.

You have now finished with the front of the patient's chest as far as inspection and palpation are concerned, and later you must sit him up and look at the back. Look for swellings, oedema, curvature of the spine, or asymmetry, and carefully watch the chest movements. Stand over the patient while he is sitting up and look down on the apices of his lungs from above (Fig. 1). First, you should note the relative height of the two shoulders and then you should look down the front of the chest below the clavicles; in this way you may detect minor degrees of muscle wasting over or flattening of an apex. Next look down the back in order to see the posterior curve of the ribs; collapse of a lung or part of a lung from any cause leads to a flattening of that backward convexity. Test the expansion of the lower parts of the lungs by the method shown in Fig. 2. Test the tactile fremitus. Its significant absence will be found more easily at the back than at the front, and you should attach more importance to its elicitation there.

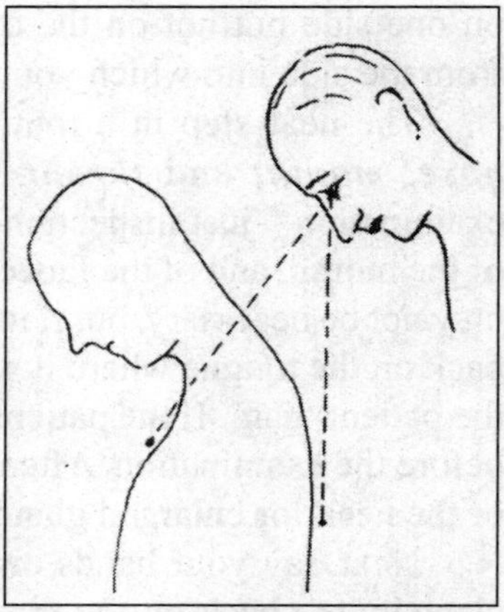

Fig. 1: Inspection of apices from above.

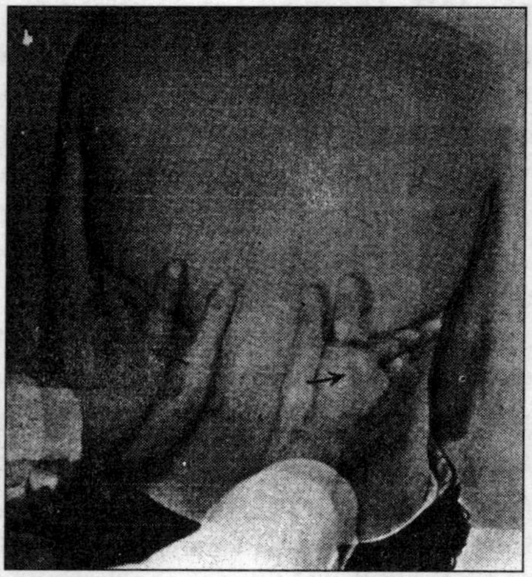

Fig. 2: Expansion of lung bases. Index finger placed firmly along intercostal space, thumbs vertical. Observe movement of the two thumbs away from the midline on deep inspiration.

Percussion

Percussion can be done in more than one way. Sometimes it is a good plan gently to slap the back and front of the chest with the volar surfaces of the fingers. By doing this, grosser abnormalities in the percussion note will be obvious at once.

To map out the areas of percussion dullness accurately

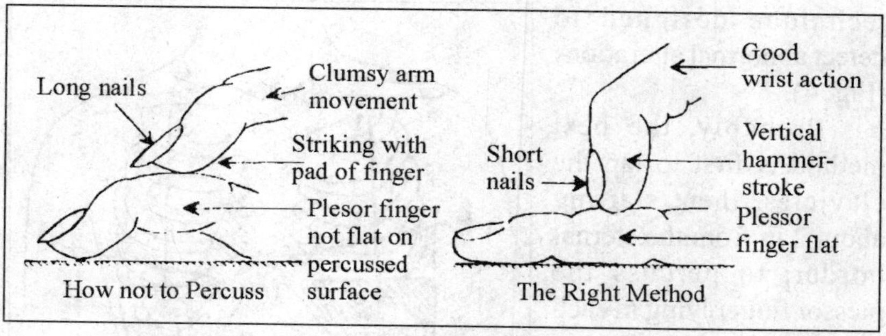

Fig. 3: The wrong and the right way to percuss.

and to elicit slight changes in note, it is best to use the left middle finger as a plessor and the right middle finger as a percussor. But percussion must be done carefully and according to certain rules, if you use this more indirect but more accurate method (Fig. 3). First, the plessor finger must be laid flush with the chest and not allowed to arch itself; it should lie in the intercostal spaces if percussing up and down, or firmly across the line of the ribs if percussing across the chest. The percussing finger should strike the plessor finger on the dorsal surface of its middle phalanx twice in quick succession and then be lifted clear. The percussing finger must strike vertically and the action of the percussing hand must be wristy and sure. You should practise in order to gain flexibility of your wrist. Percuss the furniture at home, your muscles, your bones, and your friends. There is no short cut towards learning the art of percussion; practice is essential. A word of advice we would offer, particularly to the fairer sex; don't try to percuss with long finger-nails, for if you do so, you will either hurt the plessor finger with the nail of the percussing finger, or, to avoid pain, you will start percussing with the volar surface of your finger-pad, and so lose the inestimable value of a vertical hammer stroke.

Study and think about the noises you hear, and listen to the variations in note which can be obtained simply by bending the plessor finger over a fixed spot. Learn the variations in percussion note to be expected over a normal chest, over an infantile chest, a senile emphysematous chest, and a chest covered by a thick layer of muscle and fat. Percuss chests in full inspiration and in full expiration, percuss between the ribs and across the ribs. When you know all the possible variations in note to be expected normally, you can begin to develop a technique designed to detect abnormal alterations (Fig. 4).

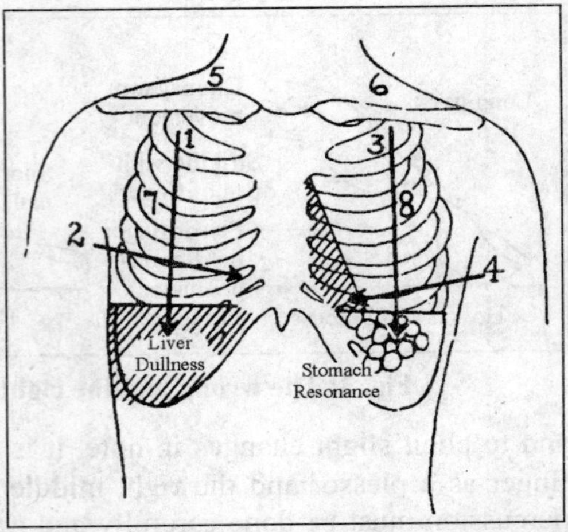

Fig. 4.: The order of percussion.

Probably, the best method is first to tap the clavicles, then, starting about 2 in from the sternal border, to percuss the plessor finger lying in each anterior intercostal space from above downwards, first on the right side and then on the left side. When you reach the liver dullness on-the right, percuss across the ribs in the right axilla and towards the right border of the heart, then percuss down the left side to the stomach resonance and then from the left axilla across to the left border of the heart. Next, by percussing lightly, compare the note over the upper intercostal spaces on the two sides. Slight variations in percussion note are difficult to elicit and percussion must be light if you are to hear them. This is most important where percussion of the lung apices is concerned, since gross tuberculous disease in these regions may give rise to only slight impairments of percussion note. At the back you should percuss with a firmer stroke and go right down to the hepatic or splenic dullness at the bases. It is usually not worth while percussing directly over the scapula as the thick layer of muscle and bone interferes with the note too much.

Normal lung resonance may be impaired or it may be lost completely. Complete loss of lung resonance is usually known as 'stony dullness'. The note is flat and high pitched, as it is over the liver, and there is a lack of vibration in the underlying structures which the plessor finger can sometimes detect more easily than the ear.

Increased or boxy lung resonance is found when percussing emphysematous lungs, and an extremely drum-like note is obtained over a pneumothorax. It may be said, in fact, that the note obtained by percussion over the lungs depends on the relative quantities of air and fluid beneath the percussing finger. The dullest note is obtained over a pleural effusion, a less dull note over a consolidated or collapsed lung; a normally resonant note over normal lung, a hyper-resonant note over a ballooned, emphysematous lung, and a drum-like note over a pneumothorax.

Auscultation

Yet again, we must stress the importance of knowing the normal. Before trying to listen to your patients' chests, listen to those of your friends, and always take the opportunity of examining and listening to the chests of patients suffering from other diseases. You will find that the normal respiratory murmur is often difficult to hear, is easily lost in extraneous noises and varies according to the part of the chest where you place your stethoscope (Fig. 6). If you settle the ear-pieces of your stethoscope snugly into your ears, if you yourself are comfortable and unhurried, and if you try to visualize as you listen what is happening to the air within the lungs, the sounds you hear will become clear to both the senses and the mind. Some find it a help in the earliest stage of their apprenticeship to close their eyes as they listen, the better to conjure up a picture of what is going on in the lung beneath. It is a pity, however, to make a permanent habit of this, since one of the most valuable features of the binaural stethoscope is the opportunity which it gives to the wearer of watching the movements of any part of the chest at the same time as he is listening to the air entering the lung beneath.

Certain conceptions are fundamental, if the sounds heard are to be understood.

(a) **The normal vesicular breath-sound** is a compound noise produced by the entry of air into myriads of tiny alveoli. It is a low

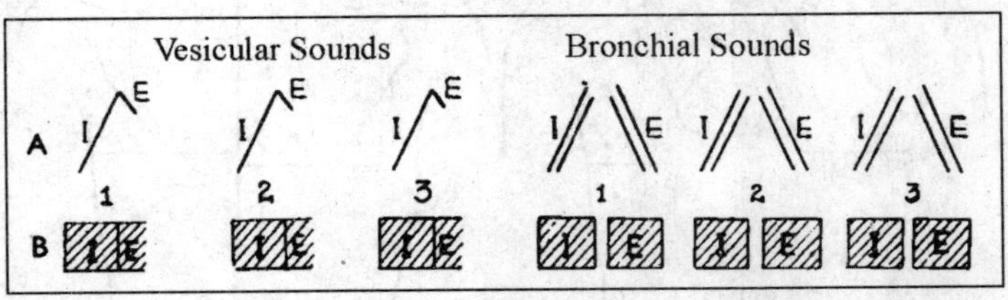

Fig. 5: A, B, Diagrammatic representations of respiratory murmurs. (The first is that most commonly used.) I, Inspiration; E, Expiration; 1, 2, 3, Respiratory cycles.

rustling sound which reaches a peak of intensity towards the end of inspiration and then dies away in a short low expiratory hum; there is no pause between the inspiratory and expiratory sounds. This type of sound is heard best over normal expansile lung tissue, for example, in the axillary region or posteriorly below the inferior angle of the scapula.

(b) **The tracheal or bronchial breath-sound** is a relatively simple or pure noise produced by air rushing up and down those hollow cylinders and being deflected by the larynx and the carinae at bronchial divisions. It is comparable to the noise you can make by blowing down any hollow tube which is partially obstructed. Try making in-and-out strokes of the plunger of a bicycle pump to which the flexible connexion has been attached, or breathing in and out through the mouth with the lips forming the consonant K, and you will hear two very passable imitations of bronchial breathing. Better still, to hear the natural sound at its loudest, listen with a stethoscope over the trachea or over the spine of the 6th cervical vertebra.

It is a hollow, rushing noise, heard equally throughout inspiration and expiration, but only very faintly in the intervals between these phases of respiration (Fig. 5). Any condition which leads to alveolar consolidation (as in pneumonia) or collapse, but which leaves the bronchi patent, will cause bronchial breathing to be heard in that area.

(c) **The normal respiratory murmur** (Fig. 6) is a mixture between vesicular and bronchial components, but the vesicular noise is so much more obvious that the bronchial sounds are obscured, except directly over the trachea or large superficial bronchi. Bronchial sounds

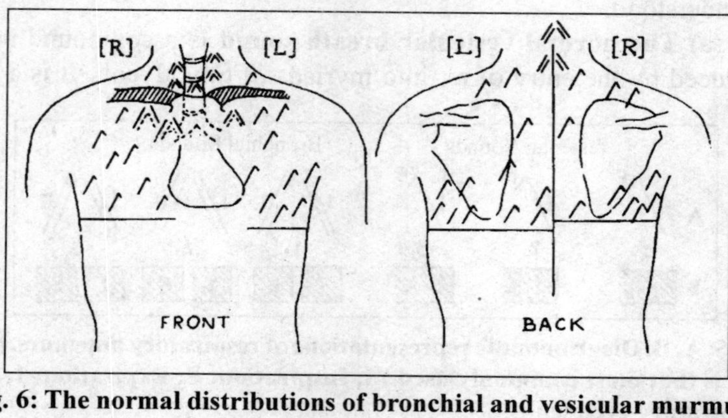

Fig. 6: The normal distributions of bronchial and vesicular murmurs.

are also damped down by the static sound-insulating effect of patent alveoli. At the right apex, beneath the clavicle, the bronchial sounds from the nearby trachea and upper lobe bronchus may be so loud that the resulting murmur is bronchovesicular in quality. By the same token the exact quality of the respiratory murmur varies somewhat over different areas of a normal chest, because of the proximity or otherwise of large bronchi. In infants the murmur is bronchovesicular in *all* areas.

(d) **The intensity or volume of the breath-sounds** depends on: (1) the amount of air entering the underlying lung, (2) the thickness of the chest wall; and (3) the presence of a sufficient number of alveoli to cause the rustling noise. Breath-sounds may, therefore, (1) be abolished by bronchial occlusion, (2) diminished by pleural thickening or fat, or (3) diminished due to emphysematous or fibrotic destruction of the normal alveolar pattern (Fig. 7).

Alterations in Breath-sounds

Condition of Bronchus	Condition of Alveoli	Breath-sounds
Collapsed	Collapsed	Absent
Patent	Collapsed [or consolidated]	Bronchial
Patent	Patent	Vesicular

As with chest movements, a most significant finding is inequality of the respiratory murmur on the two sides.

Variations in Respiratory Murmurs

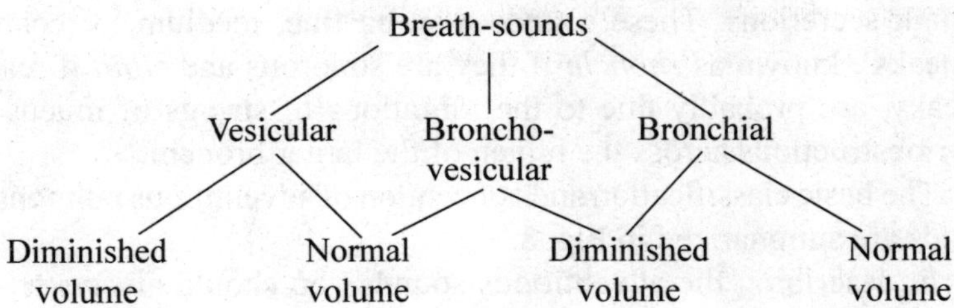

Adventitious Sounds—The exact mechanism by which adventitious or added sounds are produced in the chest cannot be known

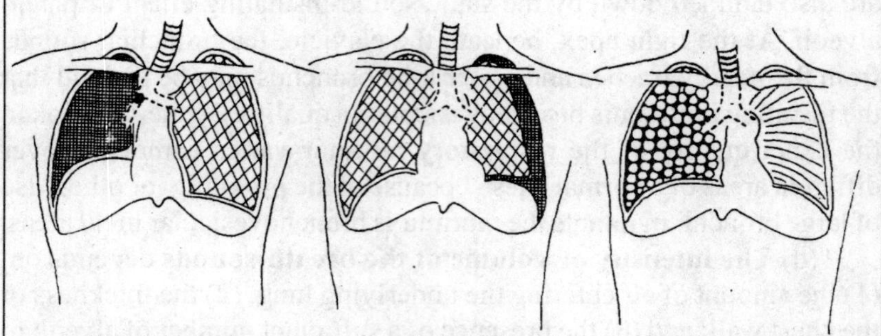

Fig. 7: Some causes of diminished respiratory murmur.

for certain, but we do know that the sounds may come from inside or outside the lung (Fig. 8). Extra-pulmonary sounds are produced either by the creaking of thoracic muscles or by the friction of pleural surfaces rubbing together. Muscle creaks are inconstant leathery sounds which vary with the patient's position. Pleural friction sounds are superficial, discontinuous, rubbing sounds, heard equally on inspiration and expiration. The sounds are often crescendo on inspiration and diminuendo on expiration.

Intrapulmonary sounds are probably produced by the flow of air over secretions in the bronchial tree, and they may be divided into 'bubbles' and 'squeaks'. 'Bubbles', known either as *rales* or *crepitations,* according to the whim of the nominator, are *discontinuous* moist sounds probably caused by air in the bronchioles bubbling through secretions. These sounds may be fine, medium, or coarse. 'Squeaks', known as *rhonchi* if they are sonorous and *sibili* if really squeaky, are probably due to the vibrations of strings of mucus or other obstructions across the lumen of the larger bronchi.

The basic classification and conception of adventitious pulmonary sounds are summarized in Fig. 8.

In describing the adventitious sounds you should always try to place the sounds in one of the categories shown in the rather rigid classifications of Fig. 8. After doing that, you may use your powers of expression and knowledge of the English language to colour your description—for example, "medium rales heard in small area beneath the left clavicle anteriorly; these were tinkling and musical in quality".

If you hear adventitious sounds in a certain area, make quite certain that they are really confined to that area. It may be that, in reality, they are to be heard all over the chest if you listen carefully and long enough.

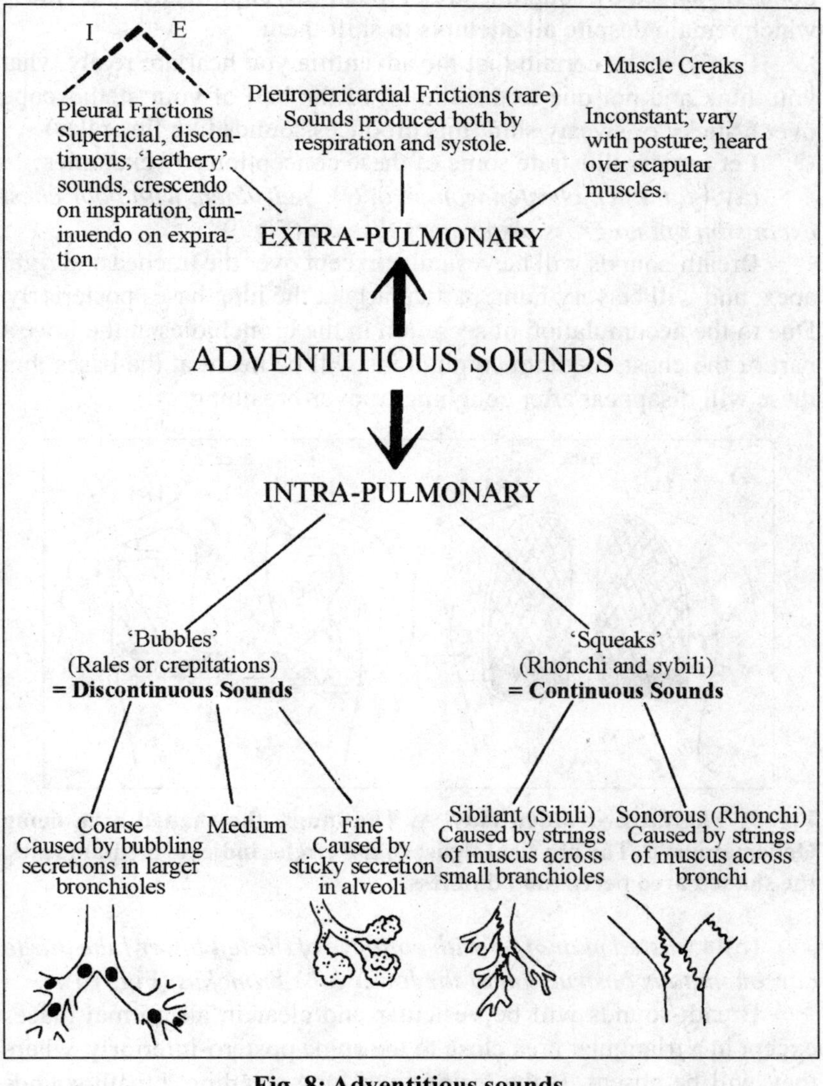

Fig. 8: Adventitious sounds.

The distinction between localized and generalized adventitious sounds is vitally important in diagnosis.

Secondly, if you hear adventitious sounds in a certain localized area, do your best to make them disappear. Make the patient cough and take deep breaths and then listen again. Inconstant adventitious bones dispersed by coughing are of much less significance than those which remain despite all attempts to shift them.

Lastly, make certain that the adventitia you hear are really what you think and not due to the sliding of the bell of your stethoscope over a sticky or sweaty skin (this produces sounds like fine rales).

Let us now illustrate some of these conceptions by examples:

(a) *A fat, thick-chested woman of* 60, *bedridden, with poor chest expansion but no gross respiratory disease* (Fig. 9).

Breath-sounds will be vesicular except over the trachea and right apex, and will be very faint, particularly at the lung bases posteriorly. Due to the accumulation of secretion in the bronchioles at the lowest part of the chest, medium crepitations will be heard at the bases, but these will disappear after coughing or over-breathing.

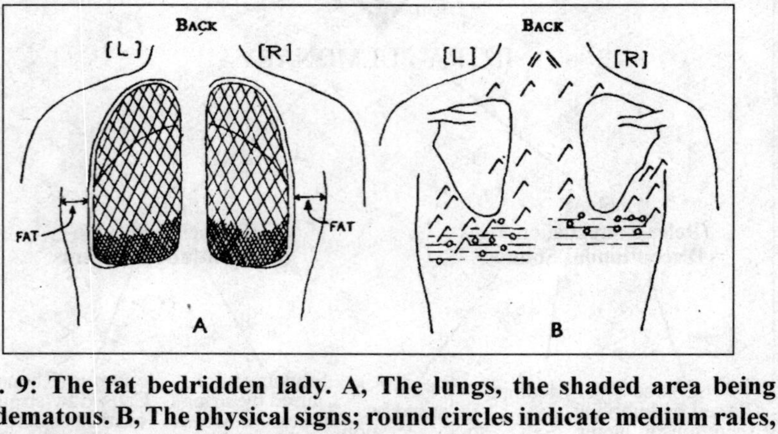

Fig. 9: The fat bedridden lady. A, The lungs, the shaded area being Oedematous. B, The physical signs; round circles indicate medium rales, the shaded area percussion dullness.

(b) *A wasted man of* 55 *with collapse of the left lower lobe due to carcinomatous obstruction of the lower lobe bronchus* (Fig. 10).

Breath-sounds will be vesicular and clear in all normal places except in a triangular area close to the spine postero-inferiorly, where they will be absent. If the lesion is of long standing, breath-sounds

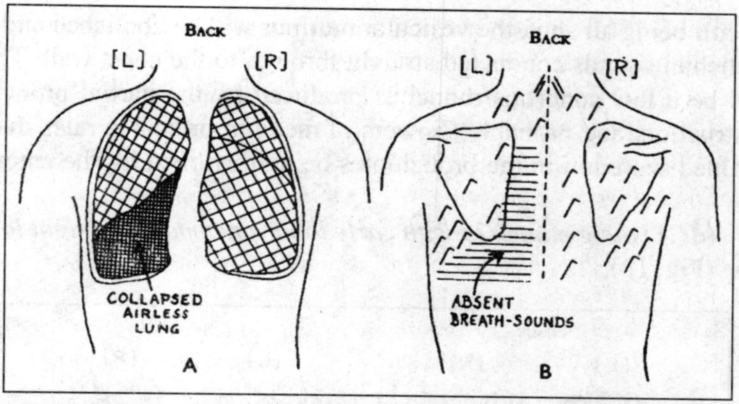

Fig. 10: Complete collapse of left lower lobe. A, The lungs. B, Physical signs; the shaded area represents percussion dullness.

will be diminished over the lung tissue close to this area (due to compensatory emphysema developing there and so reducing the total number of alveoli contributing to the vesicular murmur).

(c) *As (b), but with only partial obstruction and inflammatory consolidation of lung tissue distal to the growth* (Fig. 11).

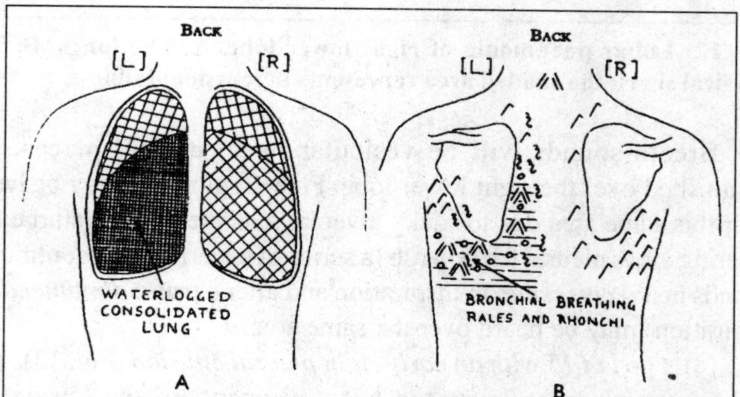

Fig. 11: Partial obstruction of left lower lobe bronchus. A, The lungs. B, The physical signs; the shaded area indicates percussion dullness, the short wavy lines denote rhonchi.

Breath-sounds will be diminished over the surface markings of the left lower lobe; they will be bronchial in character because, the alveoli being all shut, the vesicular murmur will be abolished and the bronchial sounds conducted straight through to the chest wall. There will be a low sonorous rhonchus produced by the partial bronchial obstruction, and probably showers of medium or coarse rales due to retained secretion in the bronchioles being disturbed by the entering air.

(d) *A young man 0/25 with early lobar pneumonia of right lower lobe* (Fig. 12).

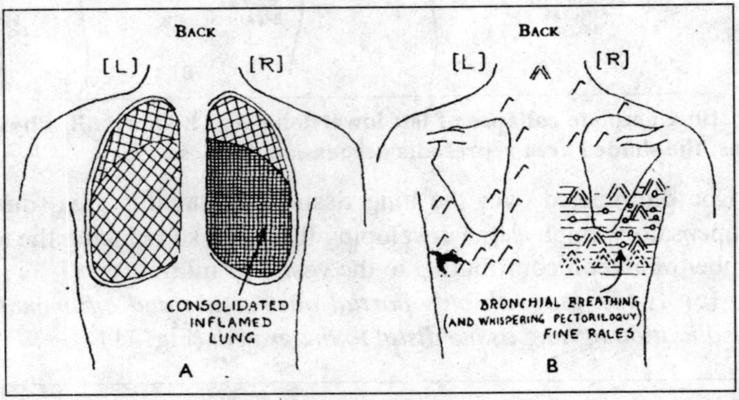

Fig. 12: Lobar pneumonia of right lower lobe. A, The lungs. B, The physical signs; the shaded area represents percussion dullness.

Breath-sounds will be vesicular in all normal places, but diminished over the right lower lobe. Fine crepitations may be heard over this same area due to sticky alveolar exudate being disturbed by entering air. A pleural friction rub (a series of superficial discontinuous sounds heard *crescendo* in inspiration and after a pause *diminuendo* in expiration) may be heard over the same area.

(e) *A girl of 15 with an early right pleural effusion* (Fig. 13). *This is big enough to collapse the basal segments of the lower lobe completely, but the bronchus to the dorsal segment of the lobe remains patent.*

Due to the complete closure of the basal bronchi, breath-sounds will be absent up to about the level of the angle of the scapular posteriorly. Above this they will be heard faintly but will be bronchial in character due to the collapse of the alveoli but patency of the bronchus. Fine or medium rales may also be heard in this area due to the partial opening of sticky alveoli.

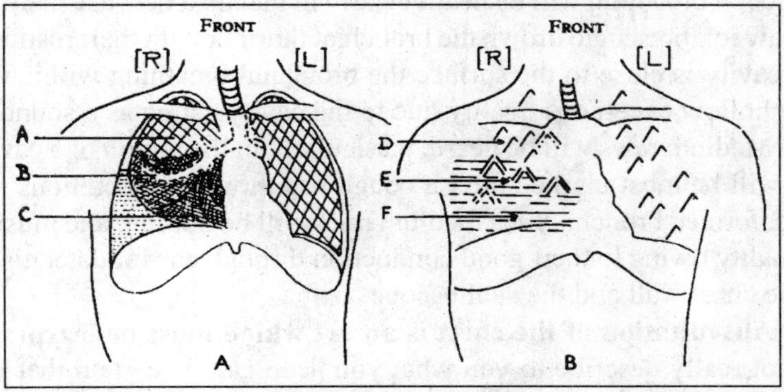

Fig. 13: Right pleural effusion. A, The lungs. B, The physical signs; the shaded area indicates percussion dullness. A, Expansile lung; B, Compressed lung, patent bronchus; C, Compressed lung, collapsed bronchi; D, Vesicular murmur; E, Bronchial murmur; F, Absent murmur.

(f) *A woman of 21 with caseating and cavitating tuberculosis of the right upper lobe* (Fig. 14).

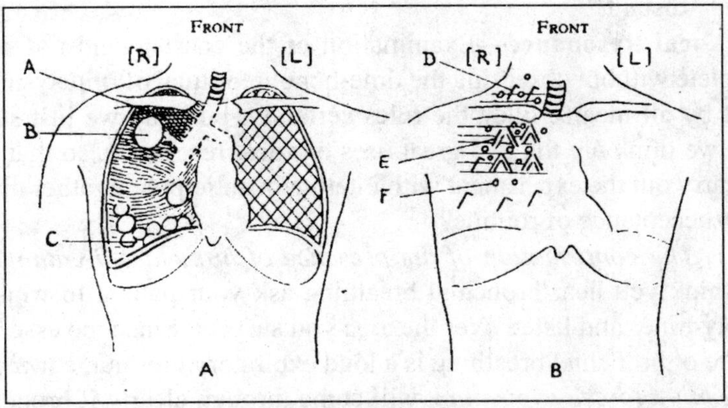

Fig. 14: Tuberculosis of right upper lobe. A, The lungs. B, The physical signs; the shaded area represents percussion dullness. A, Fibrosed and consolidated lung; B, Cavity; C, Emphysema D, Weak respiratory murmur; E, Bronchial murmur (cavernous type) F, Medium rales (tinkling quality).

Breath-sounds will be moderately diminished all over the affected area due to loss of alveolar tissue. If a bronchus passes over the surface, bronchial breathing will be heard clearly in that area because there are few alveoli present to drown the bronchial murmur with their rustlings. If a cavity is close to the surface the bronchial breathing will have a very hollow cavernous quality due to the cavity acting as a sounding box. Medium rales will be heard, particularly in the region of a cavity, and will be most marked after a cough has thrust the secretions into the deformed bronchi. Such medium rales will be tinkling and musical in quality owing to their good conduction through consolidated tissue to the chest wall and the stethoscope.

Auscultation of the chest is an art which must be learnt; we cannot really describe to you what you hear. But be certain that you know the normal before you suspect the abnormal, and obey the rules of examination laid down for your guidance. We summarize them now:

1. Note the intensity of the breath-sounds in all areas.
2. Note the character of the breath-sounds, bronchial or vesicular.
3. Note adventitious sounds.
4. Classify the adventitious sounds according to whether they are continuous or discontinuous, dry or moist, superficial or distant.

Vocal Resonance—Examination of the chest would not seem complete without observing the time-honoured ritual of 'ninety-nine'. Do it by all means, obey the rules certainly; but may we just stress what we think are the two great uses of vocal resonance, so that you can carry out the experiment with intelligent anticipation rather than a dumb acceptance of routine?

1. *The confirmation of the presence of bronchial breathing.* If you think you hear bronchial breathing ask your patient to whisper 'ninety-nine' and listen over the area you suspect. Since the essential feature of bronchial breathing is a loud expiratory murmur, a *whisper, being but a forced expiration,* will come through clearly if bronchial breathing is present. The same applies to the special form of bronchial breathing known as cavernous breathing; here the whispered 'ninety-nine will sound cavernous too.

2. *The detection of a thin layer of fluid in the pleura.* We don't know why you should, but if you have ever listened to someone's voice

while your head is under water you will know that the sound is altered in character. The fluid has eliminated certain overtones. Sometimes, when there is a thin layer of fluid separating the two layers of the pleura, the voice sounds will be conducted across this fluid, but are so altered in passage that they sound nasal to the listener with the stethoscope (aegophony). This sort of bleating or nasal sound can be imitated by saying 'ninety-nine' while pinching your own nose. Aegophony, then, is a special physical finding which may occur in the course of the development of pleural effusions or at the upper level of larger ones. Once heard it can usually be easily recognized thereafter. It is important because it may enable you to diagnose a pleural effusion or empyema when other physical signs which depend on the accumulation of larger quantities of fluid (stony percussion dullness) or the collapse of the underlying lung (absent breath-sounds) have not yet developed. Aegophony is not properly understood, but for all practical purposes if you hear aegophony over the lower zones of the lung, fluid is present there.

The Sputum

Patients, with a dry cough, but anxious to please, often tender their saliva to the doctor who really wants to examine their sputum. You should be able to recognize such watery specimens for what they are, and not waste time in examining them. From bedside observations, there are three important things to know about a patient's sputum.

First, you want to know the *daily quantity* of sputum produced. Secondly, you want to know whether the sputum contains *pus,* and if so, how much. Thirdly, you want to know whether the sputum contains *blood,* and if so, how much. We hope you can recognize pus when you see it. Smell it. If it is offensive it probably comes from a necrotic area of lung tissue infected by anaerobes, or from stagnant pools in dilated bronchi. Blood, bright and frothy, may fill the sputum-pot, or a few streaks of blood may be seen on blobs of mucus. Brownish, scanty, purulent sputum is produced by those with pneumonia; such a sputum is composed of altered blood and pus, and should be examined microscopically for organisms. A smear of sputum on a slide taken at the height of an acute pulmonary infection is always of value, even if there must be some delay before the smear can be stained and examined.

Summary

Observe the patient's respiratory behaviour, noting depth and frequency of respiration, as well as interruptions to breathing, or adventitious sounds such as stridor and cough.

Inspect the chest and its movements as a whole from the foot of the bed; do this most thoroughly. Then approach the patient, look to see if his fingers are clubbed, determine the position of the apex beat and the trachea. Inspect the inside of the mouth and throat, palpating the neck and supra-clavicular fossae at the same time.

Systematically palpate both sides of the chest with the left and right hands simultaneously, noting inequalities of movement, the presence of palpable thrills or rubs, or the decrease of tactile fremitus.

Percuss the chest carefully, making sure to use exactly the right technique.

Listen to the respiratory murmur in all areas, noting intensity and character of breath-sounds, and the presence of adventitious noises; then listen to the vocal resonance.

Then sit the patient up and make the same series of observations at the back.

Examine the sputum, noting particularly the daily quantity, the amount of pus, the presence of blood, and the smell.

□

CHAPTER VI

EXAMINATION OF ALIMENTARY SYSTEM

This chapter is chiefly about symptoms, and there is little in it concerning the technique of examination. When you want to read about the examination of the abdomen turn to the next chapter. But pause awhile, if you will to consider why this chapter is chiefly about the study of symptoms.

Let us bear in mind the elementary fact that the digestive system consists of a long tube, much coiled in places, into which empty many secretory glands. Disturbances in and around the tube tend to lead to striking alterations in bodily function of which a patient cannot easily remain unaware. For example, blockage of the upper part of the tube leads to difficulty in swallowing and the sensation of food sticking at a certain definite place; blockage nearer the middle part of the tube, shall we say at the pylorus, leads to copious vomiting and constipation; blockage of the lower part of the tube, in the colon for instance, leads to abdominal distension and constipation. Furthermore, inflammation of the upper part of the tube tends to cause dysphagia, of the middle part vomiting, and of the lower part diarrhoea. You will find therefore that, by listening carefully to the patient's story, you gain some idea as to the site of the disturbance of alimentary function.

Physical signs, on the other hand, are often absent in disease of the alimentary system. A tumour obstructing the aesophagus is certainly impalpable, while a tumour of the colon may remain so for a very long time. Peptic ulcers rarely produce physical signs, though they are spendthrift of symptoms. When you also realize that this intestinal tube is particularly susceptible to disturbances of movement and function, conditioned by emotion rather than organic disease, you will understand why this chapter is chiefly about symptoms and so little about physical signs.

It is difficult to talk about symptoms without entering upon the problem of diagnosis. This is a book of methods rather than diagnosis, but, in order to illustrate the importance of a good history in alimentary disorders, we shall have to describe the salient features of certain diseases and abnormalities of function. These descriptions are purely illustrative; they are not complete.

Pain

Pain is probably the most frequent manifestation of alimentary disorder. The description of such a purely subjective sensation can, without other clues, often provide a complete diagnosis. It is obviously, therefore, a symptom which must be studied completely. If pain is present remember to determine:

Two things about the pain itself—its character and its severity;

Three things about the location of the pain—its point of maximal intensity, its distribution, and its radiation;

Three things about the time relations of the pain—its date of onset, the duration of attacks, and their frequency of occurrence;

And, lastly, what eases the pain and what makes the pain worse. When you know all this about your patient's pain you are a long way towards locating its origin.

What else must you know before you can say that this pain is from the stomach and that from the gall-bladder? You must know certain generalizations about abdominal pains which have been deduced through years of medical experience, and certain facts which have been learnt from physiological experiments. You must learn to recognize pain by its description. You must know from which organ a particular type of pain is likely to arise, and what disorder of function this pain suggests. We give you below a few generalizations which may help you to begin your studies and give you an interest in symptoms.

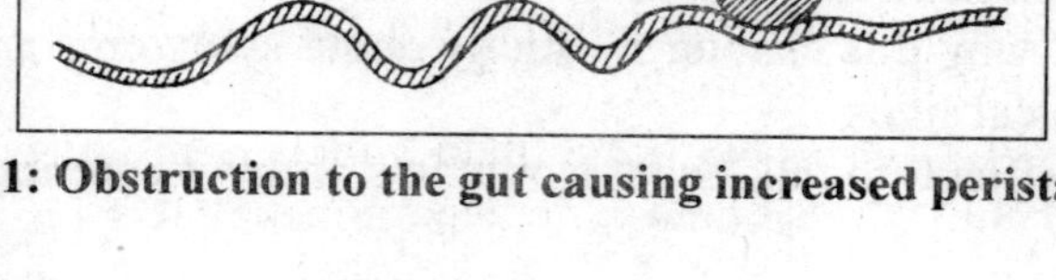

Fig. 1: Obstruction to the gut causing increased peristalsis.

'Colicky Pain'—Typically, this is a pain which makes the patient want to roll about to procure ease. It is a pain which comes on in spasms and passes off, and then comes on again. It is believed that colicky pain is caused by the excessive and spasmodic contraction of plain muscle, as happens, for example, in the segment of bowel just above an obstruction (Fig. 1). Certain varieties are fairly easily recognized.

(a) *Oesophageal Colic*—An intermittent, burning pain in the centre of the lower chest. The pain is deeply situated and may be quite severe.

(b) *Gastric Colic*—Aching or sharp in character, epigastric in position, and tends to occur at a set time after meals.

(c) *Small-intestine Colic*—Typically, occurs in the centre of the abdomen, severe, sharp in character, and gives rise to much restlessness. The fluctuations in intensity of pain are rapid and violent.

(d) *Large-intestine Colic*—A 'dragging' pain, with slow fluctuations in intensity. The lower the site of origin of the colic the more easily can the patient localize the pain, for example, to the transverse colon, the sigmoid, or the rectum.

(e) *Biliary Colic*—Pain very severe, "like a red-hot poker", maximal in the right hypochondrium but spreads all over the right side of the abdomen and chest and radiates through to the back and to between the two shoulder-blades. The pain usually remains constant for several hours, and then passes off fairly suddenly.

There are other colics arising from abdominal organs not part of the alimentary system. For comparison, here are the main features of the important ones.

Renal Colic—Very severe, knife-like pain, maximal in the loin; radiates down the course of the ureter towards the genitalia or the inner side of the thigh.

Ureteric Colic—Severe or moderate pain, aching in character, increasing up to a maximum and then dying away, maximal low down in the pelvis or in the sacrum.

Peritoneal Pain—This is the pain which is produced by the inflammation or irritation of the parietal peritoneum. It is a pain which tends either to be constant, or to change very slowly in its severity and character; a pain which is felt superficially and is associated with tenderness and rigidity of the over-lying muscles. The patient with such a pain avoids movement lest the contraction of abdominal muscles should, by disturbing the parietal peritoneum, aggravate his discomfort. As a general rule, it may be said that pain of this character means that the peritoneum underlying that particular area is irritated or is inflamed so that the site of the pain is of great value in locating the disease. If the peritoneum lining the under-surface of the diaphragm is inflamed, breathing will be painful, and, because sensation from the centre of the diaphragm is carried by the phrenic nerve (C.4-5), inflammation in that area may cause pain to be referred to the tip of the shoulder on the same side. Such a finding can be of great diagnostic value.

Mesenteric Pain—Enlarged or inflamed lymphatic glands in the mesentery undoubtedly give rise to pain, but the characteristics of such a pain are less surely known than those of visceral or peritoneal pain. An intermittent aching pain associated with deep tenderness but without marked abdominal rigidity may suggest mesenteric disease.

Nerve-root Pain—Abdominal pain may be due to irritation of, or pressure upon, the spinal nerve-roots supplying the abdominal wall—that is, those arising between the 5th dorsal and the 2nd lumbar segments of the spinal cord. Such a pain tends to be quite constant, aching or gripping in character, and to occur in the exact band of distribution of the affected sensory root. Owing to this type of distribution the pain is often called a 'girdle pain'.

Peripheral Nerve Pain—Involvement of peripheral sensory nerves by tabes or peripheral neuritis may cause various sorts of abdominal pain, but their description is beyond the scope of this book.

Dysphagia

Dysphagia means painful or difficult swallowing. Hysteria, bulbar palsy, and certain anaemias may give rise to difficulty, in swallowing, but dysphagia is usually due to disease of the pharynx or oesophagus. Everyone must have experienced the pain on swallowing food which is such a feature of the common sore throat.

It is strange that adults will sometimes have considerable difficulty in swallowing, and yet complain only of 'indigestion', so you may have difficulty in getting at the truth. On the other hand, a patient may be able to point his finger to the exact spot where the food seems to stick. Any pain or obstruction in the pharynx is usually referred to the region of the cricoid cartilage, but below this the patient's localization of the lesion is often very accurate. Be sure to ask the patient if he finds greater difficulty in swallowing solid food or liquids. When solid food won't 'go down' at all but liquids will, an organic narrowing of the oesophagus is probably present. When solids go down better than liquids neurological disease is likely.

Vomiting

When a patient vomits you have to consider the symptom in relation to his whole body and mind. Severe giddiness, fever, uraemia, drugs, abdominal pain, raised intracranial pressure, and hysteria may all cause vomiting. There is, however, a particular sort of vomiting which occurs when the alimentary canal is obstructed; it is persistent and copious and accompanied by considerable flatulence; the vomitus may contain food eaten a day or two previously or even fecal material. Obstructive vomiting, wherever the site of the obstruction, tends to be accompanied by colicky pains.

If the obstruction is in the oesophagus the vomitus is alkaline and frothy. Temporary spasm of the cardiac sphincter often occurs in patients with gastric neurosis or peptic ulcer, so that watery, tasteless fluid wells up into their mouths from time to time. 'Waterbrash' is the name given to this type of eructation; it is hardly a vomit, though the patient will often say it is. If the obstruction is at the pylorus, the act of vomiting is usually sudden and sometimes projectile in quality, the vomitus is copious and perhaps contains fermenting foodstuffs eaten several days previously. If the obstruction is low down in the small or large intestine the vomitus may be faecal, but this is a sign of obstruction which the surgeon never delays to see.

Appetite

Anorexia or loss of appetite is more often a symptom of general than of alimentary disease. Just as when considering loss of weight, your first concern should be to find out exactly when the symptom was first noticed, and to imagine what the patient looked like before the symptom began. Find out whether the anorexia is complete, involving an active distaste for food, or whether it is incomplete due to general lassitude and apathy, to weakness, or to abdominal pain made worse by food.

Indigestion

People mean very different things by the word 'indigestion'. One man means pain, another means an uncomfortable feeling in the abdomen, another means flatulence. What the majority mean to say is that they have a dull, heavy feeling in the stomach which makes them lose their appetite and eructate uncomfortably soon after beginning a meal. This full uncomfortable sensation is very unpleasant but, luckily, it is far more often the result of a neurosis, of heavy drinking, or of heavy smoking for that matter, than of a serious organic disease. Pregnancy is likely to begin with this sort of indigestion, and anyone with unsuspected fever or heart failure may also complain of it. The best general rule to have in mind when faced with a patient complaining of indigestion of this type is to study his general health rather than his stomach.

Heartburn

This is really a sensation arising from the oesophagus. Most people have suffered from it and know what it is. But in case you are exceptionally eupeptic, heartburn is a hot burning feeling in the lower chest or upper abdomen. Probably, it is due to acid from the stomach regurgitating past the cardiac orifice and irritating the sensitive mucosa at the lower end of the oesophagus. It occurs normally, especially in pregnancy, but may be severe with organic disease of the oesophagus.

Haematemesis

Blood vomited from the oesophagus is bright red in colour and alkaline to litmus; whereas blood which has stayed even a short time in the stomach is partly digested by the gastric juice, so that when vomited it looks black or brown and granular like coffee-grounds and is acid to litmus.

Flatulence

Upward flatulence is the expulsion of air swallowed previously. Air swallowing is a bad habit, but difficult to avoid if one is suffering from any abdominal discomfort or nausea. The short-lived and spurious relief which a good belch brings to the performer must be well known to all. It is a symptom which is particularly common in gastric or biliary disease and after operations. The old-style out-patient's flatulence was a remarkable phenomenon which made the rafters ring and the consultant smile, for he knew that it was done to please or impress him.

Downward flatulence is caused by increased fermentation in the large intestine and occurs after the eating of large quantities of roughage, peas, onions, or drinking beer. It is rarely a symptom of importance in diagnosis of disease.

Constipation

If a patient complains of constipation, you must try to find out whether he:

1. Is a life long sufferer from constipation (habitual constipation).
2. Is ill with a general disorder such as diabetes mellitus or a fever.
3. Has noticed a recent change in bowel habits not attributable to general disease.

If the last-named, regard the symptom as of the very greatest significance, for it may mean organic obstruction of the bowel.

Diarrhoea

Diarrhoea is often a symptom of general disease. This is true particularly of children, for an infection anywhere in a child's body, whether in the alimentary tract or remote from it, may cause most violent diarrhoea. The bowel habits of an adult are rather more stable, but an anxiety neurosis, thyrotoxicosis, starvation, vitamin deficiencies, and uraemia are all examples of conditions in which a general disorder may give rise to a severe local symptom. The character of the stool is all-important in the differentiation of diarrhoea due to local disease of the bowel, to abnormalities of absorption in the small intestine, and to general disease.

Tenesmus and Pain on Defecation

Tenesmus is a deep-seated spasmodic type of pain arising from the rectum. It is a painful 'drawing' sensation which occurs immediately after defecation, and lasts for a few minutes afterwards. A sharp pain occurring during the act of defalcation usually means an anal lesion.

Melaena

Blood arising from a haemorrhage high up in the alimentary tract (as from a duodenal ulcer) is partly digested before it is passed. Usually, it is passed by frequent bowel actions as black, tarry, or sticky stools. The black stools which are passed by patients taking iron or bismuth by mouth are small, well formed, and not sticky. Blood arising from the large intestine is dark red, jelly-like, and streakily mixed with the stool. Blood arising from the rectum or the anus tends to be bright red in colour, and either to be separate from or to coat the surface of the stool.

Physical Examination

Your patient's chief symptom determines where the emphasis is to be laid in your examination of his alimentary system. If he complains of diarrhoea you must examine the anal region, inspect the inside of the rectum with your proctoscope, palpate the inside of the rectum with your finger, and examine the stool. There is a minimum which must be done in all cases, however.

The Tongue and Mouth—The tongue is said to be the mirror of the stomach. Certainly, it is a striking fact that a patient with a smooth shiny tongue usually has an atrophic gastric mucosa, and a patient with a peptic ulcer and a congested gastric mucosa has a red 'beefy' tongue. When looking at the tongue, see whether it has been indented by the teeth or has any superficial ulcers upon it. A furred tongue usually means that the patient has not been eating normal food, which would by its abrasive action have cleared the dead epithelium (fur) from the surface of the tongue; any ill-patient who is not eating well may therefore have a furred tongue. Let it also be remembered that many people even in health always show a furred tongue; it is worth while, then, asking the patient about the usual state of his tongue; he will be sure to know. A cracked or fissured tongue may also be a normal finding, especially in old age; it doesn't mean a fissured stomach!

Look carefully at the lingual papillae. Sometimes they are completely absent, sometimes they are badly formed, flattened, and smooth. Papillae tend to disappear from the outer margins of the tongue before disappearing from its centre. A smooth tongue is often found in patients with iron deficiency or Addisonian anaemia, and is in some way associated with the atrophic gastritis and achlorhydria from which these patients suffer. A sore red or magenta tongue covered by badly formed papillae is found in patients with Vitamin B deficiency; such patients also may have cracks or sores at the corners of their lips, and these you should notice. Manifestations of Vitamin B deficiency are not uncommon in those with alimentary disorders.

Look carefully at the back of the throat, always remembering that a haematemesis may be due to vomiting of blood which has trickled down from the nasopharynx, and that you may actually be able to see this happening.

The Neck—Look for swellings of the neck, and palpate carefully for enlarged lymphatic glands. Secondary metas tases from abdominal carcinomata sometimes develop in the cervical lymphatic glands.

The Abdomen—Much can be learned from inspection alone, and you should be prepared to devote considerable time to discovering whether you can detect the outlines of any abdominal viscus. These are never visible in healthy subjects. Their presence can be easily overlooked if inspection is either too hurried or carried out in a bad light, and it is extremely important to inspect the abdomen at every phase of respiration and from several angles. When a patient complains of persistent vomiting or other symptoms suggestive of a partial obstruction of the alimentary canal you should set out deliberately to encourage the excessive peristalsis which tends to occur in the part of the alimentary canal cranial to the obstruction, and which may be visible through the abdominal wall. Give the patient a glassful of water to drink, or flick the surface of the abdomen with the finger and then watch with your eyes at the level of the abdomen.

Hypertrophic pyloric stenosis of infancy is an example of high intestinal obstruction which presents special problems. The child must be examined during a good feed, preferably the type of feed to which it is accustomed—a breast feed if necessary—and its abdomen must be inspected as the child lies on the mother's or the nurse's lap. The 'golf-ball' waves of peristalsis pass across the epigastrium from left to right, ending at the right border of the right rectus sheath. To feel the hypertrophied pylorus in spasm you must for once disobey the usual rules for palpation of the abdomen. Sit on the left-hand side of the child and use your left hand. On the tiny belly of the infant the left hand can conveniently hook round the rectus muscles, so that the middle finger and fore-finger come naturally into the position where the tumour is likely to be felt. The right hand would be at a disadvantage in this situation. You should feel for the swelling after observing the peristaltic waves and in the region where the waves come to a stop. Above all, feel for this acorn-shaped tumour at the moment when the infant is about to vomit or is actually vomiting. Your clothes must suffer if need be, for a pylorus felt, albeit for a moment only, is sufficient evidence for a firm diagnosis.

With obstruction low down in the small intestine, a zig-zag or 'step-ladder' pattern of distended gut is seen in the centre of the abdomen, while with obstruction of the large intestine, the colon stands out in huge coils, but in these two conditions peristalsis is very rarely visible.

The Anus and Rectum—In most alimentary disorders, it is essential to examine the anus and rectum.

Inspection of the anus may reveal fissures—a common cause of nagging, lower abdominal or back pain—external haemorrhoids, a discharging sinus, or a fistula. Proctoscopic examination of the lower rectum—so simply done—provides much useful information in cases of chronic diarrhoea. Inflammatory diseases of the colon such as the dysenteries and ulcerative colitis usually show visible changes in the rectal mucosa, while hemorrhoidal varicosities, polypi, and carcinomata may all be seen through the proctoscope. If ulcers are present in the mucosa of the rectum you should note particularly their characteristics, shape, depth, type of edge, and whether the ulcers are separated from each other by healthy-looking or inflamed mucosa. Swabs taken from the rectum are often of greater value to the pathologist than a specimen of stool.

Digital examination of the rectum should always be made if there is doubt about the diagnosis of alimentary, pelvic, or abdominal disease. Not only may information about the internal condition of the lower rectum be obtained, but also other pelvic and lower abdominal masses may be felt and defined. Many are the aphorisms—"Put your pride in your pocket and your finger in the rectum".... **"If you don't put your finger in the rectum, you will put your foot in it"**—which have been composed to illustrate the importance of the manoeuvre. Nevertheless, it is strange how often doctors forget to do it. If you don't want to be misled, therefore, be sure that a good rubber glove or a large finger stall is always ready for your use. Too often for the want of a glove the examination is not made. **When you intend to make a rectal examination tell the patient exactly what you are going to do,** then ask him to curl up on his left side so that his chin comes as close as possible to his knees. To insert the index finger as painlessly as possible into the rectum you should first press gently on the anal orifice with the volar surface of the tip of your finger for a second or two, after which you will find that by altering the direction of your finger it enters easily. Wait a moment to allow the patient to relax, and then palpate as far up in the pelvis as you can. Polypi are not usually palpable, so don't fall into the common trap of diagnosing polypi after feeling the soft edges of the rectal valves. If a mass is felt make sure of its exact position and relation to the rectum, test its mobility, and if possible, with the other hand on the abdomen, try to examine it bimanually. Next, turn the finger round so that the sensitive volar surface of the tip faces anteriorly, and define the prostate in the male and the cervix uteri in the female. You should feel the two lobes of the prostate and the raphe between them quite clearly. If the prostate feels abnormal it is often worth-while to move the patient into the knee-elbow position, as with the patient in this position you can best feel the gland.

Examination of the Stools

Unpleasant as it may seem to the uninitiated, much information can be obtained by inspection of the stools. In the ordinary case it is enough to ask the patient to describe his stools, but if they are excessively dark or light in colour, are blood-stained or loose, it is always as well to look at them yourself.

Dark Stools—These may be due to drugs such as bismuth, iron, or charcoal, or to altered blood passed into the alimentary tract somewhere above the ileocaecal valve. It is most important to distinguish between the one and the other, and this can be done partly after listening to the history and partly by inspecting the stools. Altered blood makes the stools tarry and sticky in consistency, whereas the dark stools due to drugs are essentially normal except for their colour.

Blood in Stools—Streaking of a normally-formed stool by bright blood is usually due to bleeding haemorrhoids or an anal fissure. Darker blood more or less intermingled with the stool probably comes from higher up in the large intestine.

Loose Stools—

(a) *Inflammatory diarrhoea*—If acute this may produce only loose, watery, and offensive stools containing many particles of undigested food. A stool due to chronic inflammatory diarrhoea, on the other hand, has certain characteristics which you can see. The stool is not only loose and offensive, but also contains an excess of mucus and either streaks of dark jelly-like blood or thin pus. This sort of stool may also be passed by patients with cancer of the colon or rectum, and is then due to the degeneration in and inflammation around the growth.

(b) *Fatty diarrhoea*—This occurs either when the bile or pancreatic juices fail to enter the duodenum, or when there is some failure of the small intestine to absorb fat. If the bile does not reach the duodenum the stool tends to be fairly firm and very pale owing to the absence from it of pigments derived from the bile. On the other hand, when there is failure of absorption of fat due to causes other than the absence of bile, the stools tend to be rather darker in colour, looser, frothy, soapy, bulky, and very offensive.

(c) *Symptomatic diarrhoea*—Due to general diseases has he special characteristics. The stools are loose and probably offensive.

The Stools in Children—The napkins of infants can provide important information; but, alas, many doctors evidently fall between two stools, for they never trouble to examine them.

To learn to know the normal make the most of your opportunities while in hospital if you look at the stools of infants in the ward you will begin to understand the meaning of those variations in colour and consistency which are of such value in diagnosis.

Meconium is the scanty, blackish-green, sticky, and odourless material passed by the infant in its first few days of life. Before the end of the first week the stools become golden-yellow but remain unformed and with little odour. In the breast-fed infant the stools should be a semi-liquid paste. In the artificially-fed infant, who takes more protein and fat in his diet, the stools are paler and drier and more like a putty than a paste. As the infant grows older and takes less milk but more solid food, the stools naturally become darker, fewer, and more odorous.

Disturbances of function may be inferred from various changes in the stools. For example, *starvation* and *under-feeding* make the stools revert to their neonatal condition. In such cases, there is almost no residue, and all that is seen upon the napkin is a green smear consisting mainly of debris and derivatives of bile. The yellow colour of normal stools is produced by partly unchanged bilirubin. The colour may change to pale green either before or after being passed, but this is a normal process resulting from the oxidation of bilirubin to biliverdin, and the colour depends on the time which is taken before the stool is passed and examined. In *infantile diarrhoea*, the colour of the stools may vary from dark spinach-green in mild cases to an ominous orange-red which portends the approach of death. These changes are partly the result of normal oxidative processes, and partly the result of changes in the bile due to the liver damage which occurs in such moribund patients.

The *number* of the stools is of less importance than their character, since the number varies so much with the habit, temperament, and circumstances of the infant. Prolonged sucking, for example, tends to promote intestinal peristalsis, which culminates in the passage of a motion.

The *consistency* and bulk of the stools will prove of some diagnostic help to you. In particular, the soft, bulky, clay-like stools of cocliac disease bear witness to abnormal fat-absorption. Frothy stools are due to fermentation (formation of carbon dioxide + water) of excess carbohydrates in the diet. Too much starch or sugar in the feeds will cause the infant to pass such stools. Undigested protein causes large yellow-grey curds in the stools. Small white curds are due to soaps and are therefore merely a normal product of fat digestion. The faster the passage of the stools the less water is absorbed and consequently the more liquid will the stools appear. If the speedy passage is due to inflammatory bowel conditions the loose stools will contain more than the normal small amount of mucus. In dysenteric conditions the mucus is blood-stained. Blood may also result from other causes; in the first few days of life melaena neonatorum is by far the commonest cause. Intussusception causes the passage of almost pure blood like 'red-currant jelly'.

The normal sour *odour* of infants' stools is mainly due to the presence of fatty acids from the milk diet. With the addition of more solid foods, especially proteins, the odour of putrefaction becomes pronounced. With excess protein in the diet, or where digestion is impaired, the stools stink.

Summary

Study your patient's symptoms with a view to determining what error of alimentary function is producing those symptoms.

Examine the patient's abdomen and rectum and stools with a view to confirming your functional diagnosis and in the hope of reaching a more exact pathological diagnosis.

□

CHAPTER VII

EXAMINATION OF ABDOMEN

The common masses to be felt in the abdomen are physiological: they are the gravid uterus, the distended bladder, and faces. You will be spared some humiliation if you carry these possibilities in your mind, and an enema syringe and a catheter in your diagnostic armamentarium. Consider this triad in every case before you set about the systematic examination of the abdomen in the way to be described now.

The traditional routine of inspection, palpation, percussion, and auscultation is followed for the abdomen as for other regions, but with one marked emphasis: palpation is far and away the most important of these methods in abdominal diagnosis. For this reason, you are advised to concentrate on palpation, as you will see has been done in the following description. A good history and a practised right hand will take you a long way in abdominal diagnosis.

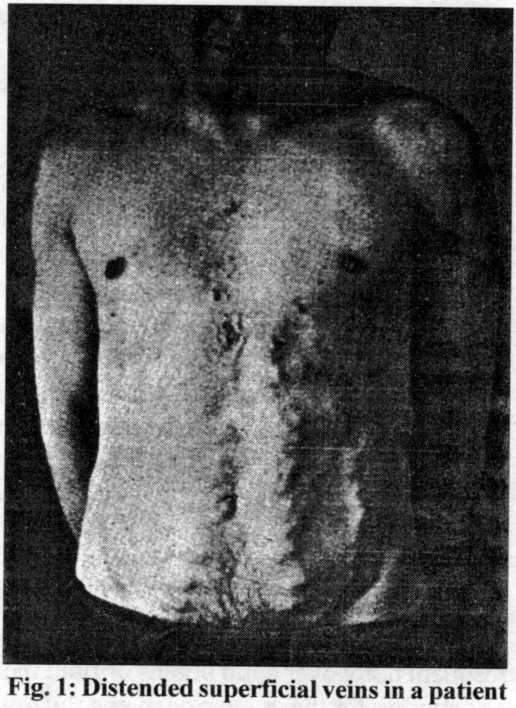

Fig. 1: Distended superficial veins in a patient with an abdominal tumour.

I. Inspection

Look not only at the abdomen, but also at the whole patient: a rickety child appears to be pot-bellied partly because of its flabby muscles. Inspect the patient's abdomen in a good light, paying attention to three features: *shape, surface,* and *movement.*

Shape—The entire abdomen may appear big, because of fat, ascites, or gaseous distension. Alternatively, the abdomen may appear irregularly enlarged, as occurs with a distended bladder, other large organs, or localized distension of the alimentary canal.

Inspect the back as well as the front: it is not rare for an apparently swollen abdomen to be produced by unsuspected lordosis.

Surface—Enlarged veins are always abnormal. The classical, but rare 'caput Medusae', with veins radiating out from the umbilicus, compensates for obstruction to the portal veins. Obstruction of the systemic veins (as by a tumour, or even ascites) tends to enlarge superficial veins all over the abdomen, and you will find that the blood courses upwards in this collateral circulation (Fig. 1).

Occasionally, you may observe such rarities as carcinomatous nodules or a discharging sinus on the surface, providing an indication of what you are likely to find in the depths.

Movement—The abdomen normally expands with inspiration. Absence of movement may be bilateral, as in widespread peritonitis or with the diaphragmatic paralysis of interior poliomyelitis; or it may be unilateral, as with one-sided diaphragmatic paralysis.

It is extremely important to observe whether the intestinal movements are visible through the abdominal wall. Peristalsis may become visible merely because of extreme wasting; otherwise it is pathognomonic of some form of intestinal obstruction. You can by looking carefully, judge which part of the intestine is obstructed.

Percussion and auscultation are briefly described next, to dispose of them quickly and leave you fresh to concentrate on the delicate and rewarding art of palpation.

II. Percussion

Percussion, over gas in the intestines produces a drum-like resonant note; over solid organs or fluid the note is dull. It is, however, so common for the gut to ride over solid organs that only the diagnosis of free peritoneal fluid really depends on percussion. For example, the spleen is rarely percussible unless it is grossly enlarged, and other large masses may not lend themselves to accurate percussion because of overlying intestine. Do not, therefore, rely too much on percussion, but remember when you do use it to employ moderately heavy strokes and to percuss from resonant to dull, roughly parallel to the border of what is suspected to be abnormal.

III. Auscultation

You are likely to find auscultation of real help in only one type of condition. The faint irregular gurgling noise which accompanies normal peristalsis can be heard over most of the abdomen, though you should be prepared to listen intently with your stethoscope for several minutes to hear it. In such conditions as peritonitis and paralytic ileus no sounds are heard.

In thin patients with renal artery stenosis you might hear a murmur below the costal cartilages an either side at the level of kidneys.

IV. Palpation

Those who approach palpation wrongly may be divided into three groups: the casual prodders, the ponderous pushers, and the persistent pokers.

To achieve success make the examination as easy as possible, both for your patient and for yourself. Your chief does these things almost instinctively: you must practise them consciously and deliberately.

Start by attending to the patient. He should be reassured and at ease mentally—your success in achieving this desirable state depends on the depth of your sympathy and under-standing. He must be lying perfectly comfortably, with the trunk flat, and the head supported on one or two pillows. The arms should be resting loosely at the sides, and it sometimes helps if you place a pillow under his knees. He should be told to breathe naturally and easily, out rather more deeply than usual.

The patient must be relaxed and warm, and so must you. Above all, be sure your hands are warm, because they are then more sensitive. Cold hands also prevent relaxation in the patient. Stand or seat yourself comfortably at the patient's right side, so that your flat right hand is naturally on a level with his abdomen. Touch his skin gently (almost caressingly!) for a few moments, and then gradually permit most of your hand (not merely the finger-tips) to sink deeper and deeper into the abdomen each time it softens as the patient breathes out! This procedure can be so gentle and undisturbing that it may be carried out on a sleeping child without waking him; in intussusception, for example, it may provide your only available means of diagnosis. You must be prepared to take time; if you are, you will achieve a sensation as if your hand had become almost part of the patient's abdomen. Once your hand is comfortably established in the abdomen, it moves naturally with the patient's respiration, and any other movement you make must be gentle though deliberate. **It is important to start palpation in a part of the abdomen known to be free from pain, and gradually and systematically to explore the remainder of the abdomen, leaving any possibly painful area until the last.**

For abdominal palpation a planned approach should be made: proceed from wide to localized examination, from superficial to deep, and from painless to painful.

1. Ascites

Ascites is defined as a collection of fluid in the abdominal cavity. Keep clearly in mind two aspects of the diagnosis: first, *the recognition of ascites*; and, second, *the determination of its cause.* Only the former will be described here.

On inspection a large effusion should be easily recognized if you pause to look before plunging into troubled waters. If the amount of fluid is not excessively large, the flanks bulge between the ribs and pelvis, and the bulge varies with the position of the patient. A very large effusion not only bulges the flanks, but also causes protrusion of the entire abdominal wall, so that it appears like the dome of St. Paul's, but with the stretched or everted umbilicus perched on its summit (Fig. 2). The skin may be stretched tight, possibly with the formation of the thin long scars called striae atrophicae, and the veins of the abdominal wall may be visible.

On *palpation,* two diagnostic signs may be elicited. Where there is sufficient fluid to form a continuous pool from one side of the

Ascites

Underfill	**Overflow**	**Vasodilation**
	Cirrhosis	
↓	↓	↓
Portal hypertension	Primary renal sodium retention (? stimulus)	Peripheral arterial vasodilatation
↓		
Ascites		Decreased effective intravacular volume
↓		
Decreased effective intravascular volume		
↓		
Reneal sodium retention →	Increased blood volume	← Renal sodium retention
	↓	
	Ascites	

abdomen to the other a '*fluid thrill*' can be obtained. Ask a colleague to press firmly on the centre of the patient's abdomen, with his hand in a vertical direction, in order to eliminate the transmission of impulses through the subcutaneous tissues. Now place a hand on one flank and flick the other firmly with a finger: the 'flick' is transmitted by the fluid and is felt very distinctly by the palpating hand. Where there is so much fluid that the abdomen is greatly

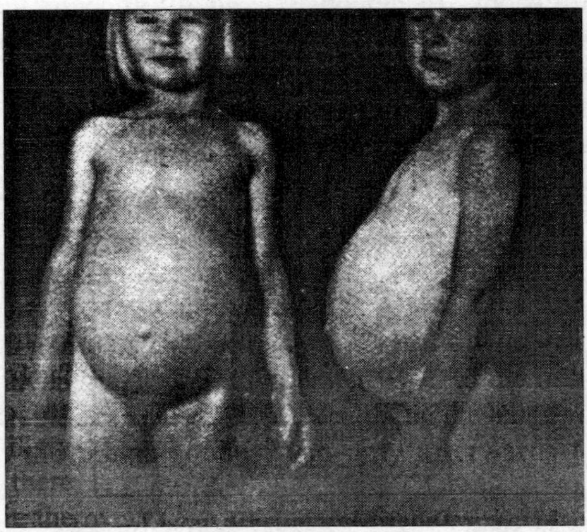

Fig. 2: Ascites.

distended '*dipping the liver*' is almost pathognomonic. The fingers of the right hand are firmly tapped on the anterior abdominal wall in the liver area, and almost instantaneously removed; the action is that of tapping a loud but short note on a big bass drum. The sensation of 'ballottement' is quite characteristic: the liver seems to bounce off your fingers.

On *percussion,* dullness characteristic of ascites will be obtained (Fig. 3). With the patient supine, and with a large effusion, the dullness is in the form of a horseshoe which includes the suprapubic area and both flanks; with moderate effusions you will find dullness only in the flanks. In both cases the central area, where the gas-filled intestines float, is resonant. To clinch me diagnosis you must prove that *the dullness shifts* according to the position of the patient. To do this, percuss into one flank until your pleximeter finger reaches an area which is definitely dull. Keep your finger firmly in position while the patient rolls on to the other flank then percuss again; the fluid will have gravitated to the lowermost flank, and percussion over your unmoved pleximeter finger will now produce a resonant note. This method is accurate, but can demonstrate only fairly considerable effusions. To demonstrate small effusions there appears to be no consistently reliable method; percussion in the periumbilical area, with the patient in the knee-elbow position, seems logical enough in theory, but in practice we have found it less logical than ludicrous. Try it for yourself, and try also to diagnose ascites by the spongy feel obtained on rectal examination, with the patient's shoulders tilted up, a recent method for which great precision has been claimed.

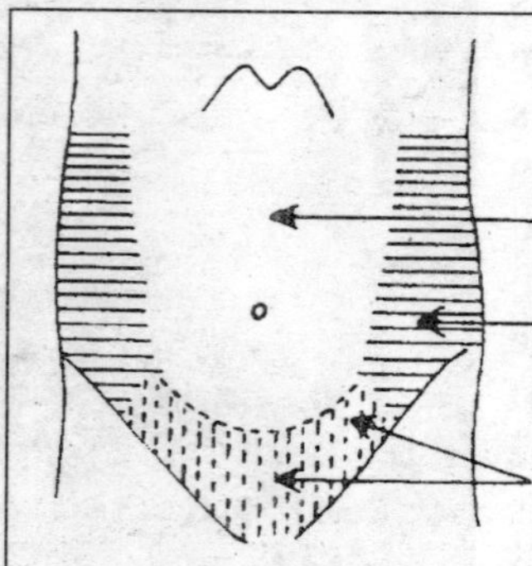

Fig. 3: Ascites demonstrated by percussion (patient in supine position). Note that the fluid gravitates to the lowest parts of the abdomen; with changes in position of the patient the limits of dullness therefore shift.

There are a few conditions in which the signs may be

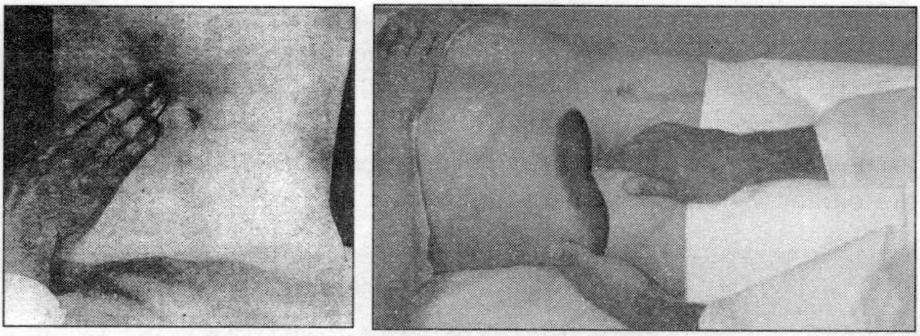

Fig. 4: Palpation of the liver.

confused with those of ascites. With omental and hydatid cysts, for example, you may elicit a 'fluid thrill', and with a bilateral hydronephrosis there may be dullness in both flanks. Curiously enough, a distended bladder most frequently causes confusion, although it is difficult to understand why. The combination of horseshoe dullness which shifts, and a fluid thrill, is pathognomonic of ascites.

2. Enlargement of Viscera

Before you decide that an organ is abnormal, ask yourself if you know the normal. Check on your estimates repeatedly by examining a wide range of normal abdomens.

Liver—In healthy adults, and especially if they are fat, the liver may not be palpable at all. Frequently, however, the edge is felt a finger-breadth or more below the ribs. The liver is an organ of firm consistency, with a smooth sharp lower border, lying mainly in the right hypochondrium but passing across the epigastrium, and moving with respiration. On palpation it is impossible to get above the liver; in health, as a rule, only the lower edge can be felt, passing across and upwards towards the left costal margin.

Palpating the liver is not a casual affair; it should be done correctly and carefully (Figs. 4 and 5). Start with your right hand low down in the abdomen, in the right iliac fossa, with the fingers pointing obliquely upwards across the abdomen. Each time the patient breathes out slide your hand a little farther up towards his chesty and eventually the liver edge may strike your hand as the patient breathes in (Fig. 4). At that stage try to feel along the edge of the liver as far to right and left as you can. In this way, you will detect not only generalized enlargement (as in chronic venous congestion) but also localized enlargement (as with neoplastic deposits). Gauge also if the liver is tender, but first try palpating your own liver to remind yourself that firm pressure on even a normal liver is not exactly comfortable. If the liver is large enough try now to palpate its surface; it may be grossly irregular (e.g. syphilis) or nodular (e.g. neoplastic infiltration).

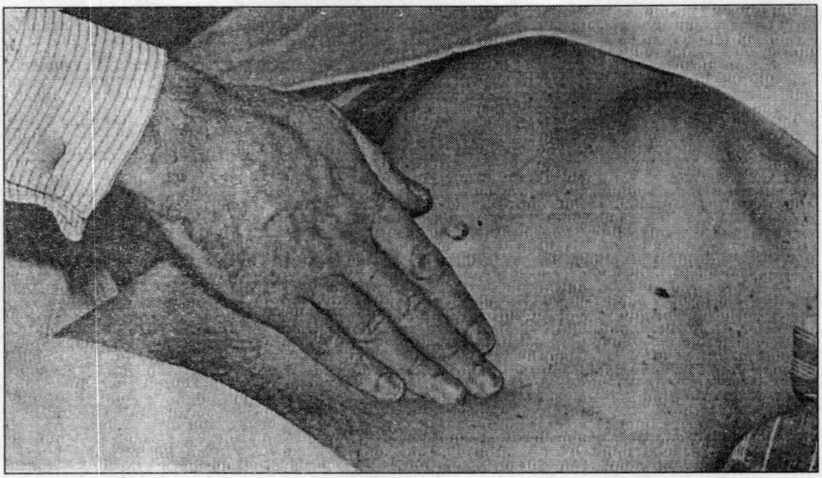

Fig. 5: Incorrect method of palpation. The hand is held rigid and mostly not in contact with the abdominal wall.

Gall-bladder—Only rarely is this organ palpably enlarged; in these cases it is felt as a smooth, tense mass projecting beneath the liver, more or less in the nipple line. More often pathological tenderness alone is elicited in the region of the gall-bladder. To elicit this sign, sit the patient up and lean him forward; seat yourself behind him on the examination couch, and insert the ringers of your upturned right hand deeply beneath his ribs in front. When he takes a deep breath the inflamed gall-bladder comes against your firmly-held fingers and causes the patient severe pain. Try this on your friends and you will find that even in healthy subjects it is an uncomfortable proceeding, though it does not produce the unmistakedly severe pain of an inflamed gall-bladder.

Spleen—It can be accepted that a palpable spleen is considerably enlarged, and is always pathological. To palpate the spleen stand or sit on the right side of the recumbent patient, and use your right hand.

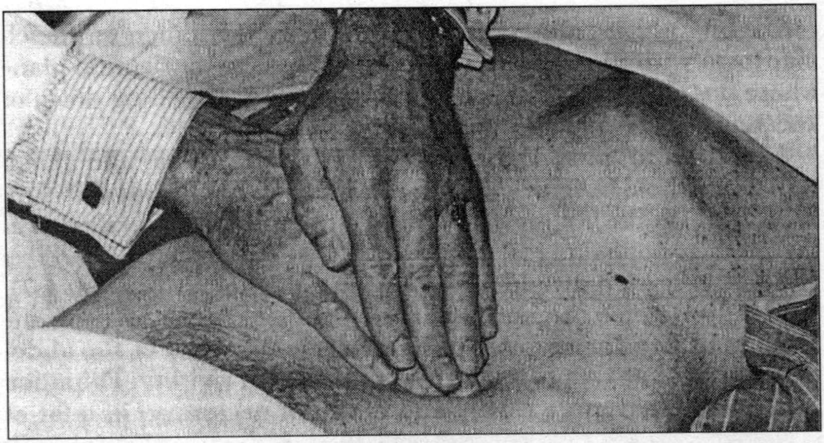

Fig. 6: Method of deep palpation in an obese, muscular or poorly relaxed patient.

Start to palpate for the spleen at about the level of the umbilicus, with the lingers of your right hand pointing towards the patient's left axilla. Slide the hand gently a little way in that direction each time the patient breathes out. A considerably enlarged spleen can be felt striking against your hand when the patient breathes in (Fig. 7). If only slightly enlarged it may call for a further manoeuvre to bring it within reach.

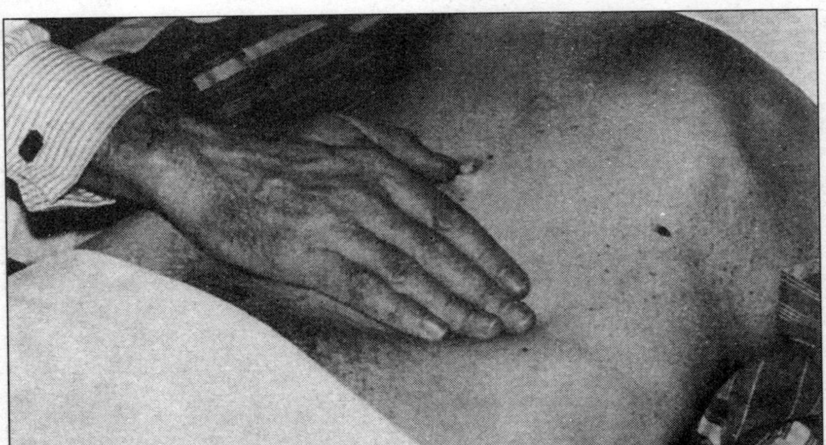

Fig. 7: Palpation of the spleen.

Pass your left hand round the patient's left axilla until it lies behind the left lower ribs. Press these ribs firmly towards you, and as they are moved forward they render the spleen more accessible to your right hand. One further precaution is necessary, because in acute infections the enlarged spleen may be so that firm palpation fails to differentiate the organ from the surrounding tissues. In this type of illness (e.g. septicaemia, typhoid) you should palpate gently and rather superficially

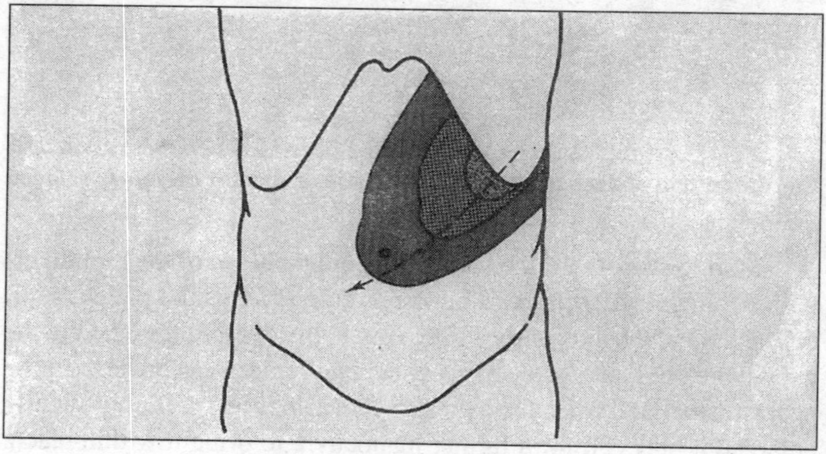

Fig. 8: The direction of enlargment of the spleen.

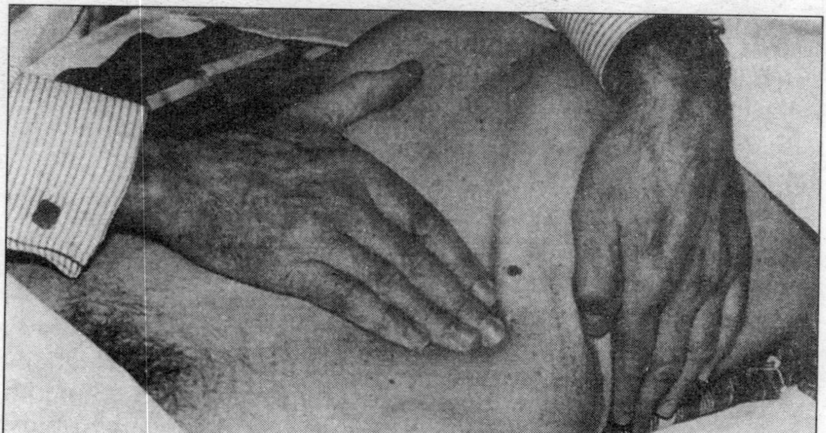

Fig. 9: Palpation of the spleen. Start well out to the left.

to feel the spleen. In children an enlarged spleen is sometimes palpable considerably "more laterally than you might expect, so feel first in the same way as for adults, and then repeat your routine but aiming this time at the posterior axillary line.

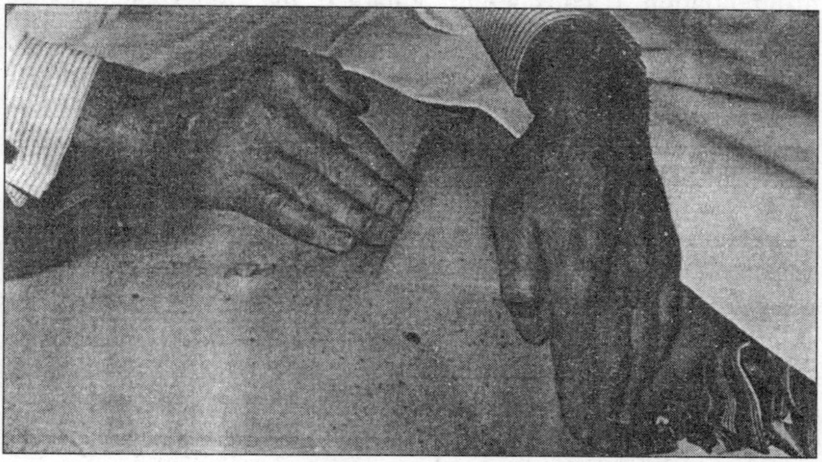

Fig. 10: Palpation of the spleen more medially than in Fig. 9.

However, large it grows, the spleen conveniently tends to retain its original shape. It moves with respiration; it has a sharp medial edge,

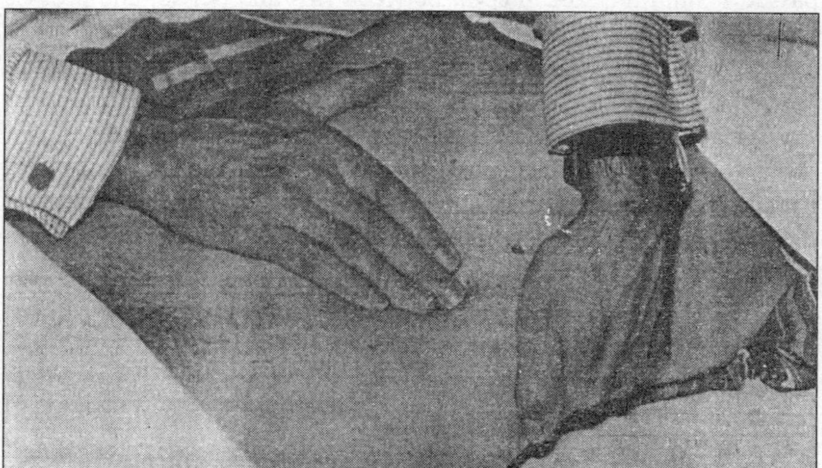

Fig. 11: Palpation of the left kidney.

in which the notch may often be felt; it enlarges downwards and obliquely across the abdomen; and it can be followed up under the rib margin. If you feel a mass with all these features it can be only the spleen, but in doubtful cases an enlarged left kidney may need careful differentiation. If considerably enlarged, the kidney tumour may become wedged under the ribs and appear to arise from there. It tends, however, to enlarge across the abdomen instead of downwards, has no sharp edge or notch, and can generally be followed back into the loin. Percussion may help in distinguishing between the two; the resonant descending colon may sometimes be percussed in front of the kidney tumour, but lies to the side of and behind a splenic tumour.

Kidney—Because they lie so deeply the kidneys are difficult to palpate. The lower pole of the right kidney can sometimes be felt in healthy adults. In infants, the lower part of both kidneys may be palpable, and often foetal lobulation can be made out, especially in a marasmic infant.

Again, you are advised to palpate for either kidney with your right hand, and from the patient's right side. As in the case of the spleen, you will need to use your left hand for the less accurate task of narrowing the space in which the kidneys move. The right hand presses firmly into the abdomen in the flank you are examining, with fingers pointing up towards the nipple on that side. Meanwhile the left hand is passed behind the soft interval between ribs and pelvis, and presses equally firmly up towards the palpating hand. When the patient takes a deep breath the kidney comes down into the narrowed space between the two hands, where it is felt.

The normal kidney is moderately firm, smooth, and not tender. With practice you can assess any enlargement, and you may feel irregularities of the surface. A really large renal tumour does not retain the shape of the kidney and has the characteristics listed above when discussing the differentiation from splenic enlargement.

Remember you are dealing with three-dimensional objects, not photographs, and examine the back as well as the front. You may find an apparent renal tumour arises from a dis-eased spine; or you may see oedema and redness in the renal area behind—vital evidence of extrarenal infection which may easily be missed.

Bladder—This is an abdominal organ in infants, but becomes pelvic in adults. If pathologically distended it may be seen, felt, and percussed. Having looked for the bulge it may produce, start percussion or palpation well away from the suspected area and proceed towards it; but you must proceed delicately, or you will miss the soft, rounded swelling arising from the pelvis and varying m position as the patient moves. A certain diagnosis is made by catheterization, but remember that once the bladder has been successfully emptied you must still find out why it became enlarged in the first place.

Gravid Uterus—You will have ample opportunity in the obstetric department for learning to diagnose enlargement of the uterus. Remember it as a possibility in every female of child-bearing age.

3. Abdominal Tumours not Arising from Viscera

To diagnose an abdominal tumour get away from it. In other words, diagnose by considering *all* the evidence and not merely the lump. This chapter describes only methods of examining the abdomen, but you will derive the essential additional evidence from the history (e.g. duration of symptoms, such as disturbed function) and from the general examination of the patient.

Certain characteristics of abdominal tumours are of great value in diagnosis. There are five main features; of these the **position in the abdomen** is probably the most important single one, but **size, multiplicity, mobility,** and **consistency** also provide helpful evidence.

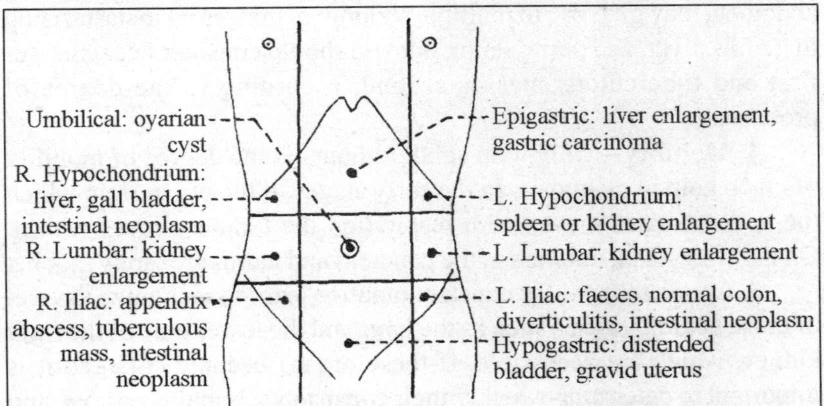

Fig. 12: Abdominal masses. Diagram illustrating the importance of the site in diagnosis. (Note: The examples given emphasize probabilities, but exceptions frequently occur.)

Before proceeding to discuss these characteristics it is helpful to recall the features of faecal masses; they indent on deliberate pressure with the finger, and they vary in position from time to time, and an enema may dissolve away both the mass and your doubts.

1. Position—The position of a tumour must be determined precisely. Your next task is to make out whether the mass is part of an abdominal viscus; to do this try to determine whether the neighbouring viscera can be separated from it. If the tumour is not in the region of any organ think, as always, of feces first of all, then consider neoplastic growths and inflammatory masses.

The accompanying diagram (Fig. 12) illustrates which are the commonest masses in particular regions of the abdomen.

If the tumour arises in the abdominal wall you will observe variations in the size, shape, and consistency when you ask the patient to tighten up his muscles, as he does by lifting his head when he is in the prone position.

2. Size—If the tumour is extremely large clinical diagnosis may be impossible. A large cyst, for example, whatever its origin, tends to occupy the middle of the abdomen. In practice, however, it is found that an extremely large central cyst usually arises from the ovary.

3. Multiplicity—The presence of many lumps rules out many diagnoses. A primary intestinal tumour, or a growth arising outside the abdomen, may give rise to multiple abdominal masses by metastasizing in glands, liver, and peritoneum; but you should consider fæcal masses first and tuberculous masses second, according to the degree of probability.

4. Mobility—Only with small tumours is the degree of mobility of much help in diagnosis. In the early stages, if the organ from which the tumour arises moves with respiration the tumour moves with it. On the other hand, tumours of the pancreas and uterus are rarely mobile.

5. Consistency—By constant practice learn to recognize the feel of those healthy organs such as the liver and the lower pole of the right kidney, which are accessible. If these organs become enlarged it is important to determine whether their consistency remains normal, and only your experience of normal organs will enable you to decide. If the consistency of any enlarged organ is not uniform it suggests neoplastic deposits or degenerative changes. Most malignant tumours are hard and tend to be irregular, so you must not be content to feel only that part of the organ which comes easily to hand.

In a large cyst you can elicit fluctuation. To do this place both forefingers firmly on the mass, at a considerable distance from each other, then press sharply with one finger. If a fluid wave impinges on the other finger the mass is said to fluctuate. You can produce the same sensation by the same method across the fibres of normal muscle. This is, in fact, a good way to learn the feel of fluctuation, and you should try it on your own thigh or calf muscles. If the cyst is under very great tension fluctuation is, however, difficult to demonstrate. Paget's test will then help to differentiate it from a solid tumour, in which the hardest part is in the centre, whereas in a cyst the centre is the softest part.

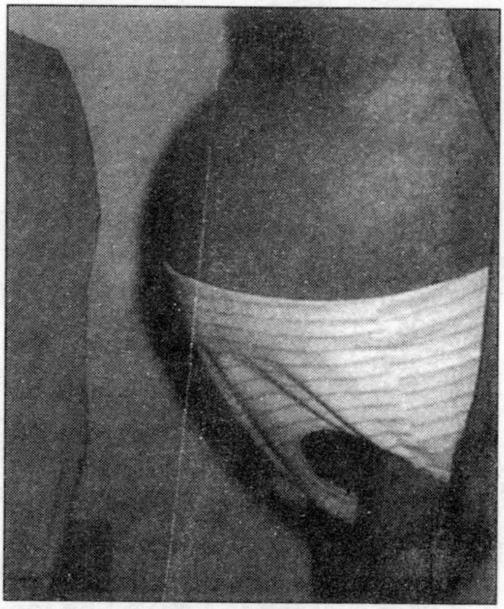

Fig. 13: A patient with end-stage liver cirrhosis disease, demonstrating muscle wasting and gross abdominal distension due to ascites.

Summary

Inspection, palpation, percussion, and auscultation are all useful in the diagnosis of abdominal abnormalities; but of these palpation is by far the most important, and deserves special study and practice.

Ascites can be recognized by its characteristic signs, but examination is not complete until the cause of the ascites is also determined.

The commonest palpable masses in the abdomen are formed by faeces, distended bladder, and gravid uterus. Pathological masses in the abdomen may be due either to enlargement of viscera or to other causes. Five features must be determined in the examination of any mass—namely: position, size, multiplicity, mobility, and consistency.

□

CHAPTER VIII

THE UROGENITAL SYSTEM

Though the physicians and surgeons, urologists, and even endocrinologists have divided urogenital disease among themselves, the general practitioner more than anyone remains the first judge and preserves that integrated view of the patient and his disease which is so important. As a student you should try to see things with a general practitioner's eyes.

As with disease of the alimentary system, intelligent hearing of the patient's symptoms and an intelligent inquiry will often be of more value in diagnosis than physical examination. Renal colic, for instance, that dramatic event which may within a few moments make a strong man writhe in agony, may produce no more physical signs than a cold sweat on the forehead and pallor. But listen to the patient's description of a pain like a red-hot knife shooting through and through his loin close to the spine, and darting down towards the groin so that the inner aspect of his thigh and his scrotum and his penis may burn in sympathy, and you know for certain that there has been some obstruction to the normal peristaltic action of the ureter on that side.

Vagaries in the habits and processes of micturition are legion. *Frequency of micturition* may be due to *polyuria* or to an irritable bladder which cannot hold more than a few ounces of urine at a time. It is your first job to find out by inquiry which of these two types of frequency troubles your patient. How often does he pass water during the day? And during the night? How much approximately does he pass at a time?

Painful or difficult micturition is known as *dysuria*; when your patient complains of it you will want to know whether the pain occurs throughout the act, at the beginning or at the end.

Difficulty in starting micturition is far commoner in men than women—it may be due to psychological or neurological cause—

whereas *incontinence,* particularly temporary incontinence after laughing or straining, is far commoner in women. This difference is related to the different lengths of the urethra in a man and woman. A long urethra is more easily obstructed, a short urethra more easily rendered patulous. If incontinence is present you must find out whether it occurs chiefly after straining, coughing, laughing, etc—if so, it is probably due to a mechanical weakness of the urethral sphincters. If it occurs without the patient being aware of the urine coming away, the cause is likely to be found in disease of the nervous system. If it occurs owing to the patient not having sufficient warning of the desire to micturate (*precipitancy* of micturition), the cause is also likely to be neurological.

Men may complain of a poor and *feeble stream of urine,* or dribbling at the end of micturition. These symptoms mean some obstruction in the urethra itself either in the prostatic region or lower down.

Discharge from the urethra may be watery or mucinous or purulent. Don't forget that watery discharges may be physiological in young men, but may cause much anxiety which you can easily allay.

Scheme of Examination

This is essentially simple:

1. Inspection and Palpation of the Abdomen—Pay particular attention to the loins (Figs. 1 and 2).

2. Inspection and Palpation of the External Genitalia—Examine the urethral orifice, whether your patient be male or female, and look for evidences of inflammation or purulent discharge. In the female you may see a small raspberry-like granuloma—a caruncle—at the urethral orifice. Such a tiny lesion may cause most

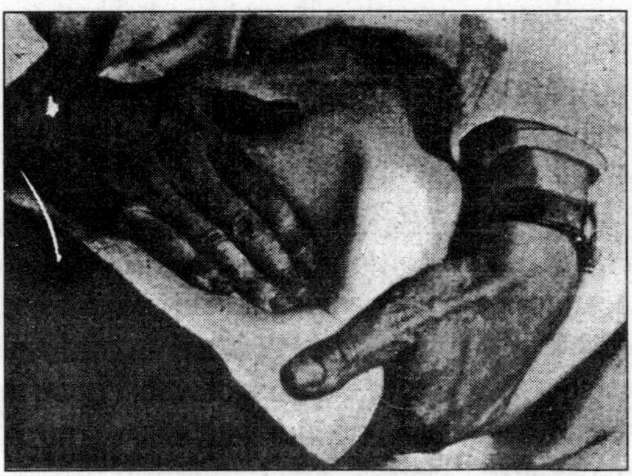

Fig. 1: Palpating the left loin.

distressing symptoms, and since the patient probably won't know it is there and won't point it out to you, you will miss finding a treatable condition if you don't look for it.

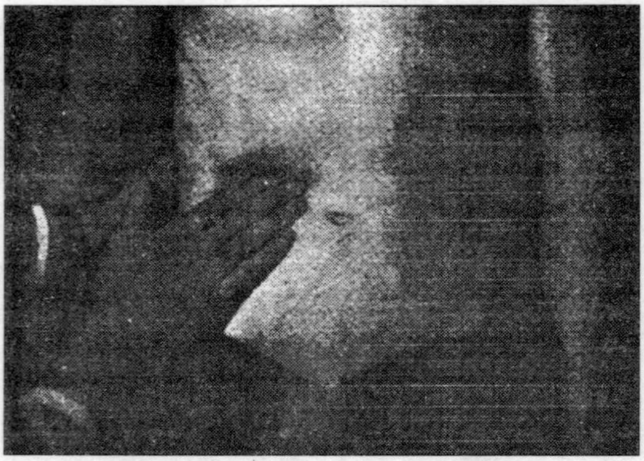

Fig. 2: Palpating the right loin.

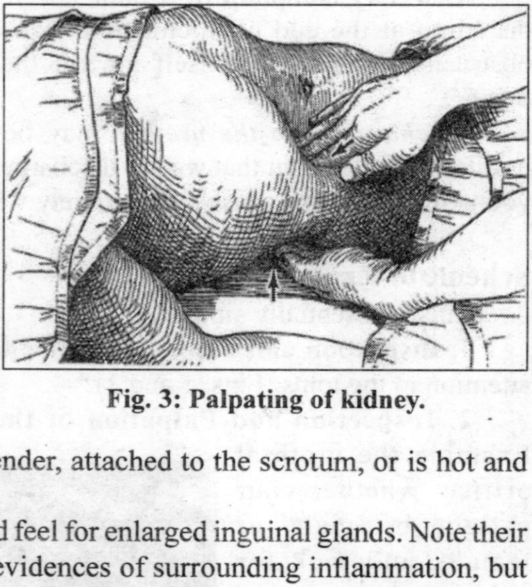

Fig. 3: Palpating of kidney.

Inspect and palpate the testicles and spermatic cord. You can make out the shape of the testis itself, of the epididymis behind, and of the spermatic cord. If a swelling is present note its shape, size, consistency, and surface, and try to determine whether it arises from the testis (anterior) or epididymis (posterior) or the cord (superior). Cystic swellings will transmit light. Note whether the swelling is tender, attached to the scrotum, or is hot and surrounded by oedema.

3. Glands—Look and feel for enlarged inguinal glands. Note their number, tenderness, and evidences of surrounding inflammation, but remember that small glands are palpable in most normal people.

4. Rectal Examination—This is best done with the patient in the knee-elbow position. Sweep the pad of your index finger over the posterior surface of the prostate. You should feel two smooth lobes, each about a centimetre in diameter and separated by a shallow valley, the median raphe. The consistency of the normal prostate should be firm but not hard; and it should not be tender, though very firm pressure may cause a deep-seated discomfort.

Sweeping your finger higher you may feel on either side and above the prostate the two seminal vesicles, and between them the posterior surface of the base of the bladder. It is useless, by the way, to try to make a satisfactory rectal examination of the prostate and the bladder neck if the bladder is full.

Examination of the Central Nervous System

Whether a complete examination is necessary or not depends upon the history of the case. A history of incontinence or of precipitancy of micturition is a direct indication for such an examination.

The Urine

Long before that time doctors had taken a great interest in the colour and composition of the urine, and rightly so, since the urine, as a modified filtrate of the blood, reflects the condition of the body fluids. The patient with a bleeding disease may pass a bloody urine, the dehydrated patient a dark-coloured concentrated urine, the patient with alkalosis an alkaline urine, while normal people pass an acid urine because their diet contains an excess of acid radicles. These are just a few of the more patent examples of the way in which the composition of the urine reflects the state of the blood.

Inspection—The first thing you must do when examining a patient's urine is to look at it! A clear amber liquid may suggest nothing abnormal to you and may indeed be quite normal. But if you see threads of epithelial debris floating there, it should make you think that the urine comes from a patient with some infection of the lower urinary tract such as urethritis, prostatitis, or cystitis. Faint 'cumulus' clouds suspended in the urine are formed of mucus from the bladder and are only a manifestation of a physiological process. An infected urine is sometimes frankly purulent, but most often is just faintly hazy. When you hold it up to the light and the haziness shimmers, the presence of pus cells is suggested. Urine which contains blood is sometimes dark red, but more often a dull smoky-brown colour. Urine containing bile-pigments is a dark mahogany brown and froths easily.

When the urine has stood for an hour or so, insoluble matter settles to the bottom of the vessel, but this deposit may be obtained more quickly by centrifuging. Sometimes, particularly in a concentrated or an infected urine, the deposit is very heavy. The commonest is of whitish material, phosphates, which are soluble in acetic acid. A deposit of a light pink or brick-dust colour, composed chiefly of insoluble urates, may come down in the urine of normal infants or in the highly concentrated urine of patients with heart failure or fever. It disappears on heating. Where there is disease of the uro-genital system the deposit may contain pus cells, red cells, or casts; these can be recognized only by microscopical examination.

Physical Examination—

(a) *Measurement of Specific Gravity*—Test the specific gravity of the urine, with the following precautions. Let the urine cool before testing; then remove surface froth. Use a vessel wide enough for the urinometer to float clear from the sides, lower yourself so that your eyes look along the level of the surface of the urine, and read off the figure on the shaft of the urinometer at exactly this level.

(b) *Measurement of Quantity*—A twenty-four hour specimen is valuable. The total quantity of urine passed in that time varies with the weather (less in hot weather) and the age of the patient (less from a child), but significant departures from the normal 1½ 1 should be recorded. The secretion of urine falls when the arterial pulse pressure falls, as in conditions of shock or haemorrhage; or when the venous pressure rises, as in heart failure; or when the body loses fluids from other sources, as in diarrhoea, vomiting, or with the development of subcutaneous oedema. The urinary volume is also decreased in acute nephritis where the inflammation and swelling of the kidney probably act as a mechanical bar to glomerular filtration.

The volume of urine secreted increases when kidney function begins to fail, as in chronic nephritis (since the kidney cannot concentrate solids a copious dilute urine is passed to get rid of the equivalent amount of solid waste). There is also increased secretion when the urine contains excess quantities of sugar, or when the body is unloading oedema fluid.

About twice the amount of urine is passed by day as by night. The night urine is dark and concentrated. This is not so, however, in infants, or in adults with chronic nephritis, none of whom have the power of concentrating their urine to the same degree. If possible, therefore, collect the night urine and the day urine separately.

(c) *pH*—Test the reaction of the urine with litmus paper.

Chemical Examination of the Urine—Only the five commonly used chemical tests are described here.

1. *For Protein*—Fill the test-tube three quarters full of urine. Hold it by the base and heat the top half-inch of urine over a flame till it boils. If cloudiness appears in the boiled area add a few drops of acetic acid and boil again; a phosphatic cloud then disappears while a protein cloud remains.

2. *For Sugar*—Quickly invert over the sink the test-tube used in the test for protein, so that nearly all the urine runs away. Enough remains on the side walls of the tube for the sugar test. Add to it about 3 c.c. of Benedict's solution and boil again, this time holding the top of the test-tube with a slip of paper or metal holder. Boil for a least a minute, noting any reduction of the copper salts to cuprous oxide which will colour the blue reagent green, yellow, or red, according to its quantity. A more accurate method is to add eight drops of urine to 5 c.c. of Benedict's solution and boil for two minutes.

3. *For Ketones*—Pour 10 c.c. of fresh urine in a tube and dissolve in it about 5 g of crystalline ammonium sulphate. Add a crystal of sodium nitroprusside or a few drops of a 5 per cent nitroprusside solution and then 2 c.c. of a strong ammonia solution. Invert the tube over your thumb a few times and leave to stand. If a purple, 'permanganate' colour develops, acetone bodies are present.

4. *For Bile-pigments*—Dilute 1 c.c. of tincture of iodine with 5 c.c. of water in a test-tube. Almost fill another test-tube with urine, then run the dilute iodine solution gently down onto the surface of the urine. If a green ring develops at the junction of the two fluids bile-pigments are present.

5. *Urinary Chlorides*—Using a pipette, measure 10 drops of urine into a test-tube. Rinse the pipette in distilled water and add one drop of a 20 per cent potassium chromate solution. Rinse the pipette again and add, drop by drop, shaking the tube after each drop, a 2.9 per cent silver nitrate solution. The end point is reached when the colour changes from red to brown. Roughly, the number of drops of silver nitrate solution added indicates the concentration of chlorides in grammes per litre of urine.

Microscopy—It is wrong to diagnose the presence of pus or blood in the urine by chemical tests, since these are by no means accurate.

Pus, blood, and urinary casts should be searched for under the microscope. The urinary deposit obtained by sedimentation or centrifuging provides you with suspended solid matter. Place one drop of this on a clean glass slide, cover with a slip and focus on it with the low-power objective of the microscope. Change then to the high-power objective and search amongst the debris and crystalline material which are almost inevitably present in such a urinary deposit for red cells, pus cells, or casts. Motile coliform organisms are often seen, but are not of significance unless the urine was passed by catheter into a sterile container. Red cells are seen as small round, doubly retractile bodies. Pus cells are slightly larger, are not so retractile, and have a granular cystoplasm and often a crenated edge. Casts are at first difficult to recognize and to distinguish from cotton-wool fibres or other cellular material in the urine. Casts are cylindrical bodies, ¼—1 mm in length, sometimes hyaline and homogeneous, sometimes made up of packed cells.

Summary

Listen carefully to the patient's story and inquire about all aspects of urinary function—the quantity and quality of urine, and the ability to pass it normally.

Examine the abdomen, particularly in the kidney regions, the external genitalia, and the inguinal lymphatic glands. Make a rectal examination and examine the central nervous system, if necessary.

Lastly, examine the urine, first with the naked eye, then by physical, chemical, and microscopical methods.

CHAPTER IX

EXAMINATION OF NERVOUS SYSTEM

It is not your chief's responsibility to teach you anatomy or physiology; nor, fortunately, is it ours. But it is our concern to insist that you must never lose that familiarity with the broad principles of these subjects which you have laboured until now to acquire.

On the basis of this knowledge the great bulk of nervous diseases can be understood and diagnosed; without it you will find that they must remain irrational and uninteresting. Diagnosis based on empirical facts is an unsatisfying substitute for diagnosis which rests on an understanding of structure and function.

You should, for example, know the ways in which lesions affecting *upper and lower motor neurones* differ. What you have learnt about the *tracts in the spinal cord*—their relative positions, the directions they take, their connexions, and their functions—is vital in the diagnosis of many nervous diseases. It is equally essential to remember the *localization of functions in the brain* and the *paths of the tracts in the internal capsule.*

"Writing maketh an exact man"—try to write down what you know about the examples we have chosen, or, better still, make diagrams to illustrate them. It is encouraging to note how few, and how elementary, are the examples quoted—only four so far. You may add to this irreducible minimum as you find it necessary; in this chapter we propose to illustrate very few additional examples.

Not only your interpretation of physical signs, but even the methods of eliciting them, may depend on your knowledge of anatomy and physiology. In the following section let us consider the reflexes from these aspects.

The Reflexes

Knee-jerk—The knee-jerk is taken as an example and will be discussed first in some detail.

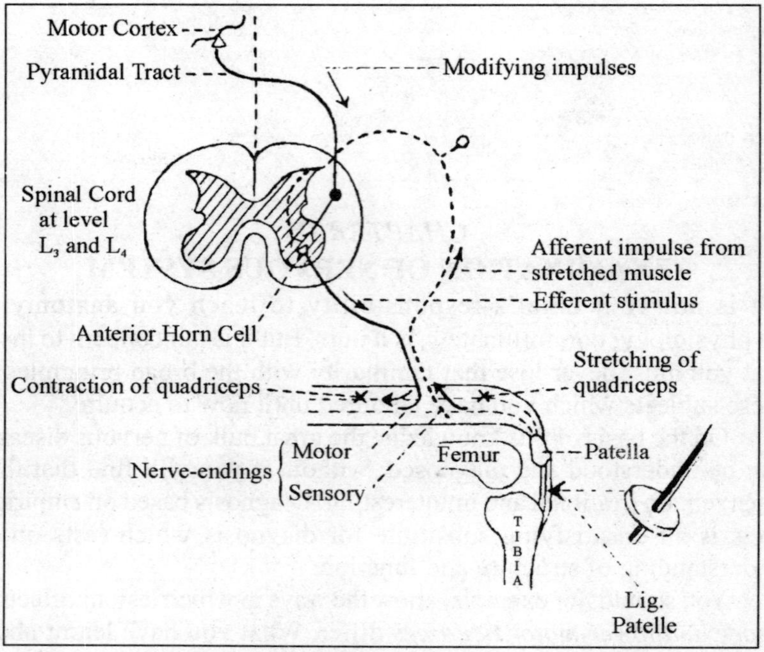

Fig. 1: Diagram to illustrate the knee-jerk.

Mechanism—The knee-jerk is a 'stretch reflex' (Fig. 1). A sharp blow on the ligamentum patellae stretches the quadriceps muscle. As a result, the sensory nerve-endings in the muscle are stimulated, and afferent impulses pass to the spinal cord at the level of the 3rd and 4th lumbar segments. From the anterior horn cells in which the afferent nerves end an efferent stimulus passes down to the motor-fibres serving the quadriceps, and gives rise to a contraction. At the same time, a stimulus passes to the antagonistic muscles, so that the hamstrings are simultaneously relaxed. Passing down the pyramidal tract impulses constantly lessen muscle tone, so that in normal health the 'stretch reflex' is a moderate one.

Practiced Applications—Obviously, any force which stretches the quadriceps may produce the reflex, but a short, sharply applied force will be most effective. The position of the leg is important; it is advisable to ensure that the leg muscles are completely relaxed, so that the quadriceps is in the optimum position to respond to stretching while the hamstrings do not inhibit the resulting movement. These

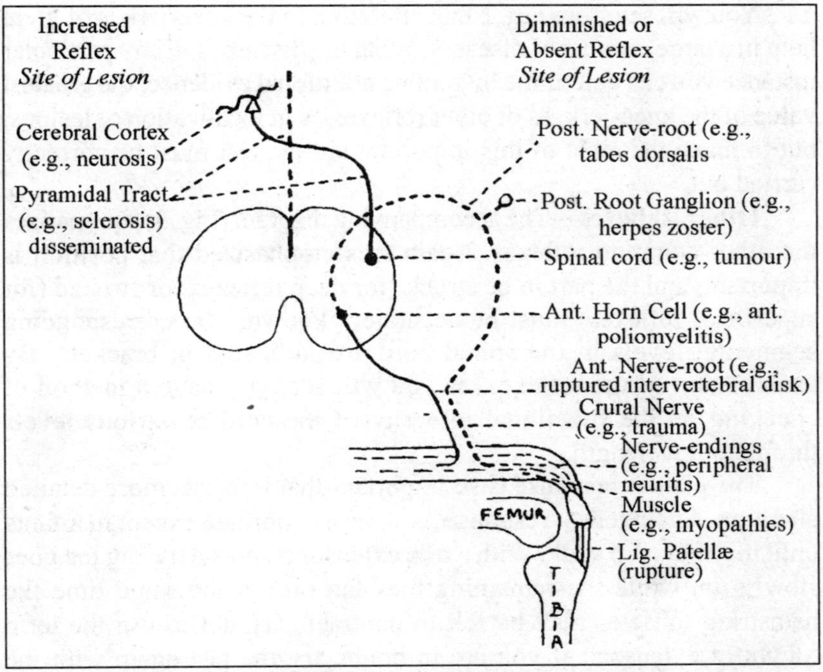

Fig. 2: Diagram to illustrate causes of alterations in the knee-jerk.

requirements are best met if the knee is flexed at a right angle, and if the ligamentum patellae is struck sharply. If relaxation is difficult to obtain, the patient's attention should be diverted, as by forced pressure of one hand against the other.

When the knee-jerk is weak or absent remember to feel the quadriceps; contraction of the quadriceps is the essential feature, and the extension of the knee is only secondary to it.

Alterations in the Knee-jerk—The accompanying diagram (Fig. 2) illustrates some of the causes of alteration in the knee-jerk, not as a diagnostic list, but to remind you of possible abnormalities while you are carrying out the test.

It is important to note that unilateral changes are of greater diagnostic importance than are bilateral, and that exaggeration of both knee-jerks without supporting evidence should not be attributed to lesions of the pyramidal tract.

You will see from Fig. 2 that alteration in the knee-jerk is of great help in a large number of diseases. What the disease is in any particular instance you can determine by finding additional evidence; the greatest value of the knee-jerk, as of other reflexes, is in localization of lesions, but to make the most of this important aid the test must be correctly carried out.

Other Reflexes—The accompanying diagram (Fig. 3) summarizes the other common reflexes. Again it is emphasized that position is important, and the part to be struck (for deep reflexes) or stroked (for superficial reflexes) must be accurately known. The corresponding segmental levels in the spinal cord are indicated in brackets. By examination of the reflexes, as you will see, you have a method of checking on the functional integrity of the cord at various levels throughout its length.

The plantar response is so important that it merits more detailed attention. An 'extensor response' is always abnormal, except in infants until they begin to walk. With a true extensor response the big toe goes slowly up, while the remaining toes fan out; at the same time the hamstring muscles may be felt to contract. Try not to use the term 'doubtful extensor'; if you are in doubt, try the test again with the knee extended, and after warming the foot by brisk rubbing, and compare it with the response of the other foot. If you cannot elicit a definite sign say 'no definite response obtained'.

C.N.S. Examination

You must aim at making a routine of the correct methods of examination; this can become a habit if you repeatedly watch and imitate the practised physician at work.

Assessment of Mentality—A considerable part of C.N.S. examination entails the co-operation of the patient. Neither a comatose patient nor an infant can provide this co-operation, and diagnosis in these cases is correspondingly more difficult. Where the patient can reasonably be expected to co-operate, however, you must know to what extent his efforts are reliable; for this reason you must obviously make a preliminary assessment of his mental capacity, and you can estimate it quite well during the course of your conversation.

Observe how the patient responds to your gambits. Does he understand your meaning?—the senile or mentally defective patient

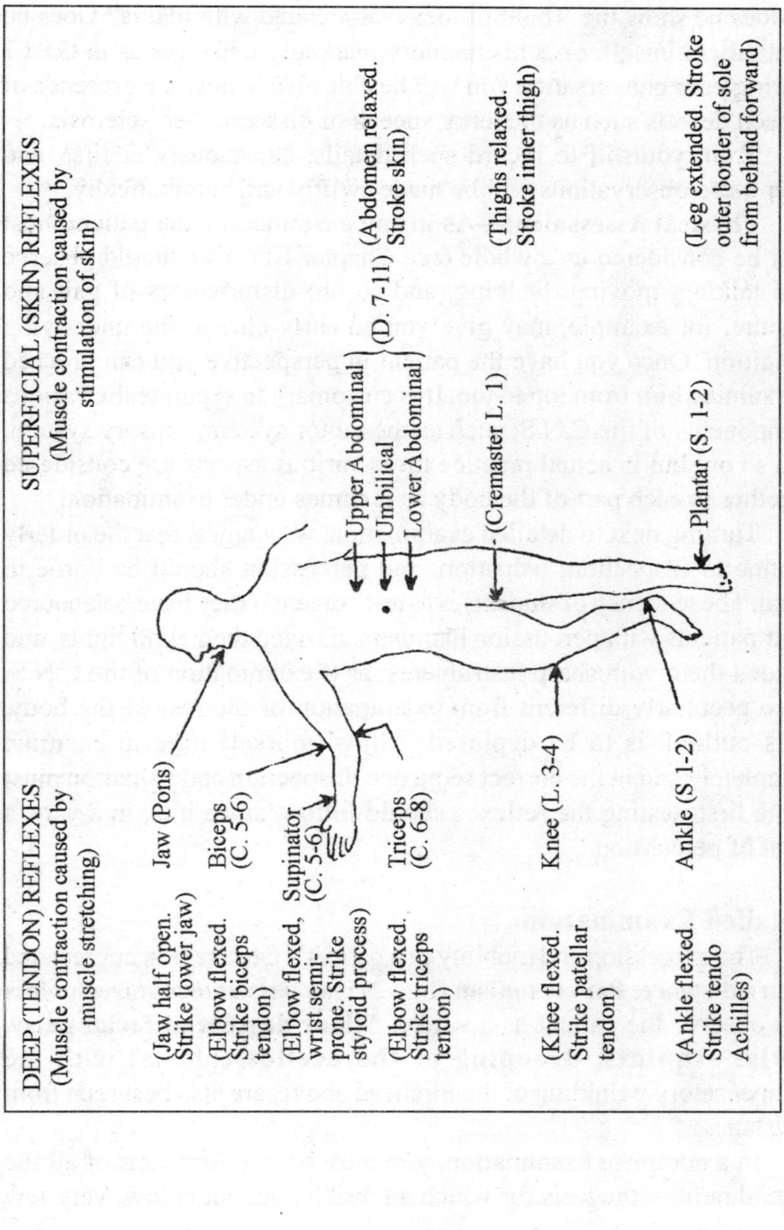

Fig. 3: Muscle reflexes. To show segmental level, position of part, and where to apply stimulus.

may do so only with difficulty. Is he unduly exalted or depressed, or nervous, or resentful? Is he reasonably well orientated, or incoherent, or does he show the 'flight of ideas' associated with mania? Does he contradict himself, or is his memory markedly defective as in G.P.I.? During your conversation you will be able also to note the presence of speech defects such as the jerky speech of disseminated sclerosis.

Train yourself to record such details, consciously at first, and later these observations will be made swiftly and automatically.

Physical Assessment—As in any examination, the patient must first be considered as a whole (*see* Chapter III). You should observe him talking, moving, walking, and so on; disturbances of gait and posture, for example, may give you an early clue to the underlying condition. Once you have the patient in perspective you can proceed to examine him from top to toe. It is customary to separate the various components of the C.N.S. such as the motor system, sensory system, and so on; but in actual practice these various aspects are considered together in each part of the body as it comes under examination.

Turning next to detailed examination, we suggest that the orderly routine of inspection, palpation, and percussion should be borne in mind. The tendency of students is to rest content if they have belaboured their patients with percussion hammers, dazzled them with lights, and goaded them with sharp instruments, as if examination of the C.N.S. were peculiarly different from examination of the rest of the body. This outlook is to be deplored. Allow yourself time to examine completely and in the correct sequence. Inspection and palpation must come first; testing the reflexes should follow, since it is, in a way, a form of percussion.

Detailed Examination

The expression and mobility of a patient's face are best appreciated from a distance. **Parkinsonism** (Fig. 2) may pass unrecognized unless you observe the patient as a whole. **Minor degrees of facial palsy, ocular' squints, drooping of the eyelids** (ptosis) with the compensatory wrinkling of the forehead above, are also best seen from a distance.

In a complete examination, you must try the functions of all the cranial nerves, the tests for which are briefly set out below. Very few of these tests may safely be omitted; the test for smell is, however, usually left out in the absence of a precise indication for it.

1. Cranial Nerves—

1st Nerve—First exclude obstructive nasal conditions such as the common cold. Test for smell by using common substances such as peppermint, which the patient can recognize.

2nd Nerve—Note the size and regularity of both pupils. To test their reaction to *light* shine a bright light on each pupil in turn, holding the light at the corresponding side so that it illuminates only one pupil at a time. To test for *accommodation,* ask the patient to look at your finger, held at a distance, then quickly to look at his own nose, while you observe whether the pupils contract.

Now you should carry out *ophthalmoscopic examination.* Efficient and easy use of the ophthalmoscope is entirely a matter of practice; if you can afford it, buy a 'Wide-Angle' ophthalmoscope and use it every day on as many people as possible. Learn to relax your own accommodation, and approach the patient's pupil from the side, not directly from the front, in order to minimize pupillary contraction. Where a good view cannot be obtained the pupils should be dilated, but this is not usually necessary if the examination is carried out in the dark, either by darkening the room or by draping a dark cloth over both the patient's head and your own.

The *optic nerve head* must be examined with great care; you will find it by following one of the retinal arteries. Note four main features: the colour, edge, depth of the cup, and state of the blood-vessels. As large a part as possible of the retina should also be inspected, paying particular attention to the blood-vessels, and observing exudates or hemorrhages.

A rough test for *fields of vision* should be carried out. It is based on a comparison between the patient's fields and your own. Ask him to cover one eye with his hand, while you, seated directly opposite him, close your corresponding eye. As your test object use a piece of white paper, about 1 in square, held in the nib. of an ordinary pen. Move it slowly from the periphery across the field of vision, repeating the manoeuvre from various directions. The patient's open eye and your own should stare one at the other. The test object should come into the patient's field of vision at about the same time as into your own, unless he has a marked visual defect.

3rd, 4th, and 6th Nerves—Observe the presence of *ptosis* (drooping of the eyelid) (Fig. 4) or any inequality in the palpebral fissures; if the difference between the two sides is only slight it may be insignificant because an asymmetry of the skull can produce it.

Notice the presence of a *squint*; it may be due to muscle paralysis, and is then of diagnostic importance. It may, however, be due to relative divergence of the visual axes of the eyes; in this case the two eyes move equally well in all directions, though there is a constant divergence.

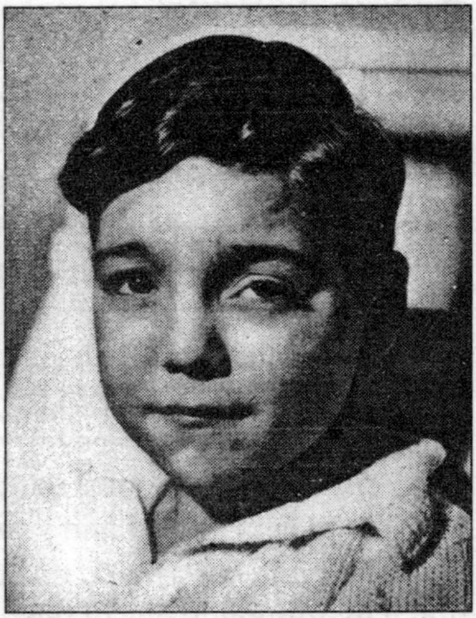

Fig. 4: Ptosis, left-sided.

When testing the *movements of the eyes* by asking the patient to follow your finger in all directions, look also for *nystagmus,* a wavering about the point of fixation. Do not carry your testing finger too far to the side, because in that position you may produce equivocal movements even in normal subjects. It is useful to bear nystagmus in mind when examining the fundus with your ophthalmoscope; in slight cases it may be best detected by the wavering of the patient's eye under ophthalmoscopic examination. While testing for eye movements ask the patient if he sees double, and remember to test for convergence.

5th Nerve—Ask about pain and numbness in the face, tongue, and eyes. Test the *sensibility to light touch* of the face, tongue, and cornea. To test the *corneal reflex* (blinking when the cornea is touched) approach the cornea from the side with a wisp of cotton-wool, in order to avoid provoking the visual reflex. The sensibility of the face to *light pin-prick* should also be tested: in tabes dorsalis there may be loss of sensation over the nose and neighbouring parts.

The *muscle functions* are assessed by palpating the masseters and temporal muscles on both sides while you ask the patient to bite. Next ask the patient to open his mouth widely; with one-sided weakness of the pterygoids the jaw deviates to one side.

Test the *jaw-jerk* with the mouth slightly opened; the normal response is almost imperceptible.

7th Nerve—Note carefully any asymmetry of the face; in slight cases you will observe it best by comparing the two naso-labial folds. Watch while the patient, at your request, wrinkles up the forehead, then screws up the eyes, then grins forcibly.

You will remember that there is bilateral cortical control of the 7th nerve nuclei, supplying the muscles of the upper face. An intranuclear lesion abolishes all movements on that side of the face; but a supranuclear lesion diminishes voluntary movements only of the lower half of the face, and permits emotional movements over the whole area.

8th Nerve—Test hearing with a watch and by whispering, comparing the distance at which they are heard on the two sides. With a tuning-fork compare air and bone conduction; when the patient ceases to hear the sound of the fork held at a short distance from his ear rest its base firmly on his mastoid process. If air conduction is defective as compared with bone conduction the sound produced by the fork will then again become audible to him.

Never omit examination of both ear drums.

9th, 10th, 11th, and 12th Nerves—It is difficult to carry out precise tests for each of these nerves without special experience, but a few simple tests will suffice.

Ask about difficulty in swallowing, and whether fluids are regurgitated through the nose.

Note if the uvula is in the mid-line. Ask the patient to say 'Ah' while you observe if the palate moves symmetrically. Tell him to put out his tongue, and note if there is any wasting or tremor, comparing both sides, or if it deviates to one side. Observe drooping of either shoulder or asymmetry of the scapulae (lesion affecting the lower two-thirds of trapezius). Test the sternomastoids by asking the patient to touch his shoulder with the ear on that side, while you feel the muscle, and compare its action on the two sides.

To complete the examination of the head, palpate it for bony swellings which may be caused by tumour infiltration. In infants, it is extremely important to feel the anterior fontanelle and estimate its tension. In infants and young children, it is also helpful to measure the maximum diameter of the skull.

Before passing on you should test for neck rigidity.

2. The Limbs—Look at the limbs before you pick them up to examine them. You may observe *involuntary movements*: in habit spasm the same set of movements is continually repeated; in chorea the movements are manifestly purposeless, vary from one part to another, and give the impression of being incomplete; in athetosis the movements affect whole limbs, as well as the trunk in many instances, and are writhing in character.

Turn now to more detailed observation. In syringomyelia, you may see on the fingers scars due to burns, resulting from the loss of sensation to heat in this condition; in syphilis the thin, papery scars of healed ulcers may be present on the outer aspect of the calves.

Note the presence of contractures, or of wasting or any difference in size on the two sides. At the same time, the limb girdles should be inspected; in the muscular dystrophies wasting often commences in these regions. An important observation to make at this stage is to note the presence of fibrillation, or twitching of bands of muscle-fibres. A normal person may show fibrillation if he is cold, but if fibrillation is marked it indicates rapid wasting of the muscles, and in its most severe form is usually associated with the disease known as progressive muscular atrophy.

Next, examine the limbs for *ataxia.* The 'finger-nose test', in which the forefinger is brought from as far away as possible to touch the tip of the nose, is the simplest of these tests and will also demonstrate 'intention tremor', a vacillation on either side of the object aimed at; but before you attach too much importance to minor deviations try the tests on yourself. For the legs a similar test consists in placing the heel of one leg on the knee of the opposite leg and sliding the heel down the front of the shin. Ataxia is usually due either to a cerebellar lesion or to damage of the sensory tracts; in the latter case it can be compensated by visual effort, so that ataxy which is caused by sensory loss is made appreciably worse if the eyes are shut.

Now pick up each limb in turn, and move it, noting any abnormality in *tone.* A spastic limb is resistant to movement and to bending at the joints; if tone is deficient the limb feels flabby and responds rather like a piece of string to shaking. In Parkinsonian conditions jerky rigidity, described as 'cog-wheel' in type, is produced on flexing the joints.

Next test the limbs for *power*. Get the patient to go through various movements—such as gripping your hand, flexing and extending the elbow, bending and straightening the knee against resistance—to estimate the power in each main group of muscles.

Now carry out simple tests for *sensation*. First outline any subjective sensory symptoms such as pain, numbness, or tingling; their precise distribution is frequently of great importance. Next, test sensibility with pin-prick and cotton-wool in turn. These tests need to be carried out quickly, or the patient's attention lapses and his answers become unreliable. To assess deep sensation you will use tests which demonstrate the sense of passive movement and of the position of the fingers and toes. For example, with the patient looking away, flex or straighten his fore-finger or big toe, and ask him to state whether it is or is not bent. Deep sensation is also assessed by testing perception to the vibration of a large tuning fork in large bones such as the tibia, which lie immediately beneath the skin. Small objects may also be placed in the patient's hand and the patient asked to name them, or the tendo Achillis may be forcibly pinched to ascertain if pain is felt. Sensation to heat and cold is tested by the use of test-tubes containing hot and cold water respectively. They are applied to the patient's hands, feet, and trunk; but the difference in temperature must be clearly appreciable to you before you judge the patient by his responses.

In infants pain is the only form of sensation which can be tested. This should be done by pinching the skin and noting if there is any resultant movement or crying; pricking the skin of infants is not to be encouraged, since they are so prone to infection.

The tests for sensation are useless unless certain elementary facts of anatomy and physiology are borne in mind. The distribution of the main sensory nerves in the skin must be known, particularly of such nerves as the radial, ulnar, and medial in the arm. The main segmentary sensory levels in the spine should also be known: a simple diagram such as that in Fig. 5 will serve to refresh your memory.

The reflexes should be tested in the manner already described, when all the foregoing tests have been carried out.

3. The Trunk—Extensive tattooing on the chest is claimed by cynics to be as diagnostic as a positive Wasserman reaction; the pale scar of a chancre on the penis syphilis is a more certain sign, and you should look for it in any case in which syphilis appears possible.

Tests for sensory appreciation and for the abdominal reflexes are carried out in the usual way, with the same appreciation of their significance as regards the level of any underlying lesion. The abdominal reflexes may be of limited diagnostic value. A positive response is shown by deviation of the linea alba and umbilicus to the side of the abdomen which is stroked. In obese subjects, or where the abdominal wall is lax, the absence of reflexes may possess no diagnostic significance. A full bladder also seems to produce anomalous responses. Repeated stroking of the skin to obtain or confirm the responses appears to tire the abdominal reflexes, so that a decision should be made quickly.

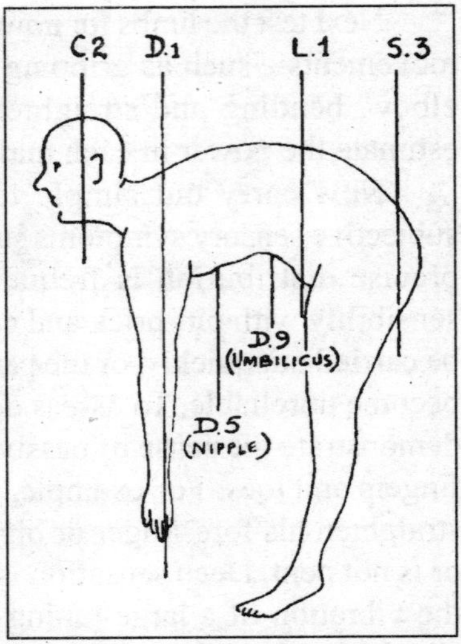

Fig. 5. Sensory levels. Note that the sensory innervation of the body surface can be simply reconstructed by placing the body in the quadruped position.

4. Lumbar Puncture—The examination of the C.S.F. is an essential part of the examination in the presence of disease of the C.N.S. Its technique is described fully elsewhere and must be completely mastered. One warning is necessary: in the presence of raised intracranial tension the withdrawal of more than a small amount of C.S.F. may be dangerous, so that **lumbar puncture should not be done until papillædema has been excluded by examination of the fundus oculi.**

Summary

1. Certain essential facts of physiology and anatomy must be continuously borne in mind while you are examining the C.N.S.
2. It is important to carry out tests of the functional integrity of the C.N.S. in the correct, and not in a haphazard, manner.
3. First assess the patient's mentality, since on it depends the degree of his co-operation, and on his co-operation a large part of your examination is based.

4. Obtain a general impression of the patient; then examine him in detail from head to toe.
5. In the head and face, test the cranial nerves in orderly fashion.
6. Next examine the limbs, in each assessing the various functions (motor, sensory, etc.), and, lastly, examine the trunk.
7. Lumbar puncture may complete an examination which has revealed neurological disease.

□

CHAPTER X
EXAMINATION OF ACUTE CASES

The Unconscious Patient

When you are confronted for the first time with an unconscious patient, your mind may be as blank as the patient's. Deprived of the help afforded by the accustomed routine of history-taking and questioning, leisurely examination and investigation, you may despair. The problem seems not only impossible to solve, but equally impossible even to comprehend. Yet somehow, by observation and deduction, you must make a diagnosis and do something for the patient—and that without delay.

If you had been fortunate enough to see your chief or an experienced casualty officer dealing with such a case you would have noticed that he went about the examination swiftly, and with purpose behind every movement, very soon arriving at some satisfactory conclusion on which to base diagnosis and treatment. How can you acquire a similar skill? By experience alone, some might say, and it is certain that without experience you will never become a master of your art. Yet the ability to profit by experience—that of others, as well as your own—is important too, and with guidance it can be cultivated so that your path is made shorter and smoother.

Probabilities—The problem of how to examine an unconscious patient is entangled with the problem of diagnosis. It is, in practice, impossible to make an intelligent examination unless you base it on what is likely to have occurred; in medicine, as in life, probability is a good stick to lean on. By diagnosing cerebral malaria in Iceland you might gain a tremendous reputation, but it would hardly last long.

Alcohol once accounted for more cases of coma than all other causes added together, but this is no longer true. Nowadays, *trauma* and *cerebrovascular accidents* are the commonest causes, and together account for about half the cases of coma. Other common causes are *epilepsy, severe infections* (which may or may not be confined to the C.N.S.), *diabetes mellitus* (hyperglycæmic or hypoglycæmic coma), and *barbiturate poisoning.* These data are valuable because, knowing the likely underlying causes, you can base on them a scheme for quick examination which will include all that is essential.

History—The urge to do something quickly may make you forget that a history can sometimes be obtained from a relative or friend or the witness of an accident. It is worth pausing to obtain a history while memories are fresh. Remember, however, that the history is sometimes misleading; anxious relatives often tend to ascribe coma to some cause such as an accident, which does not imply the social slur of, say, epilepsy. Disease, like pride, may come *before* the fall.

How can the history help? Coma which comes on gradually suggests a slowly developing cause such as diabetes mellitus; a sudden onset is more likely to be due to a sudden gross cerebral haemorrhage, for example. If the story you obtain is that of sudden coma, with recovery of consciousness followed by the recurrence of coma, it will suggest increasing intra-cranial pressure due to haemorrhage, as from rupture of the middle meningeal artery; this condition demands urgent operation and is difficult to diagnose in the absence of a history. These examples illustrate the importance of trying to obtain an accurate history.

Scheme of Examination (Fig. 1)

1. Surroundings—If you are called to the room where the patient became unconscious, look around for clues. The popularity of detective stories makes it unlikely that you will miss such an obvious clue as an empty bottle of sleeping tablets.

2. Position and General Appearance of Patient—Before proceeding to touch the patient make what you can of his position and appearance.

After a fall or other accident the position sometimes indicates a fracture of the vertebral column or limbs. In hysterical simulation of coma, on the other hand, the position may appear artificial. A child with meningitis may show head retraction or opisthotonos. At this stage also make a mental note of the type of breathing, to be confirmed later

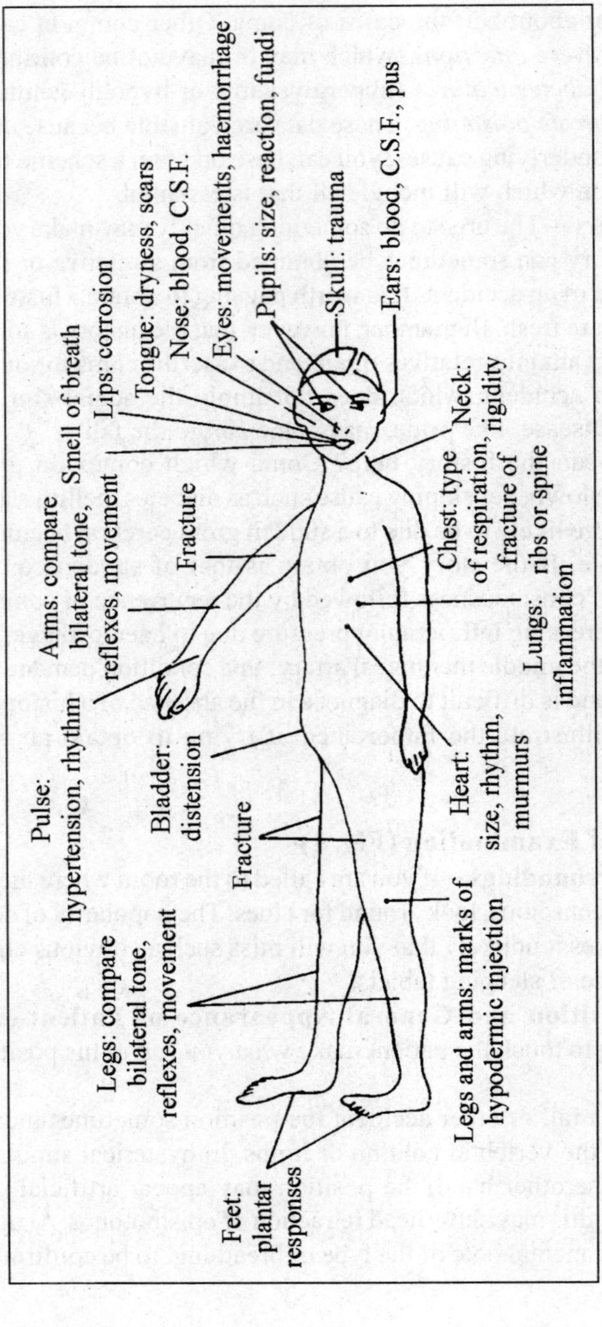

Fig. 1: Coma. Scheme for clinical examination.

facial paralysis shows by a sagging of that side, and the paralysed cheek flaps in and out with deep respirations.

The *colour* of the face may also afford some help. Pallor or greyness suggests shock, usually due to trauma; while a red face is typically seen in diabetic coma.

(c) Eyes—Inspection of the eyes often provides a clue to diagnosis early in the examination. A *subconjunctival haemorrhage,* for example, suggests the possibility of a larger haemorrhage inside the skull, due to a fracture. There may be *conjugate deviation* of the eyes, as in cerebral thrombosis or haemorrhage; both eyes turning away from the site of the lesion while it is developing (though later on they tend to turn towards it). Compare the *size of the two pupils*; with a cerebrovascular lesion, for example, one pupil alone may be dilated, and the dilatation is usually on the side of the lesion. It is important to note whether both pupils are small, because, if they are, you must consider and look for further evidence of morphine poisoning, though some vascular lesions of the brain may produce the same effect. In alcoholic coma, too, the pupils may be small, but in this condition they usually dilate if the skin is pinched firmly.

The *optic fundi* are nearly always to be seen easily in comatose patients, and they may provide the most helpful evidence. For example, papillaedema is evidence of increased intra-cranial tension, usually due to a tumour; or a characteristic retinitis may be present, as in uraemia or diabetes mellitus or in hypertension. This one examination, therefore, may provide a provisional diagnosis in many of the conditions which commonly give rise to coma.

(d) Orifices: Nostrils and Ears—Blood coming from one or both *nostrils* is strongly suggestive of a fractured skull, unless there is superficial trauma, and you should look *inside* both nostrils for it. Blood from a fractured skull may, however, have run back into the throat, instead of forward into the nose, and you will have observed it when you examined the mouth. If there is no very obvious cause of coma, your examination is certainly not complete until you have examined both *ears.* The presence of blood or of cerebrospinal fluid indicates fracture of the skull. Inflammation of a tympanic membrane is important evidence which is often missed; it obviously suggests that the coma is due to meningitis or to a brain abscess arising from the inflamed ear.

(e) Skull—Gently lift the head. At this time you can test for *neck rigidity*; it may be due to meningitis, but can also arise from intracranial haemorrhage, or obviously from a broken neck, or even from severe bruising of the superficial tissues of the neck. If there is no neck rigidity you should be able to move the head so that the chin readily touches the sternum.

While the head is lifted—and notice that we advocate moving the head only at this late stage in the examination—look and feel all over the skull for *injuries* or *wounds,* but bearing in mind that the injury may follow and not precede the illness.

5. The Limbs—It is convenient next to examine the limbs. It is, of course, best to have them completely uncovered, but at the time and site of an acute emergency this may not be possible.

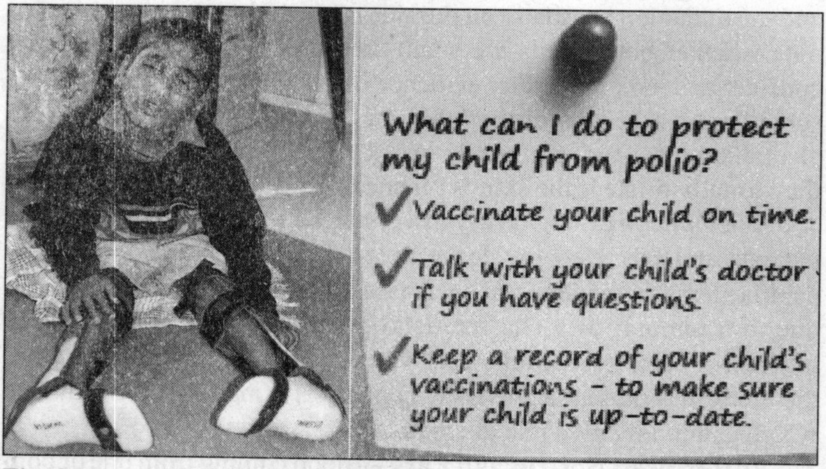

Fig. 2: A young patient with polio showing paralysis of the lower limb and paraspinal muscles causing marked scoliosis and a deformed pelvis.

Before you come to the obvious things such as looking for a fracture or for spasticity or flaccidity, feel the *radial pulse.* It is satisfying to detect an undoubted increase in the blood-pressure and thickening of the artery, and these findings may indicate the cause of the coma, but do not stop at this stage; remember what happens whenever the intracranial tension is raised—the blood-pressure tends to rise too, so that the increase in blood-pressure which you have detected may be secondary and not primary. This sort of problem is what makes diagnosis as fascinating as anything Sherlock Holmes had to do.

While you are feeling the pulse look on the surface of the limbs for the marks of hypodermic injections, often visible in diabetics and occasionally in morphine addicts.

Next compare opposite limbs for *tone.* Immediately after a cerebral accident, for example, contralateral flaccidity may be present. In general, it may be said that in coma flaccidity or spasticity is a useful guide only if it is unilateral. A similar generalization applies in the case of the *reflexes,* which should now be elicited; whatever the cause of the coma, reflexes on both sides may be absent temporarily and both plantar reflexes may also become extensor; only a difference on the two sides is therefore helpful in localizing the cause.

Although the patient cannot voluntarily co-operate, you may still be able to obtain information about loss of *movement.* In mild coma, the patient still responds to painful stimuli; if you press on a supra-orbital nerve, he will move the un-paralysed arm, and if you prick his legs or feet he will attempt to withdraw the sound limb.

6. The Chest—Before getting to grips with the chest pause again to study the *respiration,* which you first observed when you considered the general appearance of the patient. A deep breathing is seen in diabetic coma, while in uraemia the breathing is sighing or hissing in character. Irregularity of the breathing may occur with any severe intra-cranial disturbance such as meningitis. The periodic waxing and waning which constitutes 'Cheyne-Stokes respiration' is also seen with severe intracranial disturbances; it arises from such varied conditions as fractured skull or cardiac failure, for example, all of which probably produce this effect, you will remember, because of anoxaemia of the respiratory centre.

Now palpate the ribs and spine in cases where there has been a serious accident, to determine whether there is a *fracture* of these bony parts.

You will need to examine the *lungs* and *heart* with certain essentials in mind. What you are seeking is evidence of some gross lesion which may have produced coma, for minimal lesions are not likely to produce so dramatic an effect. In the lungs, tuberculosis, pneumonia, or an abscess may give rise to cerebral complications. In the heart, several conditions which can be quickly recognized may produce similar effects; cardiac enlargement, for instance, suggests hypertensive changes in the cerebral arteries, and auricular fibrillation indicates the possibility of cerebral embolism.

7. The Abdomen—Very rarely you may discover an abdominal tumour, an indication that the coma is due to secondary neoplastic deposits in the brain. Much more frequently you will find a *distended bladder*; it is no help in diagnosis, but will at least suggest one helpful form of treatment—the emptying of the bladder—and a further line of investigation by the examination of the urine.

8. Body Fluids—

(a) *Urine*—No examination is complete until the urine has been examined. You may need to obtain a specimen by catheterization, but the examination of the urine must never be omitted, and you should do it yourself without unnecessary delay. The presence of a large amount of sugar and acetone will at once indicate a diagnosis of diabetes mellitus; any serious cerebral lesion may produce a slight, transient glycosuria, but the quantity of sugar present in the urine from this cause is very small. With any cerebral lesion a trace of albumin may be present in the urine, but if albumin is present in considerable amount it suggests that the coma may be due to uræmia, and you must carry out microscopical examination of the urine for other evidence of renal disease.

(b) *Cerebrospinal Fluid*—Always carry out a lumbar puncture if, with coma, there is the least suspicion of neck rigidity, i.e., the head cannot easily be flexed so that the chin touches the chest. This essential precaution may enable you to diagnose a fulminating meningitis in time to save the patient's life by prompt treatment.

(c) *Stomach Contents*—If no diagnosis has been made and you suspect poisoning, by a barbiturate for example, do not hesitate to wash out the stomach, and keep the contents for expert examination. You will probably not come across many cases of coma due to barbiturate poisoning, but an appreciable number must be missed because of failure to carry out this simple precaution.

Summary

1. In the diagnosis of coma base your examination on probabilities.

2. Obtain a history, if possible, from witnesses or relatives.
3. Look at the patient's surroundings first.
4. Before touching or moving the patient gain all the information possible from observing him.
5. Assess the depth of coma.
6. Examine the head very thoroughly in the order suggested.
7. Obtain all the information you can from examination of the limbs.
8. Examine the chest, including heart and lungs.
9. Examine the abdomen.
10. In all cases, examine the urine. Carry out lumbar puncture and examine the cerebrospinal fluid in any case where there is neck rigidity. If no diagnosis has been made, and poisoning is a possibility, wash out the stomach and keep the contents for examination.

□

CHAPTER XI

MENINGITIS IN CHILDREN

In medicine, increased power brings with it increased responsibility. Since the advent of chemotherapy, and the power which it confers of curing septic meningitis, the responsibility for making an early diagnosis has become a pressing one. Delay in diagnosis entails delay in starting the correct treatment, and so increases the possibility of death or of serious residua such as paralysis or mental deficiency. Meningitis has thus become an acute medical emergency.

The diagnosis of meningitis depends on the recognition of a characteristic 'meningitic syndrome'. You must learn to recognize—or at least to suspect—this syndrome at an early stage in its development. Cultivate the attitude of suspicion in this, as in any curable disease, so that you consider the diagnosis without waiting for the ominous late features. The meningitic syndrome is not confined to conditions in which the meninges are actively inflamed, and in some cases your suspicions will prove unfounded; but you will not have wasted your time, for often promptness will save lives.

The Meningitic Syndrome

The first essential in the diagnosis of meningitis is to be on the watch for it; the second is to understand the mechanism giving rise to the signs and symptoms which you can recognize.

The characteristic features are produced by *meningeal irritation.* Compare the results of irritation of the meninges and irritation of the peritoneum, and you will see that they are strictly comparable. In both the main features are: (1) Pain; (2) Hyperaesthesia; (3) Muscular rigidity.

1. Pain—In meningitis, the pain is usually described as a headache, though pain may also be felt down the spine. The headache is continuous, though it may fluctuate in severity; it may be deep-seated or referred to the surface, usually the back of the neck and occipital region; it is aggravated by movement or by coughing or straining, or by any test which stretches the meninges or increases the intracranial pressure. The shrill 'meningitic cry' of an inarticulate child is probably initiated by severe headache, but limited by the necessity to avoid stretching the meninges.

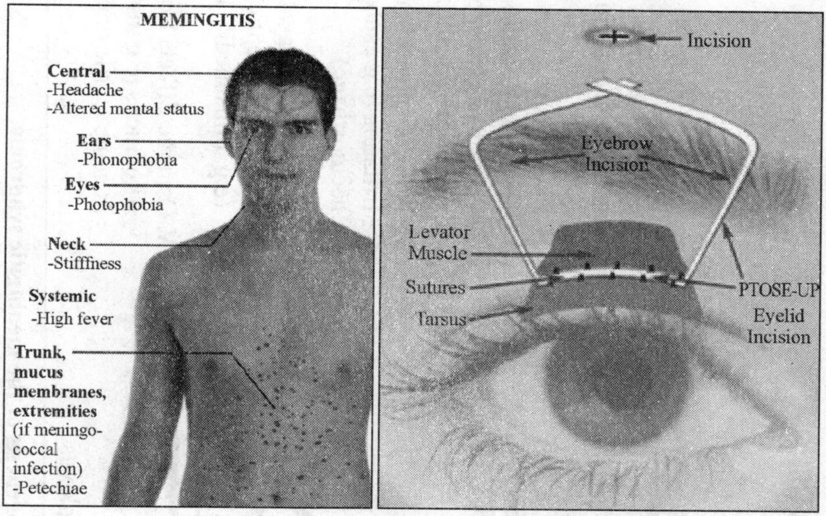

Fig. 1: Symptoms of Meningitis.

2. Hyperaesthesia—Local and general hyperesthesia may be present early, though evidence of this is not as a rule very precise. The patient may resent touching of any part, but especially of the back of the head and neck.

3. Muscle Rigidity—This important sign is nearly always demonstrable. In the early stages, it is often localized, and, since meningitis is commonly maximal at the base of the brain, neck rigidity is frequently present even when other signs are equivocal. Later, the back may become rigid, the head retracted, and the thighs flexed on to the abdomen (Fig. 1).

Before going any further, it is important to recall that though meningeal irritation, with its three characteristic features, may be, and often is, produced by infection of the meninges, it may be due to other causes. It is of more than academic interest to understand and separate

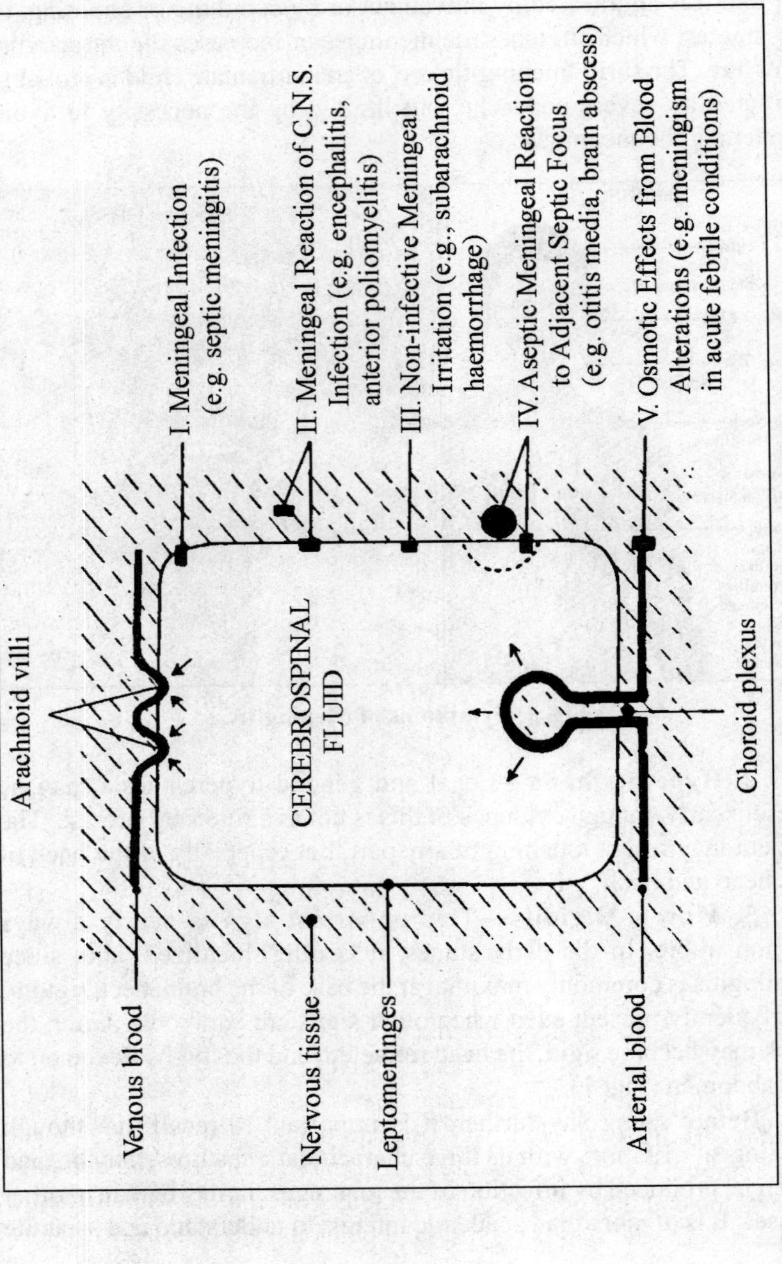

Figs. 2: The pathogenesis of the meningitic syndrome.

these causes, because otherwise your differential diagnosis will be irrational and may be misleading. For example, many acute infections of childhood are accompanied by signs of meningeal irritation, although the meninges are not infected. This condition, which is known as *meningism,* is commonest with pneumonia and tonsillitis.

The accompanying diagram (Fig. 2) has been drawn to show the different groups of conditions which may produce the syndrome of meningeal irritation.

The Complete Syndrome of Meningeal Infection—What has been said so far is essential for the understanding of meningitis, and as a basis on which to plan your examination of the patient; but it broadens the discussion, and may seem to you at first glance to make the subject more difficult because of the many conditions which are included. It is now necessary to separate the group of conditions comprehended in the term 'septic meningitis', which includes infections by the meningococcus, streptococcus, staphylococcus, pneumococcus, *Bacillus coli* and *Haemophilus influenza.* In septic meningitis, the syndrome of meningeal irritation is only one part of the complete clinical picture; in the natural history of the disease process three stages can often be observed: (1) Stage of invasion; (2) Stage of meningeal irritation; (3) Stage of raised intracranial tension, with irritative and paralytic phenomena. These stages are most clearly seen in slowly progressing cases, and they are best observed in tuberculous meningitis; but, in essence, most varieties of meningitis follow the same pattern, though the stages may overlap, or be compressed, if the disease progresses rapidly.

1. *Invasion*—Since most forms of septic meningitis are secondary to infection elsewhere, systemic effects may provide the earliest manifestations. For example, in the rare fulminating cases of meningococcal infection death from *adrenal failure* may occur within a few hours. *Petechial eruptions* in the skin are also frequently observed, especially with meningococcal infections.

But, whatever the infection, the first signs of the disease, occurring even before the signs of meningeal irritation, may be *changes in the mentality.* In extreme cases, delirium may accompany a rise in temperature. In mild cases the patient may be languid and irritable. A common combination is that of irritability alternating with drowsiness. It has been said that if you pull the blanket off a patient with typhoid he will not blink an eyelid, whereas a meningitic patient will replace the blanket with an oath. Think of meningitis whenever you see a patient who has developed acute mental confusion with a raised temperature.

2. *Meningeal Irritation*—The three essential features of meningeal irritation have already been outlined. Among these, headache and unwillingness to flex the spine are of outstanding importance because they occur so constantly.

The type of *headache* should be remembered. In meningitis, it is continuous and, unlike a 'feverish' headache, does not vary with the degree of pyrexia. There are, of course, innumerable varieties of headache. Learning them off parrot-fashion would be as useless to you as a list of the names of King Solomon's concubines to a theology student. Instead, learn from your clinical experience.

Unwillingness to permit flexion of the spine is of vital importance in diagnosis, and a host of eponymous signs has been described to demonstrate it. All depend on stretching the meninges and thereby increasing meningeal irritation. We have found that the demonstration of *neck rigidity* is the most simple and clear-cut of all, but you should try it out and compare it with other signs before you decide for yourself.

To demonstrate slight degrees of neck rigidity, ask the patient to touch his chest with his chin. In the earliest stages, he may succeed, but complains of pain in the back of the neck, and at the same time you will feel stiffness of the muscles in this region. At a later stage of the illness he will be quite unable to reach the chest with his chin; if you try to do it for him he will cry out with pain, and you will feel in the neck an unmistakable resistance to flexion. With a child, or an unconscious patient, place the palm of your hand under the patient's head and gently lift it; the head fails to flex, and you will find yourself lifting the shoulders, and, indeed, the whole body, off the bed. This can be very strikingly seen in children, who may be raised like a board until only the heels remain on the bed.

There are other useful methods of demonstrating resistance to spinal flexion. The patient may be asked to sit up in bed, and does so with both arms outstretched stiffly behind to take the weight off the spine and prevent its flexion: this is called the '*tripod sign*', and is frequently seen in the early stages of anterior poliomyelitis when irritation of the spinal meninges occurs. Or a child may be asked to kiss its knee and fail to reach it; this sign is also demonstrable when the spinal meninges are involved.

Another method of demonstrating resistance to spinal flexion is by *Kernig's sign* (Fig. 3), but it is often difficult to assess accurately unless the underlying disease process is advanced. Kernig's sign is best elicited by first flexing the hip, and only then attempting to straighten the knee. In the presence of meningeal irritation, the spinal flexion produced by this manoeuvre produces pain, extension at the knee is resisted, and the hamstring muscles go into spasm. These results constitute a **'positive' Kernig's sign.**

3. *Raised Intracranial Tension, with Irritative and Paralytic Phenomena*—With the natural development of meningeal infection, certain mechanical factors come later into operation. As the infective

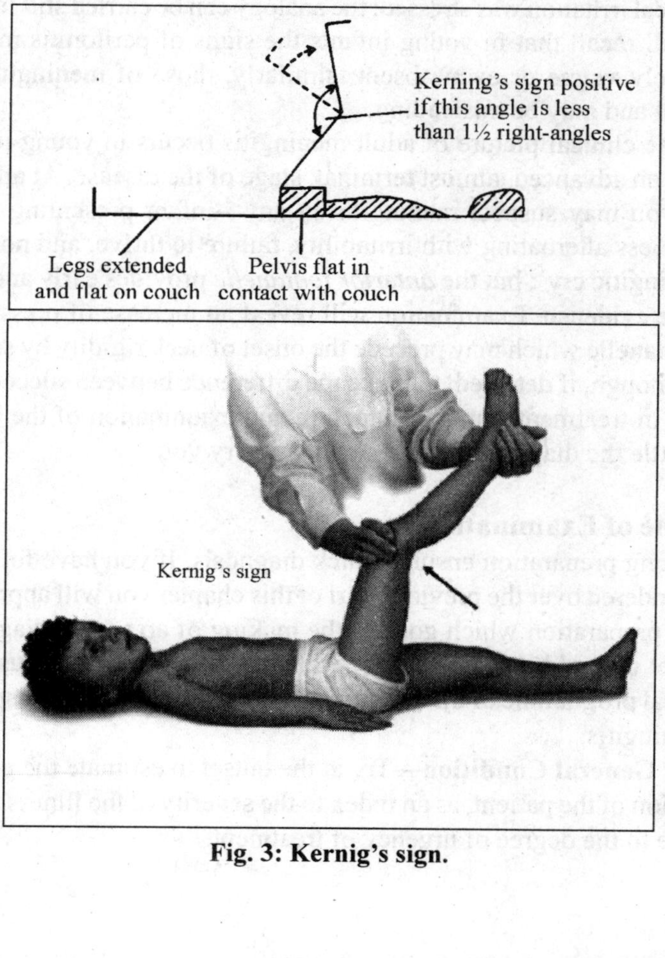

Fig. 3: Kernig's sign.

process spreads on the brain surface irritative phenomena occur; the exudate may become organized; obstruction to the flow of C.S.F. may occur; and the final picture is that of increasing intracranial tension, with failure of cerebral function.

You may observe the classical features associated with *raised intracranial tension*—headache, vomiting, and papilloedema, though as a rule papilloedema does not have time to develop. *Cerebral irritation* may produce convulsions or muscle twitchings, and the pulse and respiration may become irregular. *Depression of cerebral function* may show as strabismus, inequality of the pupils, paralysis of the limbs, coma, and finally death.

Meningitis in Infancy—The similarity between meningeal and peritoneal irritation was stressed; the analogy can be carried still further. You will recall that in young infants the signs of peritonitis may be extremely vague or even absent; similarly, those of meningitis are atypical and may be misleading.

The clinical picture of adult meningitis occurs in young infants only at an advanced, almost terminal, stage of the disease. At an early stage you may suspect meningitis in any—infant presenting fever, drowsiness alternating with irritability, failure to thrive, and possibly a 'meningitic cry'; but the *anterior fontanelle* provides early and very definite evidence. Examination will reveal an increase of pressure in the fontanelle which may precede the onset of neck rigidity by several days, enough, if detected, to make the difference between success and failure in treatment. Lumbar puncture and examination of the C.S.F. will settle the diagnosis in cases which worry you.

Scheme of Examination

Long preparation ensures quick diagnosis. If you have followed and pondered over the previous part of this chapter you will appreciate all the preparation which goes to the making of an urgent diagnosis. Now let us build, on the basis of what we have already discussed, a practical programme of the essentials in examining a patient suspected of meningitis.

1. General Condition—Try at the outset to estimate the general condition of the patient, as an index to the severity of the illness and as a guide to the degree of urgency of treatment.

A collapsed, cold child with the meningitic syndrome probably has a severe septicaemia (you will remember that meningitis is almost always secondary to infection elsewhere). He will not have long to live if treatment is not immediate and effective. The depth of coma, if it occurs, is an index of the severity of the illness.

2. The Meningitic Syndrome—Examine the patient to determine what degree of meningeal irritation is present, carefully carrying out the simple tests which have been described above.

3. Temperature, Pulse, and Respiration—These should, of course, be noted and recorded; any changes which occur may guide you both as regards treatment and prognosis.

Either a very low or an excessively high temperature is an ominous sign. The temperature may rise steeply when death is imminent.

Slowness of the pulse in relation to the temperature may occur if the intracranial tension is high; on the other hand, the pulse is weak and extremely rapid if septicaemia is present.

Rapid respiration should suggest the possibility of pneumonia. This may occur as an accompaniment of meningitis, but remember that in children pneumonia alone is often associated with meningism. Irregularity of respiration may occur in any severe meningitis and is almost invariable in the late stages of the tuberculous form.

4. Skin—Since meningitis is often secondary to infection elsewhere, look for a *septic focus* in the skin. A 'boil' on the lip or in the nostril may be of significance.

Any severe septicaemia is likely to produce a petechial rash on the skin; this occurs much more frequently with a meningococcal than with any other variety of meningitis. The *types of rash* which occur with meningococcal meningitis are extremely varied, but they have one feature in common: somewhere you will find evidence of a minute haemorrhage in the skin. There may be a few of these petechiae on the dorsum of the foot and nowhere else, but more commonly they occur also around the elbows, wrists, and other joints, on the flanks, and in the sacral region.

5. Skull, Nose, Ears, and Throat—Still hunting for a primary infective focus, examine these regions carefully. You may find evidence of abrasions or a fracture, or a purulent discharge from one nostril which suggests a severe sinusitis. Much more commonly, however, the examination of *both* ears, not merely one as a token, will reveal the causative inflammatory process. Until you have seen both ear drums you have not properly examined any case of suspected meningitis. In children, acute tonsillitis may be found; occasionally this is the source of a streptococcal meningitis, but remember that simple tonsillitis may cause meningism.

6. Neck—Examine the neck for rigidity and for enlarged glands suggesting local sepsis.

7. Chest—Pneumonia may cause or complicate meningitis, though in young children meningism is a more likely complication of pneumonia. Lesions in the lungs may also occur in tuberculous meningitis.

8. Abdomen—May be retracted. The enlarged spleen of septicaemia is often too soft to be felt.

9. Bones and Joints—If you have failed to find a primary focus examine the bones and joints for evidence of infection.

10. C.N.S. Examination—Owing to the patient's condition it is generally impossible to carry out a detailed examination of the central nervous system. Obvious features such as the presence of a squint or of pupillary changes, should, however, be noted, and the reflexes should be tested. Where the diagnosis is not certain, in an early case of anterior polio-myelitis for example, a more thorough examination should be attempted, and the examination should be repeated frequently.

11. Lumbar Puncture—In any case with the meningitic syndrome diagnosis is incomplete until the cerebrospinal fluid has been examined. You should, therefore, train yourself to carry out lumbar puncture efficiently; it should be easier to perform than venepuncture, because there are no elusively movable parts and the landmarks are bony.

Lumbar puncture should always be performed with the patient in the left lateral position; the pressure of the cerebrospinal fluid cannot be accurately estimated in the upright position, and this estimation is important. As you are about to start, needle in hand, say to yourself: "If I fail to obtain a satisfactory specimen it is my own fault, and no excuses will be accepted".

Almost all the difficulties which arise are due to faulty positioning—either of the patient or of your needle. It should take longer to get the patient into the correct position than to puncture his theca. See that your assistant flexes the patient's knees well into his abdomen, and flexes the whole spine well, to open up the intervertebral spaces for you. Clean the skin over the lumbar vertebrae with two or three changes of spirit or betadine. Pause to make sure that the spine is in one horizontally straight line, preferably with a pillow to support the head in this line. Now make equally certain that the pelvis is vertical and at right-angles to the spine. Dip a piece of sterile gauze in iodine, and with it make two lines on the skin—a horizontal one along the tips of the vertebral processes, and a vertical one down from the most cranial part of the uppermost iliac crest. These two lines should cross at right angles at about the level of the fourth lumbar spine, and your puncture may be performed either in the space immediately above or below it (Fig. 4). Now infiltrate the skin over the space you select with 2 per cent sterile xylocaine, and aim at producing a distinct wheal with the anaesthetic. With the fingers of your left hand delineate the vertebral spines above and below the space again, at the same time confirming that the spine and pelvis have not altered their relative positions. With a sharp movement penetrate the wheal and the skin with your lumbar-puncture needle, making sure it lies between the vertebral spines and in the midline. Holding the needle at its far end produces instability, so hold the needle around its middle by a piece of sterile gauze and push forward and slightly cranially. At this stage, the commonest error is inadvertently to lower the head of the needle; make sure your needle remains truly in the horizontal plane. With your hand steadied on the patient's back, push the needle deliberately and you will feel a 'giving' sensation when the dura mater is pierced (Fig. 5). If you are uncertain of the depth do not go on

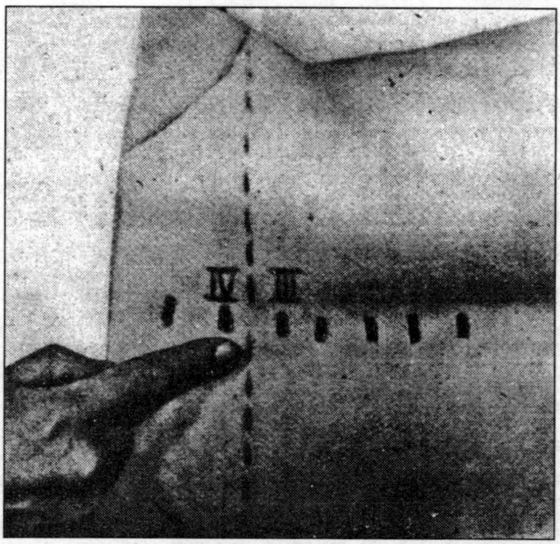

Fig. 4: Surface markings for lumbar puncture (finger pointing towards site of puncture).

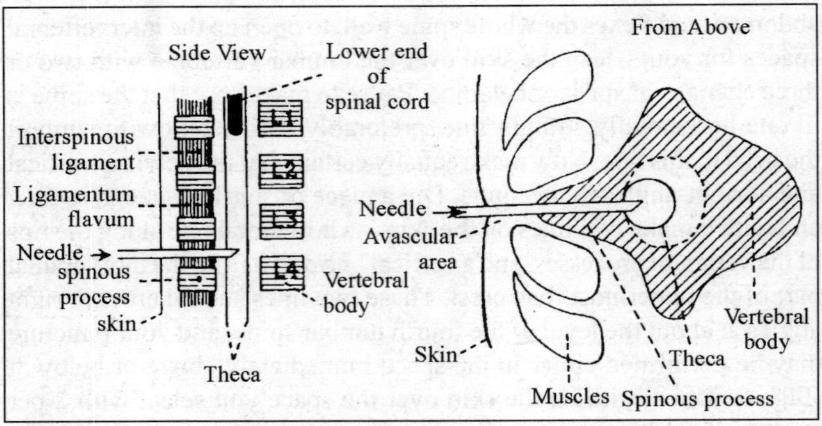

Fig. 5: Lumbar puncture.

pushing; wait until you have withdrawn the stylet to observe if fluid escapes; if the needle goes too far and touches the anterior wall of the spinal canal it may pierce the venous plexus and so contaminate the fluid with blood. (If this mishap does occur, withdraw the needle slightly, to permit the bloody fluid to run out, and it may become clear.) In children, and especially in infants, the common tendency is to push the needle in too deeply.

As soon as fluid is obtained replace the stylet and attach the manometer, avoiding flexion of the head at this stage, since it alters the C.S.F. pressure, then withdraw the stylet to permit the fluid to flow into the measuring tube. The normal pres-sure is 90-160 mm of water. Get your assistant to compress and then release the jugular veins, when, in the absence of obstruction in the cerebrospinal space, the pressure will rise and fall quickly. This done, disconnect the manometer, collecting the fluid which flows from it in your first specimen bottle for chemical tests. In a further bottle collect 1—2 c.c. of fluid for cytological and bacteriological examination. Then replace the stylet and, holding the skin down through a piece of sterile gauze, withdraw the needle rapidly.

For accurate estimation of cells and organisms, it is your responsibility to ensure that the fluid is examined within one hour of withdrawal.

Naked-eye Appearances of C.S.F—It is unnecessary to wait for all your information for the pathologist's report; naked-eye examination may furnish enough information to enable you to start treatment at once.

If the fluid is clear but under increased pressure let it run only slowly; urgent treatment is not so necessary, and rapid lowering of the pressure may produce the fatal 'pressure cone', due to depression of the cranial contents into the foramen magnum.

If the fluid is slightly cloudy or frankly turbid let a drop fall on to a clean slide which is put aside for the time being. Slight haziness is best detected by looking through the fluid in a small bottle or test-tube. Haziness or turbidity almost invariably signifies a septic meningitis.

The drop of cloudy fluid which you set aside will dry by the time you have finished the puncture; it can be stained very quickly and simply, and under the microscope you will almost certainly see a mass of polymorphonuclear leucocytes and, often, the offending cocci, especially if they are extracellular (streptococci, staphylococci, and pneumococci) but less easily if they are intracellular (meningococci). If the fluid remains blood-stained, despite letting it run as described previously, try to determine whether the bleeding is due to faulty puncture or to subarachnoid hemorrhage. If the blood arises from accidental contamination, the specimens in different bottles will not be stained to the same depth, and the supernatant fluid will be clear.

Summary

1. Learn to watch for and to recognize the meningitic syndrome at a very early stage.
2. The essential and most constant features of the meningitic syndrome are headache and resistance to spinal flexion. Mental changes or skin rashes may precede these, and the signs of cerebral irritation or paralysis may follow.
3. Separate true meningitis from conditions which simulate it by a careful physical examination, especially for a primary focus, and never omit lumbar puncture in any case of the meningitic syndrome.

□

CHAPTER XII

HIGH TEMPERATURES

High fevers are always startling phenomena and often puzzling to those who try to find their cause. The adult man is a homothermic animal who does not readily tolerate changes in internal temperature. Marked pyrexia is, therefore, in an adult, a sign of some gross bodily disturbance, usually an infection. Children are less stable. Though their temperature may be high and their appearance alarming, pyrexia often means less than in an adult. Nevertheless, a child has so little reserve of strength that the diagnosis of conditions causing high fever may be a matter of some urgency.

In all such cases, the taking of the history and the examination must be thorough and painstaking, but the attention of the doctor should be focused on certain *key points* in the history and on certain *key areas* during the examination. For instance, a detailed examination of the central nervous system is rarely necessary, but the clinician who fails to look in the nose or the ears of a child with unexplained pyrexia invites diagnostic catastrophe. A careful search of the skin for any early rash is equally important because many acute exanthemata begin with high fever. The hands and joints should always be inspected for nodules or arthritis, and the bones percussed for evidences of osteomyelitis. The neck, axillae, and groins should always be palpated for evidence of glandular tenderness or enlargement. This special emphasis on examination of the skin, joints, lymphatic glands, and upper respiratory tract is necessary because these are so often forgotten. The systematic examination of the chest, heart, and abdomen are no less important.

The reason for the special bias in considering the case of a patient with a high temperature becomes obvious when the chief causes are remembered:

1. Any acute exanthema such as scarlet fever, variola, typhoid, or typhus.
2. Upper respiratory tract infections such as tonsillitis, otitis media, or sinusitis.
3. Lung conditions such as pneumonia, abscess, empyema, or tuberculosis.
4. Abdominal conditions such as subdiaphragmatic or perinephric abscess, tuberculosis, or renal infections.
5. Cardiac conditions such as acute rheumatism, bacterial endocarditis, or pericarditis.
6. Septicaemias—often associated with pneumonia, meningitis, pericarditis, arthritis, or osteitis.
7. Reticuloendothelial diseases—such as glandular fever or leukaemia.
6. Tropical protozoal diseases such as malaria or amoebiasis.

The History

Try to find out something about the patient's environment and occupation: certain infections are more common amongst the poor and badly housed. A family history of infectious diseases such as 'sore throat' or tuberculosis may also prove an important diagnostic clue. Ask the patient about his previous health, previous diseases, and especially about any sojourn in foreign countries.

The Onset—The time and the type of onset of the illness must be determined most accurately. To do so it is necessary often to cross-question the patient and relatives with great persistence. Like a lawyer you must press for details. The first essential is to know the exact day on which the patient last felt well, ate well, slept well, and worked normally. This knowledge will usually enable you not only to say *when* the illness began but also *how* it began. There are various possibilities. For example, the onset may be abrupt; the patient becomes ill suddenly on his way home from work (as in pneumonia or malaria). On the other hand, the onset may be rapid but not sudden, in which case the patient usually fights his illness for a day or so before taking to bed (as in typhoid fever). Lastly, the onset may be insidious, in which case the patient finds very great difficulty in stating just when he began to feel ill (as in most forms of tuberculosis). Make up your mind into which category the onset of your patient's illness falls. You will find the knowledge of very great value in diagnosis.

The rest of the history should be about the waxing and waning of the symptoms from day to day. At the end you should be able to make a list of the chief symptoms suffered in order of their severity, and be able to state exactly how long each one has been present.

The Examination

1. Taking the Temperature—Most English clinical thermometers are measured in degrees Fahrenheit from 95° up to about 107°. The passage of the mercury column in the calibrated tube is retarded by a constriction which prevents the mercury column from dropping away into the bulb when the thermometer is removed from the patient to the cool air of a room. The patient's temperature can therefore be read at leisure. The mercury column must be shaken down into the bulb after use or else some careless person, possibly even yourself, will take the temperature of another patient with a thermometer which is already reading perhaps 102°F. To guard against possible mistakes by others always read the temperature *before* using a thermometer and always shake down the mercury column after use. In babies, the thermometer should be greased, then placed in the rectum and held there for at least two

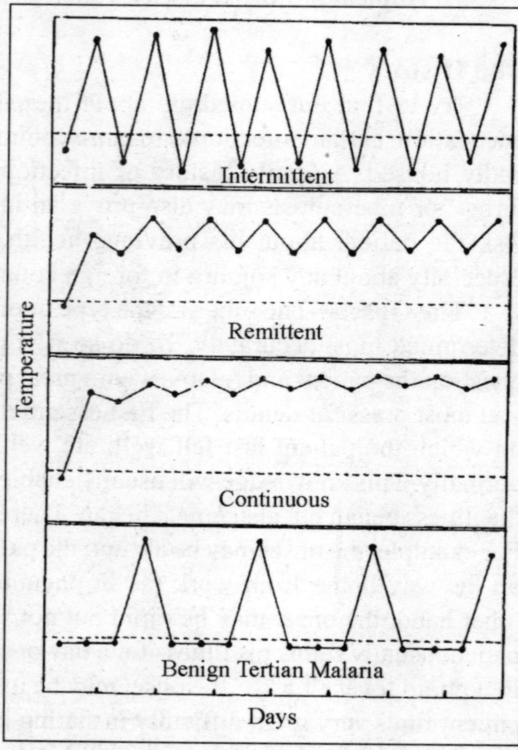

Fig. 1: Temperature curves.

minutes. Rectal temperatures are usually 1°F. higher than oral, and about 1.5°F. higher than axillary temperatures. In small children between the ages of 2 and 6 the temperature is best taken in the axilla or groin; the thermometer must be held in place while the arm is adducted or the thigh flexed so as to enclose the thermometer in a warm pocket of skin. Older children and adults can usually hold a thermometer with its bulb underneath the tongue. The thermometer must be left in place for at least two minutes, even though it is advertised as a 'half-minute thermometer'. By removing the thermometer after only half a minute an inaccurate unduly low reading may be obtained. Patients should be watched while the temperature is being taken; malingerers can, by various subterfuges, even produce a temperature reading of 106°. Remember that the 'normal temperature' of 98.4° is not really a normal, but an average. One man's normal temperature may be 99°; another's may be 97°.

If you are lucky enough to have a series of temperature readings taken during the forty-eight hours prior to your examination, you can learn much by charting the readings and studying the shape of the curve. Three main types of curve are recognized (Fig. 1), though there are many inter-mediate types:

(a) *Intermittent Pyrexia*—Here the temperature is raised in the evening, but normal or subnormal in the morning. Low intermittent pyrexia is common and may mean much or nothing at all. A high swinging intermittent pyrexia is always suggestive of undrained suppuration, septicaemia, or tuberculous infections.

(b) *Remittent Pyrexia*—Here the temperature varies by about 2° or 3° daily, but never reaches normal levels.

(c) *Continuous Pyrexia*—The temperature remains high and varies very little during the course of each day.

'Diagnostic' temperature charts are obtained in certain tropical diseases, but the only one with which at the moment you need be familiar is the sudden rise of temperature every forty-eight hours which occurs in benign tertian malaria.

2. The Pulse and Respiratory Rates—A considerable rise in the respiratory rate is always an important finding which suggests respiratory disease. This is particularly true in children, but first you must know what is the normal respiratory rate for a child of any given age. A newborn infant's respiratory rate varies from 60 to 40 per minute, but falls to 30 per minute in a few weeks, gradually dropping to the adult rate in the course of years. Children's respiratory rates are readily increased by any disturbance and minor deviations from the normal may mean very little.

The *relation of the pulse-rate to the temperature* is a most useful ratio. Diseases vary in their capacity to cause pyrexia or tachycardia; some, like diphtheria, cause very rapid pulse-rate with only moderate pyrexia; others, like typhoid, cause a high pyrexia with a comparatively slow pulse-rate. The pulse-rate of an adult usually rises 10 per minute for every degree Fahrenheit above 98°. The expected pulse-rate for a temperature of 103° is therefore about 120. This general rule, however, must not be accepted too literally. The degree of tachycardia obviously depends on the patient as well as upon the nature of the disease.

3. The General Appearance—Notice particularly whether the patient looks well in spite of the pyrexia, or whether he is dull, apathetic, and inactive. Excitement or mental confusion are usually obvious.

4. The Head and Neck—(The upper respiratory tract comes last.) Look for evidence of cranial nerve palsies which may occur as a result of intracranial infections, and test for neck rigidity. Always remember to look for neck rigidity. With a child it is a good plan to make a game of it and ask the child to kiss its own knee. The child with meningeal irritation cannot do this. The adult should be asked to put his chin forward on to his chest.

5. The Skin—Some acute infections tend to cause generalized flushing; others cause pallor due to constriction of the arterioles to the skin. Look carefully at the colour and estimate the warmth of the skin around the face and hands, and notice the amount of sweating which is occurring. A small infected wound, pimple, or boil, may have been the beginning of a severe septicaemia, so even these must be searched for carefully and noted. Herpes simplex (herpes febrilis), in which small clusters of vesicles form on the lips, may occur in any fever, but it is particularly common in pneumococcal and meningococcal infections.

A good doctor can see a rash before his colleagues. He knows where to look and how to look. Most rashes begin with a mild erythema in macular formation (red spots, not raised above skin level, which blanch on pressure) and they cannot be seen except in a good light. Look at the neck, the scalp, the post-auricular region, the chest, the abdomen, and the upper arms under these conditions. Petechial spots (subcutaneous pin-point haemorrhages which do not fade on pressure) are often first seen over the dorsum of the feet or at the bend of the elbows, but you should also look closely at the nails to see if there are any beneath them (Fig. 2).

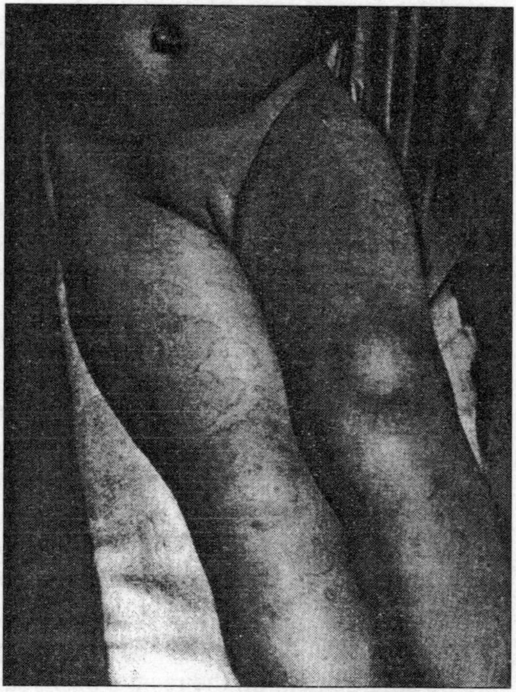

Fig. 2: The rheumatic rash.

6. The Lymphatic Glands—Palpate the neck, the occipital and pre-auricular regions, the axillae, and the groins for enlarged lymphatic glands. A small gland which is tender is of more significance than a slightly larger one which is painless. Many children have palpable lymphatic glands, particularly in the upper cervical region, so do not attach too much importance to small painless palpable glands. If any glands are felt note their size, shape, consistency, and attachments.

7. **The Joints** and **Bones**—Examine the main joints not only for redness, swelling, tenderness, and mobility, but also for particular nodules. The nodules of acute rheu-matism may be found around the knee- and elbow-joints or along the palmar tendons and knuckles. A special technique is necessary to demonstrate them: flex the child's knees and elbows and let there be a good light upon them. The nodules are more easily seen than felt. If you think you see a nodule, while taking care not to cast a shadow on it, you should gently slide the skin so as to demonstrate the roundness of the nodule and its attachment to deeper structures.

While examining the joints you should notice any redness or swelling or tenderness over the superficial bones. In young children it is also well-worth while systematically to palpate the thighs, legs, arms, and spine in a search for tender areas. Furthermore, *percussion* of the spine, and the ends of each long bone, may elicit evidence of deep-seated tenderness which could not be elicited simply by palpation. Such deep tenderness may be the only pointer to early osteomyelitis.

8. The Chest—Make a careful examination of the lungs and heart. Be especially careful and painstaking when examining the patient's lungs, remembering that inflammatory lesions of the lungs may cause severe pyrexia and toxaemia without producing much in the way of local physical signs. A raised respiratory rate may, especially in children, be the only sign of a lung infection. Unless you are very careful you may miss the slight percussion dullness, poor air entry, and aegophony at one lung base which indicate an empyema, or you may miss the generalized tinkling crepitations which are found in miliary tuberculosis.

9. The Abdomen—Inspect and palpate the abdomen thoroughly. The shape of the abdomen may be the best indication of the presence of ascites. The abdomen containing an effusion bulges in the flanks, the umbilicus is stretched out to its full width, and the abdominal girth is increased. Small quantities of fluid insufficient to cause an alteration in the shape of the abdomen are often equally difficult to detect by percussion.

Make a special attempt to palpate the spleen, but never diagnose; splenic enlargement on the results of percussion alone.

10. The Upper Respiratory Tract—With a child this examination should be left to the last because your attempts to see into his nose, throat, and ears may provoke him to howl and to resist throughout the rest of your time with him. Inspection of the throat and ears, therefore, come last in sequence, but not in importance.

Look carefully at the child's tongue, noting whether it is moist or dry and the distribution of fur upon it. Look for ulceration on the tongue and the inside of the cheeks, and also for Koplik's spots (a grain of salt on an erythematous base). Then gently placing a tongue depressor in position and using a good torch, obtain a good view of the fauces, tonsils, and posterior pharyngeal wall. Experience alone can teach you how best to look into the throat of a difficult child, but it is easier if you have tried to make friends first and if you explain just what you are going to do before you do it. With a child who is difficult, wrap its limbs and trunk firmly in a blanket. You will then have a better chance of getting that clear view of the throat which is so essential.

Next look at the ears; inspect the pinna to see whether it is displaced forwards or swollen, then examine the skin over the mastoid

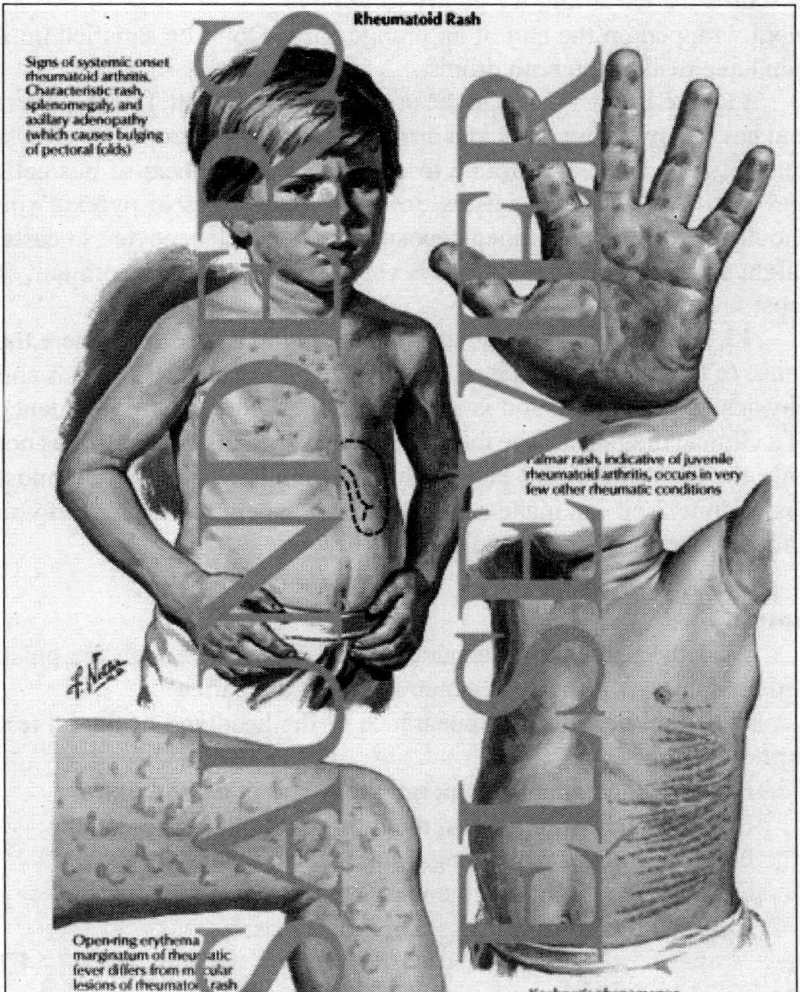

Fig. 3: Rheumatoid rash.

processes. Compare the effect of an even finger pressure over the mastoid antrum on the two sides. Use a good auriscope to look within the ears. This in children may be a difficult process and much resented, so use a speculum which is small enough for the child's external meatus and insert it very gently while pulling the pinna backwards. A specially narrow speculum is often necessary for baby's ears. If wax or debris obscures the ear drum, try gently to remove it with wisps of cotton-wool wrapped on the end of an orange stick. Don't be satisfied until you have really seen both drums.

11. The Urine—Look at the urine against the light. If it shimmers and has a fishy odour, look at a drop under the microscope, for almost certainly it will then be found to contain large numbers of pus cells and motile coliform organisms. In all difficult cases of pyrexia you should examine a centrifuged deposit for red cells, leucocytes, or casts. Slight albuminuria by itself means very little, as it is a concomitant of most fevers.

12. The Blood—Examination of the blood is essential where the cause of the pyrexia cannot be determined by the history analysis and physical examination, and is always useful as confirmatory evidence of a clinical diagnosis. The micro-scopical study of a blood-film is not only the most important part of this examination, but also the most easily done. You can make a blood-film anywhere in the world if you have a glass slide and a needle.

Summary

Take the temperature accurately and compare it with the pulse and respiratory rate and the general state of the patient.

Examine the external appearance of the head and neck and test for neck rigidity.

Examine the patient's skin, minutely, and in a good light.

Examine the lymph-nodes, the joints, and the long bones.

Examine the heart, the lungs, and the abdomen.

Examine the throat and then the ears.

Examine the urine, and the blood if necessary.

INDEX

□□□